MANCHESTER
MEDIEVAL
LITERATURE
AND CULTURE

The heat of *Beowulf*

Manchester University Press

MANCHESTER
MEDIEVAL
LITERATURE
AND CULTURE

Manchester Medieval Literature and Culture publishes monographs and essay collections comprising new research informed by current critical methodologies on the literary cultures of the global Middle Ages. We are interested in all periods, from the early Middle Ages through to the late, and we include post-medieval engagements with and representations of the medieval period (or 'medievalism'). 'Literature' is taken in a broad sense, to include the many different medieval genres: imaginative, historical, political, scientific and religious.

Titles available in the series

The heat of *Beowulf*

Daniel C. Remein

MANCHESTER UNIVERSITY PRESS

The right of Daniel C. Remein to be identified as the author of this work has been asserted by them in accordance with the Copyright, Designs and Patents Act 1988.

Published by Manchester University Press
Oxford Road, Manchester M13 9PL
www.manchesteruniversitypress.co.uk

British Library Cataloguing-in-Publication Data
A catalogue record for this book is available from the British Library

ISBN   978 1 5261 5058 5   hardback

First published 2022

The publisher has no responsibility for the persistence or accuracy of URLs for any external or third-party internet websites referred to in this book, and does not guarantee that any content on such websites is, or will remain, accurate or appropriate.

Typeset
by New Best-set Typesetters Ltd

Contents

Figures

Acknowledgments

With a great deal of humility, I recall that I once expressed serious incredulity to a graduate school adviser who relished taking one's 'own sweet time' in composing a monograph. Now, here I am, having taken at least a decade of not only my own sweet time but also that of so many others. Such a great number of people have contributed to this book that I am confident I cannot name them all here.

It is, nevertheless, my pleasure to try, and to start by thanking the libraries, museums, and—most crucially—the librarians and staff that made this book possible. I offer my gratitude to the intrepid staff at Healey Library at UMass Boston and especially everyone Interlibrary Loan. I'm also grateful to the staff at the Bancroft Library, the staff at the Beinecke Library, Tony Power and the Bennett Library Special Collections & Rare Books at Simon Fraser University, Amanda Faehnel and the Kent State University Library Special Collections, Sue Brunning and the British Museum, and James Maynard and the University of Buffalo Poetry Collection.

I remain grateful for my teachers at NYU. Hal Momma—my north star in Old English studies—always shows me what it means to be an adventurous, patient, and precise reader of Old English poetry. My enduring thanks to Carolyn Dinshaw for pushing me towards more capacious scholarship. I want to thank Lytle Shaw for continuing conversations about moving between fields. Thanks as well to Mary Carruthers (for instruction and support), Peter Nicholls (for guidance on all things modernism), Martha Rust, Patrick Deer, and Robert Young.

One strand of this book was first published in *postmedieval*, and I thank the editors of that issue, David Hadbawnik and Sean Reynolds. David—you are what Blaser would call a 'great companion' in the traffic between medieval and modern poetics. A great deal of this book would never have even been drafted without the material, intellectual, and friendly support of my roving writing-group companions, Arthur Russell, Myra Seaman, and Lara Farina. I especially want to thank Erica Weaver, a collaborator on whose brilliance and friendship I have come to depend. I want to thank Susan Oldrieve here, too, who first introduced me to Old English and whose support has continued for so long.

Many friends, colleagues, teachers, students, and family have provided support, insight, questions, and suggestions: Ada Smailbegović, Adam Darisse, Alex Mueller, Anna Kelner, Ármann Jakobsson, Audrey Walton, August Smith, Bryan Hart, Bob Stanton, Chris Jones, Chris Piuma, Chrissy Remein, Christie Towers, Dale Smith, Dan Najork, Daniel Donoghue, Daniel O'Neil, Danny O'Hara, Dianne Berg, Don Manas, Donna Beth Ellard, Eileen Fradenburg Joy, Elizabeth Leigh, Emilio Sauri, Eric Weiskott, Georgia Henley, Gillian Overing, H. M. Cushman, Haun Saussy, Hugh O'Connell, Isabel Gómez, Jeffrey J. Cohen, Jessica Hart, Joe Torra, Joey McMullen, John Leigh, Jonathan McCurdy, Joy Baker, Julie Orlemanski, Karl Steel, Kate Glavin, Katie Baima, Kent Rodzwicz, Laura Yoder, Laurie Finke, Leonard Von Morzé, Lisa Ampleman, Lisa Weston, Lowell Duckert, Martin Shichtman, Mary Dockray-Miller, Mary Kate Hurley, Megan Cook, Michael Sells, Mo Pareles, Nahir Otaño Gracia, Neal Bruss, Nicholas Watson, Nick Matlin, Nicole Carpenter, Pam Manas, Patrick Barron, Peter Buchanan, Renee Hudson, Renée Trilling, Roberta Frank, Samantha Zacher, Sarah Hamblin, Scott Maisano, Susan Tomlinson, Susie Nakley, Taylor Cowdery, and Warren Remein.

I want to extend my gratitude to UMass Boston, my English Department colleagues, the Faculty Staff Union (MTA, NEA), and the College of Liberal Arts Dean's Research grant fund. I'm particularly grateful to the TAs that taught *Beowulf* alongside me during this work: Rose Mooney, Hannah Piasecki, Lana Corrigan, Agata Caluj, and Claire Prasad. My thanks as well to the students in my graduate Old English seminars during Spring 2018, Fall 2019, and Fall 2021; those of my Spring 2017 seminar on coterie poetics and my Spring 2016 undergraduate Poetics course.

Early versions of parts of this book first took the form of talks at several institutions. I thank the hosts and interlocutors at the Comparative Literature Department at the University of Chicago, the University of Denver English Department, the Harvard Medieval Colloquium, and the UMass Boston English Department. Although the onset of the global pandemic in 2019 prevented me from speaking at the University of Wisconsin, Madison, I'm grateful to Jordan Zweck and Martin Foys for an invitation that spurred me to complete a draft of the final chapter. The project also benefited from conference panels and meetings of the BABEL Working Group, and the 2016 New Chaucer Society meeting in London.

I'm grateful to the literary estates of Jack Spicer and Robin Blaser for permission to quote and reprint images—but I cannot limit this remark to a conventional acknowledgment. Peter Gizzi and Miriam Nichols have always been generous and helpful. I am particularly grateful for Miriam Nichols' enthusiasm for the project and for ongoing correspondence about a number of difficulties of Blaser's biography and his handwriting. It's heartbreaking to me that Kevin Killian will not be able to see this book since I owe him such an immense debt. He was always enthusiastically helpful, pointing me to notebooks and documents, sorting out chronologies, and corresponding at length whenever I had a question. Without this help, and his warm invitation to cross the Bay and meet up when I first came to Berkeley to sift through Spicer's papers, this book would not exist.

I thank Jack Herndon and the Fran Herndon estate for their generous permission to use the image of Fran Herndon's woodcut that appears on cover of this book (originally done for Blaser's 'Apparitors' broadside, printed by Auerhahn Press for the San Francisco Arts Festival Poetry Folio, 1963), as well as the Altman Siegel Gallery in San Francisco. Thanks to the Bennett Library Special Collections & Rare Books, Simon Fraser University for providing the image of the print. I'm additionally grateful to Margaret Sloan and Christopher Wagstaff, co-trustees of the Jess Collins Trust, as well as Elizabeth Ivers and Andrew Arnot at the Tibor de Nagy Gallery in New York for generous help with, and permissions to use, materials that were not, after all, included in the final manuscript but were nonetheless important for its completion.

There is another difficult acknowledgment to make. The late Carol Braun Pasternack's mentoring and support in the field of Old English studies were crucial to the protean stages of this book and

I am deeply indebted to her in ways that will long outlast this project.

Manchester University Press has been a great partner in developing this book, especially the series editors, Anke Bernau, David Matthews, and James Paz, and the three anonymous readers for the press who, at different moments of completion, gave the project a committed reading that clarified my arguments, corrected errors, and provided concrete suggestions. I cannot thank Meredith Carroll enough—for her advice, but especially for her patience. Thanks, as well, to Alun Richards, David Appleyard, and to the production team; and my serious gratitude to Rachel Goodyear for excellent copy-editing (any remaining errors are surely my own).

A special thanks to Laura Yoder for compiling the index.

Above all, I offer my deepest gratitude to Meagan Manas, whose support, love, labor, and intellect made this book possible more than anything else. My working habits can be difficult to live with. This book has taken up at least as much of your time as it has mine; its completion is a testament to your reliability and care.

Abbreviations

ACMRS	Arizona Center for Medieval and Renaissance Studies
AOB	Arthur G. Brodeur, *The art of Beowulf* (Berkeley, CA: University of California Press, 1959)
ASE	*Anglo-Saxon England*
ASPR	George Philip Krapp and Elliott Van Kirk Dobbie (eds), *The Anglo-Saxon poetic records: a collective edition*, 6 vols (New York: Columbia University Press, 1931–53)
AT	Robin Blaser, *The astonishment tapes: talks on poetry and poetics with Robin Blaser and friends*, ed. Miriam Nichols (Tuscaloosa, AL: University of Alabama Press, 2015)
BT	Joseph Bosworth, *An Anglo-Saxon dictionary*, ed. T. Northcote Toller (Oxford: Oxford University Press, 1898; repr. 1976); and T. Northcote Toller, *An Anglo-Saxon dictionary: supplement. With revisions and enlarged addenda by Allistair Cambell* (Oxford: Oxford University Press, 1972)
DOE	Angus Cameron, Ashley Crandell Amos, Antonette diPaolo Healey, et al. (eds), *The dictionary of Old English, A to I online* (Toronto: Dictionary of Old English Project, 2018)
House	Jack Spicer, *The house that Jack built: the collected lectures of Jack Spicer*, ed. Peter Gizzi (Middletown, CT: Wesleyan University Press, 1998)
JEGP	*Journal of English and Germanic Philology*
JH	J. R. Clark Hall, *A concise Anglo-Saxon dictionary*, 4th edn, with supplement by H. D. Meritt (Cambridge:

	Cambridge University Press, 1960; repr., Toronto: University of Toronto Press, 2002)
JSB	'Jack Spicer's *Beowulf*', Jack Spicer, translation of *Beowulf* (notes and manuscripts), Jack Spicer Papers, BANC MSS 2004/209, the Bancroft Library, University of California, Berkeley, Box 26, folders 7–9
JSP	Jack Spicer Papers, BANC MSS 2004/209, the Bancroft Library, University of California, Berkeley
Kl. 3	Frederick Klaeber (ed.), *Beowulf and the fight at Finnsburg*, 3rd edn (Boston, MA: D. C. Heath, 1936)
Kl. 4	R. D. Fulk, Robert E. Bjork, and John D. Niles (eds), *Klaeber's Beowulf*, 4th edn (Toronto: University of Toronto Press, 2008)
MV	Jack Spicer, *My vocabulary did this to me: the collected poetry of Jack Spicer*, ed. Peter Gizzi and Kevin Killian (Middletown, CT: Wesleyan University Press, 2008)
NM	*Neuphilologische Mitteilungen*
PBLG	Lewis Ellingham and Kevin Killian, *Poet be like god: Jack Spicer and the San Francisco Renaissance* (Hanover, NH: Wesleyan University Press, 1998)
PMLA	*Publications of the Modern Language Association*
postmedieval	*postmedieval: a journal of medieval cultural studies*
RBB	'Robin Blaser's *Beowulf*', Robin Blaser, translation of *Beowulf* (notes and manuscript), Jack Spicer Papers, BANC MSS 2004/209, the Bancroft Library, University of California, Berkeley, Box 20, folder 14
SFR	Davidson, Michael, *The San Francisco Renaissance: poetics and community at mid-century* (Cambridge: Cambridge University Press, 1989)
TF	Robin Blaser, *The fire: the collected essays of Robin Blaser*, ed. Miriam Nichols (Berkeley, CA: University of California Press, 2006)

Introduction: translative comparative poetics

I taught the *Beowulfs*. I know something about it.
Jack Spicer, Lecture on 'Poetry and politics', July 14, 1965[1]

This book emerges from what has become, for me, a nearly inexhaustibly remarkable incident in literary history that is probably obscure in almost equal measure—even among some specialists of the academic sub-fields to which it would most obviously pertain. The incident, or scene, in question involves two mid-century American avant-garde poets, Robin Blaser and Jack Spicer, constructing their own self-styled 'Renaissance' of poetics and queer community while simultaneously participating—with a notable degree of devotion—in the graduate-level *Beowulf* seminar of Germanic philologist Arthur G. Brodeur at the University of California, Berkeley, sometime between 1948 and 1950.[2] In this book, this scene coalesces as a micro-intellectual-history of avant-garde poetics and Old English studies that, in tandem with readings of *Beowulf* informed by those histories, develops a poetics that is at once modern and medieval. The result will be a series of new readings of *Beowulf* on a topic that has been neglected, avoided, or only periodically taken up by scholars of the poem since the middle of the twentieth century: aesthetics. *The heat of Beowulf* explores *Beowulf*'s non-representational capacities—relying on Blaser and Spicer's encounter with the poem under Brodeur's tutelage as a framework capable of furnishing questions, theories, and critical obsessions for reading the poem anew.

Blaser and Spicer, along with their then-friend, the poet Robert Duncan, were the center of what came to be known as the Berkeley Renaissance. Although a relatively small literary and visual arts coterie, this self-styled 'Renaissance' fed into the larger, more famous, and often incommensurately heterogeneous San Francisco Renaissance in the 1950s, itself a part of the much looser and bi-coastal set of tendencies that were anthologized by Donald Allen as the New American Poetry.[3] By the late 1940s, when Blaser and Spicer were Brodeur's students, the two were both working on MA degrees. Following Brodeur's *Beowulf* seminar, they would go on to take a full year in Germanic linguistic history. Both Blaser and Spicer produced near-complete translations of *Beowulf* for the seminar, which are housed among Spicer's papers at the Bancroft Library at Berkeley.

On completing his MA, Spicer would go on to teach Old English at the University of Minnesota for two years after refusing to sign the most infamous version of the California State employee loyalty oath, and then return to complete all his coursework, but never a thesis, for a PhD in Germanic linguistics. He became a central, if highly contentious, figure of the San Francisco poetry scene at mid-century, working various teaching and research jobs, before he died in 1965 from complications of alcoholism. Blaser would go on to complete his MA and a Master of Library Science degree at Berkeley (by 1955), subsequently working as a librarian at Harvard before returning to California and then taking a job in the English department at Simon Fraser University in British Columbia in 1966. He remained a key figure in the world of North American poetry and poetics until his death in 2009.

Devoid of context, Blaser's and Spicer's translations might seem merely like two of so many graduate student level exercises in reading Old English but, when understood at the confluence of particular literary, critical, and pedagogical histories, they generate fascinating questions about both *Beowulf* and mid-century poetry. Offering rare material traces of an Old English graduate classroom at mid-century, Blaser's and Spicer's *Beowulf* notebooks are all the more valuable for additionally preserving traces of avant-garde queer poets in such a classroom, and in California, no less. As David Hadbawnik (the co-editor, with Sean Reynolds, of an edition of selections from Spicer's translation) records, Spicer's notebooks indicate that the arguments set out in print in Brodeur's 1959 monograph, *The art of Beowulf*, were shaping his pedagogy at least a decade earlier.[4] A series of assignments recorded by Spicer is particularly telling. These include directives to 'discuss design and structure', to 'comment on tone, style, and diction, of [the] poem', and to discuss 'structure, style and diction'.[5] Another assignment recorded by Spicer, which Hadbawnik takes as 'the single biggest clue to the importance of this project for Spicer's later development',[6] is also particularly important. The assignment concerns the so-called 'Finn episode' of *Beowulf*—a digression on a heroic Scandinavian feud-narrative with an analog in a fragmentary Old English poem on the same subject known as the 'Finnsburg fragment' or 'The fight at Finnsburg'. The last two parts of the five-part assignment are particularly intriguing:

4. Analyze the previous passage [*Beowulf*, ll. 1107–1124] *as you would a modern poem* both as a unit in itself and as part of the *Beowulf* poem.

5. How does the Finn episode fit into *Beowulf* as an aesthetic whole? Compare the use of this episode with the use of other episodes. If the Finnsburgh [*sic*] fragment had been inserted in place of the Finn episode, how would you show that it did not fit aesthetically into the poem as a whole? [italics mine][7]

Unfortunately, aside from their translations, there are no extant formal written responses by Blaser or Spicer to these particular assignments. However, if a curiosity about avant-garde poets in the classroom of an accomplished mid-century philologist is a critical lure, this phrase, 'as you would a modern poem', is a very sharp hook, catching us wondering not only what Blaser and Spicer might have thought Brodeur meant but also how the phrase might have registered differently in their poetics community than in Brodeur's classroom, as well as how the poets negotiated these competing frameworks. Whatever Blaser and Spicer may have thought that Brodeur meant by 'a modern poem', how might they have brought the sensibilities of their poetics community to the assignment and into Brodeur's seminar (or, might they have brought the assignment into their poetics community and worked out these questions differently there than in the classroom)? Alternately, how might the philology classroom have informed avant-garde practices? To simply ask 'What might Brodeur's assignment to read a passage of Beowulf "as you would a modern poem" have meant to Blaser and Spicer?' would elide a whole array of questions, as well as the subtleties of literary and critical history that might supply the answers.

An account of Brodeur's classroom in Blaser's 1967 essay 'The fire' links the development of his poetics explicitly to those of *Beowulf*.

Blaser has just explained that 'since 1955 I have worked to find a line which will hold what I see and hear, and which will tie a reader to the poem, not to me', when he then insists that his preoccupation with this sort of line actually developed much earlier—that he had already found this sort of line in *Beowulf* when he translated the poem with Spicer for Brodeur's seminar:

> This fascination precedes my great debt to Charles Olson, for it is in a schoolbook problem, Plato's description of the power of music over the body and the dangers of poetry in *The Republic*, and it was the fantastic pull of hearing Brodeur read *Beowulf*, a hundred lines at a whack on a good day, which led Spicer and me to compete in our translations to bring over the heat of that story. I am greatly moved by what is received and held with force in a poet's work. And sometimes that work promises that a great deal more will be held.[8]

By the late 1940s, neither Blaser nor Spicer had yet directly taken on the work of Charles Olson—perhaps the most major figure of post-war American avant-garde poetry—whose variously didactic, archaeological, historiographical, and geographical poetics looked so little like the post-war mainstream along its entire range from Richard Wilbur to Robert Lowell. Olson's Field Poetics, or Projective Verse, would eventually become hugely important to both Blaser and Spicer, and certain aspects of Blaser's work are especially redolent of Olson's influence. But here, astonishingly, Blaser claims that Brodeur's *Beowulf* seminar—alongside nothing less monumental than reading *Plato* for the first time—led him to a poetics akin to Projective Verse before he actually encountered Olson or his work. As Blaser writes, 'the heat of that story'—the *heat* of *Beowulf*— motivates these basic strains of his poetics. It is from this characterization of *Beowulf* that I have taken my title, and this book is about that 'heat'.

Especially given its age, its supposedly foundational placement near the beginning of anthologies of British literature, it is easy to imagine the aesthetics of *Beowulf* as immobile, cold, sluggish, as a 'simple and static structure, solid and strong'.[9] But for Blaser at least, *Beowulf* is a poem of *heat*; a poem of energy, the sort of text that is *active* and entangled in multiple times and multiple histories, the sort of poem that behaves as if it is actively perceiving—*receiving and holding with force*, promising that a great deal more will be held. *Heat*, for Blaser, as we will come to see, is used here as a term of art in his poetics, a marker for a non-expressive poetics of translation and phenomenology, comprehending medieval conceptions of aesthetics and entangling vulnerable human corporeality with the non-human world.

Blaser's appeals to the 'pull' of Brodeur reading the poem, the 'power of music over the body', and the phenomenologically charged language about what a poem might 'receive and hold with force' have marked aesthetic implications. But what do these aesthetics involve, what is their history, and what precisely is meant by heat? As the first chapter will explore, Brodeur's contribution to mid-century *Beowulf* studies was focused directly on the possibility of a critical approach to the aesthetics of the poem but was hampered by its theoretical assumptions and its place in intellectual history—an odd alembic of mainstream English department poetics largely against which Blaser and Spicer were constituting their avant-garde practices. What, then, about this mid-century interest in the aesthetics of the poem, about Brodeur's scholarly and pedagogical approach, and about the Old English text itself and the labor of translating it made it possible for Blaser to make such a stunning claim about it all those years later, and for Spicer, just over a month before his death and already seriously unwell, to claim the poem as he does in the epigraph above? Assuming that these small but significant moments of literary history owe something to some capacity of the Old English text of *Beowulf* itself as well as some impulse or aspect of Brodeur's place in the mid-century critical genealogies of the study of *Beowulf,* and reading Blaser's and Spicer's poetics as a comparative and conceptually translative horizon for the aesthetics of the poem, this book activates an alternative—perhaps counterfactual—trajectory for the mid-century interest in the poem's aesthetics, 'rebooting' Brodeur's project along a route not yet taken and under the sway of a stranger poetics.

How might these mid-century poetics reshape our understanding of Old English poetry? After first constructing a context out of which this question crystallizes, I then attempt to answer it with new readings of the aesthetics of *Beowulf* that are ignited by Blaser's and Spicer's engagement with the poem. This book is thus structured to permit Blaser's and Spicer's encounter with *Beowulf* to furnish a series of critical frames for an intervention in the contemporary study of the Old English poem, strategically deploying Blaser's and Spicer's encounter with *Beowulf* to launch readings of the poem's aesthetics along a new trajectory. This process is not unlike the dynamics that art historian Alexander Nagel identifies in the relationship of modern and medieval arts, of 'the interactivity of artists acting on historians and historians acting on artists'.[10] What—to recall Blaser's phrase—is 'received and held with force' in the heat of *Beowulf*, and what more might it hold? In brief, in the arc of the book, relatively recent literary history will raise theoretical questions about the medieval, articulating conditions under which a comparative process becomes necessary. The book will then turn from context, critical genealogy, and signification to a comparative process that will yield, alongside more traditional claims about the poem's aesthetics, primarily a *description* (a kind of 'close surface' reading?) of the poem's aesthetic textures and operations on distinct scales of composition. While I will make plenty of arguments that construct contexts for reading *Beowulf*, when it comes to the poem itself, I am less invested in making claims about the poem than I am curious about trying to describe what it is like, and how Blaser's and Spicer's encounter with the poem can render that process newly strange and rewarding.

What reading the poetics of *Beowulf* comparatively with the poetics it helped to shape in the work of Blaser and Spicer offers is *the activity of the poem as a multisensory phenomenological aesthetics*—not conceived of as figure but as non-representational activity and process. Blaser's and Spicer's encounter with *Beowulf* will invite us, as Mary Carruthers puts it, to focus on 'the first stage of understanding, as it were, that of "making sense" of physical sensations derived from human encounters with their own crafted artefacts'.[11] Radicalized, this is in part what Blaser refers to as the *heat* of *Beowulf*—a phenomenological process of the poem's encounter with the non-human world that is not the poem *and* the human experience of reading the poem. To phrase it another way, the heat of *Beowulf* is a non-representational poetics of perceptual translation. Taking Blaser's and Spicer's encounter with *Beowulf*—positioned concretely within its own post-war intellectual geologies and literary histories—as a comparative horizon for the Old English poem will suggest the usefulness of cultivating a greater critical capacity to detect, comprehend, and explore the non-representational capacities and orientations of medieval poems without immediately re-inscribing them within a representational teleology. As a return to aesthetics that cannot be reduced to formalism, a naive account of a Kantian exhibition of aesthetic ideas, or a transhistorical sensualism, this effort will remain tied to language, materiality, and the historical. This analysis will be variously rooted in a sensology of medieval practices and discourses of rhetoric and physiology, as well as, at times, thinking about sensory impairment—and as a direct function of these discourses it will constantly bleed over into questions I want to mark as ecopoetical. In contemporary English-language poetics, self-consciously theorized ecopoetics has always been aware, as Jonathan Skinner explains, that it has 'no choice but to resist simply, and instrumentally, stepping over language'; that as such, 'poetry frank about the materiality of language ... is a step in the right direction, but not enough if it does not move beyond an uncritical mimesis'; and that 'the first source needs to be outside'.[12] This means, as my readings of *Beowulf* will bear out, that the phenomenological and sensological processes of a poem are never far from its ecopoetical dimensions—coalescing as a question of what the poem takes in from Outside and what that feels like, of how the poem renders it materially sensible as processes of the language.

Rather than survey the critical discourses germane to all these topics (any one of which could come with its own dedicated introduction), before turning to the heat of *Beowulf* in earnest, I want to address what I see as the larger critical intervention implicit not so much in the book's findings as in its conceptual and practical structure: this encounter of Old English studies with modern avant-garde poetics that constitutes its occasion and the framing of a comparative critical protocol. While, for some readers, this may seem unnecessary or less topically connected to the chapters that follow, the conceptual and practical structure will not be immediately legible in all sectors of medieval studies and will benefit from more purposefully constructing the terrain in which it makes sense to ask these questions. So after a further preliminary excursion into the world of Blaser and Spicer below, the remainder of the introduction will turn primarily on the disciplinary complexity of allowing modern avant-garde poetics to shape the process of Old English studies, including the slippery senses in which I have already been invoking the term *poetics*. Even so, the importance of translation—conceptually and practically—to what follows is such that I address it directly below, while sensology, phenomenology, and medieval rhetorical and psychological discourses receive extended attention in their own right early in the book. However, in pride of place: a little more intellectual context for Blaser's and Spicer's encounter with *Beowulf* alongside a sketch of the germane aspects of their earlier poetics.

Blaser and Spicer in the classroom of Arthur G. Brodeur

Blaser and Spicer were quite 'minor' poets when they met Brodeur, and they would remain more or less minor until a relatively recent critical mass of publications on their work spurred the attentions of literary critics in addition to their perennial admirers among avant-garde poets.[13] The 'Berkeley Renaissance' poetics community was conceived from the first in the context of avant-garde activity. Spicer introduced Blaser to Duncan after meeting Duncan while the two were taking the train back to Berkeley from an anarchist meeting at the San Francisco home of the poet Kenneth Rexroth.[14] And when the self-named Berkeley Renaissance got underway in 1946, a group of poets including Duncan and Spicer composed a 'Canto for Ezra Pound' to send to the poet, then in St Elizabeth's Hospital.[15] Blaser, Duncan, and Spicer were, by the late 1940s, known among the English department community at UC Berkeley as purveyors of an avant-garde poetry guided by their markedly academic and intellectual medievalism and antiquarianism, garnering the epithet 'the museum poets' from their teacher Josephine Miles.[16] All three poets took a number of courses, including independent studies, from the renowned medieval historian Ernst Kantorowicz, who took them into his relatively exclusive coterie of gay male intellectuals that he set up in deferential mimicry of the famous Stefan George *Kreis* of which he was a part before his flight from Nazi Germany.[17] And prior to the *Beowulf* seminar, Blaser and Spicer had already attempted an ambitious Old English lexicography project as undergraduates using Holthausen's dictionary, employing statistical historical linguistics research methods in an attempt to trace the distribution of Old English borrowings from non-religious Latin in a number of semantic categories.[18] In 1954, Blaser compiled the work as a project, titled 'Non-learned, non-ecclesiastical words in Old English from Latin and Romance sources: a quantitative approach', for a 'Librarianship' course towards his MLS degree, citing Spicer as his authority on proto-Old English forms and linguistic statistical calculations, and noting in pencil on the typescript that it is 'really Jack's <u>work</u> used by me'.[19] Along with his later linguistics work, Spicer's archive is full of odd bits of notes on general Germanic linguistic history, Old English, and student translations of Old Norse.[20]

Living queer in post-war America constituted a major component of the community inaugurated and sustained by the poetics of the Berkeley Renaissance—and while the potential queerness of the aesthetics of *Beowulf* as such is not the most salient focus of the chapters that follow (although queerness and *Beowulf* have been and should continue to be considered), the queerness of Blaser's and Spicer's poetics community is important both to the stakes of their more general medievalism and to the question of why Blaser and Spicer would look to *Beowulf* for a model of an aesthetics alternative to and much stranger than those of mainstream mid-century poetry and criticism—as well as what this would mean in an avant-garde ineluctably under the shadow of Ezra Pound.[21] Already, before meeting Blaser and Spicer, Duncan had published his landmark pre-Stonewall essay on queer politics, 'The homosexual in society', and Spicer would take a very active role in the early gay rights organization, the Mattachine Society.[22] Closer to the UC Berkeley campus, the poets met resistance to the association of their queerness with their commitments to poetry when they helped to organize and serve as volunteer instructors in the Berkeley Writer's Conference, an early non-credit experiment in 'creative writing' pedagogy and programming sponsored by the English department—shut down because it was perceived to be an organization run by a gay clique.[23]

The importance of Kantorowicz to the Berkeley Renaissance is better documented and more widely known to readers and critics of Blaser, Duncan, and Spicer than that of Brodeur.[24] There is a certain glamour to the connection between Kantorowicz and the Berkeley Renaissance that I cannot begrudge any critic. The alembic of Kantorowicz's own biography and intellectual contributions, including his involvement with George's Maximin cult, his flight from Nazi Germany, his stand against a notorious version of the California State employee loyalty oath (he left Berkeley rather than sign), and his academic work on nothing less monumental than the political theology of Medieval Kingship—perhaps all this generates a critical allure that Brodeur, whose name comes loaded with the freight of Germanic philology, has not yet carried for many readers of the Berkeley Renaissance. As an anecdote of Blaser's suggests, the name of Kantorowicz obtains just about as much of an air of Hollywood aristocracy as is possible for medieval historians:

> He was a, well, what? A Polish, Jewish, German nobleman. The rumor was he was a count, and I remember once when I was looking for friends and accidentally bumped into his apartment—this is before I really knew him well, I was taking courses—anyway I bump into his apartment, he's giving a party, there he is with a room full of people standing, drinks in their hands, and he is stretched out on a couch with a cigarette holder and everyone else. It looked like a court scene from the flicks.[25]

Blaser's biographer, Miriam Nichols, describes the impression he made on the young poets as 'irresistibly perfumed with scandal'.[26] Aside from the attraction of this apparent extravagance, shrouded behind some supposed lost 'Old World' nobility, the immediate issue of meeting Kantorowicz, Blaser would later explain, was so monumental in scope as 'to suddenly make us historical'.[27] Kantorowicz's investments in George's aestheticism and his work on medieval political authority directly shaped the loudest of Spicer's and Duncan's public performative contests of poetic authority in what Spicer called their 'intra-poetic feudatories'.[28] Brodeur's importance, by contrast, has gone less noticed by whole orders of magnitude. If it took the intellectual and stylistic grandeur of Kantorowicz to command the attention of the two young poets, what was it that Brodeur, and *Beowulf*, offered them?

Brodeur was a Harvard-educated philologist who had also studied in Sweden at the University of Uppsala in the early 1920s. His academic work was perennially preoccupied with Old Norse and Old English poetic diction. He published a translation of the bulk of the Old Norse *Prose Edda* that remains in print to this day (he received the honorary Knight of the Order of Vasa, first class, from the Swedish crown for this work), as well as a large number of articles on English and Scandinavian medieval literature with special attention to the Old English poem *Beowulf* and to Old Norse poetic diction.[29] And, in an almost uncanny echo of his now ultra-famous British counterpart J. R. R. Tolkien, Brodeur was also an author and co-author of science fiction and fantasy stories that appeared in the pulps in the late 1920s.[30] He was a decidedly nerdy, erudite, but charismatic sort of professor, emerging from privileged East Coast educational preening to head irrevocably west, teaching for the bulk of his career at Berkeley (including a stint as a visiting professor at the University of Chicago) until retirement in the late 1950s, after which he taught for a few years at the University of Oregon until 1963. His involvements at Berkeley relevant to the present discussion included participation in groups such as the Berkeley Communist faculty group (even as late as the early 1940s), The Adventure Campfire (a folksong and 'adventure' society, cited in John and Alan Lomax's landmark *American ballads and folksongs*, that Brodeur co-led with the folklorist Robert Winslow Gordon), and a group of agitators against the loyalty oath.[31] Brodeur was in the early phases of work on his monograph, *The art of Beowulf*, which would appear in 1959, when Blaser and Spicer took his seminar a decade before.

By the late 1940s, elements of Brodeur's project—larger assumptions, guiding questions, and specific points—were already salient aspects of his approach to the poem in the classroom.[32] As Chapter 3 will more closely examine, Spicer's notes reproduce, almost verbatim, material from Brodeur's appendix on Old English poetic diction. They record Brodeur's not uncontested parsing of cryptic references early in the poem to a future civil war in Denmark and the so-called 'Ingeld Episode', both elements crucial to Brodeur's interpretations of the poem's use of anticipation and its thematic unity.[33] As Hadbawnik already discovered, Spicer records assignments that include 'quintessentially Brodeurian questions',[34] including directives that guide students through the poem with an alertness to 'the *Beowulf* poet's famously fragmented approach', tracking the 'legendary', 'historical' and 'folktale' material in the notoriously-labeled 'episodes and digressions' of the poem.[35] Hadbawnik highlights a series of general directives that are worth rehearsing here, too: 'Discuss design and structure of B.[eowulf]. How affected by use of episodes and narratives ... Comment on tone, style, and diction of poem ... *Beowulf* as courtly epic ... Summarize two episodes ... Folk tale or legend. How does poet use? ... What [are] the folk tale elements. Distinguish from legendary material. How are both types blended?'[36] Evidence of what seems to be not only directives for class preparation but specific writing assignments includes instructions to 'write on one a. Finn + Hengest, b. Sigemund + Heremod, [c.] the Scylding dynasty'.[37] Another prompt includes options to write on 'structure, style, & diction of *B.[eowulf]*' and 'use & value of episodic material'.[38] An assignment on the famous illustration of the old warrior mourning for a hanged son (Kl. 3, ll. 2444–2462)[39]—a passage Brodeur takes, in his monograph, as part of a long monologue by Beowulf, with important implications for his overall argument—poses the question, 'who is [the] speaker?'[40] Students are asked to 'comment on place & artistic purpose' of the passage that introduces the Freawaru-Ingeld digression (Kl. 3, ll. 2020–2040). In Brodeur's book, this digression is the subject of an extended debate with the positions of critic Kemp Malone.[41] In the same block of notes, not attributed to any specific passage, we also find the seemingly redundant general direction, 'Discuss design & structure. What are [the] more striking poetic figures & artistic devices'.[42]

These notes and assignments are a decent, if disordered, itinerary through *The art of Beowulf*, which professes to be a 'prolegomenon' to an 'examination of the poet's gifts and powers, of the effects for which he strove and the means he used to achieve them'.[43] Brodeur lays out his argument thus:

> *Beowulf* is the work of a great artist, a work carefully planned and organized, excellent in form and structure, and composed with a sense of style unique in the poet's age. It will appear that I regard the work as composed in writing, and the author as trained in the art of the scop and educated as a clerk. In him the best of pagan antiquity and of the Christian culture of his time had fused; and we have in his work an achievement unequaled in English poetry before Chaucer.[44]

The chapters then proceed through 'The diction of *Beowulf*', 'Variation', 'Structure and unity', 'Design for terror', 'Setting and action', 'Episodes and digressions', 'Christian and pagan', and 'Anticipation, contrast, irony'. Not incidentally, in allowing Blaser's and Spicer's encounter with *Beowulf* to reframe and deform Brodeur's project, the macro-organization of the present book follows the organization of Brodeur's monograph to the extent possible. After a chapter on intellectual and literary history and another chapter theorizing medieval aesthetics, the remainder of the book is purposefully constructed to consider the aesthetics of the poem on the scale of incrementally larger units of composition, moving through diction, variation, and narrative.

Between these larger categories of inquiry in *The art of Beowulf* and the unique evidence of Spicer's notebook, we catch a remarkably concrete sense of the relationship between the development of Brodeur's arguments and their place in his pedagogy. But the assignment on the Finn episode cited above, to analyze the episode 'as you would a modern poem',[45] is perhaps the most immediately catalyzing. This assignment appears at a crucial moment in the history of teaching the 'modern poem' in North American English departments, and so, unless Brodeur drafted it with the utmost naivete, the assignment implicitly encodes a complex set of debates without marking out a simple position.

In his history of the discipline of literary studies in English, Gerald Graff notes that it is in the immediate wake of World War Two that both professional publications and department course offerings suddenly began assimilating modern literature into the curriculum and the disciplinary discourse 'so quietly ... that most students and perhaps most professors hardly noticed what happened'.[46] As one of the many public institutions—if a prestigious one—undergoing tremendous post-war shifts in undergraduate class demographics, UC Berkeley would have been at the forefront of such trends. In the last years of the 1940s, Brodeur's assignment would have been poised at a moment precisely between when teaching or researching a 'modern poem' (or evincing a desire to do so) was first quietly legitimized and when curricula began to concretely reflect this new situation. Graff's description of this moment thus frames the oddity of thinking about Blaser and Spicer, as ostensible composers of 'modern poems', approaching Brodeur's assignment:

> Before the fifties, even had literature departments wanted to increase their commitment to modern literature, they would have been hard pressed to find instructors competent to teach the subject, because the emphasis in doctoral programs was still overwhelmingly antiquarian. Those who did teach modern literature tended to be recruited from earlier periods, and their versatility did not always earn them the respect they hoped for.[47]

Brodeur was not, of course, teaching modern literature, but he was invoking the terms and at least some of the protocols of literary study that were in part developed for that purpose. The assignments quoted above indicate an investment in a particular lexicon for the appreciation of literary aesthetics (i.e. categories like *style, diction, tone*) and a preoccupation with structure and unity. Tellingly, an early title of Brodeur's *Beowulf* monograph was probably 'The structural unity of *Beowulf*'.[48] Brodeur's assignment signals an investment in—or perhaps a test-run of—categories that the New Criticism had initially developed for the study of 'modern' poetry and had begun to normalize as the dominant terms of all literary analysis in the North American English department.

Here was a professor of 'antiquarian' literature, not recruited to teach 'modern poetry' but teaching his 'antiquarian' literature 'as if a modern poem'—teaching it, moreover, to two students especially given to reading 'modern' poems (inasmuch as they were producers of them), even if they were equally eager to devote their time to seminars on medieval literature. In one sense, of course, Brodeur is merely ahead of a trend that spread New Critical reading to the whole English department (although, as we will see, the advent of oral-formulaic criticism would make Old English studies an embattled exception on this count).[49] Even so, at the moment in which Spicer records Brodeur's assignment, to read *Beowulf* 'as a modern poem' in a graduate seminar might have been the nearest some students had come to reading actual modern poems for an assignment in an English department (something that Spicer and Blaser, along with Duncan, were doing in a private para-academic coterie setting all along).[50] This timing of Blaser's and Spicer's encounter with Brodeur's assignment thus frames it as a site for thinking about comparative critical relationships between medieval and modern poetics.

It is not, of course, entirely certain that Brodeur's sense of 'modern' here does not merely refer to a larger category of periodization by which Keats and Wordsworth are 'modern' (as opposed to premodern) and the poetry of the twentieth-century is not even on the table—a usage that certainly persisted in British university settings well past mid-century. But I seriously doubt that Blaser or Spicer understood the term in that way, and this is precisely the point at which, especially in public American universities, the term was up for grabs. As Graff explains, by the 1960s, 'students had come to know more modern literature than any other kind; yet because they rarely studied it in conjunction with any earlier literature they did not acquire the contrastive perspective that would have enabled them to see what was "modern" about modern literature'.[51] Blaser and Spicer, on the other hand, were already reading and writing 'modern' literature in deliberate coordination with their 'antiquarian' studies of medieval poetry.

As the first chapter traces it out, a more precise bearing on the location of Blaser's and Spicer's encounter with *Beowulf* within literary and intellectual history will be taken at the intersections of, and gaps between, this critical and pedagogical genealogy of *Beowulf* in post-war North America and the poem's place in the English-language Poundian avant-garde. But also looming over this more strictly historical terrain are Blaser's and Spicer's later, more developed poetics, which, in their marginality from mainstream American post-war English departments, implicitly delineate roughly contemporary alternatives to Brodeur's assumptions about the relationship of his categories of inquiry to the question of aesthetics. Blaser, for example, would eventually come to write that 'no serious poetry can be explained as self-expression'.[52] As Chapter 4 will explore in the process of reframing Brodeur's approach to rhetorical variation, one of Spicer's most famous books, *After Lorca*, was to actively theorize poetic diction as a problem of a fundamentally non-representational and deeply historical compositional process in which '[w]ords are what sticks to the real. We use them to push the real, to drag the real into the poem'.[53] Blaser would later write of a 'reopening of words' which 'lets us see their solidifications'.[54] Among Spicer's most productive and difficult postures, we find his explanation of the practice of dictation, in which an intentionally ill-defined 'Outside' (Spicer claimed that 'the source is unimportant') and not the poet is responsible for the poems—to the extent that 'you feel less proud of the poem that you've written and know damn well it belongs to somebody else'.[55] This 'Outside of you which is writing poetry', which Spicer compares cheekily to Martians arranging messages out of the language in one's mind, is routinely taken as an all-out attack on Authorship, Romantic and Modern expressivism, and, in the simple insistence that 'there is an Outside to the poet',[56] a de-anthropocentric, non-representational opening of poetic language to a larger ecological order.

Blaser, who would later adapt the language of dictation and of the Outside in analyses and practices too copious to fully enumerate here, would also inflect this process specifically as an alternative to 'an anthropomorphism in tatters'[57] and as a rejection of what we might characterize as post-medieval conceptions of aesthetics. More than anything else, in this gesture, Blaser's aesthetics become much more deeply 'medieval' than those of professional critics of Old English at mid-century, closely paralleling a pattern of twentieth-century art history in which, as Nagel writes,

> [i]t is difficult to overestimate how deeply medievalism is built into the history of twentieth-century art. The modernist critiques of the museum, the academy, the easel picture, optical naturalism, the idea of the original work of art, and of the artist as a singular creator regularly produced both implicit and explicit rapports with the art that preceded these institutions and conceptions.[58]

Blaser explains that in 1957—only two years before Brodeur's monograph was to appear—'I could then hardly articulate my disbelief in the cogito of most poetics'.[59] In dealing with such an 'Outside'—wherein Blaser's statement that 'I speak entering what is speaking—at an edge' becomes a question of reframing the aesthetic in a negative dialectics with the legacy of romanticism and modernity—we find that '[s]tyle is initially a loss of personality or personality at stake'.[60] For 'the work is always the passage of a wildness',[61] and aesthetics becomes the process of encountering this wildness at/as some corporeally sensible and linguistically intelligible edge. As Chapter 2 will explore alongside medieval concepts of sensation and corporeality and a more systematic account of 'heat' as a term of art in Blaser's poetics, Blaser draws on the Greek etymology of 'aesthetics' in offering the distinctly pre-Kantian formulation of 'the aesthetic as perception'.[62]

For both poets, the dynamics introduced by an Outside eventually play out in what they call the 'serial poem'—a form and a compositional process of the discrete series that enacted an alternative to both the continuous long poem and the isolated, self-decontextualizing lyric extolled by the New Criticism. In the final chapter, the aesthetics of serial composition offer a point of departure to reconsider all the narrative and structural aesthetics of *Beowulf*'s famous and often vexing discontinuities—its 'episodes and digressions' and its variably demarcated narrative boundaries.

Despite their material imbrication within a mid-twentieth-century moment, these poetics gesture to an ontology of the poem that might be more easily recognized by a medievalist (a critic conversant with non- or un-authored, non-representational texts, styles determined by something other than individuality or the genres proper to publication under modern capitalism, etc.) than by a scholar of post-Romantic, modern western verse. A more comprehensive picture of the critical genealogies, sociological structures, and poetics discourses that articulate the intellectual context of Blaser's and Spicer's engagement with *Beowulf* will emerge *within* each of the chapters, in conversation with the elements of Brodeur's project to which they respond—and so intentionally subjected to the pressures of more literalized adjacency. A related benefit of this arrangement is that it avoids both laying out the Blaser and Spicer elements as an assumed stable 'background' or an abstracted 'methodology', leaving *Beowulf* as merely an object of study rather than a pole along a comparative axis. *The heat of Beowulf* is admittedly not a purely comparative project—Blaser's and Spicer's poetics are instrumentalized in reading *Beowulf* more than the reverse. But the project veers towards the comparative, and comparative work, of necessity, involves a series of chicken-and-egg organizational problems whose processes may benefit from being foregrounded rather than smoothed over, so this structuring is an effort to preserve as much as possible the comparative impulse of the book.

Avant-garde/Old English

Yet, why should we allow twentieth-century poetry—however informed by an encounter with an early medieval poem—to shape Old English studies in the first place? And where would this maneuver fit within contemporary lines of disciplinary study? Even 'comparative literature' may seem ill fitting, since the diachronic comparative axis in question remains within the history of what is ostensibly a 'single' language, and movement between medieval and modern poetics rarely structures conversations in that field today. But literary history can be recalcitrant, often exceeding the resources and routines of even the fields that most directly construct it. In discussing the difficulties of producing a Present Day English translation of *Beowulf* with a wide and lasting appeal, Nicholas Howe wrote that 'there is a history to be written of the influence that Old English poetry has had on nineteenth- and twentieth-century poetry in English'.[63] Howe may not have known that the writing of this history and the expansion of its archive was already well underway even before his untimely death in 2006, following especially from Chris Jones' *Strange likeness: the use of Old English in twentieth-century poetry*.[64] In the most important expansion of this archive for our purposes here, David Hadbawnik and Sean Reynolds brought to print a selection of Spicer's translation of *Beowulf* for Brodeur's seminar.[65] The translation was initially printed only as excerpts in the CUNY *Lost and Found* series, an important but limited-run periodical. However, this appearance of Spicer's *Beowulf* heralded a growing, if still little understood, awareness (among medievalists, poets, and critics of twentieth-century poetry) of an engagement with Old English poetics from within the more avant-garde precincts of North American English-language post-war poetry—rather than in the work of a Nobel Prize winner (where medievalists had long begun to celebrate it).[66]

Medievalists have—for some time—keenly engaged the crucial role played by the study of medieval thought in the development of some of the most radical contributions to twentieth-century philosophy and literary theory,[67] and some of the most persuasive critiques of traditional literary periodization and temporality have emerged from debates in medieval studies.[68] Two recent volumes edited by Gillian R. Overing and Ulrike Wiethaus have also begun to put the 'American' into 'deeper conversational exchange with the "Medieval"'.[69] Considerations of the importance of Old English literature to twentieth-century poetics, now moving beyond conventional reception and 'medievalism studies', continue apace.[70] Closer to the critical posture that precipitated this project, Seeta Chaganti has read Old English poetry alongside the poetry of J. H. Prynne because—in a formalism that I think moves towards the comparative—Prynne's work 'illuminates a structure for a premodern poetics'.[71] Clare A. Lees and Overing's emphasis on translation 'as both practice and concept' in proposing a 'dynamic and fluid exchange' of medieval studies and a variety of contemporary arts practices (visual, performative, poetic, conceptual) stakes out another related intellectual terrain.[72]

Yet, even among such persuasive and varied considerations of how modern and contemporary poetics might shape the questions of medievalists, only on rare occasions has the field of Old English studies comprehended avant-garde strains of twentieth-century or contemporary poetry specifically by taking the measure of their oppositional and disruptive, or simply wild or strange functions and histories as integral to either their status as shaped by Old English poetics or their capacity to shape Old English studies. The small but rich body of work that does take up this problem— addressing topics including temporality, orality and textuality, identity and migration, language history, and queerness—remains at an emergent phase,[73] and has not been met without either general perplexity in some sectors of early medieval studies or the general challenges of negotiating comparative methodologies for audiences that may perceive not only their expertise (both in terms of object of study and critical practices) but their very aesthetic sensibilities as disparate. In the introduction to a special issue of *postmedieval* on 'Contemporary poetics and the medieval muse', Reynolds and Hadbawnik write that the project was often met with a 'double-edged bewilderment that cut between medievalist scholars and scholars of contemporary poetry'.[74] Reflecting back on this moment more recently, Hadbawnik recalls that for those of us involved in that project (the present author included), 'engagements with medieval material undertaken by contemporary poets' had become 'vital, even political, as competing visions of what poetry is and was'.[75] And yet, Hadbawnik laments, in hoping this effort would be only one in a whole series of projects that never quite materialized, we may have been 'naïve'.[76]

In the case of the discovery and partial publication of Spicer's *Beowulf* translation, an enthusiastic response on the part of the field of Old English studies was accompanied by an apparent difficulty in fully comprehending this particular medieval node of avant-garde literary history and its material context. While I hope I have already made clear that I find Spicer's text fascinating and generative within the specific context in which it was produced and the horizon of his larger corpus, the glimpses of it in what follows will implicitly support my sense—as a critic of both Old English and post-war poetics—that it should not be taken as a polished, masterful achievement of translation or scholarship. Hadbawnik even remarks that

Spicer's translation lacks the 'freedom and wildness' of his later work.[77] Both Blaser's and Spicer's translations are most interesting and generative when understood for what they are—incomplete, in-process student work, predating their major poetic contributions, prepared, as we will see, for the tiniest of audiences, as one node of a much larger set of emergent avant-garde activities. It was thus—at least to my mind—odd and a little puzzling when in 2015 the *Old English Newsletter* announced that Spicer's incomplete translation of *Beowulf,* published only in excerpt, had posthumously received the 2016 Howell D. Chickering Prize in Translation—awarded to the 'best translation of an Old English work'.[78] I was thrilled by the attention this brought to Spicer's encounter with the poem but curious about how the field understood it. It is of course important to allow that a non-contemporary translation published for the first time might be considered the 'best' that appears in a given year. But without further context, giving the award to Spicer seems to obscure the place of his translation in his overall corpus, its place in the specifically avant-garde context in which it functioned (well outside of either established or emergent 'literary' publishing markets), and the nature of its particular importance to Old English studies.

It should not surprise us that more mainstream poets, like the late, Nobel Prize-winning Irish poet Seamus Heaney, have historically been more swiftly and easily comprehended, if not universally lauded, by the field of Old English studies—a field deeply invested in tradition(s) and sometimes tenuously anchored within English departments at least partly by an appeal to the place of *Beowulf* within the curriculum as a mythical point of origin for canonical English literature.[79] How this same field might comprehend an intentionally marginal, North American avant-garde's investment in Old English literature and Old English studies turns out to be considerably less automatic, and sometimes even a little awkward. Of course, these dynamics can cut both ways, and *The heat of Beowulf* takes up both the strangeness of Blaser's and Spicer's poetics and the strange and sometimes technically precise process of philology. There is a great deal of philological detail and some technical linguistic terminology in the readings of *Beowulf* that follow and, as mentioned, a cache of technically oriented, 'extra poetic' notes and translations in Blaser's and Spicer's archives.[80] These disciplinary protocols for reading *Beowulf* interested Blaser and Spicer immensely, and we miss a rich element of their intellectual formation and the conditions of their poetics—as well as the reminder that philology and contemporary poetics have often been intimates rather than strangers—if we avoid their complexities.

The heat of Beowulf could perhaps have been a simple addition to the project Howe described as 'a history of the influence that Old English poetry has had on nineteenth- and twentieth-century poetry in English'. A literary history configured around influences that obtain across traditional literary periods would not be all that unconventional a task for a more strictly historicist mode of medieval studies. Much of that particular discipline and its history lean heavily on what is sometimes called 'source study', and its practitioners are often at home moving between late antiquity or early modernity and the 1,000 years conventionally given over to the 'medieval period' proper. The shape of my inquiry, however, will not satisfy the positivism of a source-criticism purist. Such criticism is diachronic in scope, but it is not necessarily comparative. The epistemological trajectory of such work tends towards the unidirectional.

Instead, this is an effort to take up the influence that mid-century poetry and poetics *have just begun to have* on the study, the translation, and the teaching of Old English poetry—a task that may, in turn, make *Beowulf* itself more available to the practice of poetics in the present. Some time ago, Eileen A. Fradenburg Joy proposed 'the necessity of a scholarly *affect* of openness with regard to the possible interrelations (or in Walter Benjamin's terms, *constellations*)' between Old English texts and 'frankly, almost anything else that might lie in our path of pilgrimage to the past and back again'.[81] Partly because translation will emerge as a crucial conceptual element of Blaser's and Spicer's poetics as they reframe the aesthetics of *Beowulf*, and partly because the term is simply apt, I tend to think of this feedback loop between modern poetics, contemporary critical practice, and Old English poetry in terms of translation—as both a concept and a practice. There is a significant and persuasive body of work in Old English studies on translation as a textual and cultural practice in early medieval England[82] and, as we will see below, a great deal of energy spent on debating the merits of particular translations (especially in *Beowulf*)—as the existence of the aforementioned Chickering Prize also attests. Critics have even taken up the most salient strains of modern and contemporary translation

theory in thinking about specific translations of *Beowulf,* as well
as the translative logic at work in the Old English text of *Beowulf*
despite the fact that the poem is not a translation of anything.[83] But
Old English studies might more consistently heed translation as its
ineluctable link with particular histories and practices of modern
and contemporary poetics—translation as a term that points to
ways in which assumptions about modern and contemporary poetics
inflect all readings of Old English poetry.

In lockstep with this attention to translation, Old English studies
might entertain a concept of *poetics* that is at once more capacious
and more sensitive to more recent literary history—as simultaneously
a process and an object of study shuttling between the theory and
practice of poetry. Anecdotally, I often hear my medievalist colleagues
use 'poetics' as a much narrower reference to 'prosody' or rhetorical
devices specific to a given historical poetic form or style, but much
more rarely in the senses that we will see Blaser's or Spicer's readers
use it—in a manner dating at least to Aristotle, with reference to a
concrete condition, function, process, or ontology of *poesis.* Since
how we understand these two terms—translation and poetics—will
inevitably structure our assumptions about an encounter between
a mid-century avant-garde and Old English studies, I want to consider
each of them a little more before offering a more schematized map
of the chapters.

Translative criticism and the 'hypercanonical' text

That *any* instance of more recent poetics should inform the study
of the aesthetics of *Beowulf* will doubtless appear as anathema to
some number of Old English specialists. At the same time, precisely
as such a relatively conservative field whose literature relatively few
scholars have the training to read, Old English studies may not seem
like a likely candidate to be taken up by any avant-garde, especially
in the post-conceptual landscape of contemporary experimental
poetry. Despite a growing list of adventurous contemporary poetries
invested in Old English (some of which I hope to address in the
future),[84] for some experimental poets with marked investments in
longer literary histories,[85] early modern literature, along with its

attendant claims on the literature of western antiquity, continues to remain a more obvious site for developing a poetics in the present.[86] And yet, Old English studies does not wholly fail to comprehend its dependence on contemporary poetics for its very survival as a discipline, even if only for the translations by which most students encounter Old English literature and the role of more 'standard' translations in shaping scholarly assumptions. Work on Old English and some of the least easily assimilable writers of the previous century—Gertrude Stein, Basil Bunting, etc.—and recent experimental collaborations by artists, writers, and academics have gone some way to demonstrate that the continuing reception of early medieval literature and culture depends on acts of translation and transformative cultural memory.[87] The revered critic and influential translator of *Beowulf* R. M. Liuzza goes a little further and insists on the inescapability of thinking *Beowulf* apart from the frames of more contemporary poetics, asserting that 'our experience of the poem [*Beowulf*] occurs only within the framework of expectations given to us by the literary world in which we live and move'.[88]

We might radicalize that impulse, drawing on the capacity of more elastic—if not always the most recent—forms of translation theory to usefully entangle the most basic gestures of literary poetics and generalized critical practice. In this respect, it is worth noting that in his process of revising Ezra Pound's influential theories of translation within a postcolonial context, Brazilian poet, translator, and theorist Haroldo de Campos initially developed his theory of translation as a task of re-creation and of criticism, in which the best translations become 'both criticism and pedagogy'.[89] Taken seriously, Liuzza's remark above implicitly posits a similar relationship between criticism, translation, and pedagogy, but from the side of critical discourse—namely, the ineluctably translative dimension of all *critical* attention to an early medieval poem like *Beowulf*: criticism as translation and poetics. Even critical readings of *Beowulf* that refer exclusively to an edition of the Old English text, without providing any translation, remain inescapably conditioned by particular scenes of translation that are in turn governed by a particular poetics. Particular instances of more narrowly defined inter-lingual translation of *Beowulf* then become privileged, specially charged sites for identifying and debating the more general translative functions of *Beowulf* criticism as well as the translative qualities already in the Old English text.

Almost immediately, however, the student of twentieth-century and contemporary poetry and poetics will respond to Liuzza's above-cited claim with a rejoinder in the form of a question that might baffle many trained as medievalists: *which literary world, which twentieth-century poetry?* For we do not all live in the same literary world; there was not only one 'poetry world' in twentieth-century English-language poetics, nor is there only one now, and this fact bears significantly on how the study of Old English and modern poetics can mutually inform each other. So much is demonstrated by, for example, Rebecca Barr's study of the engagement with Old English poetry in poet and self-identified 'nasty man' Peter Reading's work (to take an example of a poet whose formalism sets it relatively far afield from my own interests). In 'eschewing avant-gardism, intellectual verse, and commercial success', Reading's investment in Old English may only be rescued from 'abject idiosyncrasy' when placed in a much longer literary genealogy, and even then, it can only surface as a 'commodity' within 'dystopian modernity'.[90] If modern and contemporary poetics constitutes an ineluctable horizon for the study of Old English poetry by virtue of the field's *dependence* on translation, then it is crucial that the field harbor a capacity to distinguish among the varieties of modern and contemporary poetics that pursue differing accounts of poesis and literary history.

But, historically, much of the critical debate about the translation of *Beowulf* into Present Day English betrays a fundamental misapprehension of the institutional, aesthetic, and political territories that constitute(d) modern and contemporary poetry and poetics.[91] Scholars who (not incorrectly) insist on the heterogeneity of the Old English literary world may all too easily mistake a single dominant idiom of contemporary poetry as a homogenizing synecdoche for poetics since modernity. Consider, for example, comments by critic Nicholas Howe on the occasion of a debate among prominent *Beowulf* scholars about translating the poem at the moment that Heaney's popular translation had just appeared. Despite a keen awareness of the importance of Old English verse to both mainstream and avant-garde twentieth-century poetry,[92] Howe evinces a desire for a translation of *Beowulf* with pretensions to a kind of—however necessarily attenuated—universality. In his essay, 'Who's afraid of translating *Beowulf*', Howe asserts that 'we should all be afraid of translating *Beowulf*. Very Afraid'.[93] This prescribed trepidation follows from Howe's sense that no one has been able to produce *the* translation of *Beowulf*. Articulating this concern on the heels of the competing releases of Nobel Laureate Heaney's translation (Norton, 2000) and Liuzza's attempt (Broadview, 2001), Howe implicitly posits a metaphor of *Beowulf* translation as a deadly hazard, pointing to what he calls the 'causality rate' among *Beowulf* translators—the failure for *Beowulf* translations in Present Day English to maintain an appeal to a wide audience for very long: 'almost all of the translations done of the poem in the past, especially before 1960 or so, are unreadable today and were probably unreadable when they first appeared'.[94] *Beowulf* lacks, Howe laments, 'that much-desired achievement: a version of *Beowulf* to match those of Homer by Richard Lattimore, Robert Fitzgerald, or Robert Fagles'.[95] In other words, Howe would like a *Beowulf* that we can 'all' agree on, whose pre-eminence is obvious. But this lament is only possible in the first place by assuming that the field of contemporary poetry is capable of or interested in yielding universally accessible and eminently 'readable' poems and, relatedly, that contemporary poetry could consist of a single, obvious idiom.

For Howe, Heaney's translation of *Beowulf* fails because it funnels the poem into too narrow a target idiom, taking up only those features of the poem most amenable to 'his [Heaney's] gifts' as a poet and leaving others forgotten, 'to let the remainder of the poem fade off in ways that only specialists will notice'.[96] This strategy, Howe writes, 'betrays not only the Old English poem of *Beowulf* but also the possibilities of contemporary poetry in modern English'.[97] While coming perhaps closer than any of his contemporaries to recognizing the heterogeneity of contemporary poetry from within Old English studies, what Howe misses here is the possibility that this mutual betrayal of the linguistic resources of both Old and Present Day English alike might stem not from the narrowness of the target idiom but rather from pretensions to poetics as an uncontested and universalizing process and the attendant expectation of one 'lasting' translation.

Heaney himself claims the easy syntax of his verse aims at a Wordsworthian 'directness of utterance' that would try to elide the heterogeneous orders and inevitable remainders of translation, courting, as I argue elsewhere, a curiously imperialist and colonialist linguistic ideology.[98] However potentially revolutionary during the Romantic period, the image of a 'man speaking to men' in even-handed and eminently legible dictions and meters (not to mention a gendered pretension to universality) may not strike us as the most adventurous edge of Present Day English poetics. For example, Thomas Meyer (whose translation of *Beowulf* first appeared in 2012 but was completed in the 1970s as a formal collage of several specific modernisms, long before Heaney's was commissioned) explains, '[t]here's not a translation of *Beowulf* that doesn't have me yawning. Having said that, Edwin Morgan's and Michael Alexander's are maybe my favorites. The Seamus Heaney strikes me as somehow pedestrian, at the same time somehow overbearing.'[99] By his account, Meyer attempted his translation as a response to a historically conditioned and contested site of English-language poetics. He explains his decision to sink the poem deeply into typography and to compose in the physical space of 'the page as a unit/recto-verso idea' as a response to the promptings of the International Concrete Poetry movement of the time as well as the then still-unassimilated late modernism of Objectivist-related poetics: 'Jonathan [Williams'] and [Basil] Bunting's "end of the long poem" tipped me over from oral to visual as the answer, how to put across and old (epic) poem in 1972'.[100] Where medievalists have classically sought a universal idiom (for which Heaney's translation here seems to function as a short-hand, simultaneously failing to capture Meyer's attention and sucking the air out of the room), Meyer seems to assume—if not privilege—multiply contested spaces of modern and contemporary poetry.

To the extent that these tendencies can tacitly shape the translative functions of *Beowulf* criticism, literary readings of *Beowulf,* I would thus contend, require a special vigilance with respect to their inherently comparative and translative capacities. This vigilance would in turn include, at very least, accounting for the ways that *Beowulf* criticism is implicitly conditioned by the assumptions of what poet and poetics theorist Charles Bernstein calls, in a broad stroke, 'official verse culture', as distinct from the heterogeneous and contested tangle of 'formally innovative and "otherstream" poetries that form the inchoate heart of the art of poetry'.[101] That is, Beowulf criticism is implicitly shaped not only by contemporary assumptions about what poetry is and does but by the assumptions of *particular* contemporary poetry communities. Left unexamined, hegemonic, mainstream ideologies of 'official verse culture' will shape basic assumptions about what poetry is within Old English studies—no matter whether its practitioners are of an oral-formulaic school, theoretically adventurous, or statistically or linguistically minded.

While this polemic might seem to some Old English scholars a mere squabble within contemporary poetry-world politics, if Liuzza is right in claiming that contemporary literary horizons inevitably inflect our encounters with *Beowulf*, then the stakes of this problem concern the very capacity for the reading of Old English poetry to continue to have stakes at all. Bernstein satirically claims that the 'program' of official verse culture is to 'promote safe reading experiences and is based on ... [the] founding principle that safe poetry is the best prophylactic against aesthetic experience'.[102] Most scholars of Old English verse, especially those who devote a significant portion of their scholarly energies to *Beowulf*, would probably *not* contend that the poetics of *Beowulf* should be understood or somehow re-rendered as 'safe' or incapable of yielding an aesthetically difficult and complicated experience for a reader—modern or medieval. The medievalist holds very dearly to a maxim to not 'patronise the past'.[103] And serious students of *Beowulf*—one at least imagines—would prefer that the poem survive as something other than an antiquarian curiosity, kept behind glass to keep both the poem and any reader safe.

This situation is further complicated in that, at this point in English-language literary history, the status of *Beowulf* within the English literary canon might be described as analogous to what comparativist Jonathan Arac has called the 'hypercanonical' in American literature.[104] Arac uses the term 'hypercanonical' to describe a select group of nineteenth-century American fiction texts (especially Mark Twain's *The Adventures of Huckleberry Finn*) whose reception dramatically shifted during the middle of the twentieth century when the texts were re-framed as High Literary Masterpieces in the construction of a National Literature—a process that at once relied on and newly required that such texts be 'extravagantly praised and studied primarily through close reading'.[105] *Huckleberry Finn*, Arac points out, was transformed from 'a beloved boy's book' into 'a masterpiece of world literature and ... the highest image of America'.[106]

In this way, '[h]ypercanonization involved teaching students to appreciate *Huckleberry Finn* in ways that it had never been appreciated before'.[107] Especially in the case of *Huckleberry Finn*, this hypercanonization sacralized the text, rendering it at once idol and target, hampering struggles against racism and important debates about morality, censorship, and Americanness.[108]

Beowulf is obviously not an example of hypercanonization narrowly defined with respect to the construction of Americanness within an exclusively *American* National Literature, and the stakes here should not be taken as equivalent. However—especially through the vector of J. R. R. Tolkien's lecture '*Beowulf*: the monsters and the critics'—the poem was similarly transformed during the post-war period from a disappointing specimen of antique barbarian poetry ('a poem so poor that only its accidental historical interest can still recommend it', as Tolkien ventriloquized the consensus to which he objected[109]) into an object for mandatory appreciation as the very point of origin for English literature surveys. As Nicholas Howe writes, recalling the likely centuries-long neglect of the poem's single surviving manuscript, 'that the poem made it into the canon, much less into the cliché "from *Beowulf* to Virginia Woolf", is something of a miracle'.[110] The mandate for teachers of medieval literature to *teach students to appreciate* Beowulf *as it never was before* has been further reaffirmed in that the poem is currently more widely read than at any time during its entire history—still as a bestseller; not long ago in Heaney's translation (2000) and, more recently, in Maria Dahvana Headley's undeniably significant translation of the poem (2020). Headley's text even led a reviewer for National Public Radio to declare that after so many translations, '[t]here is no *real* Beowulf. Not anymore', while yet still confidently avowing that what *Beowulf* '*always* was' is this '*Hamilton* for the Geats and Scyldings' that '[d]emands ... to be taught as the thing that it is—the Marvel movie of its time'.[111] This overleveraged status of the poem remains a liability, with increasingly high stakes. Scholars might object that these examples speak only to 'popular' reading practices. However, we risk kidding ourselves if we think that such widely read translations never inflect professionalized readings (even if only in imagined negations or refusals). Surely, they appear on countless syllabuses— where their very contemporaneity is often deployed as a blunt lure for student interest, and in which context 'professionals' presumably *do* read them as instructors. A desire for a univocal, mandatory, and supposedly universal *Beowulf* not only produces invisible distortions for even the most positivist work on the poem. It also impedes the discussions of the poem with the highest stakes, for example, guaranteeing a site within medieval studies and English-language literary culture that will at best slow the effort to render early medieval studies incompatible with white supremacy.[112]

A critically responsible attempt to open the aesthetics of *Beowulf* to modern poetics might thus emerge from the position of a secular critic—de-sacralizing our relationship to the poem and guarding against appeals to either a fantasy of democratized or scientified legibility or spiritualized transcendence).[113] Especially for scholars of hypercanonical, or pseudo-hypercanonical poems situated at a mythical origin of a 'national' literary history (e.g. the *Iliad*, the *Divine comedy*, *Beowulf*, *Le chanson de Roland*), an investment in such a 'foundational' poem's 'universal appeal' (no matter how weak, disguised, or tacit) may often come more easily than a willingness to negotiate poetries that not only reject the possibility of their universality but in fact foreground and leverage their concrete and contingent horizons.

For our purposes, aesthetics are an early causality of criticism whose translative dimension tends towards a universalizing poetics. In developing the idea of translation as 'creation and criticism', de Campos points to critic and philosopher Max Bense's observation that, while semantic (and related types of) information in a literary text may exhibit high levels of redundancy because, in contrast, 'aesthetic information is identical to its original codification', the translator must reckon with the reality that '*the fragility* of aesthetic information, is, therefore, colossal'.[114] The implications of this special status that de Campos assigns to aesthetic information—that it 'cannot be semantically interpreted'—are what, in the first place, lead him to postulate the 'impossibility of translation' and the need to reconceptualize translation as 'transcreation'.[115] In a translative account of the hypercanonical, the fragility of the aesthetic is all the more precarious as semantic or documentary dimensions become overcharged in service to activities that translate aesthetic information only insofar as it is recoded in terms of ideology. For this very reason, the translation of the hypercanonical may especially tempt scholars to tacitly rely on the assumptions of a homogenizing or universalizing poetics, or at least to ignore (or, more dispassionately, cede) the particular aesthetic dimensions of a particular present day target 'literary world'. Even as an exigent shortcut for a specialist in premodern literature, a tacit sense of contemporary poetry and poetics as a univocal field will only strengthen this temptation.

Among the lasting contributions of Spicer's poetics and their constructions of coterie—like those of Frank O'Hara—are their displacements of an assumed 'rhetoric of universality' in American poetics.[116] 'We have to get over', wrote Bernstein back in the 1990s, 'as in getting over a disease, the idea that we can "all" speak to one another in the universal voice of poetry'.[117] Spicer is known for an intensely factional poetics, while Blaser, especially in his later work, for an investment in a reconceived concept of a 'public world'.[118] Yet even Blaser's concept of 'public' marks an intense reformation of the naive modernist account, reframing the poetic image as not a universal voice but, as Andrew Mossin phrases it, the much more fragile and contingent 'site of a meeting and the instant of an interchange', where or when the poem becomes 'a site of both adjoinment and separation'.[119] In the wake of the Trump years and the (ongoing) deadly results of their conspiracy theories, a desire for some semblance of a public sphere is entirely understandable, but to expect an uncontested, immediate version of this from poetry, be it very new or very old, is to set ourselves up—at very least—for disappointment. A translative comparative poetics of *Beowulf* will at best render the poem as the site of a particularized meeting. We need many *Beowulf*s—not just in translation but also in the criticism. Blaser's and Spicer's encounter with the poem will give us such a *Beowulf* that can only be one among others.

Poetics and particularisms

To allow modern and contemporary poetics to shape how we attempt to comprehend *Beowulf,* we need to accord just as much historicity to 'modern and contemporary' poetics as a medievalist would demand for the past. To put this another way: translative comparative modes do not proceed in the manner of a controlled experiment—cannot control the variables of either past or present. This epistemological instability is partly why, in agreement with

Bernstein's argument that 'scholarship requires poetics',[120] the chapters which follow accordingly pursue the process of poetics as much as they pursue poetics as their object of study.

Bernstein's playful account of poetics, at times selectively engaged by medievalists,[121] can seem to confirm long-standing practices in the study of premodern literatures while simultaneously challenging the most basic orientations of the field. Bernstein privileges poetics as, on the one hand, a long and necessarily comparative history of rhetorical and compositional practices, procedures, and contexts, and, on the other, a field of future-oriented processes emerging or arriving only in their performance. In this usage, poetics signals not precisely a 'field', a 'discipline', or a 'genre' so much as an ineluctably performative discursive practice situated between the theorization and the practice of poetry—whose orientations to temporality and to actually extant poetry are distinct from those of conventional 'literary criticism':

> While poetics brings to mind a long history of laws of composition, poetics can also stress poiesis—the actual making or doing: poetry as process. Every doing carries the potential of something new, emergent, something not already predicated by poetics. Practice overtakes theory, practice changes. And not just writing practice but also performance.[122]

Rather than embracing a disciplinary posture of pure knowledge-production, poetics is a critical practice, with all the resources of literary criticism, oriented towards poesis-production—self-modulating as its very products overtake it. Where conventional criticism reads instances of poesis as an object of study, poetics is thus willing to comprehend them as the performance of theory. Poetics is always tied to the practice of poetry, but we need not be writing or discussing 'a poem' to be engaged in the process of poetics. One practical result: the idioms of contemporary poetics are thus unstable, often deceptively resembling professionalized critical prose but prone to lapses away from the scaffolding of the constative. Genealogically, much North American contemporary poetics writing is distinct from and yet sometimes also an extension of the category of 'nonversified poetry' that Stephen Fredman once dubbed 'poet's prose', which emerges out of a constant question of 'whether poetry, under present conditions, is possible' and in which 'American poets refuse to separate imagination and intellect' while giving up the 'prestige' of verse.[123] In practice, this means that we need to be able to comprehend apparently critical prose, composed under the sign of poetics, as the result of an intentional choice away from, or failure to produce, verse, rather than an assumption of a supposedly universal prose 'genre'.

Accordingly, Bernstein argues, the practice of poetics embraces a set of attendant stylistic values that condition a variable, heterogeneous critical idiom: 'poetics is situational, shifts with the winds, courts contradiction, feeds on inconsistency'.[124] These values additionally stem from and encourage a set of reversals of traditional orientations to the temporality of literary history:

> One of the two most important lessons of poetics is that the contemporary practice of poetry informs all readings of poetry. Poetry begins in the present moment and moves backward and forward from there. With no orientation in contemporary poetry and poetics, young scholars will remain ungrounded, without a direct connection to how works of literature are engendered in their own time. Without this knowledge, it will be all the harder to understand the relation of older works to their own times or to ours, or, for that matter, future works to the times yet to come. The absence of this visceral connection to poetic practice may be disguised by the demeanor of disinterest or clinical professionalism, but it will be betrayed in the body of the text of any scholarship produced.[125]

While, in a long history of western poetry, theory and positivist historical narrative may have, by turns, supplanted poetics as conditions of scholarly writing about literature, Bernstein would reverse or confuse these relations.[126] Scholarship under the sign of comparative poetics would yield not only readings of supposedly fixed texts but also an account of the conditions by which dynamic and mutually informative relationships arise between them.

By invoking poetics, and not merely 'literary studies', I thus mean to radicalize the uncertainty and the contingency of the outcomes of this attempt to reboot the study of the aesthetics of *Beowulf*, without abandoning claims for its effectiveness, interest, or potential historical functions. I also mean to clarify that *The heat of Beowulf* is less interested in a hermeneutic of *Beowulf*'s significance than a description of its phenomenological contours, less interested in its findings than its process. Bernstein praises scholarship enacted 'not as a predetermined ride to selected port of calls but as an exploration by association, one perception leading to the next, a network of stoppages, detours, reconnaissance'.[127] Rather than conceiving of each installment of what follows as a teleological intervention in this or that critical topic, and foregrounding those discourses, the bulk of the energy of each chapter is spent on relatively micrological readings, purposefully indexing their variable larger implications in-process and after the fact. In turning towards poetics, I turn towards generalization in a way that is meant to founder on the narrow and the idiosyncratic.

Performed under the sign of poetics, even a 'scholarly' effort 'will sometimes go out of its way to seem implausible, to exaggerate, or even to be self-deprecating'.[128] Comparative poetics would allow for, even cultivate, processes of mutual deformation. Readers of Blaser, Spicer, and their contemporaries can easily take for granted that such exaggerative or otherwise distorting performances may inevitably signpost, or even condition, a given critical argument. Spicer, after all, somewhat tantalizingly suggested that we let Martians write our poetry for us.[129] By contrast, Old English studies may be less accustomed to a purposefully implausible critical lexicon. Although I still remain, in some ways, unsatisfied with the slipperiness of terms I propose, the Old English poem and modern poets, read together, furnish us with a lexicon that may get us closer than we may have been before to concretely naming the non-representational aesthetic functions of the poem.

Habits and contexts

Even as Blaser's and Spicer's catalyzing encounter with *Beowulf* is so deeply shaped by Brodeur's classroom, Brodeur's ticks and obsessions, Brodeur's interlocutors, we do not, now, share the same literary world as Brodeur, or Blaser and Spicer. We do not even share the same *Beowulf* and, for us, the general milieu of *Beowulf* scholarship since the turn of the millennium remains an inescapable and useful horizon. As valuable as I and many of my colleagues in Old English studies probably still find Brodeur's 1959 monograph, *The art of Beowulf*, as the first chapter will explore, its critical lexicon may seem—quite legitimately—dead in the water in the twenty-first century. Yet, if the aesthetics of Old English poetry are not precisely a current critical fashion, this is not to say that attention to aesthetics in Old English poetry has been entirely neglected in the new millennium. Renée R. Trilling's *The aesthetics of nostalgia: historical representation in Old English verse* includes an elegant exploration of, among other things, how specific verse styles of Old English historical verse meditated and signaled poetry as 'both a tool of hegemonic discourse and a vehicle of dissent'.[130] Elizabeth M. Tyler's study of the 'aesthetics of the familiar' in Old English poetry is an important exploration of the 'stability of the stylistic conventions in Old English poetry', historicizing the social expectations of traditional stylistic structures in representations of familiar, pervasive objects like 'treasure'—and from the perspective of composition.[131] An entire collection on the aesthetics of (mostly) *Beowulf* appeared about a decade ago, along with a monograph devoted to the history of major translations of the poem.[132]

As Chapter 2 explains, this book differs from these contributions in taking aesthetics as a question not of criteria for incorporeal beauty or excellence, nor in terms of the function of aesthetics as a signifier, but as the site of the poem's entanglement with vulnerable biophysical corporeal experience and the non-human world. This orientation of aesthetics around sensory-affective experience—perception rather than abstraction—marks neither a turn from history nor politics, and will require a calibration of early medieval models of health, sensation, and rhetoric with twentieth-century phenomenology. Because it is rooted in human corporeality, this elaboration of the perceptual operations of the poem also has the benefit of engaging with contemporary medieval disability studies and posing questions about the relationship of sensory impairment to sensorial poetics while also implicitly redressing the customarily representational poetics of ecocriticism in Old English studies. One connection threaded variously through Chapters 2 through 5, which I will not always have space to remark on but is worth making more explicit here, is the possibility of a mode of processual perception that, on the one hand, engages in a multisensoriality that offers a corrective to the presumed dominance of vision in western aesthetics and, on the other, constantly bleeds over into a matter of ecological entanglement that differs from what posthumanist, New Materialist, or more straightforward representational ecocritical interventions in medieval studies routinely consider: the poem as a perceptual process that translates the non-human world into humanly perceptible experience. More generally, the critical milieu around *Beowulf* is ready for Blaser's and Spicer's poetics to shape a stranger lexicon for the poem's aesthetics. We are approaching the two-decade mark since, in their essay introducing *The postmodern Beowulf*, Eileen A. Fradenburg Joy and Mary K. Ramsey took *Beowulf* as 'a test case of what literary criticism is capable of saying and doing' and found the poem 'liquid and supple' in its anxieties about history, violence, community, and, even—however counterintuitively—modernity and postmodernity.[133] Unmooring us as readers of a *Beowulf* that becomes 'a poem in our time', Overing argues that *Beowulf* provokes 'a radical reconfiguration of the interconnection of time, space, and embodiment'.[134] Unmoored with *Beowulf*, I look to Blaser's and Spicer's poetics to reignite still-unrealized dimensions of mid-century *Beowulf* criticism in the midst of our current conversations about the poem. Poet and translator Lyn Hejinian points out that 'it is the task of poetry to produce the phrase *this is happening*, and thereby to provoke the sensation that corresponds to it'—namely, that of 'the liveliness of the world'—only to qualify this borderline platitude by arguing that 'to produce such a sensation is not necessarily to produce knowledge, nor even a unit of cognition, but rather to discover context and, therein, reason'.[135] Whether the discovery of 'context' yields something that goes by the name of reason lies well beyond the scope of this book, but the first step in Hejinian's argument will be indispensable: the suggestion that poetics not only ventures an incipient moment (a situation Hejinian narrates as 'along comes something, launched in context') but does so in such a way as to simultaneously render a given 'context' legible and co-ventured so that 'context too is launched … something comes into existence *qua* context'.[136] Neglected arguments, outmoded critical approaches, and critical impasses—these stand to emerge as contexts potentially 'relaunched' right into the midst of the present; as contexts newly legible as such; and as conditions that activate the scene of a poetics that is launched by *Beowulf* and, in turn, that launches *Beowulf*, into new and uncertain critical scenes.

In his watershed 1994 monograph, *Thinking about 'Beowulf'*, James W. Earl admits, 'I no longer trust those who say they know what *Beowulf* means, or even what it is about',[137] but he goes on to conclude that 'we can assume from the start that *Beowulf* bore a complex, indirect, and nonmimetic relation to any historical reality'.[138] Even years later, Earl wrote that 'the poem never gets easier, and I never stop being surprised'.[139] Overing describes a similar phenomenon, which amounts to a 'habit' of the poem that, I would argue, allows its non-representational functions to operate in a multitemporal context:

> The beginning student of the poem [*Beowulf*], I argue, encounters the same difficulties as the lifelong scholar; the poem has a habit of indeterminacy, an acceptance of contradiction, and a fluidity of definition on many levels. Time is one of these.[140]

A property inhering in the text itself, the identification of this habit prepares the way to more closely enumerate the non-representational aesthetics that it encompasses. For Earl, while some of the 'difficulties' of the poem may be explained as 'byproducts of the translation process', some are indeed 'features of *Beowulf*'s style itself'.[141] Included, for Earl, in '*Beowulf*'s beguiling aesthetic' is a '*haunting*' quality.[142] Although Earl invokes haunting here within a roughly psychoanalytic framework, his vocabulary necessarily summons, in a touch, the inescapably translational, non-present yet still-operating, deconstructive temporalities of the ghost or the specter that are an effect of translation and that Jacques Derrida famously positions as 'not docile to time'—as the dis-adjustment of any 'linking of modalized presents'.[143] This assertion of *Beowulf*'s haunting style thus implicitly links the *operations* of the poem's relationship to translation, its indeterminacies of signification, and its temporal instabilities to the question of the poem's aesthetics.

The heat of Beowulf coalesces out of concrete contingencies within this temporal unmooring. Poised at the intersection of the mid-century genealogies of the aesthetics of *Beowulf*, Chapter 1, 'The aesthetics of *Beowulf* in the middle of the twentieth century', traces the intellectual contexts of modernism and literary studies out of which we can 'reboot' the mid-century interest in the poem's aesthetics along a new trajectory. Blaser's and Spicer's encounter with *Beowulf* unfolds in the wake of, but simultaneously contests, the aesthetics of both Ezra Pound's medievalism and an emergent but delicate academic framework for aesthetic analysis of Old English poetry at mid-century. Chapter 2, '"Heat", medieval aesthetics, and multisensory complexion in *Beowulf*, begins to imagine in concrete terms the implications of the literary and critical histories of the first chapter by asking what precisely Blaser meant in referring to the 'heat' of *Beowulf*, and what this comprehends about early medieval aesthetics. Contextualizing heat within Blaser's formalized poetics, heat emerges as a term of a phenomenologically translative poetics that phrases the aesthetic as 'perception' and frames poesis as a primarily perceptual process of vulnerable corporeality. Calibrating this critical lexicon to early medieval concepts of aesthetics, the chapter constellates Blaser's engagement with the Old English poem *The dream of the rood* with the phenomenology of Maurice Merleau-Ponty, early medieval discourses of the senses, and Mary Carruthers' analysis of rhetoric in terms of medieval models of corporeality and multisensory complexion in medieval aesthetics. Carruthers' contributions to the history of medieval aesthetics and compositional rhetoric— which may not be routinely taken up as a resource by scholars of Old English literature but speak directly to compositional and rhetorical practices of the early Middle Ages—are a shaping force on the remainder of the book.[144] Phrased as a question about perception, Blaser's 'heat' occupies a convergence of the ecopoetical functions of aesthetics and the ways that sensory impairments—especially vision impairments—might shape how we understand aesthetics within western medieval hierarchies of the senses. The chapter concludes by turning this analysis on a reading of multisensoriality in *Beowulf*, where, I argue, the poem represents a world whose multisensoriality would require the kind of phenomenological translation performed by Blaser's 'heat' in order to render it sensible for the vulnerable corporeality of the human sensorium.

At the third chapter, the book shifts the critical terrain from genealogies, signification, and the representation of perception to perception itself. As suggested above, Chapters 3 through 5 are loosely but purposefully organized on the pattern of Brodeur's *The art of Beowulf*, successively considering the aesthetics of the poem on incrementally larger scales of composition. Like Brodeur, I begin with the poem's compound poetic diction before proceeding to variation and then narrative structure. I dispense with separate investments in 'setting', because the implications of each chapter concern elements traditionally conceived of as 'setting' or 'scenery'; and I skip 'unity' and thematically defined categories, simply because following the heat of *Beowulf* will lead us elsewhere. Chapter 3, 'The heat of *earmsceapen* style: translatability and compound diction', thus revisits the debates about Old English poetic diction that formed the bedrock of the mid-century interest in *Beowulf*'s aesthetics, rewound through Blaser's and Spicer's responses to Brodeur's attention to compound words in the poem. Their experiments indirectly point towards a fundamental instability *within* compound words stemming from the ease of their capacity for rephrasing, or what I come to call 'translatability'. Tending to the translatability of compound diction, the greater portion of the chapter performs an exaggeratedly close reading of Hrothgar's verbal map to the so-called 'Grendel-mere', tracking an unstable, deforming lexical 'movement' that forms the rhetorical *ductus* (path) through the passage. The resulting *earmsceapen* (ill-shaped) style resonates with the cardiocentric hydraulic model of cognitive-affective vernacular psychology in Old English verse and indexes a process by which the poem deforms the human sensorium.

In Chapter 4, '"Real cliffs": variation and lexical kinetics', I take on an incrementally larger unit of composition that builds on and modifies the translatability of compound diction: the rhetorical pattern of *variation*. While an anxiety about the possibility of lexical redundancy in variation led most critical discourses away from considering its stylistic functions, Spicer's response to a similar anxiety in literary modernism points instead towards allowing the possibility of redundancy to activate the aesthetic functions of reference and a permutational lexical kinetics. Following Spicer's lead, I reexamine well-known instances of variation in *Beowulf* across the passages that narrate the sea-crossings of Beowulf and his warriors, often read as set-piece descriptions that merely facilitate the human action of the poem. However, the internal imbalance of the compound lexemes that occur in these figures of variation interacts with the prosodical patterns of Old English verse in a way that disrupts this overt representational logic, reactivating the referential function of variation as a stylization that renders the poem more porous to the non-human world.

Finally, Chapter 5, 'Narrating heat in a hot world', proceeds to the yet larger scale of *Beowulf*'s narrative aesthetics. Against the backdrop of mid-century structuralist narratology, Blaser's and Spicer's approach to what they called 'serial composition' provides a point of departure for a reevaluation of the *interruptive* and incomplete aesthetics of a poem whose 'episodes and digressions' obsessed its mid-century critics. Rather than relitigate the episodes and digressions directly, I first turn to lyrical interruptions of the poem's narrative and, paying special attention to the poem's lexicon of fire, trace a fragmentary narrative about the aesthetics of fire and flame, arguing that the aesthetics of these instances of flame-eaten lyricism mark an attempt to render sensible the resistance of sensoriality to narrativity. I then turn to the 'Finnsburg episode', which Brodeur asked Blaser and Spicer to read as a discrete modern poem just as they were formulating their early serial poetics. Examining the narrative, formal, stylistic, and 'fitt-division' boundaries that surround either end of the episode, I trace a latent seriality conditioned by a layering of pure spacing and the intrusion of non-narrative compositions whose edges constitute the texture of a poem besieged by sensoriality on the scale of narrative. I conclude by articulating how the heat of *Beowulf* operates differently—perhaps *less humanly*—on the scale of narrative than on that of diction.

As Mary Kate Hurley argues, *Beowulf* is a poem that, while not a translation in the conventional sense, nonetheless 'deploys a myriad of translation effects' and 'partakes of the same cultural logic as traditional translations'.[145] Where Hurley examines the poem's fundamentally translative logic in terms of the human and non-human collectivities that it renders legible,[146] the heat of *Beowulf* points to a scene of conventional translation that reopens the questions of the non-representational, perceptual functions of the poem's translative operations, asking how the poem renders the non-human sensible by impinging on the human sensorium. As translative, the aesthetics of *Beowulf* are not static, solid, or strong. The aesthetic may be fragile, and conventional translative practices may tend to translate anything and everything *but* aesthetic information. De Campos' early solution to this problem was to depart from traditional figures of translation as 'carrying across' from foreign to domestic or past to present—since the aesthetic information is too fragile to survive such a journey. Rather, he posits a recreation of texts that yields two 'isomorphic bodies', which 'crystallize within the same system'.[147] In what follows, we track the heat of *Beowulf* as it recrystallizes in Blaser's and Spicer's engagement with the poem. But, as fundamentally a translative operation, we will also follow the contours and textures

of the poem's aesthetics as constituted by what the poem gives to the
human sensorium as recrystallizations of its own perceptual processes.

As avant-garde poets, Blaser and Spicer found *heat* in *Beowulf*
in the middle of the twentieth century; *The heat of Beowulf* draws
strategically from that encounter to give an account of the poem
that aims to reframe the Old English text as an active force in
twenty-first-century discussions of medieval poetics. My hope is
that the poem itself emerges as a perceptual entity in its own right,
in which its aesthetics mark attempts to translate into language
what is not the poem. If, as Merleau-Ponty argues, 'the word
"perception" indicates a *direction* more than a primitive function',[148]
then the aesthetics of *Beowulf* chart a frenetic, veering, curving
line—one that manages both to proliferate its vectors and barb its
way into bits of the energetic world before it hooks them back into
the poem itself.

Notes

1 *House,* p. 168.
2 These dates are not entirely clear. 1950 is a *terminus ad quem* for Spicer
   before he left UC Berkeley to teach in Minnesota. The date '2/14/50'
   appears on the first extant page of Blaser's *Beowulf* notebook (RBB),
   but Spicer's MA transcript logs courses from Brodeur in September
   1948 (English 211G) and February of 1949 (English 211H), dates
   confirmed by another anecdote in *PBLG,* p. 26; and we know Blaser
   and Spicer took the courses in question together (see *AT,* p. 62, *TF,* p.
   414 n. 20). Two other courses appear on Spicer's transcript as English
   211 for 'Fall 1949' and (probably) 'Spring 1950' (the handwriting
   is not clear) without an instructor listed, and this may account for
   the date in Blaser's notebook. Miriam Nichols reports the two went
   on to take a full year of Germanic linguistic history (*TF,* p. 414 n.
   20). However, Blaser's undergraduate transcript (I have not located
   any graduate records), which marks his courses from February 1949
   as counting towards graduate studies, lists none of Spicer's courses
   from 1948–49, and records English 200 (247) for 1948–49 (Blaser
   fonds, MSA-109005). It is possible that Spicer's earlier courses with
   Brodeur were linguistic history classes and not the *Beowulf* seminar,
   which would tally with a 1948 notebook on linguistic history (JSP
   Box 23, folder 11), and that the two took *Beowulf* in 1950, but not
   linguistic history, at the same time. See also Hadbawnik, 'Introduction:

"*Beowulf* is a hoax"', pp. 3–4. I am grateful that Kevin Killian shared a photocopy of Spicer's transcript with me.

3 See Allen, *The new American poetry*. The groundwork of Michael Davidson's foundational study, *The San Francisco Renaissance* (1989) informs this project throughout.
4 Hadbawnik, 'Introduction: "*Beowulf* is a hoax"', p. 4.
5 JSB.
6 Hadbawnik, 'Introduction: "*Beowulf* is a hoax"', 6.
7 JSB. An image of this passage is also reproduced and quoted in Hadbawnik, 'Introduction: "*Beowulf* is a hoax"', frontispiece, pp. 6–7.
8 *TF*, p. 9.
9 Tolkien, '*Beowulf*: the monsters and the critics', pp. 29–30. Cited hereafter as 'Monsters'.
10 Nagel, *Medieval modern*, p. 266.
11 Carruthers, *The experience of beauty*, p. 13.
12 Skinner, 'Why ecopoetics', p. 106.
13 On the complex of reasons for the tardy critical reception of Blaser and Spicer, see Katz, *The poetry*, pp. 3–4; Nichols, *Radical affections*, pp. 177–9; Spanos, 'Jack Spicer's poetry', pp. 1–2. Foundational and catalyzing studies include: *PBGL; MV; House*; Blaser, *The holy forest*; *TF; AT*; Watts and Byrne (eds), *The recovery of the public world*; and now Nichols, *A literary biography*. Before 2008, the most widely available collection of Spicer's work was the (out of print) *The collected books of Jack Spicer* (1975). Academic reception of Spicer effectively began with a special issue of *Boundary 2*, ed. William Spanos, 6.1 (1977), but Davidson's *SFR* (1989) and Ellingham and Killian's *PBLG* (1998) brought broader critical attention. Spicer's uncollected works, *Be brave to things*, only appeared during the final phases of this book. See also Vincent, *After Spicer: critical essays*.
14 *PBLG*, p. 11.
15 *Ibid.*, p. 13.
16 *Ibid.*, p. 79.
17 For varying and inconsistent accounts of Blaser's, Duncan's, and Spicer's participation in Kantorowicz's *Kreis* re-creation, see *PBLG*, pp. 19–21; Duncan, *A poet's mind*, pp. 78, 109; and *AT*, pp. 76–93.
18 *AT*, p. 59 and Blaser, 'Non-learned'.
19 Blaser, 'Non-learned'. Blaser also cites Albert Baugh's *History of the English language* as the source for the idea of the project.
20 E.g. JSP, Box 22, folder 12 (history of English notes); Box 23, folder 9 (translations of, among others, the *Poetic Edda*); Box 23, folder 11(history of English notes, including early Germanic runic inscriptions).

21 *PBLG*, p. 11; Katz, *The poetry*, p. 4. On masculinity in Spicer's constructions of homosexuality as a 'tough guy stance [that] configured homosexuality within an almost Calvinist sense of moral imperatives', see Davidson, *Guys*, pp. 28–48.

22 See Killian, 'Spicer at the Mattachine'; Duncan, 'The homosexual in society'.

23 *PBLG*, pp. 23–4; Nichols, *A literary biography*, pp. 48–50. And see Faas, *Young Robert Duncan*, pp. 274–80 (but, see *PBLG*, p. 380 n. 6, which notes this account is disputed).

24 Even German-language scholarship on the afterlife of the George *kreis* has taken note. See Raulff, *Kreis ohne Meister*, pp. 337–8. (My thanks to David Wellbery for this reference and to Len Von Morzé for help with the German). Kelly Holt's work on this subject is extensive. See Holt, 'In the sense of a lasting doctrine', see especially Chapter 1, Chapter 2 parts 2–3, and the conclusion; and Holt, 'Spicer's poetic correspondence'. And see Nichols, *A literary biography*, pp. 45–7.

25 *AT*, p. 77.

26 Nichols, *A literary biography*, p. 45.

27 *AT*, p. 78.

28 See Spicer's and Duncan's correspondence including Spicer's 'AN OPEN LETTER TO ROBERT DUNCAN FROM J. SPICER, REX ET EXUL IMMERITUS', in Spicer, *The collected books of Jack Spicer*, pp. 364–5. See also *SFR*, p. 40; *PBLG*, p. 20; Holt, 'Spicer's poetic correspondence', pp. 42–3.

29 Brodeur, *Prose Edda*. See also the following selection of relevant scholarship: Brodeur, 'The riddle of the runes'; Brodeur, 'The climax'; Brodeur, 'Design and motive'; Brodeur, 'The meaning of Snorri's categories'; Brodeur, 'The structure and unity of *Beowulf*'.

30 For an example of Brodeur's pulp/sci-fi/fantasy writing, see Brodeur, with Farnham Bishop, *The altar of the legion* (1926). For a full bibliography see Greenfield, *Studies in Old English literature in honor of Arthur G. Brodeur*, pp. vi–vii.

31 Unlike Kantorowicz, who left in protest, Brodeur elected to stay and 'fight from within' ('Statement by Arthur Brodeur'). See also Farnham and Huston, Obituary, 'Arthur Gilchrest Brodeur, English; German: Berkeley', University Archives, University of California Berkeley, Bancroft Library. Brodeur's folk-singing group, in addition to apparently acting as a gentleman's outdoors and amateur archaeology club, seem to have been compelling performers. See Kodish, 'Introduction', pp. 3–9, especially photos and captions on pp. 6, 8–9; Lomax and Lomax, *American ballads and folksongs*, p. 133.

32 Many arguments in the book were in print by the time Blaser and Spicer met Brodeur. See Brodeur, 'The climax' and 'Design and motive'.

Two more relevant essays would come out within three years of their seminar. See Brodeur, 'The meaning of Snorri's categories' (1952) and 'The structure and unity of *Beowulf*' (1953).

33 JSB, 'Reference to Ingeld say most [critics]. Kl.[laeber] says refers to the struggle of later kin of Hrōþgar. Br.[rodeur] says [ll.] 81–83 refers to the civil war; 83–85 refers to Ingeld'. Cf. *AOB*, e.g. pp. 77 n. 5, 116–17, 136.

34 Hadbawnik, 'Introduction: "*Beowulf* is a hoax"', pp. 4–7.

35 *Ibid.*, p. 5. And see *AOB*, pp. 132–7.

36 Hawbawnik, 'Introduction: "*Beowulf* is a hoax"', p. 5.

37 JSB.

38 JSB.

39 References to *Beowulf*, from either Kl. 3 or Kl. 4. will be given in-text in parenthetical citations. All in-text references are to Kl. 4 unless otherwise specified.

40 *AOB*, pp. 66, 84–5; JSB.

41 JSB; *AOB*, pp. 157–81.

42 JSB.

43 *AOB*, p. vii.

44 *Ibid.*, p. viii.

45 Hadbawnik, 'Introduction: "*Beowulf* is a hoax"', p. 6.

46 Graff, *Professing*, p. 206. I freely admit the irony of citing Graff, given his rationalist account of 'literature' and attacks on non-representational and deconstructive criticism.

47 *Ibid.*, p. 197.

48 That 'The structural unity of *Beowulf*' was an early title for Brodeur's 1959 book can be surmised from the notes by David Reed (Brodeur's colleague, Spicer's instructor and supervisor) on the sleeve of a vinyl LP recording of Brodeur reading from *Beowulf* (see Chapter 1) which refers to the project by this title.

49 See Graff, *Professing*, pp. 206, 298.

50 Yeats was read by this point in the UC Berkeley English Department. On this and Blaser's, Duncan's, and Spicer's study of radical modernist texts long before the English department would touch them, see *PBLG*, p. 14; *AT*, p. 168.

51 Graff, *Professing*, p. 207.

52 *TF*, p. 23.

53 *MV*, pp. 122–3.

54 *TF*, p. 31.

55 *House*, pp. 5, 7.

56 *Ibid.*, p. 5.

57 *TF*, p. 31.

58 Nagel, *Medieval modern*, p. 15.

59 *TF*, p. 27.
60 *Ibid.*, pp. 29, 33.
61 *Ibid.*, p. 29.
62 *TF*, 115.
63 'Who's afraid', p. 33.
64 Howe himself had already contributed to this history with his remarks on Auden, Hill, Gunn, and AIDS. See Howe, 'Praise and lament', especially p. 304. See also Jones, *Strange likeness* (2006); Jones, 'Anglo-Saxonism in nineteenth-century poetry'; Jones, 'Old English after 1066', pp. 325–30; Jones, 'While crowding memories came'; Buchanan, 'Cædemon and the gift of song'; Davies, *Visions and ruins*, pp. 38–54, 200–4; Davies, 'Re-locating Anglo-Saxon England'; Barr, 'Resurrecting Saxon things'; Hadbawnik, 'Speak like a child'; Kears, 'Eric Mottram and Old English'; Remein, 'Auden, translation, betrayal'; Remein, 'Robin Blaser, Jack Spicer, and Arthur Brodeur'; Ladrick, '*Tender* and changing'; Lees, 'In three poems'; Lees, 'Basil Bunting, *Briggflatts*, Lindisfarne'; Brooks, 'Liturgy, performance, and poetry of the passion'. And see Hadbawnik and Reynolds, 'Contemporary poetics and the medieval muse' and Hadbawnik, *Postmodern poetry and queer medievalisms.*
65 Spicer, *Jack Spicer's Beowulf.* Hadbawnik can also be credited with seeing into print contemporary poet Thomas Meyer's distinctly modernist and typographically adventurous translation of *Beowulf* (Meyer, *Beowulf*).
66 See Jones, *Strange likeness*, pp. 182–237 and Heaney, *Beowulf.*
67 On the general debt of twentieth-century theory to medieval studies and medieval thought, see e.g. Holsinger, *The premodern condition*; Ethan Knapp, 'Medieval studies, historicity, and Heidegger's early phenomenology'.
68 For foundational work on medieval studies and theories of temporality, see Dinshaw, *Getting medieval*; Dinshaw, *How soon is now*; Cohen, *Medieval identity machines*, pp. 1–34. On periodization, medieval studies, and political theory, see Davis, *Periodization and sovereignty.* On the politics of temporality and Old English studies, see [Fradenburg] Joy, 'Goodbye to all that'.
69 Overing and Wiethaus, 'Introduction', *American/medieval: nature and mind*, p. 11. See also Overing and Wiethaus (eds), *American/medieval goes north.*
70 See especially Davies, *Visions and ruins*, on 'cultural memory', pp. 3–4, 18–64; Jones, *Fossil poetry*, see pp. 30–1 on 'refraction' as an alternative to 'reception'.
71 Chaganti, 'Vestigial signs', p. 50.

72 Lees and Overing, *The contemporary medieval*, pp. 91, 1, 5.
73 E.g. Hadbawnik and Reynolds, 'All times'; Hadbawnik, 'Time mechanics'; Buchanan, 'Cædemon and the gift of song'; Lees and Overing, *The contemporary medieval*, pp. 66–70; and see note 64 above.
74 Hadbawnik and Reynolds, 'All times', pp. 115–16.
75 Hadbawnik, 'Introduction: the opening of the field', p. 1.
76 *Ibid.*
77 Hadbawnik, 'Introduction: "*Beowulf* is a hoax"', p. 3; 'Preface', p. 2.
78 *Old English newsletter* web page, News, accessed June 13 2017, www.oenewsletter.org/OEN/index.php.
79 In addition to Jones' and Lees' work on Heaney cited above, see e.g. Donoghue, 'The languages of *Beowulf*'.
80 On Spicer's philology as 'extra poetic', see Reynolds, 'Afterword', p. 37.
81 [Fradenburg] Joy, 'Goodbye to all that', §69.
82 E.g. Stanton, *The culture of translation*; Hurley, *Translation effects*.
83 E.g. Ferhatović, 'A portrait'; Magennis, *Translating Beowulf*, e.g. pp. 7–10, 140–1; Hurley, *Translation effects*, pp. 151–82.
84 E.g. Pattie McCarthy's serial poem, *queyne wifthing*, see especially notes, n.p., and p. 27. The chapbook interpolates fragments of *The wife's lament* into lyrical fragmentary references to later medieval women that construct a *longue durée* literary history reorganized around the gendering of writing and reading. See also McCaffery, *The darkness of the present*, pp. 25–40. McCaffery relies heavily on high medieval rhetorician Geoffrey of Vinsauf in triangulating his reading of Ronald Johnson's *Radi*. On Caroline Bergvall's *Drift*, see Davies, *Visions and ruins*, pp. 199–202; Hadbawnik, 'Speak like a child'; Lees and Overing, *The contemporary medieval*, pp. 49–72. And see Miller Oberman, *The unstill ones*. I refer here only to a sampling of only very contemporary work.
85 As Lytle Shaw repeatedly explores in *Fieldworks*, the New American Poets often turned to various forms of 'fieldwork' which allowed poets to 'rethink their relationship to neighboring disciplines' and in turn gave them access to a literary archive of *longue durée* (3).
86 E.g.. Robertson, *Debbie: an epic*; Smailbegović, 'Of the dense and rare'.
87 See note 64 above; and see Allfrey et. al., 'New ways to know the medieval'.
88 Liuzza, 'Lost in translation', p. 294. Howe also cites this remark in 'Who's afraid', at p. 46.

89 De Campos, 'Translation as creation and criticism', p. 313. De Campos
    later alters this isomorphic model of translating into his better-known
    'cannibalistic' approach (on the latter in a discussion of *Beowulf*
    translation, see Ferhatović, 'A portrait'). My thanks to Isabel Gómez
    for conversations informing my use of de Campos throughout. And see
    Gómez, 'Brazilian transcreation', pp. 316–18, 324–5; Gómez, 'Anti-
    surrealism?', p. 379, 379 n. 8; Gómez, 'Transcreation / transcriasção'.
90 Barr, 'Resurrecting Saxon things', pp. 255–7. I thank one of the
    anonymous readers for directing me to this essay.
91 But see Ferhatović, 'A portrait'; Hadbawnik, 'Differing intimacies'.
92 Howe, 'Who's afraid', p. 33.
93 *Ibid.*
94 *Ibid.*
95 *Ibid.*, p. 31.
96 *Ibid.*, p. 45.
97 *Ibid.*
98 Heaney, Introduction, *Beowulf*, p. xxix. Heaney's pretense to 'direct-
    ness' suggests a fantasy of poetry as the transparent and therefore
    transcendent expression of a (male) subject's interiority, and resonates
    with that famous (distinctly gendered and eurocentric) definition of
    poetry as 'a man speaking to men'. Cf. the preface to the 1802 *Lyrical
    Ballads* (Wordsworth and Coleridge, *Lyrical Ballads*, p. 98). This specific
    gendering of poetic activity is further suggested in Heaney's recollection
    of how 'big men of the family spoke'; because, Heaney suggests, in this
    'big voiced' mode, a 'simple sentence ... took on immense dignity' (pp.
    xxvi–xxvii). Ironically, he also indulges in a settler-colonial stereotype
    about Native Americans in order to underscore the gendering of those
    from whom he borrows the voice of his translation: 'they [the big
    voiced men] had a kind of Native American solemnity of utterance,
    as if they were announcing verdicts rather than making small talk' (p.
    xxvii). These moves will not surprise readers equally familiar with his
    early figuration of the task of writing in a sublimation of masculine
    phallic disseminative labor in his early poem 'Digging'. See Heaney,
    Death of a naturalist, pp. 13–14. See also Remein, 'Auden, translation,
    betrayal', 813; Howe, 'Scullionspeak'.
99 Meyer, *Beowulf*, p. 264. Comments taken from an interview with
    David Hadbawnik.
100 *Ibid.*, p. 260. Meyer describes Williams, who was his partner, as
    a 'kingpin in the International Concrete Poetry movement' at that
    time' (p. 270). On the complicated chronology of late modernism,
    see Nicholls, 'Modernising modernism'.
101 Bernstein, 'Against national poetry month as such', p. 27.

102 *Ibid.*
103 Lewis, *The allegory of love*, dedication (n.p.).
104 I also make a similar argument with Erica Weaver in 'Dons and Dragons'.
105 Arac, *Huck Finn as idol and target*, pp. vii, 137.
106 *Ibid.*, p. 6.
107 *Ibid.*
108 *Ibid.*, p. 21.
109 Tolkien, 'Monsters', p. 5.
110 Nicholas Howe, 'Scullionspeak', pp. 32–4, reprinted in *Beowulf At Kalamazoo*, p. 347.
111 Sheehan, 'Bro'.
112 There is a large body of relevant scholarship here, but in this case I am particularly indebted to Nahir I. Otaño Gracia's discussion of 'complicity' vs. 'compatibility' in Otaño Gracia, 'Towards a de-centered global North Atlantic', pp. 3, 11, 16.
113 To disambiguate this usage from projects of so-called 'secularism' aimed at the marginalization of Muslims, especially in European countries, I point out that my sense of the secular critic is not entirely coterminous with, but derives ultimately from Said's readings of Vico and Gramsci. See Said, 'Opponents'. The concept refers to the status of the literary text and the posture of the critic towards it, as 'worldly' and not 'otherworldly'—not to historical or contemporary religions, beliefs and/or practices (Said, 'Representing the colonized', p. 301). For Said, Hugh of St Victor stands beside Adorno and Auerbach in an example of the 'secular and contingent' world of the exile. See Said, 'Reflections on exile', p. 185; Buttigieg, 'The exemplary worldliness'.
114 De Campos, 'Translation as creation and criticism', p. 314.
115 *Ibid.*, pp. 314–16.
116 See Shaw, *Frank O'Hara*, p. 405. In the same period, the displacement of supposed poetic universality is also forcefully articulated not in coterie poetics but in the Black Arts Movement and Black Nationalism, as in Amiri Baraka's 'State/meant': 'The Black Artist's role in America is to aid in the destruction of America as he knows it. His role is to report and reflect so precisely the nature of the society, and of himself in that society, that other men will be moved by the exactness of his rendering and, if they are black men, grow strong through this moving, having seen their own strength, and weakness; and if they are white men, tremble, curse, and go mad, because they will be drenched with the filth of their evil'. See Baraka, 'State/meant', p. 169.
117 Bernstein, *A poetics*, p. 5. The pretense to universality is further belied by the very impossibility of staking out a functional 'public' space'

(p. 5). Since 1992, the material dynamics of social-media capitalism and its deployment by Trumpism have only thrown these conditions into further relief.

118 E.g. see Nealon, *The matter of capital*, pp. 110–14; Nichols, *A literary biography*, pp. 208–15. The phrase is taken from the title of Blaser's essay 'The recovery of the public world' in *TF*.

119 Mossin, 'Recovering,' pp. 152–3.

120 Bernstein, 'The practice of poetics', p. 74.

121 See Bergvall, *Meddle English*, p. 161.

122 Bernstein, 'The practice of poetics', p. 73.

123 Fredman, *Poet's prose*, pp. 5–8.

124 Bernstein, 'The practice of poetics', p. 73.

125 *Ibid.*, p. 76.

126 *Ibid.*

127 *Ibid.*, p. 74.

128 *Ibid.*, p. 75.

129 See, e.g., *House,* pp. 1–48; Gizzi, 'Afterword', pp. 189–92. Spicer later pointed out that 'it's obviously not martians' (*House,* p. 168).

130 Trilling, *The aesthetics of nostalgia*, p. 27.

131 Tyler, *Old English poetics*, pp. 1, 6–7.

132 See Hill (ed.), *On the aesthetics of* Beowulf *and other Old English poems*; Magennis, *Translating 'Beowulf'*.

133 [Fradenburg] Joy and Ramsey, 'Liquid *Beowulf*', pp. xxx, xl.

134 Overing, '*Beowulf*: a poem in our time', pp. 311–12, 330.

135 Hejinian, 'Reason', pp. 344–5.

136 *Ibid.*, pp. 341–2.

137 Earl, *Thinking About 'Beowulf'*, p. 11.

138 *Ibid.*, p. 167.

139 Earl, 'The Swedish wars in *Beowulf*', p. 33.

140 Overing, '*Beowulf*: a poem in our time', p. 312.

141 Earl, 'The Swedish wars in *Beowulf*', p. 36. Emphasis mine.

142 Earl, 'The forbidden *Beowulf*', pp. 303–4.

143 Derrida, *Specters of Marx*, pp. xix, 48. And see p. 21.

144 I want to thank the anonymous readers for suggesting the extent to which the application of Carruthers' work to earlier medieval literary history may appear novel to some medievalists, and may underscore certain continuities between earlier and later periods.

145 Hurley, *Translation effects*, p. 154.

146 *Ibid.*, pp. 151–82, especially 181.

147 De Campos, 'Translation as creation and criticism', p. 315.

148 Merleau-Ponty, *The phenomenology of perception*, trans. Landes, p. 12.

1

The aesthetics of *Beowulf* in the middle of the twentieth century

Why do we make ourselves alive by going backward, so far back?
Robin Blaser, in conversation with Warren Tallman[1]

Robin Blaser's and Jack Spicer's encounter with *Beowulf* marks a remarkable confluence of, on the one hand, genealogies in the history of the study and teaching of that poem in North America and, on the other, particular trajectories of post-war twentieth-century avant-garde English-language poetics. For critical and literary history alone, laying out these genealogies and trajectories side by side holds a certain promise. But this effort will also be instructive in generating new paths through *Beowulf* that take up outdated preoccupations about the poem's aesthetics in ways that render them strange to the trajectories they actually followed. If that latter operation is admittedly speculative, this chapter remains largely historical and analytical, reconsidering the study of Old English verse in the middle of the twentieth century and its historical trajectories alongside the ambivalent transformations of Ezra Pound's medievalism in the so-called 'Berkeley Renaissance'. This chapter does not revisit an earlier moment of criticism out of piety or nostalgia, nor in order to discount the criticism generated between then and now.[2] Rather, it reexamines the intellectual and institutional conditions that nurtured inquiry into the aesthetics of *Beowulf* to better comprehend the site of its intersection with a mid-century poetics avant-garde as a force to shape readings of *Beowulf* now.

'A modern poem'

As mentioned in the introduction, whether Brodeur knew it or not, Blaser's and Spicer's sense of how to approach at least their own 'modern poems' differed radically from those shaping Brodeur's project. And yet, certain critical impulses of Brodeur's project and its assumptions about poetics seem to have helped construct this encounter with *Beowulf* as a constitutive node of the young poets' later poetics. Where, then, is the overlap and where the gaps between Brodeur's sense of this assignment and that of the two young poets? In what sense did Brodeur comprehend *Beowulf* 'as a modern poem'? To whatever extent his scholarly contributions represent such an understanding, his project occupies a catalyzing and determinative place within a larger critical genealogy of the study of *Beowulf*'s aesthetics at mid-century. Brodeur's 1959 monograph crystallizes the advances, historical conditions, and structural limitations of the wave of interest in the aesthetics of *Beowulf* that would seem to some almost hopelessly antiquated by the end of the twentieth century. The study concludes on the aesthetic excellence of Beowulf with an implied metaphor of the poet as a tapestry-weaver of aesthetic unities who 'controls the threads of his designs admirably, and weaves them into a magnificent whole'.[3] The real heart of his argument lies in his meticulous, even obsessive and loving attention to poetic diction. According to Brodeur, the compound diction of *Beowulf*, which he analyzes to underwrite his assessments, is 'used in telling combinations, in which the various elements of the sentence combine into a style more vigorous, stately, and beautiful than that of any other Old English poem'.[4] The book was incredibly important at the time of its publication. Kemp Malone's review of the book insisted that it 'should be required reading for all serious students of Beowulf' despite a host of serious reservations about the book's pivotal arguments and a number of ongoing critical disagreements with Brodeur.[5]

Brodeur's appeals to wholeness—so resonant with New Critical attitudes—and comparative evaluations of literary 'beauty' are likely to strike students of *Beowulf* in the contemporary world as antiquated, if not naive.[6] *The art of Beowulf* is a perfect example of what John D. Niles calls the 'sometimes uneasy alliance with the New Criticism' found in mid-century approaches to the aesthetics of the poem.[7] Indeed, Brodeur's tapestry metaphor, implying a self-sealing unity, is one no New Critic would need despise—even as Brodeur's emphasis on the individual genius of the poet veers towards a less compatible investment in the Author.

Yet the terms with which Brodeur discussed the aesthetics of Beowulf were effectively recent additions to English-language criticism—and not, initially, articulated in support of or in conformity to an explicitly New Critical hegemony. Brodeur frames his monograph as a 'prolegomenon' specifically to formalize the 'new and significant direction' given to literary criticism of the poem by J. R. R. Tolkien.[8] Only in 1936 had Tolkien given his landmark lecture '*Beowulf*: the monsters and the critics', where, in his case for the poem's legitimacy, Tolkien characterizes it as a 'simple and static structure, solid and strong', lionizing the aesthetics of its construction as 'essentially a balance'.[9] Although the best-known contributions of the New Criticism were yet a decade away, Tolkien's lexicon of aesthetic appraisal is redolent with what we can now easily recognize as constituent of an emergent New Critical structure of feeling: this 'balance' resolves in a static 'opposition of ends and beginning'; it is only of necessity 'read in a time-sequence' and 'approaches rather to sculpture or painting'.[10] Such a poem is to be grasped and felt spatially, atemporally, and as an organic whole wherein the microstructure of the poem's lines are also 'founded on a balance; an opposition between two halves of roughly equivalent phonetic weight … more like masonry than music' and in 'parallel to the total structure'.[11] Measured by issue rather than intent, it is quite beside the point to worry over whether the characterization of Tolkien's intervention as New Critical is 'anachronistic',[12] since he gives us a *Beowulf* that is, if not a well-wrought urn, then a well-timbered fortress or a romantic subject of heroic masculinity—transcendent of, or at least uniquely resistant to, history and capable of 'enduring' critical 'treatment'.[13]

At stake here is not the viability of Tolkien's intervention in critical practice *now* but its specific status as a condition of Brodeur's project. Identifying Tolkien as 'grounded in the legacy of Edwardian middlebrow tastes', Seth Lerer identifies a shared 'fundamentally Arnoldian position' between the Oxford don and the mid-century American New Critics: an effort to recover aesthetic wholes and a false nostalgia for a society unmarred by perceptible class conflict—and, we might add, racial difference.[14] One might object to calling Tolkien *Edwardian*, aligning him instead with an odd blend of nineteenth-century Victorian 'amateurism' and Arnoldian disinterest (witness Tolkien's own loose, baggy novels, his Arnoldian fixation on balance).[15] Nevertheless, when removed from its local project of reactionary white Englishness to that of post-war, middle-class American university education, one thing that Tolkien's intervention leaves to us is a newly 'public' *Beowulf*. If, in the United Kingdom, Tolkien asserted that *Beowulf* was 'for' the English, abstracted from that context, it would become 'for' middle-class (mostly white) undergraduates. This recently literary *Beowulf* would be of interest to any that could obtain some modicum of expertise in literary reading—just at the moment that New Critical explication supposedly rendered literary criticism a universally teachable and learnable skill-set calibrated for mass higher education of students without homogeneous cultural backgrounds.[16]

By the time this 'public' *Beowulf* arrived on the West Coast, the inquiry into its aesthetics had already accrued another crucial generic convention. A year ahead of Tolkien's lecture, and in New York City, Adeline Courtney Bartlett had already argued that *Beowulf* has 'an organic unity of its own', invoking the figure of a 'tapestry' to describe the relationship between its episodes.[17] Adrien Bonjour's *The digressions of Beowulf*—the only longer study to take up Tolkien's intervention ahead of Brodeur—would appear in 1950 (completed in 1944, but delayed owing to the post-war conditions of Europe).[18] Bonjour follows Bartlett in figuring the poem as an 'elaborate and impressive tapestry' in an argument for the organic unity of the poem's so-called 'episodes and digressions'.[19] In the immediate wake of Tolkien's lecture, Joan Blomfield's study, 'The style and structure of *Beowulf*', added to its apologetics for the poem's organic unity the evaluation that 'the writer of *Beowulf* is in fact a true poet'.[20] Bonjour, too, frames the function of all his inquiries into the aesthetics of the poem as an evaluation of the poet's individuality, offering as the final, enthusiastic line of his study, 'þæt wæs god scop!' (that was a good poet!).[21] These remarks may seem merely conventional, but their implicit critical assumptions play a key role in the trajectory that follows from Brodeur's project. By the time Brodeur attempts to demonstrate that the compounds of *Beowulf* 'convey thought or feeling more freshly and vividly than the power of other Anglo-Saxon poets', despite his sense that '[c]ultural conditions in England were not so favorable [as in Norse-speaking places] to the development of individual modes of expression',[22] the individuality of the poet had become both prerequisite for and the object of the study of the poem's aesthetics. This is the specific texture of that 'uneasy alliance with the New Criticism' mentioned above—uneasy not, as one tends to expect or characterize it, because of medievalists' reluctance to endorse decontextualized formalist analysis, but because of this attachment to individuality. Despite the ascendency of T. S. Eliot's calibration of 'tradition and the individual talent' in some modernist poetry, for some early medievalists, reading a poem like a modern poem would mean an explication of beauty as a static unity linked to an individual mind.

The aesthetics of *Beowulf* in Ezra Pound's avant-garde

As Blaser and Spicer entered Brodeur's seminar amidst these shifts of *Beowulf*'s legibility within professional literary criticism, the place of *Beowulf* in English-language literary modernism and its fallout was by no means certain. As a dominant figure of radical modernism and an object of intensive study and critique in the Berkeley Renaissance, Ezra Pound is the most salient modernist precedent for Blaser's and Spicer's avant-garde medievalism. And the shifting place of *Beowulf* in Pound's own canon constitutes an important horizon for the aesthetics of the poem within post-war avant-garde poetics genealogies. Chris Jones' analysis of Pound's interest in Old English suggests that *Beowulf* was important in its earliest phases: he used A. J. Wyatt's 1894 edition of the text for his second semester of Old English at Hamilton College under the Reverend Joseph D. Ibbotson and seems likely to have encountered the ornate Kelmscott edition of William Morris' versification of Wyatt's prose translation at the British Library.[23] Pound remained interested in thinking actively about *Beowulf* at least as late as the end of the 1920s, when he produced an unpublished essay on 'The music of *Beowulf*' and accompanying notes (or so it seems) comparing scansions of lines from *Beowulf* with one of the Old English *Seafarer*.[24] This essay is an important inflection point in Pound's assessment of *Beowulf*'s aesthetics and its place within the avant-garde canon of medieval literature inherited, and contested, by Blaser and Spicer.

The essay claims that the meter of the Old English poem fits the music of a folksong from the Outer Hebrides that Pound heard performed by the Kennedy-Fraser singers in London.[25] Pound's interest in the prosody of the poem lies in his efforts to 'break the pentameter' of modern English verse, arguing that 'the misunderstood principle of alliterative verse is possibly radical in all proper vers libre in our language'.[26] With his novice sense of Old English meter, Pound recounts that he 'earnestly endeavoured to fit the words of the *Seafarer* to the tune [of the Kennedy-Fraser performance]' and, failing, 'finally turned to Skeat and tried a bit of the *Beowulf*'—the result of which seems to have been a scansion of the first fourteen lines of *Beowulf* on loose cablegram sheets.[27]

Later, in the *ABC of reading*, Pound would draw on the work of the unpublished essay in a condensed anecdote that at first glance seems to reflect favorably on the 'music' of *Beowulf*:

> An instance of how the life of a work of art is something that just won't stay nailed down in a coffin: The Kennedy-Frasers found some music in the outer Hebrides that fits the Beowulf, or at any rate that some of the Beowulf fits. It is the 'Aillte'. I heard it in concert, and racked my mind to think where it fitted. It wouldn't go to the Seafarer. Two lines fitted a bit of the Beowulf, then the next wouldn't fit. I skipped a line of the Beowulf, and went on. The Kennedy-Frasers had omitted a line at that point because it didn't seem to them to have an inherent musical interest.[28]

But Pound's attempt to 'fit' the music to an Old English poem also seems to have clarified for Pound a (quite problematic) aesthetic distinction at the level of prosody between *Beowulf* and *The seafarer* that in turn reinforced his hierarchy of their importance.[29] In his 1914 essay 'The renaissance', Pound already establishes a hierarchy of Old English poetry within the larger medieval corpus that should constitute the 'medieval songbook' for the modern poet, excluding *Beowulf*:

> I should want Dante of course, and the *Poema del Cid*, and the *Sea-farer* and one passage out of *The Wanderer*. In fact, some knowledge of the Anglo-Saxon fragments—not particularly the Beowulf—would prevent a man's sinking into contentment with a lot of wish-wash that passes for classic or 'standard' poetry.[30]

However, by Pound's 1929 essay 'How to read', which led in part to his *ABC of reading*, Pound cites his thesis about *Beowulf* and the music of the Kennedy-Fraser singers not in order to install *Beowulf* in the modernist medieval canon but only to illustrate his dubious argument that universities should take practical measures to teach medieval poetry as song, suggesting that 'each dozen Universities [should] combine in employing a couple of singers who understand the words [of the medieval languages]' on the basis that this 'would give the student more knowledge of that sort of *melopœia* than a year's work in philology'.[31] When it comes to recommending what one should actually read in this context, Pound's list of medieval texts opens with his selections from Old English: 'The Anglo-Saxon *Seafarer*, and some more cursory notice of some medieval narrative, it does not so greatly matter what narrative, possibly the *Beowulf*, the *Poema del Cid*, and the Sagas of *Grettir* and *Burnt Nial*'.[32] The very interchangeability of *Beowulf* in this list with other long poems—and even prose narratives—from entirely different languages announces Pound's ambivalence about its relative importance as a source of *melopœia*, especially in contrast to his growing attachment to *The seafarer*. And the association of *Beowulf* with Old Norse prose may suggest a further insult. If Morris' work on the poem colored Pound's sense of the Old English poem's aesthetics at all, yoking *Beowulf* here with the Icelandic *prose* sagas in particular (other prominent objects and sources of Morris' medievalism) suggests that he may have associated the poem a bit too closely with his own early investments in Pre-Raphaelite experimentation.[33]

The aesthetics that condition this account of *Beowulf*'s prosody and the hierarchies of this medieval canon traverse the racist, misogynist, and homophobic strains of Pound's earlier poetics[34]—as well as the ecological implications of his poetics, his investments in classical Chinese poetry, and his later poetics of economics along with their imbrication in his commitments to fascism. In his extended essay on 'medievalism' (revised from the introduction to his earlier translations of Guido Cavalcanti), Pound sets 'the medieval clean line' of the 'Tuscan aesthetic' as his aesthetic ideal.[35] While this 'clean line' marks an ecologically alluring trajectory in a 'radiant world … a world of moving energies … magnetisms that take form, that are seen, or that border the visible'[36]—it also enacts a program of racial and sexual hygiene. For Pound, the 'clean line' demarcates a (racist) pure European medieval tradition 'untouched by the two maladies, the Hebrew disease, [and] the Hindoo [*sic*] disease', both of which are determined as racially innate asceticism ('anti-intelligence' and 'anti-flesh', respectively): '[b]etween those diseases, existed the Mediterranean sanity'.[37] The racist knot of Pound's medievalism thus constructs a racially *heterogeneous* European Middle Ages (counter to what one might expect, a desirable 'southern' aesthetic of 'Mediterranean races', before they fell to 'renaissance-ism', and a sensorially deprived 'northern race') in order to differentiate a 'truly' European 'good' Middle Ages from those strains he is willing to deterritorialize into non-European modernity.[38]

Against the 'clean line', the orientalizing aesthetics of the 'medieval niggle'—for Pound equally that of 'Angoulême or Bengal'—is pejoratively coded as effeminate, decorative, fecal, hemorrhoidal, and homosexual; defined as 'bulging and bumping and indulging in bulbous excrescence', since 'mess, confusion in sculpture, is always symptomatic of supineness, bad hygiene, bad physique (possibly envy)'.[39] By contrast, the 'Tuscan aesthetic', coded in terms of male reproductive potency, involves 'an interactive force: the *virtu* in short'.[40] Against what Pound sees as the unchecked bulging energies of the aesthetics of 'European Hindoos [*sic*]', he posits potency *at rest*: 'interior harmony', the 'harmony *of* the sentient'.[41] However, this 'rest' takes the figure of the colonialist threat, the domestic abuser, or the playground bully: 'The force is arrested, but there is never any question about its latency, about the force being essential, and the rest "accidental" in the philosophical technical sense. The shape occurs'.[42]

It is not difficult to see how Pound fits these theories of measure and immanence, as Peter Nicholls demonstrates, into his attempt to conceive of a 'natural economic order',[43] or how he coordinates both with a construction of political legitimacy (conceived in relation to his reading of Ernest Fenollosa's work on the Chinese character) as 'one which successfully channels and contains its power' and is 'premised on "self-generated" systems' and paternalistic authority—all of which leads him to his support for Mussolini.[44] As aesthetic theories, they provide terms for what Pound thought he had 'discovered' in his exercise comparing scansions of *Beowulf* and *The seafarer*, wherein his long-growing preference for the latter may indeed have fully crystallized. A famous comparison of *The seafarer* with the so-called 'Exile's letter' of medieval Chinese poet Li Po further clarifies how Pound's account of the meter of the Old English poem mediates these aesthetic and ideological commitments while simultaneously casting *Beowulf* aside:

> I once got a man to start translating the *Seafarer* into Chinese. It came out almost directly into Chinese verse, with two solid ideograms in each half-line.
>
> Apart from the *Seafarer* I know no other European poems of the period that you can hand up with the 'Exile's Letter' of Li Po, displaying the West on par with the Orient.
>
> There are passages of Anglo-Saxon as good as paragraphs of the *Seafarer*, but I have not found any whole poem of the same value.[45]

Aside from the suspicious anecdote about Pound's unidentified translator, it is worth noting, as Jones highlights, that Pound's own translation of *The seafarer* appears smack in the middle of the *Cathay* sequence of Chinese poems in Pound's attempt to align them on (shaky) historical and rhythmic grounds.[46] The dubious adequation of the two prosodical stresses that structure a half-line of Old English poetry to two Chinese characters anticipates Pound's later attempt to employ Chinese writing as a 'deeply charismatic language of authority' in his wartime cantos, in which Pound imagines individual characters as able to 'stand alone' as an 'intrinsic affective and intentional structure'[47]—a further development of the aesthetics of potency at rest and its imbrication in the fascist state. Whatever Pound initially identified as the 'music' of *Beowulf*, it must have harbored too much of the 'supine', inharmonious energy of the 'medieval niggle' and did not accede to the preferred aesthetics that his exercise in comparative scansion would confirm for him in *The seafarer*.

The medievalism of the younger Pound—when *Beowulf* first held his interest—was not yet so ambivalent about his Pre-Raphaelite impulses and in fact turned to Old English poetry for a more diaphanous style. Take, for example, Pound's 'At the heart o' me', a poem he composed in college and that appeared in the 1909 *Personæ*—but which, as he became more circumspect about his medievalism, Pound removed from the collection from 1920 onwards.[48] The poem is a stylized, archaizing engagement with the tropes (and meters) of Old English verse. Marked under the title as set in 'A.D. 751', the poem, likely drawing on Stopford Brooke's summary of *The husband's message*,[49] veers between ballad and anticipatory elegy as the speaker, who fears their beloved will tire of waiting for them, travels through a lavishly ornamentalized world—accompanied by nothing less medievalizing than a 'Grey-Falcon'. Here, 'the twin delights/ of shore and sea' are figured as '[s]apphire and emerald with/ fine pearls between', and, the speaker reports, '[t]hrough the pale courses of/ the land-caressing in-streams/ Gilded my barge …' ('in-streams' is the subject of 'Gilded').[50] In the speaker's animating kennings for shore ('land-caressing') and either the river or some sort of tidal inlet ('in-streams') that 'gilds' the boat, the poem traces an intimate interface with the non-human world constructed precisely of the 'accidental' and unstilled aesthetics Pound would later repudiate. The speaker then proceeds to mourn that all the trappings and glamour of what we might recognize as the material Beowulfian world will lose their luster, '[a]n thou should'st grow weary/ ere my returning,/ An *"they"* should call to thee/ from out the borderland':

> What should avail me
>> booty of the whale-ways?
> What should avail me
>> gold rings or the chain mail?
> What should avail me
>> the many-twined bracelets?
> What should avail me,
>> O my beloved,
> Here in this 'Middan-gard'
>> what should avail me
> Out of the booty and
>> gain of my goings?[51]

This catalog (along with the coastal descriptions) may draw on the list of possessions at the end of *The husband's message* or even the *ubi sunt* motif in *The wanderer* rather than the treasure-laden *Beowulf* (although the Pre-Raphaelitism of this piece is suggestive of a connection to Pound's familiarity with Morris' translation), but either way, it deploys tropes (and meters) of Old English poetry to delineate a whole ecology of 'moving energies' that emanates not from a 'clean line' backed by male potency but from glittering, gauzy, littoral, interpenetrating longings, geographies, and itineraries.

Yet it was Pound's (no less archaizing) translation of *The seafarer*, and his account of that poem's equilibrium, that would long shape

his 'post-Fenollosa poetic' and become the most salient account of
Old English poetry in the historical canon of English-language
avant-garde poetry,[52] shunting *Beowulf* into an undifferentiated pile
of medieval narrative texts from a variety of languages and moments,
any one of which might suffice for the poet in training.[53] Nevertheless,
the terms on which Pound eventually settles for evaluating the aesthetics of Old English poetry (and by which he tacitly finds *Beowulf*
lacking) superficially coincide with Tolkien's vocabulary of balance,
stability, and endurance. More rigorously, of course, Tolkien's balance
is not adequate to Pound's radiant potency at rest, but without
careful study of Pound's labyrinthine corpus one could easily mistake
them as homologous. In support of radically different poetics (and
differently reactionary politics), and in importantly different senses,
Pound and Tolkien nevertheless converge on balance and stability
as the watchwords of an aesthetic lexicon. At mid-century, the most
salient horizons of the aesthetics of *Beowulf* were caught between
fascist manliness at rest and middlebrow stasis with an added investment in individuality of expression. To poets in his wake, Pound
had persuasively demonstrated that medieval literary history offered
models of aesthetics that could conceive of the poem radically
entangling the human sensorium with the 'radiant' activities of the
non-human world, but he demarcated an archive for this purpose
that excluded *Beowulf* on the ground of politico-aesthetic entanglements that Blaser and Spicer would not share. In turn, their marked
interest in *Beowulf* can be understood as rejecting Pound's commitments to masculinist, and eventually fascist, force without abandoning
his search within medieval literary history for a poetics of phenomenologically active, energetic worldliness.

Beowulf in the 'Berkeley Middle Ages'

In contrast to both Tolkien's and Pound's language for the aesthetics
of Old English poetry, the scene of Blaser and Spicer translating
Beowulf pulses vibrantly within the rhythms of a very different
sexual and sociological poetics. In a conversation with Warren Tallman
about homosexuality and the Berkeley Renaissance, Blaser interrupts
his discussion of Duncan's early influential poem 'Among my friends,

love is a great sorrow', as a poem written 'right in the midst of the sexual', to talk about *Beowulf*:

> Well, as time goes on, Jack and I will do *Beowulf* together and we work three hours a night, five nights a week, and on Friday nights we can go out to the Red Lizard. That's a bar queer bar. Once a week you can go out and have a big time. The rest of the time you're really doing this job, and I have my translations and Jack's of the *Beowulf*, and so on. They are better than anybody's so far, Jack's especially.[54]

By marking this work with *Beowulf* in post-war California as a scene of translation, Blaser ineluctably situates it against a backdrop of Poundian medievalism. As Steven Yao characterizes it, 'translation represented for the Modernists much more than either just a minor mode of literary production or an exercise of apprenticeship';[55] as a defining mode of modernism, translation 'functioned as a strategy for negotiating gender, politics, and language'—it 'helped, to generate the internationalist content of modernism', and for Pound especially, it was a 'generative writing practice'.[56] According to Daniel Katz, in Spicer's later experiments with translation in *After Lorca,* the poet 'is arguably the first major poet to take Pound's translation practice as something other than an idiosyncrasy'.[57] But as Erica Weaver I and gesture to elsewhere,[58] Blaser describes a scene of translation on several scales at once: of a text from one language to another, yes, but also of the classroom at a public university into the private space and daily habits of companionship, intellectual labor, and poetics, and then again into the pragmatics of a larger gay, avant-garde poetics coterie set within a marginalized (and illegal) but thriving pre-Stonewall queer culture.[59]

In this particular concrete location within pre-Stonewall queer life, the value of 'assimilation' was highly contested. Spicer (if not Blaser also) pursued a 'radical' queer politics at the early Mattachine Society (rejecting a construction of homosexuality in relation to a static identity and pursuing an 'alternative to an obsession with the issue of the homosexual's relation to the mainstream'),[60] and Spicer was developing a related poetics that worked to vigilantly retain its marginal status within official verse culture.[61] Missing the nightly scene at the Red Lizard most of the week, Blaser's and Spicer's translations inaugurate a micro-community whose medievalism marks it as doubly marginal to its already marginal avant-garde. They take up *Beowulf* 'as a modern poem' without positing it within a purely Poundian project, within New Critical verse culture, or within a reactionary fantasy of a hetero-medievalism opposite the 'queer bar'. Rather, the marginal modernity of this medievalism arises from its capacity to operate 'in the midst of the sexual' for those whose technical linguistic training informs a resistance to the supposed transparency of naive expressivism or fantasies of aesthetic transcendence.

Michael Davidson argues that the poetics community around Spicer was constituted by an 'almost medieval sense of loyalties and hierarchies that would secure a sense of community in a homophobic society'.[62] Given Blaser's and Spicer's apparent intensity of commitment to the task of translating *Beowulf*, Blaser's confidence about the quality of their translations, and the way that this particular corner of their coterie crystallized specifically around the poem, perhaps Davidson does not need to qualify his description of the *medieval* qualities of this community with an 'almost.' The poets' enthusiasm for *Beowulf* revises the canon and aesthetics of medievalism in avant-garde poetics even as their embrace of formal training in Old English reverses the modernist ambivalence towards expert knowledge of a language as a pre-requisite for a 'successful' translation (an ambivalence 'consecrated' in Pound's work with Chinese poetry).[63] Tending, in translation, to this particular node of the medieval, inaugurates a whole literary world in miniature: organizing and energizing its corporeal and social rhythms and orders, propelling both intellectual labor and partying in the nightly sessions of companionable translation and their relationship to the weekly 'big time' at the bar within the larger gay poetry community as functions of the same poetics. The centrality of a historically specific experience of pre-Stonewall gay life in these practices of social and literary medievalism does not mean that Blaser's and Spicer's encounter with the aesthetics of *Beowulf* will necessarily yield readings of that poem that we will want to mark as queer (although it may), but it does herald the possibility of finding there an early medieval aesthetics that was, at least, compatible with their queer poetics community.

In their effort, as Blaser puts it, to 'make ourselves feel alive by going backward',[64] the poets also find something deeply akin to the sensory and ecological attunements of Pound's 'radiant world of moving energies'—right where Pound would not have told them to

look for it. Blaser rid himself of most of his poetry written before
1955, but his *Beowulf* notebook preserves a rare unique holograph
of an early untitled poem that quivers with the Pre-Raphaelite style
experimentation of early Pound:

> We wear velvet gowns,
> bright and gold
> in their several folds
> near the ground
>
> He remembers the past with pleasure,
> takes, like Midas, immediate treasure.
> Here is a begging
> shame like sorrow
> only remembering back of tomorrow
> Here is an end of old prepossessions [presuppositions,
>   propositions?],
> seen against old possession ...
>
> We wear velvet gowns
> and hear the barking dogs. (RBB)[65]

Complete with its elegiac tone, the lyric resonates with the man-
nerist idiom of Duncan's roughly contemporary *Medieval scenes*
(in which, for example, Duncan writes, 'dark ages/ are long with
hours for the poet's tapestry').[66] Embracing the splendor of a glitzy,
gaudy, decadent medievalism, the poem is bookended by references
to regal robes (perhaps marking the poetic authority of the 'we', as
the 'poet-king' was a favorite trope of the Berkeley group).[67] The
line breaks of the otherwise restrained, nearly imagist, first stanza
luxuriate in incrementalizing the description of the robes, slowing
their cascade to the ground. The penultimate line repeats the first
verbatim but abandons the previous exultation in the majesty of
the robes for a reference to the sound of barking dogs—a sense of
foreboding? the added excitement and danger of a hunt? Among the
admittedly clumsy simile and rhymes of the middle stanza, the rhyme
of 'pleasure'/'treasure' and the reference to a 'begging/ shame like
sorrow' nonetheless infuse the emerging atmosphere of an echoing,
royal hall with a hint of sexual longing, wrenching a vague nostalgia
into a taut corporeal attunement to the contrast between the flowing
robes and the aural interruption of the sound of the dogs. That
barking, and whatever those cries herald, puncture the stasis of the

courtly scene and knock the 'balance' of the poem off kilter—despite the apparent symmetry of the refrain and the solidity of the initial image that now evaporates into deteriorating echoes.

Back at school, Brodeur's *Beowulf* classroom also provided a space in which to modify Pound's insistence on the importance of translation even to explicitly anti-fascist ends—a claim we can take quite materially. As Hadbawnik explores, Brodeur's class and mentorship, and drafts in Spicer's *Beowulf* notes, were important vectors by which Spicer first contested the notorious anti-communist version of the California State employee loyalty oath (before emulating his other medievalist teacher, Kantorowicz, in refusing to sign and thus interrupting his studies—a choice that had momentous consequences in Spicer's life and work).[68] Additionally, Brodeur's sense that *Beowulf's* simultaneously belated and avant-garde-like temporality (looking back on 'the best of pagan antiquity' from within a later, Christian perspective), which drove a 'conventional' poetics 'to experiment', would have likely appealed to Blaser's and Spicer's own sense of epochal betweenness (following the cataclysm of World War Two, at the ends of modernism, their pursuit of a 'Renaissance', etc.).[69]

Even so, Brodeur's brand of the mid-century 'public' *Beowulf* and his emphasis on individuality of expression would not quite do. Although critics tend to see it as only a later development in his corpus, Spicer's eventual insistence on a poetics of what he called 'dictation' marks his poetic development as a process of rejecting individual expression in favor of, as Katz puts it, 'a process of becoming less human, less alive, *less distinctive*'.[70] But even by the time Blaser and Spicer reached Brodeur's classroom, if 'as you would a modern poem' were interpreted, even to the slightest degree, in terms of their own efforts in poetry, neither poet would have taken the instruction as a directive to read Old English poetry like an institutional critic with a propensity for New Critical attitudes, nor with such an investment in individuality. Although we need to be careful not to project a blanket anti-academic attitude onto either poet,[71] by the late 1940s, Blaser and Spicer were already cultivating a theorized ambivalence about the hegemonic protocols of the mid-century English department.

For example, although Spicer and Blaser were both pursuing graduate degrees when they took Brodeur's *Beowulf* seminar, neither pursued literary study exclusively. Spicer's affiliations with the Linguistics department placed him in contact with some of the very discourses that would later aid in dismantling the New Criticism. After being founded in 1901 (the first such program in the United States), Linguistics was soon subsumed by the Anthropology department founded by A. L. Kroeber (a student of Franz Boas, who considered linguistics a subfield of anthropology), where it remained until 1953.[72] Spicer thus worked on historical linguistics, dialectology, medieval history, and medieval literature (at least initially), with connections to a linguistics curriculum housed in Anthropology.[73] The faculty included Brodeur on the one hand (whose position was not Professor of English, but Professor of English and Germanic Philology), the dialectologist David Reed on the other (with whom Spicer would work on the California Language Survey and publish his only scholarly paper), as well as, earlier in Spicer's studies, the anthropologist Paul Radin (another student of Boas and classmate of the famous linguist Edward Sapir).[74]

   This disciplinary constellation informs Spicer's early critiques of the New Criticism—as in an often-quoted remark from Spicer's first published statement on poetics (roughly contemporaneous to his work with *Beowulf*):

> The truth is pure poetry bores everybody. It is even a bore to the poet. The only real contribution of the New Critics is that they have demonstrated this so well. They have taken poetry (already removed from its main source of interest—the human voice) and have completed the job of denuding it of any remaining connection with person, place and time. What is left is proudly exhibited in their essays—the dull horror of naked, pure poetry.[75]

The remark combines a theorized investment in the historicity of language with a prescient understanding of the philosophical implications of structural semiotics. Here, Spicer sounds more like a continental critic of Samuel Beckett in the late 1970s than a post-war North American English major, identifying the 'dull horror' of an arbitrary signifier that can both bore and terrify when bracketed from social and historical entanglements. Dryly framing the most troubling of the New Criticism's shortcomings, from its more obvious (ahistoricity) to the more nuanced (failing to grasp the importance of performance), Spicer's take-down also presages most of the major terms of the New American Poetry's alternatives: site-specificity, embodied immanence, historiography, performativity, community, even pleasure.[76]

In pointing to the entertaining and embodying qualities of vaudeville and popular music as alternatives to the official verse culture in the same statement, Spicer laments of his fellow poets that 'we are not singers' and that 'we do not use our bodies', echoing Brodeur's own enthusiasm for folksong.[77] In 1949, at the same time that Spicer was Brodeur's student and that he drafted these early remarks on poetics, he also hosted a radio show about folk music on KPFA in Berkeley, drawing on his training in philology and source-study to trace the transformation of motifs in folksong—sometimes as far back as the end of the Middle Ages.[78] The connection of these remarks to Brodeur is even more interesting in that a draft of this early statement of poetics survives in a notebook used for a History of the English Language class (including one page on which Spicer has taken down references to R. W. Chambers' *Beowulf: an introduction* and W. W. Lawrence's *Beowulf and epic tradition*, the latter annotated as 'very useful').[79] Another notebook used for History of English assignments and notes (including practice of Old English inflectional paradigms) preserves a bibliography on folksong traditions.[80] Framing Orpheus as a kind of Woody Guthrie, Spicer explains in his statement: 'The proudest boast made about Orpheus was not that his poems were beautiful in and of themselves. There were no New Critics then. The proudest boast was that he, the singer with the songs, moved impossible audiences'.[81]

Spicer thus advocates not only for an avant-garde deforming of the bounds of high and popular culture but also for a felicitous, embodied rhetoric. Here was an early objection to the New Critics, not on the same grounds as those who initially opposed their 'modern' readings of 'modern' poetry, but on grounds more responsive to both the objects of study and the insights claimed by linguistics and anthropology. Brodeur was the professor that set up Spicer and Blaser to read *Beowulf* like a New Critic, but also an inveterate historian of language, a science fiction author, and an amateur anthropologist.

In this context, Brodeur's 'as a modern poem' assignment goes a long way towards securing the relative importance of Brodeur to Blaser's and Spicer's medievalism. It would not be sufficient to only suggest that Kantorowicz gave the poets some sense of 'history' and the background for their performances of poetic authority while Brodeur the philologist offered the poets a technical perspective on historical linguistics (although this is indeed the case). By fitting *Beowulf* to the protocols of post-war literary reading while still maintaining the interests of the historical linguist and folklorist, Brodeur gave *Beowulf* to the poets, and to their poetics, as a site where poetry could translate its others. By placing *Beowulf* within 'modern' official verse culture but performing the poem and contextualizing that performance in ways that, for these two poets, exceeded its protocols, Brodeur implicitly inaugurated a pedagogical space and a scene of translation by which to encounter the aesthetics of *Beowulf* as a potential constitutive force in a contemporary avant-garde.

Blaser's account of coming to the heat of *Beowulf* through that 'fantastic pull' of Brodeur's recitations additionally situates their in-class encounters with the poem within a particular aesthetics of performance in mid-century poetry. The 'pull' of the readings derives neither from the organic unity of the poem nor an expressive theatricality. Rather, as Blaser describes it, the corporeal, sequential, and catalyzing force of the serialized oral delivery of the poem operates on Blaser, Spicer, and their poetics as if it were an ever-incomplete translation from a non-totalized past running through the classroom of the present. In a more general way, Blaser's account of Brodeur's performance moving him and Spicer to translate would seem to describe the operation of what J. L. Austin refers to as 'perlocutionary' performative force.[82]

To read *Beowulf* 'as a modern poem', it seems, would necessitate scenes of translation and performance whose aesthetics have concrete, embodied, social functions. In this sense, Blaser's account transforms Brodeur's seminar into the scene of an avant-garde 'poetry reading' at mid-century and frames Brodeur's performance of the poem as a foundational event of the Bay Area avant-garde. As Davidson argues, in the context of the larger San Francisco Renaissance, the emphasis given to the 'poetry reading' redirected the very function of poetry, since 'the performative removes it from a realm of linguistic universals and emphasizes the uniqueness of the speech act itself'.[83] This emphasis on performance recontextualized 'the poem' such that it almost necessarily included within its expected form the event of a performed utterance as well as its (usually social) conditions and effects. Such performative poetics involve an 'operational rhetoric' that persuasively inaugurates a concrete social-formation: 'the poetic act does not stand in a specular relation to reality but creates new relationships between author and reader and, ultimately, between reader and reader'.[84] Blaser's anecdote of Brodeur reading large chunks of *Beowulf* aloud, as an integral element of his pedagogy, frames the event as a successful performative utterance inaugurating a tiny, but concrete, poetics community: Blaser and Spicer, translating together.

It is thus all the more alluring to consider the *sound* of Brodeur reading *Beowulf* aloud, especially in light of an extant recording of Brodeur reading from the poem: a limited edition, novelty translucent red vinyl LP, *Selections from Beowulf read by Arthur G. Brodeur,* released by his students in 1955 on the occasion of his retirement.[85] This recording is also tantalizing as a point of comparison to the importance of audio recording technologies to mid-century poetry avant-gardes—as sites of resistance and complicity.[86] As a more concrete parallel, we can point to the 1959 release of Allen Ginsberg's LP, *Howl and other poems,* also in translucent red vinyl, by Fantasy records (released in a run of 500). Ginsberg's record documents a benefit reading for *Big Table*, a magazine founded to print an issue of the *Chicago Review* suppressed by the University of Chicago after the magazine's publication of San Francisco beat poets elicited scandalized commentary in the *Chicago Daily News.*[87] In large print, the front of the record sleeve quotes from the ruling of the judge in the 1957 obscenity trial of Lawrence Ferlinghetti and Shigeyoshi Murao over their publication and sale of *Howl and other poems*—adding '"Honi soit qui mal y pense" *Evil to him who thinks evil*' (which readers of medieval literature will recognize as the motto ascribed to the Order of the Garter at the end of *Sir Gawain and the Green Knight*), as if to transform the consumer's purchase of the record itself into a virtuous act of resistance to censorship.[88] Ginsberg's voice opens the recording over low-level audience noise: 'now, since the reading is going reasonably well, I'd like to try to read *Howl*. If we—if we have the patience. Have we got time and patience to go through more poetry now?'[89] He is both interrupted and followed by enthusiastic applause, and then quickly slips into his characteristic vatic-like intoning. The occasion of the reading, this opening *in medias res,* and the implied spontaneity in the rationale Ginsberg gives for reading his most famous poem (despite its obvious appropriateness) operate in concert to frame the audio as an echo of an improvisational inauguration of communal countercultural resistance.

Brodeur's record, by contrast, comes off as far from improvisational, countercultural, or commercial—for a coterie of students, not a public of followers. The professor's own notes on the record's sleeve indicate that he paid a great deal of meticulous, if also convoluted, attention to his pronunciation on the recording.[90] But can we hear in these recordings that 'fantastic pull'? The recordings preserve a memorable voice, reading about twenty to fifty lines of the poem per track. There is no audience, and except for the few occasions on which the full signal of Brodeur's voice is momentarily clipped and distorted (whether because of Brodeur's unfamiliarity with microphones or simply less-than-professional engineering), we hear only the philologist. Brodeur opens with a perfunctory, unemphatic croak of a 'hwæt' (the first word of the poem) and quickly settles into a recital that occasionally modulates pitch slightly downward (usually when a b-verse coincides with the end of a clause) and consistently emphasizes the prosodical stresses as a regular pulse. But these features do not heighten the register beyond that of a diplomatic exercise in historical linguistics. To a philologist, the recording is fascinating for its attempted hybrid pronunciation. To the dedicated *Beowulf* scholar or reader of Brodeur's work, any performance of *Beowulf* may be fascinating, and Brodeur's delivery might suggest useful readings of the poem. But where is the 'heat'? There is no way to know if this recording merits comparison to Brodeur's usual classroom reading voice (we should perhaps even assume that a recording resulting from a highly constructed and socially mediated occasion might not). And we can assume that in class, Brodeur would have not only read long passages but also offered commentary as he went along. If there is 'heat' here—whatever that turns out to be—it does not lie in the conventions of vocal modulation that one might stereotypically associate with a San Francisco poetry reading at mid-century (e.g. a manic pace, vatic intonations, slow crescendos, or sudden silences).

If this recording even hints at what Brodeur's performance must have been like when Blaser and Spicer were in attendance, then Blaser's inscription of Brodeur's seminar as an inaugural event in the history of his poetics community also stands in instructive contrast to a more famous founding narrative of the larger San Francisco Renaissance—Jack Kerouac's fictionalized account of the famous '6' Gallery reading of October 13, 1955 (the same year as Brodeur's retirement and the production of his *Beowulf* recording). Kerouac describes the event as emerging almost as if by accident soon after his semi-autobiographical character, Ray Smith, arrives in San Francisco via freight car and hitchhiking:

> Anyway I followed the whole gang of howling poets to the reading at the Gallery Six that night, which was, among other important things, the night of the birth of the San Francisco Poetry Renaissance. Everyone was there. It was a mad night. And I was the one who got things jumping by going around collecting dimes and quarters from the rather stiff audience standing around in the gallery and coming back with three huge gallon jugs of California Burgundy and getting them all piffed so that by eleven o'clock when Alvah Goldbook [Allen Ginsberg] was reading his, wailing his poem 'Wail' ['Howl'] drunk with arms outspread everybody was yelling 'Go! Go! Go!' (like a jam session) and old Reinhold Cacoethes [Kenneth Rexroth] the father of the Frisco poetry scene was wiping his tears in gladness.[91]

As Davidson points out, uncritical acceptance of this account as a foundational myth is misleading: it elides the entire stream of the Berkeley Renaissance poets—who operated in significant antagonism to the expressivist beats—and homogenizes what was a highly sectarian poetry world into a single spontaneous scene.[92] Yet, however fictionalized, Kerouac's account has indelibly shaped critical reception of the moment.[93] In his portrayal of a 'mad night' the performance of the poetic act inaugurates community, but here the conditions of success seem to involve an expressivist poetics enacted through a transgressive modulation of voice ('howling', 'wailing', 'yelling') and, of course, intoxication. Nothing in the scene approaches anything like a scholarly affectation. Interestingly, Gary Snyder, whose study of Japanese and Chinese poetry had just taken a more serious academic turn, did read from his (tonally restrained) translations of Hanshan that night. And while Snyder is otherwise a major character in the novel (under the name 'Japhy Ryder'), Kerouac's narrative omits him here and avoids having to suggest that anyone's academic linguistic training should share in the credit for the evening's success.

For Blaser, by contrast, the avant-garde *poesis* lies instead in the mutual translations between the philology classroom and the concrete scenes of his and Spicer's poetics community. The voice and apparatus of philology inaugurate the scene of translation that carries the active and corporeally perceptible 'heat of that story' into their midst. These are sufficient to render *Beowulf* 'as a modern poem'. Even if Brodeur the philologist is not caught drunkenly 'wailing' out the Old English, this does not relegate *Beowulf* to mainstream mid-century verse culture. *Beowulf* itself, Blaser implicitly claims, has the capacity to pulse as a generative node of his literary world—to set an operational rhetoric to work within a performative horizon, and to generate a non-representational aesthetics of unstill corporeal energy. But at mid-century, such possibilities remained beyond the scope of the critical debates that even now cast their long shadows on what kinds of questions get asked about aesthetics in Old English poetry.

The demise of the aesthetics of *Beowulf*

Back within professionalized Old English studies, the aesthetics of *Beowulf* quickly became a fragile object of inquiry. Brodeur's approach to the aesthetic criticism of Beowulf was to be embattled on at least three critical fronts: 1) the eventual waning of the New Critical ascendency, 2) the correlated rise of structuralist and poststructuralist critiques of the Author, and 3) the development (ahead of no. 2) of so-called 'oral-formulaic' approaches Old English verse. This critical history is familiar to many readers of Old English poetry, but I rehearse it here as a genealogy of the questions Old English studies has and has not been able to ask about aesthetics.

With the routinization of the New Criticism, soon it was not only rogue, meddling critics who 'reinterpreted and reevaluated earlier literature' in the way that 'modern' poems were being read,[94] and, in publications and classrooms across the fields of English studies, an organic unity 'explication industry' took hold.[95] In Old English studies in particular, however, the case was somewhat different. As Haruko Momma chronicles, the early twentieth-century transformation of Germanic comparative philology into a monolingual 'English studies' had rendered antiquarian philology a sub-field rather

than the mainstay of English departments, and even scholars of
Beowulf's 'literariness' like Tolkien bristled both at the displacement
of historical linguistics from its former place of privilege and at
the ensuing departmental reorganizations.[96] Moreover, the work
of mid-century Old English literary scholars was, of necessity (and
as now), indebted to work in other fields: history, archaeology,
linguistics, etc. Literary scholars could not resist the famous finds at
Sutton Hoo,[97] and significant work was still underway to establish
English-language critical editions of Old English poetic codices.[98]
All of medieval literary studies was shaped by polemics advocating
the interpretation of medieval literature exclusively within a patristic
hermeneutic framework (as with, for example, the work of adherents
to D. W. Robertson's account of medieval Christian allegoresis).[99]
Brodeur's modified New Criticism thus had relatively little time
or space in the field when the shock of 'oral-formulaic' reading
offered only more weight to the arguments of scholars who may
have resented the transformation of their antiquarian objects of
study as they were 'reread in ways that to the scholars made them
no longer look familiar'.[100]

So one cannot overemphasize the extent to which Brodeur's quarrel
with Francis P. Magoun Jr.'s, adaptation of the theories of Milman
Parry and Albert Lord, which asserted the oral and 'totally formulaic'
character of Old English poetry, determined the trajectory of aesthetic
criticism of *Beowulf*.[101] Brodeur had wed his approach to the aesthetics
of *Beowulf* to a view of the poem as the literate composition of a
particular individual: 'I regard the work as composed in writing
and the author as trained in the art of the scop and educated as a
clerk';[102] and, as Daniel G. Calder puts it, Magoun's landmark
Speculum paper posed a problem for critics of Old English poetry
who assumed that 'conventional literary criticism buckles before
such a concept of poetic composition'.[103] Magoun and many of his
adherents (often in East Coast universities) understood any lexical
variation as the result of metrical expediency, cutting away the
ground on which Brodeur would take distinctive diction as a measure
of individuality and aesthetic quality.[104]

The notion that Old English verse is at least informed by oral
and/or formulaic poetics was not totally novel.[105] What was new,
in phrasing oral-formulaic poetry within the Parry–Lord framework,
was 1) the insistence that extant Old English poetry was composed

orally and extemporaneously—containing pervasive elements that can only be explained by positing an earlier oral-formulaic tradition, and 2) the perspective of anthropological-inflected (i.e. not 'literary studies') methodologies stemming from Parry and Lord's field work in Bosnia and their investments in historical linguistics and folklore studies. So, this split—*initially* falling between West Coast and East Coast, public university and Ivy League, Brodeur the one-time member of the faculty communist group and Magoun, an open supporter of Nazi Germany in the mid-1930s[106]—might be *partly* understood in light of distinct institutional and economic contexts that, on the one hand, probably helped to catalyze Brodeur's attempt to consolidate the study and teaching of a 'public' *Beowulf* and, on the other, nurtured a theory whose effects *could have* included conserving *Beowulf* as the province of especially specialized departments at elite schools.

Further critical interventions quickly nuanced the initial hard line of the oral-formulaicists (and scrambled, and then rendered immaterial, the East vs. West geography of the argument). It was thus Larry D. Benson (who had studied at Berkeley with Alain Renoir in the wake of Brodeur's presence in the department) who, in his position at Harvard, offered his account of how 'lettered' poetry can be written in a formulaic style.[107] Brodeur himself, although arguing that Magoun 'presses his case too far', does not reject outright the role of formulaic composition in *Beowulf*, but contests only that the poem is 'totally' formulaic and, anticipating Benson, that 'a lettered poet would be incapable of composing in this formulaic manner'.[108] Some critics would argue that literate composition does not have a monopoly on 'artistry',[109] yet others would refine the critical parameters of 'the formula',[110] and, crucially, later on, critics would eventually arrive at more nuanced accounts of the interrelations of orality, textuality, literacy, composition, and writing in early medieval England, rendering the polarity of the initial debate nearly moot.[111]

However modified, Magoun's intervention was indelibly transformative for the study of Old English poetry.[112] Still, things seemed more pressing at mid-century, and Brodeur framed his response to Magoun around an obsessive attention to *Beowulf*'s poetic diction, drawing on Brodeur's own earlier comparative study of taxonomies of medieval Old Norse poetic diction (via the *Prose Edda* of Snorri

Sturluson) in his appendices on 'The varieties of poetic appellation',
a 'Checklist of compounds', and 'The limits of variation' (details
from all of which will be considered in later chapters of this book).[113]
The aesthetic functions of compound lexemes underwrite almost
everything Brodeur finds wonderful about *Beowulf*, and the book's
culminating arguments all depend on poetic diction and variation
as the threads with which one weaves organic unity. In his signature
argument that the poem's 'fourfold telling of Hygelac's death' stitches
together the plot of the poem, Brodeur charts the aesthetics of the
poem's diction as a kind of integrated master-pattern, scaling up
through variation and then 'extending through, or recurring over,
larger narrative sequences ... transferred from phrasal to structural
use', so that 'main plot and subplot are knit together ... and the
unity of the entire poem [is] effectively established'.[114]

And Brodeur was not without his own apologists. Bonjour,
who gives a name to 'the aesthetic approach' that he considers
'diametrically opposed' to the oral-formulaic approach,[115] defends
Brodeur even in his French-language writings.[116] Even before Brodeur's
monograph was out, his student Stanley B. Greenfield began an
attempt to preserve the ability to detect originality in the 'tension'
between traditional expectations and specific instances of formulaic
diction. As Carol Braun Pasternack puts it, Greenfield wanted 'to
preserve the virtues of individuality and originality, and he argued that
some poets used formulas more artistically than others'.[117] Randolph
Quirk's similar argument from 1963 (which Greenfield would take
up alongside his own after it appeared) made a case that, especially
in the capacity for variation to 'extend' collocations—allowing
'some degree of independence' between conventional lexical and
grammatical connections—Old English verse can 'stretch linguistic
expression', yielding 'incongruous collocations'.[118] As a result, 'while
formulaic utterances and habitual collocations are the necessary
starting point ... they are *only* the starting point'.[119] And as late
as 1979, Greenfield's West Coast colleague Calder's 'History of
the study of style in Old English verse' played the apologist for
Brodeur, arguing that there was much still to build on Brodeur's work
and that the oral-formulaicists' overall effect had 'inhibited literary
analysis'.[120]

Yet, Katherine O'Brien O'Keeffe argues, 'in a way much different from the methods of Foucault and Barthes some twenty-five

years later, Magoun had managed, nonetheless, to kill the author of Beowulf'.[121] By 1995, Greenfield's and Calder's own protégé Pasternack[122] slammed the lid shut on individuality as a quality of Old English poetry in her monograph, *The textuality of Old English poetry*, bringing the poststructuralist study of textuality and authorship by Kristeva, Barthes, and Foucault to bear on her teachers' assumptions, and describing the conditions of extant Old English poetry as un-authored and traditional texts of inscribed verse, performed within a tissue of intertextuality.[123] As the role of Pasternack's book in the following chapters will suggest, by cutting Old English verse free from the burden of individuality and from a need to prove or disprove textual autonomy and transcendence, Pasternack implicitly preserves—or recovers the ground of—the question of style, rephrased in terms of functions of the verse that articulate textual boundaries and condition the coherent performance of Old English poetry.[124] But since Pasternack's argument was posed as a thesis about the textuality and signification of Old English verse during the heyday of 'Theory', a new critical discourse of Old English aesthetics did not coalesce to take up Brodeur's objects of inquiry anew.

Studies of style in *Beowulf* still continued along different lines,[125] more recently in Tyler's study of the poetics of the familiar and in Trilling's study of the aesthetics of nostalgia.[126] Interest in larger formal or numerical patterns and narrative structures, debates about criteria for beauty and Kantian aesthetic judgments, and, in one notable exception, a psychoanalytic reading of the aesthetics of Old English verse, have continued more or less into the present.[127] Other studies implicitly reframe aspects of *Beowulf*'s aesthetics as a function of other inquiries, such as Gillian R. Overing's study of Peircean semeiosis and gender in the poem, which considers the 'dynamic potential', and the 'speed and intensity' in the metonymic logic of the poem's compound diction and larger semiotic webs.[128] James Earl's *Thinking about Beowulf* posits a 'fractal' experience of the semiotics of *Beowulf*—which hints at a style akin to something other than stable masonry.[129] And Eileen A. Fradenburg Joy and Mary K. Ramsey's application of the word 'liquid' as a modifier for the poem surely has similar aesthetic implications.[130] So while Old English studies has not been bound to the terms of Brodeur's project for some time, neither have we tried rearticulating his project in the context of the operational rhetoric and non-representational aesthetics that Blaser and Spicer found in the poem. And in this sense, the trajectory that Brodeur's project might take if freed from the baggage of its implicit relationship to mid-century official verse culture may still have something to offer.

Arts of *Beowulf:* a counterfactual critical history

At the risk of giving too much space to these disciplinary histories, a final point about the *tenor* of these mid-century debates will help clarify both how Blaser's and Spicer's encounter with the 'heat' of *Beowulf* was possible and why I take that experience as the ground of an alternative trajectory for Brodeur's inquiry. That tenor was decidedly high-pitched—so much that Bonjour wondered in a 1967 essay whether 'any attempt to span the gap [between aesthetic and formulaic approaches] by ever so tenuous a flying bridge is doomed from the outset to utter failure or at best bound to turn into a *dialogue de sourds*'.[131] Elsewhere, Bonjour portrayed Godfrid Storms' espousal—in a lecture—of Magoun's position as a 'crossing of the Rubicon'.[132] Ridiculing Storms for the same position in a review, Malone commented that 'the *Beowulf* poet was no minstrel, strumming a harp and composing verse as he strummed'.[133] In an article from 1955, Bonjour praised a study of artistry in the use of sea-words in *Beowulf* by Caroline Brady (a former student of and collaborator with Brodeur), concluding with a veiled jab at Magoun by implicitly snubbing his position as the better-known scholar of Old English at Harvard: 'Ms. Brady has now been working for some time at Harvard—let us hope that she will soon publish more about the ways of the word in *Beowulf*.[134] And, as late as 1970, in response to Magoun positing *Beowulf* as the composite of three distinct 'folk-poems', Brodeur's argument for the poem's individuality of authorship, lettered composition, and courtly and aristocratic (not 'popular') audience crescendoed with the exclamation, 'I deplore Magoun's characterization of *Beowulf*, or any of its parts, as a "folk-poem"'.[135]

The critics of the 'aesthetic approach' were defending the legibility of Old English poetry as an object of study within the dominant modes of professional scholarship and pedagogy in the mid-century

English department, and I take it in good faith that they also believed, as scholars, in the adequacy of their account. But this rhetoric is fierce, and I cannot help but wonder if it does not also point to another motivation, operative in the logic that makes Brodeur's assignment to read *Beowulf* 'as a modern poem' possible—to position the aesthetics of *Beowulf* with respect to a living discourse of *poetics* in the sense elaborated in the Introduction to the present book.

Hard-line oral-formulaicist Robert P. Creed posed these questions in a way that underscores this possibility: 'how can a tissue of formulas, of repeated verses and significant parts of verses, be a great poem ... how can we apply the subtle techniques developed by critics of old, new and newer to this kind of text'?[136] At their most radical, these questions propose that *Beowulf* may not have anything at all to do with what we mean when we say 'poetry' in the contemporary world. By contrast, Creed's questions also reveal his opponents' positions as at least partially motivated by a nagging insistence on the possibility that the study of Old English poetry and the practice of poetics in their present world might matter to each other.

In this respect, the poetics of Blaser and Spicer might plot a kind of counterfactual critical trajectory for this impulse of the mid-century aesthetic approach. Blaser and Spicer may have even already detected a more capaciously theorized concept of aesthetics hovering in Brodeur's critical lexicon. In one of his essays on the Finn episode in *Beowulf* from the early 1940s, Brodeur argues that 'the poet of *Beowulf* was absorbed in the movements of the human mind and heart, in the springs of action, and its emotional consequence'.[137] At times, if for just a moment, it seems as if Brodeur pursues a poetics of feelings that do not resolve into spatialized figures of balance or unified beauty—as in his influential attention to a 'design for terror', which tracks 'techniques of terror' and the cultivation of 'accumulated horror' in the poem's monster-fights.[138] Mark C. Amodio goes so far as to argue that '[a]lthough he never employs the term "affective" and although his criticism reinforces rather than challenges basic New Critical tenets, Brodeur's sensitivity to the reader, if not his aim, is in many ways consonant with contemporary affective criticism'.[139]

The timing of Blaser's and Spicer's encounter with *Beowulf* also renders it the inflection point of an alternative trajectory for Brodeur's project. Brodeur's student and fierce apologist, Greenfield, completed his PhD at UC Berkeley under Brodeur in 1950, just as Spicer was finishing his MA. I have found no evidence to suggest that Spicer or Blaser and Greenfield meaningfully knew each other—but it would be difficult not to speculate on the matter.

Without, by any means, wishing to diminish Greenfield's immense contribution to the field, it is hard not to speculate about what path the mid-century interest in the aesthetics of *Beowulf* might have taken if it were shaped by a poetics not beholden to the 'uneasy alliance' with the New Criticism, if it were taken up by Blaser and Spicer in an alternate universe in which they had careers in professional medieval studies. How might Blaser's and Spicer's poetics replot Brodeur's preoccupations along an alternative trajectory? And why would we want to do this? What Old English studies missed without a critical poetics adequate to the categories and the impulse of Brodeur's study, and what Blaser's and Spicer's encounter with that poem in the context of Brodeur's classroom might still offer (and the next chapter will detail) is a framework within which to rephrase questions about the poem's aesthetics in terms of the poem's non-representational functions and what these have to do with both human corporeal experience and an unstill world of moving energies that is not the poem. Without having to prove that the poem is an original, beautiful tapestry, we can ask what it feels like, we can ask about the poem's own modes of perception. The next chapter begins to answer these questions by exploring the lexicon of aesthetics in Blaser's and Spicer's poetics—measuring its potential to comprehend the aesthetic dynamics of early medieval compositional and rhetorical practices.

Notes

1 *AT,* p. 103. The remark occurs in a discussion of Blaser's and Spicer's introduction to a certain concept of history by Kantorowicz, Pound, and Olson.

2 For relevant summaries, see O'Brien O'Keeffe, 'Diction'; Niles, 'Introduction' in *A Beowulf Handbook,* pp. 5–12; 'Some trends in literary criticism' in the introduction to *Kl.* 4, pp. cxxii–cxxix; and Kisor, 'The aesthetics of *Beowulf',* see especially pp. 230–3. For the

most exhaustive analysis of stylistic approaches to Old English verse from the eighteenth century through the late 1970s, see Calder, 'The study of style'. This project is deeply indebted to that essay.

3 *AOB*, p. 246.

4 *Ibid.*, p. 38.

5 Malone, 'Review of *The art of Beowulf*', pp. 347–53. Brodeur's earlier essays on the Finn episode are largely structured as critiques of Malone's readings. See Brodeur, 'The climax' and Brodeur, 'Design and motive'.

6 The project was not, however, forgotten. E.g. Kisor, 'The aesthetics of *Beowulf*', p. 232 n. 32; O'Brien O'Keeffe, 'Diction'; Howe, 'Who's afraid'; Liuzza, 'Iron and irony'.

7 Niles, 'Introduction' in *A Beowulf Handbook*, p. 6.

8 *AOB*, p. vii.

9 Tolkien, 'Monsters', pp. 29–30.

10 *Ibid.*, p. 32.

11 *Ibid.*, p. 31.

12 Cf. Kl. 4, p. cxxiv n. 2, for this claim. Tolkien is not a New Critic not because of timing but critical genealogy. By 1936 many of the basic assumptions of the New Criticism were already in circulation (Brooks and Warren's *Understanding poetry*, 1937; Empson's *Seven types of ambiguity*, 1930).

13 Tolkien, 'Monsters', p. 30.

14 Lerer, '*Beowulf* and contemporary critical theory', p. 331. On race and Tolkien's project, see Lavezzo, 'Whiteness, medievalism, immigration'; and Kim, 'The question of race'.

15 Thanks to Nicholas Watson for the suggestion that 'Edwardian' misreads Tolkien's own temporal affections.

16 See Graff, *Professing*, p. 173.

17 Bartlett, *The larger rhetorical patterns*, p. 7. The work began during Bartlett's graduate studies at Columbia.

18 Bonjour, *The digressions,* see Acknowledgements, n.p.

19 *Ibid.*, p. 72.

20 Blomfield, 'The style and structure', p. 402.

21 Bonjour, *The digressions*, p. 76.

22 *AOB*, p. 38. Brodeur's comparison to Norse skalds overlooks the outpouring of Skaldic verse in Cnut's court. E.g. Roberta Frank, 'King Cnut in the verse of his skalds' and 'Terminally hip and incredibly cool'.

23 Jones, *Strange likeness*, pp. 18–22; for a summary of Pound's study of OE and concurrent juvenilia see, pp. 18–27. See Wyatt, *Beowulf*; Morris and Wyatt, *The tale of Beowulf*.

24 Jones, *Strange likeness*, pp. 17, 21–2. For an online edition of Pound's essay, see Ezra Pound, '*The music of Beowulf*: *a digital critical edition and introduction*.

25 I cite here directly from the draft. Ezra Pound, 'The music of *Beowulf*', Ezra Pound papers, American literature collection, Beinecke rare book and manuscript library, Yale University, YCAL MSS 43, Box 69, folder 3045, TS, p. 1. Cited below as 'The music of *Beowulf*', TS. My thanks to Chris Jones for sharing his research on and copies of this document when the Beinecke was closed for renovations, and before Maxwell Gray's online edition was available.

26 Pound, 'The music of *Beowulf*', TS, p. 3; and see Jones, *Strange likeness*, p. 47. The full phrase, 'to break the pentameter, that was the first heave' is of course taken famously from Canto LXXXI, not the essay on *Beowulf*. See Pound, *The cantos*, p. 538.

27 Pound, 'The music of *Beowulf*', pp. 4–5. Gray takes 'Skeat' as a mistake for 'Sweet' (as in the famous OE reader). Pound's scansion of the opening lines of the poem and references in his notes suggest he was using Wyatt's edition. See Jones, *Strange likeness*, pp. 20–1; and see the images of the 'autograph documents' in Gray's online edition of Pound's essay.

28 Pound, *ABC of reading*, pp. 54–5.

29 Pound's 'discovery' is an overly facile assertion about the 'orality' of *Beowulf* in the medieval contexts of its performance. For the traditional view of the place of the harp in the meter of Beowulf, see Pope, *The rhythm of Beowulf*. Cf. O'Brien O'Keeffe, *Visible song*; Frank, 'The search for the Anlgo-Saxon oral poet'; Saussy, *The ethnography of rhythm*. The elegies of the Exeter Book do not operate on a different prosodical system; all OE poetry relies on the same poetic syntax that enables composition of prosodically acceptable lines. See Momma, *The composition of Old English poetry*.

30 Pound, *Literary essays*, pp. 215–16.

31 *Ibid.*, p. 25. On *melopœia* see p. 39: *melopœia* occurs when 'words are charged, over and above their plain meaning, with some musical property, which directs the bearing or trend of that meaning'.

32 *Ibid.*, p. 28.

33 See Morris and Magnusson, *Grettis saga*. The text was republished in 1900, in London, by Longmans, Green & Co. Morris did not publish a translation of *Njal's saga*. See also Nicholls, *Modernisms*, p. 164; Nicholls, 'The poetics of modernism', p. 55. And see Pound's essays, 'Medievalism' and 'Swinburne versus his biographers', in *Literary essays*, pp. 149–200, at 190–5.

34 For a differently focused reading of race and ethnicity in Pound's *Beowulf* essay, see Gray, 'Introduction' to Pound, *'The music of Beowulf': a digital critical edition.*

35 Pound, *Literary essays*, pp. 149–200, at 150–1.

36 *Ibid.*, p. 154.

37 *Ibid.*

38 *Ibid.*, pp. 192, 152.

39 *Ibid.*, pp. 150–1.

40 *Ibid.*, p. 152.

41 *Ibid.*, p. 154, italics original.

42 *Ibid.*, p. 154, italics original, p. 152.

43 Nicholls, *Ezra Pound*, pp. 72–3.

44 *Ibid.*, pp. 90–103, and see pp. 116–19. On the interventions Pound made into his re-working of Fenollosa's work, see Fenollosa and Pound, *The Chinese written character as a medium for poetry.*

45 Pound, *ABC of Reading*, p. 51. My thanks to Peter Nicholls for discussing this passage with me.

46 See Jones, *Strange likeness*, pp. 18, 39–40. On Pound's exploration of rhythm's function in anti-expressive 'objectification and activity', see Nicholls, 'The poetics of modernism', p. 54.

47 Nicholls, *Ezra Pound*, pp. 94, 98; and see Jones, *Strange likeness*, p. 18.

48 See Jones, *Strange likeness*, p. 24.

49 See Robinson, '"The might of the north"', pp. 207–12; on the date of Pound's composition of the poem and its Old English tropes, see Jones, *Strange likeness*, p. 24.

50 Pound, *Ezra Pound: poems and translations*, p. 85.

51 *Ibid.*

52 See Jones, *Strange likeness*, p. 18. Jones also suggests *metrical* continuity in Pound's attention to Old English (that runs from 'At the hear o' me' through *The seafarer* and into the *Cantos*) that I would not contest—the break lies in the larger affiliations of the governing aesthetics.

53 See Jones, *Strange likeness*, pp. 23–67, and references at p. 19 nn. 10–12; Robinson, '"The might of the north"'. Edwin Morgan's translation of *Beowulf* is of course a major exception.

54 *AT*, p. 62. Blaser introduces the poem as part of his response to Tallman's awkward prompt, 'I'm interested now in the homosexuality … Where does it start and what does it mean to you' (p. 60).

55 Yao, *Translation and the languages of modernism*, p. 4.

56 *Ibid.*, pp. 18, 4.

57 Katz, *The poetry*, p. 53.

58 Remein and Weaver, 'Getting intimate', p. 9.

59 On the place of the Spicer circle within the homophobia of the post-war Bay Area, and forms of exclusion within the group itself, see Davidson, *Guys*, p. 41. On Blaser, the illegality of homosexuality in the late 1940s, and the 1947 establishment of a sex offender registry, see Nichols, *A literary biography*, pp. 35–7.

60 Young, '"The queen of the mad frontier"', p. 264; Killian, 'Spicer at the Mattachine'; Davidson, *Guys*, pp. 41–3. Spicer's motivations stand in contrast to his friend Duncan's, as explored in 'The homosexual in society'.

61 Davidson, *Guys*, p. 42.

62 *SFR*, p. 28.

63 Yao, *Translation and the languages of modernism*, p. 26.

64 *AT*, p. 103.

65 My thanks to Miriam Nichols and Stan Persky for help transcribing Blaser's difficult handwriting in light pencil (any errors are mine). There are many stray pencil marks at the ends of lines (from a resting pencil) and the punctuation here is thus partly conjectural. The final word in the penultimate line of the middle stanza remains obscure.

66 Duncan, *The collected early poems*, pp. 183, 186.

67 *PBLG*, p. 20. See *AT*, p. 47 for Blaser's similar description of his robes in the DeMolay society as a youth.

68 See Hadbawnik, 'Jack Spicer and the English department', pp. 9–13; *PBLG*, pp. 32–3.

69 See *AOB*, pp. viii, 237–8, 236–46, 22. My thanks to Miriam Nichols for suggesting this point to me. And see Nichols, 'Introduction: reading Robin Blaser', pp. 30–1; *Radical affections*, pp. 20–1; *A literary biography*, pp. 38–9.

70 Katz, *The poetry*, pp. 10–11.

71 Hadbawnik, 'Jack Spicer and the English department'. As Ellingham and Killian note, in the early 1960s Spicer came to regret that his earlier ambivalence towards the 'English department' seemed to influence protégé poets—leading him to go so far as to help plan an (unrealized) 'White Rabbit College' or 'Rabbit Mountain College'—a sort of Black Mountain West, where he would teach Old English. See *PBLG*, pp. 192–4. Blaser had a long university career.

72 See the brief departmental histories at the UC Berkeley Anthropology department homepage, http://anthropology.berkeley.edu/about/history, and the UC Berkeley Linguistics department homepage, http://linguistics.berkeley.edu/about/history.

73 Spicer would have initially pursued a 'linguistics' program taught by faculty in the Anthropology and English departments. Brodeur was not

only a professor of English and of German but also a co-founder of the Scandinavian Studies department, which had begun as an experiment in 1944.

74 See *PBLG*, pp. 33–4, 122. On Spicer's work for Radin, *AT*, p. 79.
75 *House*, p. 230.
76 See Altieri, 'From symbolist thought to immanence' and Shaw, *Fieldworks.*
77 *House*, p. 228.
78 *PBLG*, p. 30.
79 JSP, Box, 22, folder 12; Box 22, folder 10. The draft precedes a long list of Old English strong verbs given with their ablaut series.
80 JSP, Box 22, folder 10. The bibliography ranges from Alexander Haggerty Krappe's *The science of folklore* to John Lomax's *Cowboy songs and other frontier ballads.* This, and the notebook cited above, also contain notes on other introduction to linguistics/HEL topics.
81 *House*, p. 230.
82 See J. L. Austin, *How to do things with words*, p. 109: 'perlocutionary acts' are 'what we bring about or achieve *by* saying something'.
83 *SFR*, p. 22.
84 *Ibid.*
85 Brodeur, Notes. Brodeur's graduate students and friends, it seems, funded its release in a limited pressing of 175 copies. Worldcat reports holdings of this item only at UC Santa Barbara and UC Santa Cruz, and documenting its publication information is difficult. I consulted the copy issued as No. 29, which is in my personal collection.
86 See Shaw, *Narrowcast.*
87 Steinhoff, 'The making of the *Chicago Review*'.
88 On a similar commercial use of Ginsberg's image by the *Evergreen Review*, see Shaw, *Narrowcast*, p. 43.
89 Ginsberg, '1. 'Howl', *Allen Ginsberg reads*. The recording is available online at Pennsound: https://writing.upenn.edu/pennsound/x/Ginsberg.php.
90 Instead of following John C. Pope and using the best approximation of the West Saxon dialect that corresponds to the later date of the extant manuscript, Brodeur, in his words, 'ventured upon a somewhat different—perhaps less justifiable—procedure' on his (debatable) assumption that *Beowulf* was originally composed in a very early Anglian dialect. He thus attempted to employ the probable earlier Anglian pronunciations of certain consonants (*g, s, sc*) while maintaining the later West Saxon vowel and inflectional system. See Brodeur, Notes.

91 Kerouac, *The Dharma bums*, pp. 13–14.

92 Not only did the reading occur late in the game but Kerouac's account also elides the complexity of Rexroth's relationships with the various groups of younger poets and overleverages the importance of the Beats. Incidentally, Blaser and Spicer—who had helped found the gallery—were not in San Francisco at the time. A letter from Spicer was read from the stage requesting help finding a job so he could return to San Francisco. See *SFR*, pp. 3–4, 150–1; *PBLG*, pp. 58, 61–2.

93 *SFR*, pp. 3–4.

94 Graff, *Professing*, p. 198.

95 *Ibid.*, p. 233.

96 Momma, *From philology to English studies*, pp. 187–90.

97 Thus, e.g., Wrenn, 'Recent work on *Beowulf* to 1958'.

98 E.g. Kl. 3; *ASPR* 4.

99 Graff, *Professing*, pp. 234–5.

100 *Ibid.*, p. 198.

101 Magoun, 'The oral-formulaic', p. 466. Cf. *AOB*, p. 3.

102 *AOB*, p.viii.

103 Calder, 'The study of style', p. 47.

104 Magoun, 'The oral-formulaic', see pp. 450, 454, 461.

105 See Stanley's comments to this effect regarding Vilmar, *Deutsche Alterümer im Heliand*, etc., cited in Stanley, 'Beowulf', pp. 127–9.

106 See Norwood, *The Third Reich in the ivory tower*, pp. 35–45. For contemporaneous reporting on the scandal of Magoun's relationship with Nazi Ernst ('Putzi') Hanfstaengl, see 'Professors regret Hanfstaengl snub'; 'Magoun perplexed at publication of cable'; 'Translation of "Deutsche Allgemeine Zeuitung" story gives cables sent by Mellon and Magoun'.

107 Benson, 'The literary character of Anglo-Saxon poetry'. Brodeur, Malone, and Stanley all anticipate Benson in various ways. See *AOB*, p. 4; Malone, 'Review of Godfrid Storms, *Compounded names of peoples in Beowulf*', pp. 200–5; Stanley, 'Beowulf', pp. 127–9. Later work nuancing the idea of the formula is vast—a selection includes Russom, 'Artful avoidance of the useful phrase'; Whitman, 'The meaning of "formulaic" in Old English verse composition'.

108 *AOB*, p. 3.

109 E.g. Bonner, 'Toward a unified critical approach to Old English poetic composition'; Renoir, 'Old English formulas as themes and tools for textual interpretation'.

110 E.g. Niles, 'Formula and formulaic system'.

111 E.g. O'Brien O'Keeffe, *Visible song*; Amodio, *Writing the oral tradition*, pp. 1–47.

112 Alain Renoir's work provides a good example of this shift. He admits the formulaic quality of OE verse early on, but see also his formalist readings, experimental comparisons of Old English aesthetics and cinematic techniques (recalling his father, the famous director), and later work on reception of oral-formulaic verse. See Renoir, 'Wulf and Eadwacer'; and 'The Old English *Ruin*'. Regarding cinematic techniques, see, e.g., Renoir, 'Point of view'. And see Renoir, *A key to old poems.*

113 Brodeur's study of Old Norse poetic diction dates to Brodeur, *Prose Edda* (1916) and Brodeur, 'The meaning of Snorri's categories' (1952).

114 *AOB*, p. 221. There is evidence that his argument had a special appeal to Blaser's and Spicer's poetic companionship. See Remein and Weaver, 'Getting intimate', pp. 9–10.

115 Bonjour, 'Jottings on *Beowulf* and the aesthetic approach', p. 179.

116 Bonjour, *Twelve Beowulf papers*, p. 170.

117 Pasternack, *Textuality*, p. 6. And see Greenfield, 'Formulaic expression'.

118 Quirk, 'Poetic language and Old English meter', pp. 152, 154. And see Greenfield, 'Grendel's approach', pp. 275–6, 283, 283 n. 5; Greenfield, *Interpretation*, pp. 115–16.

119 Quirk, 'Poetic language and Old English meter', p. 171.

120 Greenfield, 'Formulaic expression'; Greenfield, 'Grendel's approach', pp. 283, 283 n. 5; Calder, 'The study of style', pp. 50, 47.

121 O'Brien O'Keeffe, 'Diction', p. 91.

122 On the relationship to Greenfield and Calder, see Pasternack's dissertation, 'Disjunction', p. v. Calder directed the dissertation.

123 Pasternack, *Textuality*, see especially pp. 1–32.

124 In fact, the project emerges from Pasternack's interest in disjunctive aesthetics in Old English verse. See Pasternack, 'Stylistic disjunctions in *The dream of the rood*'.

125 Robinson, *Beowulf and the appositive style*; Donoghue, *Style in Old English poetry*.

126 Tyler, *Old English poetics*; Trilling, *The aesthetics of nostalgia*, pp. 3–28.

127 These topics are all represented in Hill, *On the aesthetics of Beowulf*. See especially: Hill, 'On aesthetics'; Geoffrey Russom, 'Aesthetic criteria in Old English form and style'; Peggy A. Knapp, '*Beowulf* and the strange necessity of beauty'; Stevick, 'Hunting the Anglo-Saxon aesthetic'; Thomas E. Hart, '*Beowulf* and Boethius on beauty and truth'; Janet Thormann, 'The subject of language: a psychoanalytic approach to the aesthetics of Old English poetry'.

128 Overing, *Language*, p. 22.

129 Earl, *Thinking about 'Beowulf'*, pp. 12–15.

130 Joy and Ramsey, 'Liquid *Beowulf*', p. xl. This quality is discussed in the experience of reading the poem in the digital age, but obviously is meant to extend beyond this context.
131 Bonjour, *Twelve Beowulf papers*, p. 179.
132 *Ibid.*, p. 148.
133 Malone, 'Review of Storms, *Compounded names*', p. 204; quoted by Bonjour, *Twelve Beowulf papers*, p. 148.
134 Bonjour, *The digressions*, p. 119. Brady was at Harvard as a Marion Talbot Fellow of the American Association of University Women. See 'Fellowship awards, 1952–53', p. 226.
135 Brodeur, '*Beowulf*: one poem, or three?', p. 25.
136 Creed, 'On the possibility of criticizing Old English poetry', p. 98.
137 Brodeur, 'Design and motive', p. 42.
138 *AOB*, pp. 88–106, at pp. 102, 89.
139 Amodio, 'Affective criticism', p 57.

2

'Heat', early medieval aesthetics, and multisensory complexion in *Beowulf*

Heat, translation, and corporeal sensoriality

Neither *Beowulf* nor Brodeur's instruction was soon forgotten by either Blaser or Spicer. As noted, Blaser returned to their undergraduate Old English lexicography project in 1954. A variety of references to Old English language and literature (and Old Norse) in Spicer's later work are well documented.[1] During Spicer's time teaching Old English at the University of Minnesota for two years (1950–52), Spicer had Blaser send him what he referred to as 'the Beowulf notes' (in all likelihood both his and Blaser's translations).[2] Even in the last months of Spicer's life, struggling with alcoholism, Spicer had the wherewithal and the motivation to admonish an interlocutor from his lecture at the Berkeley Poetry Conference in 1965 who casually implied that *Beowulf* was composed as a popular/folk song, restating Brodeur's position as he had recorded it in his notes fifteen years before: '[w]ell, to begin with, *Beowulf* was a court poem, probably not sung although it might have been. I've taught the *Beowulfs* [*sic*], I know something about it'.[3] What might Spicer have known about it—or what might he have said about it if he had continued on the trajectory of professional philologist? What might a systematized approach to the aesthetics of *Beowulf* have looked like if launched from the positions it catalyzed in Blaser's and Spicer's poetics?

This chapter takes up the question of to what exactly Blaser refers in phrasing the target of his and Spicer's translations of *Beowulf* as 'the heat of that story' and what it might comprehend about the poem's aesthetics. *Heat*, in this case, is not merely a loose colloquialism from a mid-century avant-garde speech community but a term of art in Blaser's poetics and one that, I argue, implicitly articulates a useful relationship between early medieval concepts of sensory-affective perception and a poetics of translative process. This chapter outlines the assumptions of an alternative 'aesthetic approach' to *Beowulf* implicit in this sense of heat, reading aesthetics as a complex of multisensory and affective perceptual activities that condition the poem's phenomenological and ecological poetics, as well as the relationship between the poem's aesthetics and the question of sensory impairment. The first half of the chapter takes a closer look at heat in Blaser's poetics—especially in terms of his interest in the phenomenology of Maurice Merleau-Ponty and his use of fragmentary translations of the Old English poem *The dream of the rood*—alongside Mary Carruthers' work on early medieval aesthetics and early medieval English discourses of the senses. To round out this constellation as a reference point for reading *Beowulf*, the latter portion of the chapter surveys the multisensory and often synesthetic phenomenal field of the poem.

Aside from the likelihood that Blaser's 'heat' may owe something to all the references to fire in a poem in which, as Christine Rauer argues, 'Beowulf's fight against the dragon is mainly one against fire and heat' (a point explored further in Chapter 5),[4] the larger context of Blaser's remark goes a long way to clarifying the importance of the term and the implications of its application to *Beowulf*. The anecdote appears in his 1967 essay (initially a lecture), 'The fire'. The essay marks Blaser's first effort to formalize his poetics in print and constitutes an implicit response to Robert Duncan's public attack in *Poetry/Audit* on Blaser's 1965 translation of Gérard de Nerval's *Les chimères*, which includes a call for Blaser to bring his 'poetics into action as theory'.[5] Among accounts sympathetic to one side of the dispute or the other,[6] as Andrew Mossin suggests, it can be understood as displaced fight over the poetic legacy and authority of their late companion, Spicer.[7] Duncan objects to what he perceives as Blaser's 'omissions' of hermetic and occult references in Nerval's text and takes this as symptomatic of a fetishization of individuality that the late Spicer, and his still allegiant Blaser, would abhor—a 'poetics in which the poem is to be authentic, i.e. an expression of what is really his own'.[8] Blaser's attribution of heat to *Beowulf* is nestled within what unfurls as a dialectical reversal of those charges (quoted more fully here than earlier in the book):

I am thirty years old before I begin even tentatively to accept the title
of poet. In San Francisco, I was tied to two other poets who, it was
my superstition, wrote my poems for me. When that notion become
sentimental, I dropped it, and became another poet. I have worked
since 1955 to find a line which will hold what I see and hear, and
which will tie a reader to the poems, not to me. This fascination
precedes my great debt to Charles Olson, for it is in a schoolbook
problem, Plato's description of the power of music over the body and
the dangers of poetry in *The Republic*, and it was the fantastic pull
of hearing Brodeur read *Beowulf*, a hundred lines at a whack on a
good day, which led Spicer and me to compete in our translations to
bring over the heat of that story. I am greatly moved by what is
received and held with force in a poet's work. And sometimes that
work promises that a great deal more will be held.[9]

What looks at first like a literary autobiography in miniature proceeds
to undermine the fetishization of the individual poet latent in that
form by gesturing to a series of performative fictions that accede
'to the title of poet'. Then, the search for 'a line which will hold
what I see and hear'—which might at first glance look like a poetics
of individual expression—becomes merely the scaffolding for the
activity of the poem quite apart from Blaser's own individuality:
what will 'tie a reader to the poems, not to me'. Although the phrase
functions as a synecdoche for an entire poetics, the search for 'a
line' also places special emphasis on aesthetics by invoking a prosodical unit (i.e. a line of a poem) as what 'will hold' not significance,
but concrete sensory experience. Blaser's admission that he remains
'greatly moved' by a given poet's work may sound at first like a
desire for bourgeois individual expression, but this capacity too
aligns aesthetic experience with the activity of the poem. The account
of Orphic poetics as 'the power of music over the body and the
dangers of poetry' as feared by Plato similarly marks the capacities
of an operational rhetoric—not an individual singer—to vitally shape
the human sensorium.

This usage of 'heat' contests and refines a term that already had
currency in mid-century poetics. Duncan's initial attack invokes heat
in a more idiomatic manner: 'I set my version of *Les Chimères* at
war with your version. Raising ideas in the heat of battle.'[10] But in
an earlier moment, Charles Olson's essay 'Against wisdom as such'—a
friendly critique of a creeping hermeticism and spiritualism in

Duncan's poetry—had already leveraged the word 'heat' to very different ends within that community. Olson explains, 'I said to Duncan "heat, all but heat, is symbolic, and thus all but heat is reductive"'.[11] Tacitly invoking Pound's 'world of moving energies', Olson identifies heat as a constitutive property of a poem—'a poem is the issue of two factors: (1) heat, and (2) time'.[12] Olson further distinguishes the implied sense of heat as an unstable, worldly, energetic process from conventional western associations of light with the symbolic, the transcendent, and epistemological illumination: 'Light is reductive. Fire isn't'.[13] At one other point, Olson comes very close to a functional definition of heat, before characteristically veering away: 'I'm so foolish. A Song is heat. There may be light, but light and beauty is not the *state* of: the state is the grip of (and it is not feverish, is very cool, is—the eyes are—how did they get that way?'[14] Here, the sense of 'heat' is clarified less by its status as a verbal complement of 'song' than by the syntactic performance of the attempted statement. The admission that 'I'm so foolish' is played out not in that Olson could simply rest his definitional efforts with the deceptively simple equation of heat and song, but in the displacement of this static claim in the ensuing exchange of (syntactic? corporeal?) forces by which the sensorium emerges in a series of overlapping digressive fragments ('... not feverish ... cool ... the eyes are'). These fragments of terms for thermal qualities and sensory organs are themselves caught in and constitute a process of ('is the grip of') we know not what ('the eyes are—how did they get that way?').

Further developing Olson's usage,[15] Blaser's response to Duncan opens by refusing the idiomatic 'heat of battle' in favor of heat in this other sense, at once technical and strategically murky:

... Burning myself up, I would leave fire behind me.
To hold an image within the line by sound and heat is to have caught something that passed out there. The psychological accuracy of this perception is not enough; the sculptural imagistic quality is not enough; and the very aesthetic quality of taking the one image, or even three images as a whole, the beauty of the idea that you can write a single poem, is a lie. The processional aspect of the world has to be caught in the language also. The body hears the world, and the power of the earth over the body, the city over the body, is in terms of rhythms, meters, phrasing, picked up—the body's own rhythms

compose those or it would shake to pieces.—The music of the spheres is quite real, but the sound of the earth must meet it. I suppose I want to say that the real business of poetry is cosmology, and I'm claiming my own stake in this. And this is the activity of telling the story—the necessity is chemical—it is *not* invented, but it is original, personal, singular, and even domestic ... No symbols.[16]

Playfully invoking the heat of fire as what Miriam Nichols calls '*Blase*-r's signature element',[17] Blaser describes a process of overlapping the human sensorium with energies from 'out there'—a recalibration of William Carlos Williams' demand for 'some proximate co-extension of the universe' so that the poem becomes the site of what Nichols calls a 'complicated nonequivalence.'[18] As an index of this 'procession' that does not take for granted the relationship between the non-human world and the human sensorium, heat marks a phenomenological poesis that becomes the primary target of Blaser's translation—whether of *Beowulf* or Nerval:

Though I consider most of my work as a kind of translation, I have moved toward translation in the ordinary sense. My Nerval is an effort to bring over the chimeras of another poet, because the recognition was word for word. In doing so, I spent months trying to find words in English to carry the heat of the Nerval world, which is cosmic, but also most personal. And it is this content which must be translated—not the word-for-word crib, but the actual heat of the process which gave form to the poems.[19]

Thus doubled—as both a quality of the world and the process that constitutes a poem—heat is what the perceiving poem, constituted as a process of encountering the world, feels like.

Heat thus aestheticizes poesis as other than transcendence. Blaser casts it as a quality of emotion even as he recasts emotion as a fugitive specter not transparently legible to the human sensorium:

I'm haunted by a sense of the invisibility of everything that comes into me (aware that nothing is more invisible than emotion—by emotion, I mean the heat of one's sense of the war or a place, or a body, or of the extensions of these, the earth, the existence of gods ...[20]

Wresting emotion from the domain of the individual human subject, Blaser thus folds it back into aesthetics as a process of rendering perceptible the encounter of human corporeality with energies of factical experience ('everything that comes into me') that exceed and/or insensibly traverse it—material, abstract, real, imagined.[21]

As Norma Cole explains in her analysis of this essay, it is the 'resistance of the image to *being seen* that generates the poem'.[22]
Anticipating his engagement with Merleau-Ponty that began a few years later, Blaser's dialectic is that of the phenomenological reflection, wherein '[a] philosophy becomes transcendental, or radical, not by taking its place in absolute consciousness without mentioning the ways by which this is reached, but by considering itself as a problem; not by postulating a knowledge rendered totally explicit, but by recognizing as the fundamental philosophical problem this *presumption* on reason's part'.[23] By the time we learn that the promise of a poem lies in the possibility that 'a great deal more will be held', poems become active perceptual entities beyond the conventional sense in which a poem performatively *does* this or that. Beyond the conventional senses of 'heat', the term functions as an index of the poem's capacity to comprehend the human sensorium—as if the process of 'receiving and holding' were both (literally) energetic and not without resistance or loss, as if heat were not manifested in representation or imitation of aesthetic experience but by recognizing as a fundamental problem of poetics this presumption on the part of literary convention.

Heat thus becomes a function of—the experience of—the translation of the invisible into the stuff of the poem. For Blaser, as a generalized mode of poesis, translation harbors a non-representational, perceptual (although not undeconstructible) dimension alongside its more conventional recoding functions:

> I am trying to describe the foreignness, the outsideness, as a kind of metaphor for the sense I have of the process that leads to a poem, which again is outside, when made, and it is akin to translation, a word which in its parts holds the meaning of the word *metaphor*, the bringing over. This is here a problem of describing the process of inclusions, which as a man's work extends, enlarges and must take in both earth and sky. The heat I'm after is not simply the personal heat of the meeting, the recognition, but a heat and a passion which are of the nature of existence itself. The personal, yes, but then the translation of the personal to correspond with larger and larger elements, images of earth, is a process of inclusion—a growth of sensibility in Valéry's phrase, but also a making which is not self-expressive. To be included, to be caught, to be brought over.[24]

Whether between languages or between the poem and whatever is not the poem, heat issues from 'the meeting' or 'the recognition' as only one term in a recursive series of 'inclusions' (a word used here twice) that constitute the poem. The movement of these inclusions reconfigures the traditional etymological sense of translation as 'carrying across' and its equivalence with metaphor. Rather than figuring translation as a form of 'communication' or representation—as resolutely 'not self-expressive'—the poem becomes the site not of relationships of equivalence between linguistic systems or linguistic and non-verbal semiotic systems,[25] but a phenomenological tangle between language and a-semiotic orders.

It is worth remarking that this phenomenological tangle, as a function of the poem's sensological relationship to the non-human world, would precipitate a profoundly ecopoetical moment—especially in that it would constitute an alternative to both more traditional ecocritical questions of representation and the strains of 'New Materialist' thought that tend towards neglecting language and the human in leaping to a too-often respiritualized world.[26] Registering the heat of the poem's mutual translation of the world and the human sensorium as a potentially assistive function may also have implications for how we conceptualize the relationship of *Beowulf* to sensory impairment, disability, and prosthesis. Jonathan Hsy, Tory V. Pearman, and Joshua R. Eyler suggest that Richard Newhauser's concept of medieval 'sensory communities' implicitly articulates embodied contexts of disability.[27] As Richard Godden and Hsy explore, the notion of poesis as prosthesis is not new in medieval studies, nor unrelated to either style or the non-human.[28] If, as Julie Orlemanski's analysis of later medieval exempla suggests, 'disability is the figurative friction of personhood resisting narrative subsumption',[29] then, given the phenomenological friction inherent in the aesthetic implications of Blaser's sense of heat, it is not impossible that the relationship of ecological and sensological dimensions of the heat of *Beowulf* might *at times* enable what Orlemanski calls 'tendentious solidarity' with otherwise invisible aesthetics of sensory impairment, meeting and modulating (extending or deforming) the incompleteness of the human sensorium. We need to be careful not to assume any simple adequation of a professionalized reading of a poem with the assistive devices that 'supplement and complete disabled bodies'.[30] But at very least, the logic of the aesthetic process described above would affirm a fundamental concept of disability studies—which Godden phrases as the 'immanent vulnerability' of all bodies—while entangling that vulnerable corporeality with a larger non-human world.[31] In this way, the ecopoetical and multi-sensory functions of heat are inseparable from the possibility and ubiquity of sensory impairment. As the next section explores, the embodied, sensory-affective vulnerability implied by this heat lies at the heart of its congruency with early medieval aesthetics.

Sensory complexion in early medieval literature and the phenomenology of the poem

Blaser associates a distinctly premodern concept of aesthetics with the mechanisms of his translative poetics. In 'The practice of outside', his influential essay on Spicer's corpus, Blaser phrases it as 'the aesthetic as perception relating directly to the formation of the public, political and social life',[32] as contrasted with an 'untied beauty' or 'the aesthetics of only-feeling or ideality'.[33] For Blaser, the latter involves the modern subsumptions of aesthetics under adequation to a given abstract value: such 'untied' aesthetic values belong to 'an agreement of logical structure that turns out to be our imposition of an order' which 'does not entangle us with the world'.[34] By contrast, 'the aesthetic as perception' bespeaks the perceptual vulnerability of the body to the operational rhetoric of the poem and its capacity for worldly perception.

While Blaser's phrasing here draws heavily on his readings of Merleau-Ponty (as explored below),[35] it resonates profoundly with the larger concepts of aesthetics in premodern compositional practices, and it surely issues in part from his training in medieval studies and premodern rhetorical traditions. In a conversation with Warren Tallman, Blaser makes the etymological argument for this formulation in describing an 'appalling course on aesthetics from Stephen C. Pepper' that he took at Berkeley: 'nobody should teach aesthetics that does not perceive, and he did not perceive. The word "aesthetic" in Greek means perception, and he didn't perceive anything.'[36] By this point, Blaser had already studied some Greek language as well as Byzantine rhetoric on a special course that he, Duncan, and Spicer took together from Kantorowicz on tenth-century emperor Constantine VII,[37] and, as Kelly Holt explores, Kantorowicz's instruction in medieval rhetoric and especially the *ars dictaminis* would eventually influence the epistolary rhetoric and serial poetics of Blaser's and Spicer's (as well as Duncan's) later work.[38] More to the point, Blaser's phrasing here, and the dynamics of heat above, adhere closely to the conceptions of aesthetics inherent in medieval compositional and reading practices. As Mary Carruthers articulates, similarly pointing out the etymological sense of 'aesthetics' in opposition to the sense it accrued in eighteenth- and nineteenth-century transcendental philosophy, 'human senses are what medieval aesthetics is all about'.[39] Strictly speaking, a transcendent or mathematic sense of beauty (or, we might add, unity) 'is not an aesthetic concept'.[40]

Reminding us that 'medieval art is not only explained by considerations of semiology and representation, *mimesis* ... but also by persuasion', Carruthers urges the practice of what she calls a rhetorical analysis: 'our first question could then be not "What is it (and what does it represent)?" but "What is it doing (and what is it asking us to do)?"'.[41] With the added sense that 'persuasion is a process not a state', the embodied vulnerability that accompanies medieval concepts of aesthetics is strikingly legible to Blaser's poetics. As Carruthers argues:

> modern notions of a fully autonomous self are profoundly unmedieval. Indeed it is a peculiarly modern western idea, bound in, I think, equally modern ideas about autonomous Beauty and the primarily self-referential aesthetic values which accompany it ('I know what I like') ... this 'self' is malleable and in motion, always penetrated by the world. The biophysical world of compounds, mixtures, flux, affect, and continuous movement among opposites is also the realm of medieval aesthetic experience.[42]

Viable aesthetic qualities are accordingly 'attributes of *style*, intended effects of the artefact on the perceiver', and these take for granted that the composition in question has a 'direct agency' far beyond its status as 'media'.[43] Congruently, in *The astonishment tapes,* Blaser rejects 'the view that style in language is my personality', defining style instead as 'the distance traveled in the language'.[44] This formulation recalls a medieval rhetorical concept that will be important to each of the remaining chapters: *ductus* (guides, paths)—the articulation of the *intentio* (intention, in the formal philosophical sense) of the work, conceived of as an *iter* (journey) through its stylistic variation.[45] The scholastic philosophy most famous for theorizing *intentio* belongs to a moment after *Beowulf*, but the debt of modern(ist) phenomenology to that term (especially through Husserl's engagement with scholasticism via his teacher, Franz Brentano) renders it useful in imagining the activity of a medieval poem in terms of perceptual experience.[46]

As they develop across the Middle Ages, terms for such aesthetic experience (later on, as borrowed from Roman rhetorical tradition) are drawn from adjectives that 'articulate and qualify modes of perception by describing particular effects on the perceiver'.[47] Not words for entities, but modulations of perception, this lexicon is not uniformly 'positive'; it ranges between and conflates the senses, from the gustatory and/or olfactory (*dulcis* [sweet], *foedus* [foul]), to the tactile and/or olfactory (*pinguis* [plump, juicy]), as well as into the more expected realm of the visual (*clarus* [clear, brilliant]).[48] On their own, and in combination, plications of sensation with affective experience structure such aesthetic qualities. As Carruthers explains, 'all sensations, like all human beings, are complexions',[49] and 'aesthetic experience "makes sense" as a complexion of formal qualities and sensory perceptions'.[50] This logic is crucial to conceptions of aesthetic experience in compositional practices throughout the earlier Middle Ages[51] in which the *varietas* (variety) necessary for good composition adheres to *diversitas* (diversity) rather than *dignitas* (fittingness).[52] By the logic of *complexion*—'not fusion'—heterogeneous perceptual fields accede to the status of an attribute of style.[53] That is, for example, in the 'sweetness' or 'clearness' of a text, a variety of tactile, olfactory, and rhythmic or even syntactic patterns combine—perhaps with positively or negatively affecting references—*without dissolving into a single abstracted value*.

Blaser's poetics comprehend such premodern concepts of aesthetic complexion in part through Merleau-Ponty's discussion of what he calls 'the chiasm': the 'hinge' between the body and the world, sensation and the idea, the sensed and the sentient.[54] In his essay on Spicer's poetics, for example, Blaser explicates 'a reversal of language into experience' explicitly as a 'chiasma—a crossing, an "intertwining"'.[55] For Merleau-Ponty, the chiasm maps 'the most difficult point ... the bond between the flesh and the idea'.[56] The chiasm is not precisely a medieval aesthetic complexion, but by its logic the sensing and the sensed meet as a plication rather than fusion, as in the expression of the body as 'this fold, this central cavity of the visible which is my vision'—a vision which occurs 'in our flesh' by means of 'a folding back, [or] invagination'.[57]

Blaser would also later turn to Deleuze's treatise on Leibniz, *The fold*, when discussing a poetics of folding in both verse and prose,[58] and, as Steve McCaffery explains, he initially arrives at his concept of the fold 'through a genealogy via Blake rather than Deleuze or the Baroque',[59] but these earlier invocations of Merleau-Ponty's chiasm are especially useful for framing a medieval aesthetics of complexion as a performance of perception.[60] As McCaffery suggests, a poetics of the fold applies the processes of sensation to the poem just as it entangles the poem with the body by a logic aloof to representation: 'these choreographies of folds and detours lead back to the skin, that most quotidian and insistent organ, enveloping us ... the fold is antiextensional, antidialectical, and intransigently inclusive'.[61] Nichols characterizes Blaser's practice of Merleau-Ponty's thought in a similar vein: '[i]f the chiasmus is primary, there is neither transparency of representation (naive realism) nor disembodied textuality: there is only the Möbius twist of inner and outer'.[62] Placing poesis 'at the end of thought as description and logical structure', Blaser describes 'a commotion between the visible and the invisible'.[63] As Peter Middleton observes, both 'flesh', as Merleau-Ponty conceives it, and this horizon of performance in Blaser's poetics, insist that 'both world and language are activities, and not conditions, entities, or systems'.[64] In the performance of the poem's style, the reader is, as Blaser puts it, 'set loose in the invisibility where the text leads him [*sic*] ... [they are] after all a perception of the text'.[65]

Further movements of Merleau-Ponty's phenomenology can also help translate the specifically *multisensory* world of medieval aesthetics.[66] In *The visible and the invisible*, the chiasmic dialectic of body and sensation, sensation and idea, grows out of similar entanglements between the senses:

> We must habituate ourselves to think that every visible is cut out in the tangible, every tactile being in some manner promised to visibility, and that there is encroachment, infringement, not only between the touched and the touching, but also between the tangible and the visible ... the tangible itself is not a nothingness of visibility, is not without visual existence.[67]

For Merleau-Ponty, even a single sense already comprises an intertwining of distinct experiences that we take for granted, as in, for example, touch, always pregnant with 'three distinct experiences which subtend one another, three dimensions which overlap but are distinct: a touching of the sleek and of the rough, a touching of the things … and finally a veritable touching of the touch, when my right hand touches my left hand while it is palpating the things'.[68] Sensations themselves are not inert substance and any individual quality is already a process: 'before becoming an objective spectacle, quality is revealed by a type of behaviour which is directed towards its essence'.[69] As considered at length in *The phenomenology of perception*, 'the unity and the diversity of the senses are truths of the same order'.[70]

It is, finally, the corporeal, kinetic, and invisibly spatial dimensions of the senses that enable them to 'translate each other without any need of an interpreter'.[71] Countering what we now recognize as the ableist assumption that blind people do not experience space properly, Merleau-Ponty tracks the manner in which '[e]very sensation is spatial … not because the quality as an object cannot be thought otherwise than in space, but because, as the primordial contact with being … it is itself constitutive of a setting for co-existence, in other words, a space'.[72] Georgina Kleege, disabilities studies scholar and self-described 'blind sight-seer married to a medievalist, Nick Howe [d. 2006]', describes the spatiality of her visits to medieval sites with her late spouse:

> When I accompanied Nick on research visits to England and European cathedrals and other sites, I found many ways to experience these places nonvisually … the average cathedral offers many opportunities for tactile exploration. If one is willing to climb towers, or explore crypts, catacombs and other subterranean areas, one not only gains a vivid kinetic sense of scale and grandeur; one may encounter many examples of carving and sculpture with no barriers to exploration. Attending a service or concert allows one to map the interior through acoustics, while the scents of incense and candles create an olfactory atmosphere … These places were meant to be experienced through as many senses as possible.[73]

And for Merleau-Ponty, the experiential configuration of such sensory spatiality is exemplified in a stunning two-part reflection on music in a concert hall:

> When, in the concert hall, I open my eyes, visible space seems to me cramped compared to that other space through which, a moment ago, the music was being unfolded, and even if I keep my eyes open while the piece is being played, I have the impression that the music

is not really contained within the circumscribed and unimpressive space. It brings a new dimension stealing through visible space, and in this it surges forward ...'[74]

...

Music is not in visible space, but it besieges ['erodes it'], undermines and displaces that space, so that soon these overdressed listeners who take on a judicial air and exchange remarks or smiles, unaware that the floor is trembling beneath their feet, are like a ship's crew buffeted about on the surface of a tempestuous sea ... Sensory experience is unstable, and alien to natural perception, which we achieve with our whole body all at once, and which opens on a world of inter-acting senses.[75]

From a radically different philosophical position, Michel Serres makes a similar point in and around his reading of the famous 'unicorn tapestries' (ca. 1500) held by the Musée de Cluny: the senses are 'unstable ... because they are mingled'.[76]

Such a burrowing of the senses through mutually transverse trajectories at once deconstructs the perennial primacy of the visual field in western poetics and makes possible a potentially prosthetic perceptual activity of the poem—all of which can be grounded in Merleau-Ponty's sense of the primacy of synesthesia:

Synaesthetic perception is the rule, and we are unaware of it only because scientific knowledge shifts the centre of gravity of experience, so that we have unlearned how to see, hear, and generally speaking, feel, in order to deduce, from our bodily organization and the world as the physicist conceives it, what we are to see, hear and feel.[77]

Thus conceived, synesthesia operates on the same logic whereby sound cuts across visual space—with the addition that it posits a kinetic corporeality. Rather than an inert representational medium in which the senses might merge, Merleau-Ponty posits a virtual kinesis as a de-ontologized form of their entanglement: '[m]ovement, understood not as objective movement and transference in space, but as a project towards movement or "potential movement" forms the basis for the unity of the senses'.[78] When a sound is experienced as sight, *'the subject does not say only that he* [sic] *has the sensation both of a sound and a colour: it is the sound itself that he sees where colours are formed'.*[79] When sound is experienced visually, 'I echo the vibration of the sound with my whole sensory being, and particularly with that sector of myself which is susceptible to colours.'[80] This possibility is already important in considering the variable functions of complexional aesthetics (medieval or modern) in their relationship to sensory impairments (to what extent can a poetic complexion extend, assist, sharpen, obscure, or enfold experiences of impaired or absent senses?)—as in Kleege's experience above—especially in light of the casual ubiquity of 'imagery' in the contemporary critical idiom. And it is by a similar logic that a poem could include both corporeal sensation and the otherwise insensible 'something that passed out there': the poem's aesthetics must entangle the sensory body, as 'the common texture of all objects'.[81]

Without positing an ahistorical equivalence, this phrasing of Blaser's *heat* in terms of a phenomenological sensology provides a heuristic congruency with specific instances of early medieval discourses that construct the body in its vulnerability to rhetorical complexions. If, as Deleuze opens his treatise on Leibniz, 'the Baroque refers not to an essence but to an operative function' that 'endlessly produces folds' even unto infinity,[82] then the heat of *Beowulf* may refer us to another plicative function, accompanied by medieval doctrines of the senses, the body, and health, rather than Leibniz's discourses of body and soul. After all, even on a purely terminological level, heat has a part to play in the classical doctrine of the humors, a discourse of bodily health crucial to medieval aesthetic experience.[83] Although perhaps associated more often with the later Middle Ages, the doctrine is not absent from early medieval England, appearing in the context of computistical texts like Bede's eight-century *De temporum ratione* and Byrhtferth's eleventh-century *Enchiridion*.[84] The precise medical understanding and application of humoral theory in early medieval England remain contested, and Old English itself does not appear to employ a consistent set of terms for the four humors, but it seems that Old English translations of Latin medical texts attempt to retain humoral concepts with explanatory circumlocutions, and there is evidence that *Bald's leechbook* considers humoral etiology in its diagnoses and treatments.[85] The doctrine of the humors was additionally extant in Isidore of Seville's *Etymologiae*, whose 'eclectic' approach to medical and psychological traditions easily combined with vernacular models of the mind and later theological models of the soul's incorporeality.[86] As the next chapter will explore, heat, in a different sense, is a crucial element in the cardiocentric 'hydraulic' model of the mind and the emotions in Old English vernacular psychology.[87]

Tucked within Blaser's sense of the heat of *Beowulf* is thus a renewed potential responsiveness to the poem's performance of what Newhauser calls an 'elasticity in understanding the relationship between the senses'.[88] Of course, Merleau-Ponty is responding to a modern, Cartesian disembodied ego. And Merleau-Ponty's analyses of multisensoriality (curiously amnesiac of olfactory and gustatory sensations even while besieging the primacy of vision), with its emphasis on the 'unity of the body', is not without its problems. Much of contemporary sensology orients itself around contesting that very notion, and Merleau-Ponty's discussion of blindness (like his famous analysis of the phantom limb) is surely a *pharmakon* from the perspective of disability and impairment (the communication of the senses in their distinctiveness refuses to impoverish the world of persons with impairments but depends on the 'unified' body). Nonetheless, especially as refracted through Blaser's poetics, this phenomenology returns us to a multisensory world in which we can comprehend a non-representational poesis—one that is not identical to its early medieval catalysts, but whose affinity with them can still help translate the perceptual activities of *Beowulf*.

Contexts of complexion in Old English poetry/complexion as translation

Yet, surviving discursive constructions of the senses and the organs of sense specific to early medieval England do not provide an unequivocal context for multisensory complexion in Old English poetry. The visual register of Old English poetry retains its assumed prominence in the scholarship,[89] and productive analogies between the aesthetics and structure of Old English poetry to early medieval visual art remain long-lived critical touchstones.[90] Even when the role of a wider 'non-visual' sensorium is acknowledged in these contexts, it remains secondary to an assumed primacy of the visual.[91]

According to Katherine O'Brien O'Keeffe's analysis of appraisals of the senses in Old English prose, Old English homiletic and learned texts follow classical and patristic hierarchies of the five senses with only minor variations, routinely holding up eyes and sight as the least corporeal of the classical 'five senses' and most aligned with spiritual domains of knowledge—against touch and hands as the lowest and most bodily of senses and sense-organs.[92] The differential valuation of the senses, as measured by compensation for damage to organs of sense in the Old English legal tradition is somewhat more complicated,[93] yet, especially as realized in the *Domboc* of King Alfred, O'Brien O'Keeffe detects 'an increased appreciation of the role of the senses and the organs of sense' in legal discourse across the period.[94] Later on, Wulfstan would combine the developments of legal and homiletic valuations of the senses in his codes for Æthelred II and Cnut, assigning value to the *destruction* of organs of sense as a payment for both legal and spiritual offenses.[95] This last innovation—more or less contemporary to the unique manuscript of *Beowulf*—would seem to register a paradoxical increased valuation of the senses alongside a heightened anxiety about their spiritual, and perhaps civil, liability, encoding a kind of reversibility of the senses with both value (in the performance of legal retribution) and the invisible realm of the spiritual.[96]

Old English learned prose may also seem more directly averse to positing what we would call synesthesia. As O'Brien O'Keeffe points out, by contrast with the discussion of the senses in the Latin text of Boethius' *Consolation*—in which the language of the grammatical tradition emphasizes the 'diametrically opposite ways' that the higher and lower senses operate—the Old English Boethius is marked by a shift to a concrete language of appraising the senses more akin to the Old English legal tradition.[97] Yet, I would argue, the Old English text conserves the implicit anti-synesthetic perspective of its source on the silo-like separateness of the senses:

> Hwæt ðu wast þæt gesihð and gehernes and gefrednes ongitað þone lichoman þæs monnes and þeah ne ongitaþ hi hine no gelicne. Þa earan ongitað þæt hi gehiorað, and ne ongitað hi þeah þone lichoman eallunga swylcne swylce he bið. Sio gefrednes hine mæg gegrapian and gefredan þæt hit lichoma bið, ac hio ne mæg gefredan hwæþer he bið þe blac þe hwit, ðe fæger ðe unfæger. Ac sio gesihð fruman cerre swa þa eagan on besioð, hi ongitað ealle þone andwlitan ðæs lichoman ... se an monn angitt þæt þæt he on oðrum ongit synderlice. He hine ongit þurh þa eagan, synderlice þurh þa earan, synderlice þurh his rædelsan, synderlice þurh gesceadwisnesse, synderlice þurh gewis andgit.[98]

You know that sight and hearing and touch perceive the body of a
man, and yet they do not perceive it at all similarly. The ears perceive
what they hear, and yet they do not perceive the body in totality such
as it is. [Tactile] feeling can grope it and feel that it is a body, but it
cannot feel whether it is black or white, whether pleasing or unpleasing.
But sight—from the first moment the eyes see it, they perceive completely the appearance of the body … a man perceives what he perceives
in another in diverse ways: he perceives him through the eyes, separately
through the ears, separately through his imagination, separately through
discretion, separately through intelligent understanding/perception.

This explication of the presumed superiority of the eye might be
easily missed amidst the repetitions of *synderlice* (separately, variously,
distinctly) that pile up at the end of Lady Philosophy's lesson—where
the separateness of different sensory as well as cognitive perceptual
processes are asserted like a drumbeat. By this logic, one cannot
perceive, through tactile texture, whether a face is visually *fæger*
(pleasing, beautiful) or *unfæger* (unpleasing). Here, there is no
perception of sound 'where colors are formed'.

Even so, as Newhauser argues, the later record of the medieval
discourse of the five senses suggests that 'it allowed for more multisensoriality than a static hierarchy might be taken to permit'.[99]
And, during the period of Old English literature, lived experience
surely required it—despite the ocularcentrism of medieval European
Christianity.[100] As Martin Foys argues, our contemporary privileging
of visual media can yield a modern ocularcentrism that fails to register
early medieval networks of bodies, technologies, and non-visual
senses—even as he suggests that words *can*, 'if only faintly', index
a wider range of 'sensory perceptive play'.[101] Even more crucially,
alongside the ideological primacy and separateness of vision, Old
English medical texts attest to the ubiquity and seriousness of
diseases and impairments of the eye—including frequent infection
and irritation from unsanitary and smoke-filled domestic spaces,
and a host of problems (like astigmatism or poor accommodation)
often described as *eagena miste* ('dimness of the eyes')—as well
as the normal presbyopia of aging.[102] This historical conjunction
introduces at least some complexity to the vision-dominated sensory
hierarchy, if not also the trace of a counternarrative of assistive or
supplemental multisensoriality and a certain pressure on the position
and function of sensory poetics with respect to this historically
particular corporeality.

At least one famous example of metalwork from this earlier period (and another object of O'Brien O'Keeffe's analysis) offers a material context for multisensoriality in Old English poetry, especially since, as Newhauser argues, 'sensory communities are subject to resistance by conflicting or insurgent or "reinterpretive" understandings of the senses'.[103] Although a patristic reading of the famous late Trewhiddle style 'Fuller brooch' (Figure 2.1) leads us to the ostensible centrality of sight through the gestures of the hands (as a metonym for touch) that identify each of the 'outer senses',[104] it also enacts a parallel program of multisensoriality starting with how the hands of each figure are positioned. 'Smell', with its hands behind its back, gives the impression that touch may need to be restrained in order to

Figure 2.1 The Fuller brooch. The British Museum, museum number 1952,0404.1.

artificially isolate olfactory sensation. The gustatory and/or tactile intensity of the entire hand stuffed into the mouth of 'Taste' seems to also heighten the receptivity of sight and touch for the figure as it tightly clutches a vine, with bulging eyes that are entirely outlined by a line trailing towards the ear.[105] The cupped hand of 'Hearing' may suggest an attempt to hear a faint noise, but it may also remind us of the tactile vibrations that accompany low-pitched or loud sounds—as well as the 'broad range of sensory experiences that existed along the hearing [and hearing-impairments] spectrum' in early medieval England, which Lori Ann Garner uncovers in analysis of medical and legal texts.[106] The foliate vines that 'Smell' seems to smell spread across the entire central roundel—presumably with their odors. And what precisely, we may ask, is 'Hearing' trying to listen to (or through)? Offstage music? The rustle of the vines and their leaves entangling all the figures—especially Hearing's, possibly dancing, leg?[107] The mouth of the central figure of 'Sight' is closed, but the ears are prominent and the strong grasp it has on the thick terminals of the aromatic vines suggests that the space bursts with multisensoriality, making it difficult if not impossible to distinguish sensations *synderlice* (separately). Each of the main figures representing the four 'outer' senses presses against the frame of their respective lentoid fields as if they might burst out of them. Perhaps the central figure's concerned or even supplicating look, with upturned brows, marks sight as less bodily and more spiritual—but perhaps it registers a corporeal sensory overload.

Conventionally read as a 'variety of creation' motif,[108] the Trewhiddle style ornaments that occupy the open-work outer ring (lobed plant ornaments as well as ornimorphic and—equine or leonine?—creatures) also address the senses to a multisensory and at times synesthetic world. Especially the ornimorphic creatures suggest a cacophony of sounds that surrounds all the figures in the central roundel (birdsong occupies especially compelling sites of Old English poetic history) as well as, perhaps, an onslaught of bestial odors.[109] The otherwise conventional self-biting animals present a non-human echo of the figure of 'Taste' with its hand in its mouth, and may invite speculation about how the meat of such marvelous creatures would taste. Their interlaced (sometimes foliate) tails, mouths, beaks, legs, claws, etc., become icons of multisensoriality, or even of synesthetic sensory entanglement or confusion. The lobed designs that appear one per quadrant in this outer ring then stand out like synesthetic *puncta*; they mark popping or piercing sounds, creeping odors, and curious textures, *perceived in the place where vision is formed.* This synesthetic program is underscored in (at least my own) factical experience of the brooch itself. With the front of the brooch restored to a high polish, the intricate niello inlay is difficult to trace when light hits the silver at certain angles, and it is easy to imagine having to handle the brooch to distinguish all its figures under variable light.[110] Moreover, the not-quite symmetrical distribution and various orientations of the animals and abstract designs, along with the motion implied in the human figures (especially 'Hearing') all resolve in *both* 1) a movement *inwards,* that traces a process of bodily orientation in space, or what we recognize in modernity as proprioception, and 2) a movement *outwards*, towards the varied and tumultuous intricacies of the multisensory world.

One can, then, imagine compelling material multisensory and even synesthetic contexts for Old English poetry as well as the shaping and positioning of these contexts with respect to sensory—especially visual—impairment. And so as an additional context for the 'heat' of *Beowulf*, I want to turn to Blaser's engagement with the multi-sensorial aesthetics in the Old English poem known as *The dream of the rood*, a dream-vision poem in which the speaker reports an encounter with a marvelous, speaking cross. As Carruthers argues, '[t]he poem is conceived as a rhetorical action'.[111] Singling out the poem as a paradigmatic example of the kind of experience to which the medieval aesthetic lexicon is directed, Carruthers argues that multisensory and conceptual complexion becomes primary to the function of the poem itself:

> As a work of art, the poem is most significant not as it expresses doctrinal content—though of course it does that. It does not even seek, I think, to *represent* (in the sense of imitate) a psychological action. It is far more active than that. The poem directly *produces* in us a variously sensory, complex aesthetic experience that, through its enacted stages, occasions 'warm' belief, confidence, and joy, not only in the dreamer and the cross, but in us, its readers.[112]

Furthermore, since, as Carruthers points out, by opening the ekphrasis of the 'swefna cyst' (best of dreams) as 'hwæt me gemætte, to midre nihte' (what I dreamed in the middle of the night), when the speaker is alone[113] and in 'an ambiguous state ... conventional for medieval dream vision composition', the poem additionally calls attention to the rhetorical process of composing such experiences.[114]

Blaser's poem, 'Image-Nation 11 (the poēsis' [*sic*] (part of a series of 'Image-Nation' poems that recur throughout the corpus of his lifelong *Holy forest*), takes up—and partially translates—these complexions of *The dream of the rood* as emblematic of poesis itself.[115] The architectural space invoked in the poem's opening, 'inside the tower ot a broken tower',[116] evinces a kind of soft medievalism (perhaps a jocular inversion of Tolkien's characterization of *Beowulf* as a broken tower)[117] before the first-person lyric goes on to narrate a pyrotechnic encounter (or witnessed encounter) of 'one • passing/ the other • not named' within a contemplatively composed 'space' not alien to that of *The dream of the rood*.[118] At the climax of the encounter, an 'explosion' enfolds an unstable, pulsing sensory field constituted in part by inclusions of fragmentary translations of the Old English poem:

                in the explosion   the rings became
                a constellation
                          the moving angel
                    changed raiment

    and colours   at times   soaked with the blood going
    or *adorned with treasure*   turning   now   transparent [119]

The phrase '*adorned with treasure*' highlights its status as a formula belonging to Old English verse by intruding typographically into the poem as italicized text, and as a conventional translation of *since gegyrwed*,[120] it is sure to catch the eye of a reader lucky enough to have had a course in Old English, and to point them to *The dream of the rood* as a likely source.[121] Yet the entire couplet in which the italicized phrase appears is a fragmentary translation of the hypermetric lines narrating the moment just after the 'wood' later to be revealed as the cross first appears:

                          Geseah ic þæt fuse beacen
    wendan wædum ond bleom;   hwilum hit wæs mid wætan
                                bestemed,
    beswyled mid swates gange,   hwilum mid since gegyrwed. (ll.
                                21b–23)

                                          I beheld that eager signal
fluctuate in garments and colors;   sometimes it was beaded up
                                          with water,
drenched with flows of sweated blood; sometimes [it was]
                                          adorned with treasure.

The complex simultaneity of the repetition of 'hwilum' (at times, often) at the start of the b-verses of two consecutive lines in the Old English registers in Blaser's poem in the occurrence of 'at times' and 'now', also in the middle of their respective lines. Blaser's phrase 'with the blood going' suffices as an oblique reading of 'swates gange' ([with] flows of blood, streams of blood). And the phrase 'turning now transparent' merely emphasizes sensation or color over nominal reference in translating the ambiguous contrast of red blood and 'wetness' or 'water' (*wæta*). Both Blaser's reordering of clauses (from 'wetness'-'blood'-'treasure' to 'blood'-'treasure'-'wetness') and the extra typographical space between phrases translate the pulsing quality of the lines and their prosodical echoes and excesses as relatively rare examples of Old English hypermetric verses with inflectional end-rhymes. This reshuffling also enacts a chiasm of sorts that entangles Blaser's poem in the syntax of *The dream of the rood*. In both poems, what an ocularcentric reading might take as visual 'imagery' is actually eroded by aural, tactile, and even syntactic experiences. The prosodical elements, however mimetically, as well as the terms that comprise the 'image', also evoke the tactile sensations of fluidity as movement over the skin, fluctuating between the sense of viscous blood trickling, water sheeting down and off the body, and the feel of textiles flapping in the wind against the skin. Blaser's poem composes the 'explosion' as a complexion of the complexions first composed by *The dream of the rood*—experiences Carruthers characterizes as of 'fluctuation and porosity, in both the dreamer and the dream image'.[122]

This marked inclusion of a fragmentary translation spreads retroactively, tendril-like, into the lines that lead up to it. The Old English poem holds off on describing the rood as a cross during the dreamer's account of the initial encounter, marking it instead only as a 'fuse beacen' (rapid/hastening/eager sign/token/signal).[123] The introduction of a 'moving angel' as the subject that changes 'raiment/ and colours' ('wendan wædum ond bleom') similarly enfolds the unidentifiable, kinetic state of the thing encountered while also

The heat of Beowulf

playing on the etymological sense of 'angel' as 'messenger'—activating a partial overlap between the semantic fields of 'messenger' and 'signal/sign' and thus enacting a crease or plication whereby a fragment of *The dream of the rood* is included in/as the composition of the poem.[124] Of course, the rood in the Old English poem is also a messenger, delivering a rhetorical composition to the dreamer,[125] and there is a certain deconstructive irony in that the Old English poem characterizes humans as *reordberend* (speech-bearers), while the chief device of the poem consists of the prosopopoeia of the speaking, non-human cross—'þæt hit hleoðrode./ Ongan þa word sprecan' (ll. 26b–27a) (that it made sound. It began/ began then to speak words)—which the dreamer encounters as at once external to themself and included within their composition.[126] But this is not a question of a representational *mise en abyme*. As Pasternack argues, *The dream of the rood* relies on a 'non-mimetic, analogical method' that, as I would rephrase it, enfolds a series of discrete segments articulated by stylistic disjunctions, relying especially on shifts in syntactic patterns to stylistically 'disjoin' the narrative and render palpable an abstract 'idea'.[127] Here, then, we find the heat of Blaser's series of perceptual inclusions at work in the modern and the Old English poems alike, composing the abstract encounter with 'poesis' or a 'messenger' as a (however dream-like) multisensorial complexion—not only in the referential functions which identify the aesthetic 'explosion', but also as literalized in the inclusions of lexemes, taxis (the grammatical term), (in Blaser's case) translations, as well as multisensorial references. The fragmentary translations of Blaser's poem thus include these complexions not as grammatical referents or representational objects, but as fluctuating contours of its perceptual topology. As McCaffery explains: '[a]n applied poetics of the fold alters radically the phenomenology of the fragment. Citations figure not as textual shards in a collage but as textual nomads in serial plications upon a plenum'.[128] Accordingly, in a poetics of folding, 'the smallest material unit … is not the point but the fold', which requires a 'plicative rather than granular entry into the poem'.[129]

Continuing, then, to read recursively, more precisely synesthetic plications of *The dream of the rood* ripple through the lead-up to the aesthetic 'explosion' in Blaser's poem:

> verbs of
> the *music-footed horse*

```
                I was afraid   at the fair sight
    the dark imagined land   disappeared as they came to the edge
    in the   air   across   the verticle road   leading up to the
    sky   of that constellation   by   an explosion   •¹³⁰
```

The metrical pun in the phrase *'music-footed horse'*—a line from Jaco-
bean poet George Chapman's revenge tragedy *Bussy D'Ambois*—calls
attention to sound in the prosody of English syntax itself ('verbs
of'). This inclusion of verse from the English Renaissance does not
dilute the poem's relationship to *The dream of the rood*; rather, the
surrounding lines in Chapman's text (from a speech invoking the
Spirit of Intelligence) underscore the phrase's place in composing a
multisensory complexion that echoes fortuitously with those of the
Old English poem as the dreamer begins their composition:

> Terror of darkness! O, thou King of flames!
> That with thy music-footed horse dost strike
> The clear light out of crystal on dark earth,
> And hurl'st instructive fire about the world ...¹³¹

As a metonym for these lines, the fragment of Chapman translates—*as
a complexion*—the experience of contemplative darkness and silence
which suddenly break open onto the glam-rock aesthetics of the
rood: prosodical sound yields an experience of affective, conceptual,
as well as physical space that allows for and intrudes on the ensuing
light. So Blaser's 'dark imagined land' is partly Chapman's early
modern 'dark earth', but the paradoxical movement (of what, it is
grammatically obscure) 'in the air across the verticle road' recalls
the shape of the rood as it appears in the sky. The expression of
fear 'at the fair sight' before the movement 'up to the/ sky of that
constellation' enfolds the overwhelming affects of the dreamer,
'synnum fah,/ forwunded mid wommum' (ll. 13b–14a) (stained with
sins, badly wounded with shames), in their complexion with the
sensory experience of horizon and sky, where '[g]immas stodan/
fægere æt foldan sceatum' (ll. 7b–8a) (gems stood,/ lovely at the
corners of the earth) and 'engel dryhtnes ealle' (l. 9b) (all the angels
of God) appear 'fægere þurh forðgesceaft' (l. 10a) (lovely ['fair']
throughout the cosmos).

   Finally, as the aesthetic explosion continues to re-furl, it moves
to enfold the fluctuations of the invisible physical world in the
human sensorium—continuing to rely on fragments of *The dream
of the rood*:

>   I reached up into that space
>   to touch the enormous mobile
>   hanging from the centre   I had wanted to arrange it
>
>   from each pendant   a shining ring   which one by one
>   my fingers entered   dissolved   in the light
>   as if space looked for time
>   or the block of the image did not know the size of
>   what you are doing   •[132]

This exploded compositional space implicitly enacts a conceptual slippage between the senses of the Greek term κόσμος (cosmos), which include 'order', 'the universe' (i.e. the order of the world), and 'ornament'.[133] So if the 'enormous mobile' recalls a cosmological model that seems to belong to the poetics of a much later, Dantean vision of the heavens,[134] it also recalls the ornamental cosmology of the Old English riddles, in which 'Is þes middangeard missenlicum/ wisum gewlitegad, wrættum gefrætwad' (this middle-earth is in a variety/ of ways made-radiant, decorated with ornaments)[135]— refiguring that poem's explosion of sensation as a net of whirling, jangling, tangling jewelry. As each 'shining ring' dissolves into a transparent co-extensivity with the speaker's fingers, it does not mark the dissolution of sensation, but only a disappearance of vision within a tactile experience of conceptual movement: 'as if space looked for time/ or the block of the image did not know the size of/ what you are doing'. Here, plications of the aesthetic whirlwind in which the cross suddenly appears in *The dream of the rood* impinge tangibly on visible space, despite the ostensibly visual character of the image of light:

>   Þuhte me þæt ic gesawe   syllicre treow
>   on lyft lædan,   leohte bewunden,
>   beama beorhtost.   Eall þæt beacen wæs
>   begoten mid golde. (ll. 4–7a)

>   It seemed to me that I looked upon the best tree
>   carried into the air, entangled with light,
>   the brightest beam. All of that signal was
>   coated over with gold.

That the dreamer uses a verb of seeing ('gesawe') to report a sensation of light should not distract from the multisensory and conceptional tumult of these lines. The prosodical alliteration on *l* opposite the unvoiced consonant clusters in *lyft* (air) and *leohte* (light), forcing air to swift stops after hissing through the front and then the back of the mouth, underscores a tactile perception of air whipping over the skin. The shine of the gold that is literally poured over (*begoten*) a signal or sign (*beacen*) cannot hide a paradoxically heavy sense of weight in contrast to the lifting force of the atmosphere. The ostensible privileging of vision is thus eroded as the poem depends on multisensoriality to include the human sensorium in the perceptual activity—the heat—of the poem. These inter-burrowing sensations all corporealize the experience of something outside of human sensation, a *beacen*: a signal or a sign that is here seen in the place where tactile and proprioceptive weight is felt and touched in the place where vision is formed: *as if the block of the image* (as a visual unit) *did not know the size of what you are doing.*

As its title indicates, Blaser's poem unfurls under the sign not only of *poesis*, but—with the added specificity and gravity of the definite article—*the poesis*. Under this sign, the inclusion of fragmentary translations of an Old English poem at the height of its sensory whirlwind composes the space of the modern poem, not merely representing sensation, but performing the poem's perceptual activity so as to entangle it with the human sensorium. Blaser's poem thus not only calls on *The dream of the rood* as a kind of exemplary performance of poetics, but also performs translation as a mode of inclusion (and the ensuing sensory-affective-conceptual complexion) that stages the poem as an encounter with and a testament to the multisensoriality of the Old English poem. The homologies of translation and complexion that flow from Blaser's poetics of heat and as performed in this poem are thus not only not foreign to Old English poetics, but on full display in *The dream of the rood*.

Multisensory and synesthetic sensations in *Beowulf*

So Old English poets *do,* as Fred C. Robinson writes, 'appear to have been unusually bold in their use of synesthetic imagery';[136] and *Beowulf* too is a poem interested in occasioning multisensory and even synesthetic complexion. The remaining chapters of this book take up this possibility in relation to defined scales of non-representational composition. But as a final point of reference, I want to sketch the multisensorial and synesthetic aesthetic atmosphere within the poem's representational economy—because the world that *Beowulf* represents is a world that requires a poetics of heat in order to be actually met by a vulnerable, incomplete human sensorium in the space of the poem.

Take, for example, the description of Beowulf and his men walking up from their boat towards Heorot. At first, the 'suspicious coast-guard' perceives (visually) the approaching troop metonymically *as* armor in the form of 'beorhte randas' (l. 231b) (bright shields).[137] The *sight* of armor is crucial to the poem's ideological preoccupations with, as Overing phrases it, 'the warrior body and … [the] performative aspects of warrior masculinity',[138] even as elsewhere in the poem such equipment 'displays a life and will of its own' in the poem's personifications.[139] And, as James Paz explores, weapons in *Beowulf* can threaten and provoke anxiety not only in their capacity to injure but also as material riddles that 'disrupt a longstanding human reliance on legibility'.[140] So it is no surprise that the account makes a strong appeal to the visual register:

> Stræt wæs stanfah,   stig wisode
> gumum ætgædere.   Guðbyrne scan
> heard hondlocen;   hringiren scir
> song in searwum.   Þa hie to sele furðum
> in hyra gryregeatwum   gangan cwomon,
> setton sæmeþe   side scyldas,
> rondas regnhearde   wið þæs recedes weal;
> bugon þa to bence.   Byrnan hringdon,
> guðsearo gumena;   garas stodon,
> sæmanna searo   samod ætgædere,
> æscholt ufan græg;   wæs se irenþreat
> wæpnum gewurþad. (ll. 320–331a)

The road was stone-paved; the path directed
the warriors together. War-shirt scintillated,
hard and hand-linked; resplendent iron-rings
sang among the equipment. When, further on,
in their terrible-gear, they had come to the hall,
they planted—sea-weary—broad shields,
wondrously-strong boards, against the wall of the building;
then they sank to a bench. Mail-shirts rang out,
the war-equipment of the warriors. Spears stood,

the equipment of the sailors stacked together,
an ash-grove topped with silver; that iron-gang was
ennobled by its weapons.[141]

But, as Edward B. Irving, Jr notes, the passage also appeals conspicuously to all the senses but taste and smell.[142] Brodeur's analysis points out that the 'movement and sound' of the scene 'are conveyed by verbs of shining, hastening, gleaming, singing, marching, and ringing'.[143] Moreover, Brodeur argues that the enumeration of the men's equipment, accompanied by variations on the terms for individual items, exemplifies the poem 'utilizing variations to create a texture'—suggesting a tactile experience in the warp and weft of these signs that vies with their referential functions.[144]

A closer look at those variations opens onto an even more thickly convoluted sensorium. Brodeur identifies *guðbyrne/hringiren* (war-shirt/iron-rings), *scyldas/rondas* (shields/bosses), and *garas/searo* (spears/equipment) as three distinct variations (excluding the attendant adjectives).[145] With each variation, however, one also finds an implicit variation of sensory register. Taken conventionally, 'guðbyrne' (war-shirt) and 'hringiren' (ring-iron) share the referent *mail-shirt*, so the mail-shirts both sing and glitter, appealing to sound as well as sight. Brodeur insists that the verbs *scinan* (glitter) and *singan* (sing) do not stand in variation and denote distinct actions.[146] However, given the parallel syntax and the variation on the subject-nouns of these clauses, it seems more like a bias against the possibility of finding appeals to synesthetic experience in Old English poetry than a compelling definition of variation which would not entertain the possibility that the verbs do contribute to the variation, evoking a single synesthetic complexion that conflates visual and aural experience.

At this point, a dogmatic assumption of the strict separateness of the senses could still reinforce the enumerative force of the verbs. However, the pairing of the qualities suggested by the adjectives with those of the verbs in their respective clauses also harbors a potential confusion of the senses. Both nominal variations are modified by adjectives (although not in strict grammatical parallelism) and so, unless one needs to take 'heard hondlocen' (hard hand-linked) as a substantive in variation with 'guðbyrne' (war-shirt) (an unlikely possibility given the heavier variation in the subsequent clause), neither do we necessarily need to hold to Brodeur's assumption that

the adjectives do not participate in the variation, and we might in fact
construe an only slightly looser variation-like structure at the level
of the noun-phrase in which the synthetic construction *hard hand-
linked war-shirts* shares its referent with *resplendent iron-rings*.[147]
The shiny 'guðbyrne' (war-shirt) glitters, appealing to the visual
register, but the qualities emphasized by 'heard hondlocen' (hard
hand-linked) are tactile and implicitly invoke the hand—suggesting a
continuity between the sensation of physical hardness, the mobility
of interlocking mail-rings against the body, and the sensation of light
moving starkly over a surface of small but distinct moving rounded
edges. The total construction begins as a simple visual 'image', but
then comprehends the 'sharp' intensity of shining or glittering as
a tactile quality.

Moreover, the word *hringiren* (lit. ring-iron) is already a near-
paronomasia that, in this context, confounds the distinction of the
visual and the aural. As a simplex, *hring-* (ring, round) here refers
to shape, but the homophonic sound-verb *hringan* (to ring, as in a
bell; to sound) occurs only a few lines later, describing the sound
of mail-shirts (designated in this case by the simplex *byrnan*) (l.
316b). So the participation of *hring*, as noted by Irving, in the
onomatopoeia of 'hringiren scir'[148] intensifies the sonic suggestiveness
of this echo. While the *hringiren* makes sound, presumably echoing
in searwum (in or among the equipment), the attendant *scir* (resplendent) visual qualities, as well as the hardness and shapes of the
equipment that give rise to them, all mirror the equipment's aural
effects, entangling—if not fully conflating—an experience of the
refraction of light, the reverberation of sound, and tactility of
interlocking metal rings. As in Merleau-Ponty's description of music,
or Kleege's account of a cathedral, sound produces the experience
of shape and space, leaving us with a represented world that cannot
be entangled with the human sensorium with a conventional 'image'.

In the wake of these mutual intrusions of the senses upon each
other, the sound of the mail shirts that ring out (*hringan*, l. 326b)
erodes the vision of the men setting down their equipment and
lowering their bodies to the bench. And in the echoes of these clangs
and thumps, the spears that stand gathered or piled together become
an 'æscholt ufan græg' (ash-grove topped with silver)—a description
that evokes not only the visual sensation of flashing spear-points
but also an implicit comparison of the sounds of the spear-points
sliding against each other to the rustle of leaves—a sound that

reverberates in the place where colors are seen. This synesthetic silveryness, with its flashes of rustling, thus additionally enfolds the affective or conceptual 'sæmeþe' (sea-weary) quality of the bodies of the men as they sink to their seats.

This march to Heorot may mark a relatively brief appeal to a thicker sort of multisensorial and synesthetic complexion, but the sensory atmosphere to which it appeals is no anomaly. Take, for example, a particularly salient instance of the poem's subtle personification of weapons during Beowulf's fight with Grendel's mother, in which the warrior 'onfand/ ðæt se beadoleoma bitan nolde' (ll. 1522b–1523) (discovered/ that the battle-ray [sword] would not bite).[149] The highly adaptable semantic range of the verb onfindan (find out, discover, perceive, meet with) registers both Beowulf's cognitive realization of the sword's failure and the shuddering tactile sensation of the sword clanking to a violent stop, while beadoleoma (battle-ray), the famous kenning that refers to the sword itself, makes a memorable appeal to the visual field. Yet the personification figures the most dramatic point—the sword's refusal to bite (bitan)—in terms of (an avoidance of) gustatory experience, a sensory field easily elided even in a decently thickened literary sensorium.[150]

This multisensorial atmosphere also extends to moments of the poem not concerned with describing or narrating the actions of weapons and war-equipment. For example, a cluster of occurrences of a relatively common verb of perception and cognition, ongitan/-gytan (perceive, feel, understand), before and during Beowulf's fight with Grendel's mother, mark a wide range of complex sensory experience in the poem, often without invoking sight. Of Beowulf's swim to the bottom of the mere, through the opacity of 'dreorig ond gedrefed' (horrific and turbid) water (l. 1417a),[151] we are told that 'Ða wæs hwil dæges/ ær he þone grundwong ongytan mehte' (then it was a day's time/ before he could perceive the bottom-field) (ll. 1495b–1496). As Thomas Klein argues, 'there is no strict break in the usage of ongytan between the perceiving of abstract and physical things',[152] making it the perfect word to register complexions. Unsurprisingly, ongitan can have strongly visual connotations, and may at times refer to experiences that are not perceived corporeally, but in the Alfredian Boethius, ongitan is compatible with touch, and it is often associated with hearing.[153] In the dark waters of the mere it is not likely that Beowulf sees the bottom, nor that he experiences some spiritual realization. Rather, here the word seems to mark the tactile knowledge—physical, affective, and even philosophical—in a hand groping through the murk, suddenly plunged into the muck of the abyss.

The same word registers a similarly complex sensoriality when Beowulf first enters the home (*hof*, see l. 1507b) of Grendel's mother. The *brimwylf* (sea-wolf) herself seems to hear or otherwise feel (*onfunde*, discover) Beowulf's presence, sight unseen—during which time Beowulf can only feel that 'sædeor monig/ hildetuxum heresyrcan bræc' (ll. 1510b–1511) (many sea-beasts/ with battle-tusks broke through his fighting-shirt). Suddenly emerging in a space with a 'hrofsele' (hallroof) keeping out the water, Beowulf '*ongeat*/ þæt he in niðsele nathwylcum wæs/ þær him nænig wæter wihte ne scebede' (ll. 1512b–1514; emphasis mine) (*perceived* that he was in some sort of harm-hall/ where no water injured him at all). The associations of *ongitan* with aural experience may suggest that Beowulf perceives the space through its acoustics, while the sudden protection from water that the space affords suggests a release from surrounding pressure, a shedding of wetness, the mouth and lungs opening. Only after Beowulf 'fyrleoht geseah,/ blacne leoman beorhte scinan' (ll. 1516b–1517) (beheld firelight,/ a luminous ray shining brightly) does the sense of *ongitan* potentially include a visual sensation of the *brimwylf* (although the reader is not yet given a description of her visual appearance): '*Ongeat* þa se goda grundwyrgenne,/ merewif mihtig' (ll. 1518–1519a; emphasis mine) (then that good one *perceived* the lake-felon, the powerful water-woman).

The great *healreced* (hall-building, e.g. l. 68a), Heorot, is also a space of thick sensoriality. It provides an exhibition space for the compelling visual sensations of Grendel's hand and arm as a 'tacen sweotol' (l. 833b) (easily perceptible sign), a 'wundor' that people come from all over to visually inspect (*sceawian*) (ll. 839–840). Hrothgar too looks at the 'claw' as if it were staged and framed for a heightened aesthetic encounter when he 'geseah steapne hrof/ golde fahne, ond Grendles hond' (ll. 926b–927) (beheld the steep roof/ plated with gold, and Grendel's hand). Appropriately, however, the gripping apparatus also yields tactile experience, as when Unferth 'hand sceawedon/ feondes fingras' (ll. 983b–984a) (visually inspected the hand/ the enemy's fingers), where 'foran æghwylc wæs/ steda nægla gehwylc style gelicost,/ hæþenes handsporu, hilderinces,/ egl' unheoru' (ll. 984b–987a) (at the tip of each [finger] was,/ in the place of each nail, most like steel,/ the heathen hand-spike of the battle-warrior,/ hideous, unpleasant).[154] In a glance down the length of each finger, here the eye snags on sharp, hard tactility and disgust.

But the hall is especially a space of complex, and sometimes overwhelming, aural experiences. In Benjamin Saltzman's analysis of the hall as a space for the performance of and the sharing of sensory experiences (aural and gustatory) in the production of communal joy, the sounds of speech in storytelling and the sound of the harp interact in compelling ways, especially in the use of the compounds *healgamen* (hall-joy) for the recitation of story and song and *gomenwudu* (joy-wood) for the accompanying sound of the harp.[155] We might emphasize just how much these affective dimensions are grounded in a thick aural atmosphere of the hall as an acoustic resonator and amplifier. Of course, Heorot is truly a visual spectacle in its preparations for the celebration of Beowulf's defeat of Grendel: '[g]oldfag scinon/ web æfter wagum, wundorsiona fela/ secga gehwylcum þara þe on swylc starað' (ll. 944b–996) (gold-dyed they shone,/ tapestries on the walls, many wonder-spectacles/ to each man who gazed on such things). But all this shine is soon drenched in sound, namely the 'sang ond sweg samod ætgædere' (l. 1063) (song and sound mixed together) in which the poet recites the Finn episode. The alliterative doublet, *sang ond sweg*, implicitly contrasts two types of sound: 1) organized, musical, human vocalization, or *sang* (Present Day English reflex, *song*)—the general word for song, singing, or uncoordinated sonic phenomena, and 2) *sweg*—a word that can indicate neutral sonic phenomena in general (Ælfric's *Grammar* describes speech-sounds as *sweg*, e.g. a diphthong is a 'twyfeald sweg'[156] [twofold sound]). But especially in its implicit comparison with *sang*, *sweg* suggests tumultuous or unorganized (although *not* necessarily unpleasant) 'noise' or even a 'crash' of sound.[157] If this is a particularly joyful sonic phenomenon, it is importantly a mixture of contrasting sonic textures yielding a *loudness* that can participate in a range of affective complexions.

The specific affective tenor of this acoustic complexion is not absolute but depends upon one's conceptual and social relationships to the resonance of the hall. The structuring of the communal joy of the hall around Grendel's exclusions from it registers especially in his experience of the same loudness:[158]

Ða se ellengæst   earfoðlice
þrage geþolode,   se þe in þystrum bad,
þæt he dogora gehwam   dream gehyrde
hludne in healle.   Þær wæs hearpan sweg,
swutol sang scopes. (ll. 86–90a)

Then that powerful spirit painfully
suffered for a stint—he that waited in darkness,
that he, each day, heard joy
loud in the hall. There was the sound of the harp,
the clear song of the *scop*.

Garner points to this moment as an example in which 'hearing itself could be associated with pain and torment', deflating any monolithic account of the experience of hearing during the period.[159] For those inside Heorot, *dream* (joy) is experienced as a naively sensory phenomenon—an affect one can hear, a feeling achieved purely by the mixture of sonic textures at a sufficient volume. Outside, dispossessed, with his sight presumably attenuated by the darkness (his glowing eyes may suggest some degree of enhanced night-vision), he hears joy *in the hall,* where visual experiences of splendid decorations and the hall's concrete social-formation further modulate the complexion. It is *there* where the *sang ond sweg* enfold an exuberant collective affect. Outside, the sound is merely loud—as Christopher Abram reads it, an eco-colonial 'noise pollution'.[160]

The hall also amplifies the sound that arises in the wake of *song ond sweg*, enfolding it within an atmospheric sensoriality: 'Gamen eft astah,/ beorhtode bencsweg; byrelas sealdon/ win of wunderfatum' (ll. 1160b–1162a) (joy-sounds mounted up after,/ bench-noise glittered; cupbearers offered/ wine from wonder-cups). Here, *gamen* refers to the usually audible manifestation of people enjoying each other's company,[161] but it also takes on a tactile, atmospheric, and perhaps olfactory substance and weight, rising up (*astigan*) in a tumultuous manner. Elsewhere in the poem, *astigan* describes the clashing or billowing upward movement of waves or smoke, as in the manner that 'yðgeblond up astigeð/ won to wolcnum' (ll. 1373–1374a) (wave-tossing mounts up,/ dark to the skies) in the Grendel-mere, or that '[g]uðrec astah,/ wand to wolcnum' (ll. 1118b–1119a) (war-smoke mounted up, curled to the skies) from the pyre of Hildeburh's son and brother, or that 'wudurec astah/

sweart ofer swioðole' (ll. 3144b–3145a) (woodsmoke mounted up/ over the blaze) during Beowulf's cremation. Those inside Heorot do not hear the rising-up of *gamen* as a sinister sound, but the description of its motion and growth suggests the synesthetic and overwhelming qualities of the experience: a sense of shape and space, a tactile, vibratory feeling of loud but low-pitched thumps and thuds, and a smoke-like pervasive quality. As a finishing touch, this aesthetic atmosphere is also traversed by the precisely calibrated synesthesia Robinson notices in the glittering bench-noise,[162] a pleasant flood of sound-sparkles reflecting off the curved *wunderfatum* (wonder-cups) and the gustatory and cognitive experience contained therein.

This is not the first time that the hall has functioned as an aesthetic amplifier and refractor. Beowulf and Grendel's fight inside the hall is felt by the terrified Danes as a series of increasingly loud, unseen soundings and re-soundings:

Dryhtsele dynede;   Denum eallum wearð,
ceasterbuendum,   cenra gehwylcum,
eorlum ealuscerwen.   Yrre wæron begen,
reþe renweardas.   Reced hlynsode.
Þa wæs wundor micel   ðæt se winsele
wiðhæfde heaþodeorum,   þæt he on hrusan ne feol,
fæger foldbold;   ac he þæs fæste wæs
innan ond utan   irenbendum
searoþoncum besmiþod. (ll. 767–775a)
...
                    Sweg up astag
niwe geneahhe;   Norð-Denum stod
atelic egesa,   anra gehwylcum
þara þe of wealle   wop gehyrdon,
gryreleoþ galan   Godes andsacan,
sigeleasne sang,   sar wanigean
helle hæfton. (ll. 782b–788a)

The lordly-hall boomed. To all the Danes it became
—to the inhabitants of the town and to each valiant earl—
[like] an ale-party. Both [Grendel and Beowulf] were angry,
violent house-guards. The building resonated loudly.
It was a great wonder that the wine-hall
held up against the battle-bold ones, that it did not fall to the earth,
the lovely earthly-building; but for this it was fastened

inside and out with iron strips
forged with skillful thought.

    ...

       Noise mounted up
new and stark, again and again. There arose among the North-Danes
a horrible terror in each one
of those that heard the shrieking from wall:
God's adversary screamed a terror-lyric,
a victoryless song, (he) bewailed his pain,
the captive of hell.

The disturbing similarity of the sounds of *gomen* at a celebration
and the sounds of violence in combat is amplified at least twice
over, as the hall progressively 'dynede' (boomed, resounded), then
'hlynsode' (resounded, echoed, sounded loudly), and finally 'sweg
up astag' (noise mounted up). The iron strips that hold the walls
together against this vibratory onslaught—forged with forethought,
as if made with this sort of thing in mind—become vectors of
amplification. By the end of the fight, the waves of sound—in parodic
similarity to the sounds of celebration—enfold a horrific shrieking-
as-song that, as Foys argues, even escapes a purely representational
horizon and exhibits a 'medieval *frisson* of the visual and the auditory,
[in which] physical senses are not quarantined from each other, but
combined'.[163] The hall is truly an aesthetic amplifier, bringing
especially aural but also multisensory experience to successively
higher levels of intensity wherein synesthesia often (although not
always) crosses crashing waves of sensation—enfolding affects that
vary from joyous to terrifying, welcome to invasive.

    References to other individual senses or sensory qualities—too
numerous to catalog completely here—appear peppered throughout
the poem. Tactile experience of thermal stimuli makes an appearance
in memorable, if brief, descriptions of coldness in the elements and
weather of the non-human world, as in the 'wedera cealdost' (coldest
of weathers) that Beowulf faces in his swim (or row) with Breca (l.
546b).[164] References to literal heat, which the final chapter will take
up in detail, also appear in descriptions of the various fires that
burn in and outside the poem's main narrative, as well as in descriptions of mental states in the context of the Old English vernacular
cardiocentric psychological model, which the next chapter addresses
more directly. Only unambiguous references to olfactory sensation

seem noticeably scarce in the poem. Smell is a prominent and fascinating object of representation in other Old English poems, especially those preoccupied with religious subjects,[165] although it is perhaps the least salient of the senses represented in *Beowulf*. One can still, perhaps, catch a whiff of it in the hot gore that bubbles in the Grendel-mere, the oppressive or choking air around the same lake (*ðrysman*, l. 1375b), or the smoke of the various pyres in the poem.[166] The word *æþm* (breath, breathing, exhalation), which can refer to an odorous exhalation, does occur in the poem, but only to describe the dragon's breath held *within* its chest.[167] By and large, the small number of attested Old English verbs or nouns specifically for smelling do not appear in the poem.[168] It is possible that smell is subject to some implicit and hierarchical association with lower bestial or monstrous sensation. Some scholars read *stonc* (l. 2288a), describing the dragon's activity in his search for the thief, as 'sniffed', 'snuffled', or 'followed a scent', but other editors favor reading the term as meaning 'moved rapidly'.[169] Since the 'sniff' reading has fallen variously in and out of favor over some time,[170] it may be tempting to lean on this moment, but even if the reading of *stonc* were more decidedly settled, it is hardly enough on which to hang a robust reading of smell in *Beowulf*.

Short of embarking on an exhaustive catalog of the poem's direct and indirect references to sensory experience, these moments provide a sense of the place and the dynamics of sensory perception within the representational poetics of *Beowulf*, providing a context for thinking about the non-representational functions of the poem's aesthetics. Despite the hierarchized and separated sensorium constructed by the discursive horizons of *Beowulf*, Old English poetry is not only capable of conceiving of multisensory or even synesthetic perception in complexions with the affective and the conceptual (and without always privileging the visual register) but also, as in the case of Blaser's fragmentary translation of *The dream of the rood*, capable of underwriting modern efforts at a phenomenologically translative poetics. To represent this world in verse is simple enough—but to entangle it more radically with the human sensorium would require Blaser's heat. We will likely not find such poetics at work in every specimen of Old English verse, but its operation in two major poems and the relevant larger material culture suggest that a variety of readings of multisensoriality in other Old English poems, within or against the horizon of the early medieval hierarchy of the senses, might be possible. Moving adjacent to these representations of multisensoriality and synesthesia, the next chapter begins the process of measuring and calibrating the translative, inclusive, phenomenological poetics of heat to specific scales of *Beowulf's* composition. Following Brodeur's attention to progressively larger units of composition, we begin with the non-representational movement of compound diction.

Notes

1 E.g. Hadbawnik, 'Introduction: *"Beowulf* is a hoax"', pp. 1, 10; Reynolds, 'Afterword', p. 35; Remein, 'Human tongued', pp. 135–8.

2 Jack Spicer, letter to Robin Blaser, JSP, Box 1, folder 7. Spicer writes: 'I've been waiting for your letter so that I could answer it while thanking you for the Beowulf notes'. The letter can be dated from early to mid-May of 1952 since it references 'Gary [Bottone]' (a lover Spicer had left in Berkeley, whom he did not meet until the summer of 1951) and since it addresses Spicer's impending return to Berkeley for summer, 'in very little more than a month'. This return is later fixed as June 15. See also *PBLG*, pp. 37–9.

3 *House*, p. 168; see also *AOB*, pp. viii, 4–5; Reynolds, 'Afterword', pp. 35–6.

4 Rauer, *Beowulf and the dragon*, p. 33.

5 Duncan, 'The Chimeras', p. 60. And see Mossin, 'In the shadow of Nerval', pp. 678, 703; Nichols, *A literary biography*, pp. 124–6; Nichols, 'Love will eat the empire', p. 370. Blaser gave 'The fire' first as a lecture accompanying a reading, as early as March 1967, in San Francisco. See Miriam Nichols' notes in *TF*, p. 411 n. 2.

6 Mossin, 'In the shadow of Nerval'; Nichols, *Radical affections*, pp. 123–6; Nichols, *A literary biography*, pp. 124–6; Jarnot, *Robert Duncan*, pp. 251–3; Persky, 'Reading Robin Blaser', p. 25. For the full text of each translation, see Duncan, 'The Chimeras', pp. 38–42 and Blaser, *The holy forest*, pp. 95–108. And see *AT*, pp. 66, 70–1, 147–9.

7 Mossin, 'In the shadow of Nerval', pp. 676–7.

8 *Ibid.*, p. 694.

9 *TF*, p. 9.

10 Duncan, 'The Chimeras', p. 60. As Mossin chronicles, Duncan imagines the battle with the fiery 'blaze' of Blaser in the west—another source of figurative 'heat'. See Mossin, 'In the shadow of Nerval', pp. 701–2.

11 Olson, 'Against wisdom as such', p. 263. As a measure of the indebted-
    ness of this discourse to Pound, Duncan's response to Olson takes
    Olson as 'so keen upon the *virtu* of reality …'. See Duncan, 'From a
    notebook', p. 44; *AT*, p. 107.
12 Olson, 'Against wisdom as such', p. 263.
13 *Ibid.*, p. 262.
14 *Ibid.*, p. 264.
15 For Blaser's discussion of this term in 'The fire' in relation to Olson's
    usage, see also *AT*, p. 106.
16 *TF*, pp. 3–4.
17 *TF*, p. 411 n. 4.
18 Williams, *Spring and all*, pp. 26–7; Nichols, *Radical affections*, p.
    185.
19 *TF*, p. 10.
20 *Ibid.*, p. 3.
21 This concept of affect predates Blaser's exposure to Deleuze and
    Guattari, anticipating their *haecceity*. See Deleuze and Guattari, *A
    thousand plateaus*, p. 261.
22 Cole, 'A minimum of matter', p. 125
23 Merleau-Ponty, *The phenomenology of perception*, p. 73. Unless otherwise
    noted, I quote from the 1962 English translation by Colin Smith (Routledge,
    2003), which was available to Blaser during his lifetime.
24 *TF*, p. 10.
25 See Jakobson, 'On linguistic aspects of translation'.
26 Cf. Glofelty, 'What is ecocriticism?'; Skinner, 'Why ecopoetics', p. 106.
    On spiritualizing tendencies, see Bennett, *Vibrant matter*, pp. 110–22.
    Or compare her reading of American poetics as political philosophy
    in Bennett, *Influx and efflux* with Rasula, *This compost*.
27 Hsy, Pearman, and Eyler, 'Introduction', p. 10. And see Newhauser,
    '"Putten to ploughe"'.
28 Godden and Hsy, 'Analytic survey', p. 335. And see Mitchell and Snyder,
    Narrative prosthetics; Singer, *Blindness and therapy*; on prosthesis
    and the transhuman, see Godden, 'Prosthetic ecologies', especially p.
    1277.
29 Orlemanski, 'Literary genre', p. 1266.
30 Godden, 'Prosthetic ecologies', p. 1274.
31 See Godden, 'Prosthetic ecologies', pp. 1274, 1287 n. 3. I stress
    the conditional here because, as Godden remarks, there is risk of
    universalizing disability at the expense of occluding the experience of
    disabled persons in too-readily using prosthesis as a metaphor and/
    or identifying mere 'instruments' or extensions as prostheses. I credit
    Godden's essay with pointing me to examples of these arguments:
    Sobchack, 'A leg to stand on'; Scully, 'Disability and vulnerability'.

32 *TF*, p. 115.

33 *Ibid.*, pp. 142, 144.

34 *Ibid.*, p. 131.

35 Merleau-Ponty himself makes few comments on 'the aesthetic' as such. In *The visible and the invisible* it is 'a space of incompossibilities, of explosion, of dehiscence, and not as objective-immanent space' (p. 216). Blaser takes the title of his later book *Pell Mell* from the idea of the aesthetic as 'experiences that have not yet been "worked over"' (p. 147). But cf. Merleau-Ponty, *The phenomenology of perception*, pp. xix, 212, 335 n. 73, 498.

36 *AT*, p. 89. Pepper's 1938 monograph on aesthetics does phrase aesthetics in terms to which Blaser would object but, ironically, Pepper's later work speaks directly to Blaser's philosophical interests. See Pepper, *Aesthetic quality* and Pepper, 'Whitehead's "actual occasion"'.

37 *AT*, p. 81.

38 Holt, 'Spicer's poetic correspondence'; Holt, 'In the sense of a lasting doctrine', e.g. pp. 7, 23–5, 49, 63, 70–3, 79–80, 106–15.

39 Carruthers, *The experience of beauty*, pp. 196, 196 n 54, and see p. 17 Also relevant is the (corrective) affinity of Carruthers' previous books to Frances Yates' earlier work on memory, given Blaser's interest in the latter. See *TF*, pp. 9–10; Yates, *The art of memory*. Cf., Carruthers, *The book of memory*, e.g. pp. 331–2, 419 n. 66; Carruthers, *The craft of thought*, p. 9.

40 Carruthers, *The experience of beauty*, p. 196.

41 *Ibid.*, p. 14.

42 *Ibid.*, pp. 34–5.

43 *Ibid.*, pp. 14–15.

44 *AT*, p. 67. And see *TF*, p. 35.

45 Carruthers, *The experience of beauty*, pp. 53–4. For a more sustained treatment, see Carruthers, *The craft of thought*, pp. 61, 77–81, 253–4, 116–17; Carruthers, 'The concept of *ductus*'. For more on *ductus* in *Beowulf*, see Chapter 3 of this book.

46 The foundational study is Spiegelberg, '"Intention" and "intentionality"'. More recently, see Cesalli and Taieb, 'Brentano and medieval ontology'; Banchetti-Robino, 'Ibn Sīnā and Husserl'. On Husserl and Brentano's scholasticism in Heidegger's medievalism, see Knapp, 'Medieval studies', p. 174.

47 Carruthers, *The experience of beauty*, p. 45.

48 *Ibid.*: '*dulcis, suavis, altus, clarus, acutus, varius, pulcher, foedus, asper, amarus, pinguis, elegans, subtilis*, and many more'.

49 *Ibid.*, pp. 45–56.

50 *Ibid.*, p. 139.

51 *Ibid.*, p. 137 n. 7. Carruthers has repeatedly and convincingly argued that several key (although not all) elements of early medieval compositional practice are transmitted from antique and late antique rhetoric indirectly through their inherence in monastic orthopraxis. See Carruthers, *The craft of thought*, pp. 1–6, 9–10. On reading Bede's grammar as a rhetoric, pp. 122–30.

52 Carruthers, *The experience of beauty*, pp. 135–64, especially 137, 157: '*dignitas* … returns to the classroom together with the *Rhetorica ad herennium* (p. 157). And see Carruthers, '*Varietas*'.

53 Carruthers, *The experience of beauty*, p. 46.

54 Merleau-Ponty, *The visible and the invisible*, pp. 147–8, and see p. 146. And see Nichols, *Radical affections*, pp. 177, 192–3, 184–5; Nichols, 'Introduction: reading Robin Blaser', pp. 34–40; Nichols, *A literary biography*, pp. 77, 138, 153–4; Middleton, 'An elegy for theory', pp. 189–91, 197–8; Marriott, 'A dialectics of the real'; Carberry, *Phenomenology*, pp. 65–93.

55 *TF*, pp. 117, 134. See also pp. 29, 143–4.

56 Merleau-Ponty, *The visible and the invisible*, p. 149.

57 *Ibid.*, pp. 146, 152. And see Merleau-Ponty, *The phenomenology of perception*, pp. 49–50.

58 *TF*, p. 365; Blaser, *The holy forest*, p. 396.

59 McCaffery, 'Blaser's Deleuzian folds', p. 107. And see *TF*, pp. 154, 156; Sakkis, 'John Sakkis interviews Robin Blaser', p. 72; *AT*, p. 66. And see Bernstein, 'Afterword', p. 508; Carberry, *Phenomenology*, pp. 72–9; Nichols, 'Introduction: reading Robin Blaser', pp. 41, 69 n. 21, 70–1 n. 26; Nichols, *A literary biography*, p. 211; Nichols, *Radical affections*, pp. 220, 226–7.

60 On this point, McCaffery points to Blaser's citation of Merleau-Ponty's translator, Alphonso Lingus' (decidedly postmedieval) account of 'the imaginary' as 'the "baroque" proliferation of generating axes for visibility in the duplicity of the real'. See Alphonso Lingus, 'Translator's preface', p. liii, cited in *TF*, p. 144; and cited in McCaffery, 'Blaser's Deleuzian folds', p. 106.

61 McCaffery, 'Blaser's Deleuzian folds', p. 101.

62 Nichols, *Radical affections*, p. 193.

63 *TF*, p. 140.

64 Middleton, 'An elegy for theory', p. 202.

65 *TF*, p. 30. See also Carberry, *Phenomenology*, pp. 71–2.

66 On Merleau-Ponty's phenomenology in relation to Old English literature, see also Buchanan, 'Phenomenal Anglo-Saxons', pp. 8–10, 120–56.

67 Merleau-Ponty, *The visible and the invisible*, p. 134.

68 *Ibid.*, pp. 133–4.
69 Merleau-Ponty, *The phenomenology of perception*, p. 245.
70 *Ibid.*, p. 252.
71 *Ibid.*, p. 273.
72 *Ibid.*, pp. 256–7. The assertion that all sensation is spatial is repeated like a refrain. See pp. 252, 253.
73 Kleege, 'As if our friends felt the sun for us', pp. 474–5. On multi-sensoriality in medieval churches, see also Tuan, *Topophilia*, p. 11; Palazzo, 'Art'; Newhauser, 'The senses', p. 1571.
74 Merleau-Ponty, *The phenomenology of perception*, pp. 257–8.
75 *Ibid.*, p. 262. For 'erodes', see Landes' translation, p. 234.
76 Serres, *The five senses*, p. 56.
77 Merleau-Ponty, *The phenomenology of perception*, p. 266.
78 *Ibid.*, p. 272.
79 *Ibid.*, p. 266.
80 *Ibid.*, p. 272.
81 Merleau-Ponty, *The phenomenology of perception*, trans. Donald A. Landes, p. 244. Here I cite the newer translation. Cf. Merleau-Ponty, *The phenomenology of perception*, trans. Smith, p. 273: 'fabric into which all objects are woven'; Merleau-Ponty, *La phénoménologie de la perception*, p. 272: 'la texture commune de tous les objets'. The older translation conveys the relationship to the textile but not the pun on material/sensation.
82 Deleuze, *The fold*, p. 3.
83 Carruthers, *The experience of beauty*, pp. 27–31.
84 Hollis, 'Scientific and medical writings', pp. 200, 195, citing Ayoub, 'Old English *wæta*'; Cameron, *Anglo-Saxon medicine*, p. 28; Doyle, 'Anglo-Saxon medicine', pp. 76, 120–1. It is likely that early medieval England had many of the same Latin medical texts as the rest of western Europe, but this remains contested. See Cameron, 'The sources', p. 150; Doyle, 'Anglo-Saxon medicine', pp. 77–9.
85 Doyle, 'Anglo-Saxon medicine', pp. 185, 295–6. Cf. Ayoub, 'Old English *wæta*', p. 341; Cameron, *Anglo-Saxon Medicine*, e.g. p. 161. My thanks to an anonymous reader for pointing out the most recent references and important nuances of this debate.
86 Lockett, *Anglo-Saxon psychologies*, pp. 225–7, 440–1.
87 *Ibid.*, pp. 54–109.
88 Newhauser, 'Introduction', p. 5
89 But see aurally focused exceptions: Foys, 'A sensual philology'; Garner, 'Deaf studies'; Jorgensen, 'The trumpet and the wolf'.
90 E.g. Niles, Klein, and Wilcox, *Anglo-Saxon England and the visual imagination*; Leyerle, 'The interlace structure of *Beowulf*'.

91 E.g. Niles 'Introduction: negotiating', pp. 7–8.
92 O'Brien O'Keeffe, 'Hands and eyes', see pp. 106, 117, 119, 128.
93 Ibid., pp. 113, 116, 138, 114 table 5.
94 Ibid., pp. 113–14.
95 Ibid., pp. 139–40, 138.
96 I make no arguments here about the poem's date of composition, and defer to the dating of the manuscript in Kiernan, Beowulf and the Beowulf manuscript, pp. 13–63.
97 O'Brien O'Keeffe, 'Hands and eyes', p. 119.
98 The Old English Boethius, vol. 1, p. 378, ll. 117–130 (B text). Translation mine, but largely following O'Brien O'Keeffe, 'Hands and eyes', p. 118 n. 49.
99 Newhauser, 'Introduction', p. 5, citing Duggan and Farina, 'Intimate senses'. And see Newhauser, p. 22.
100 On ocularnormativity and ocularcentrism in medieval European Christianity, see Wheatley, 'Blindness', pp. 70–2.
101 Foys, 'A sensual philology', pp. 461, 463.
102 Cameron, Anglo-Saxon medicine, p. 11. On blindness in the Middle Ages (mostly) after the OE period (a subject distinct from the kinds of impairments listed here), see Wheatley, Stumbling blocks, and 'Blindness'.
103 Newhauser, 'The senses', p. 1573.
104 O'Brien O'Keeffe, 'Hands and eyes', p. 129; and see Pratt, 'Persuasion and invention', pp. 209–16.
105 Given that the 'exquisitely controlled decoration' of the brooch once 'duped scholars into believing it could be a fake', this seems unlikely to be a mistake of craft. See Backhouse and Webster, The making of English, p. 257.
106 Garner, 'Deaf studies', p. 28.
107 Bayless, 'The Fuller brooch'; on the figure's facial expression, see p. 212.
108 E.g. Backhouse, Turner, and Webster, The golden age of Anglo-Saxon art, p. 11.
109 On the 'recalibration' of the whole body to birdsong in The seafarer, see Ellard, 'Communicating between species', especially pp. 295, 297–303.
110 This observation is based on visits to the object (with these questions in mind) as displayed at the Walters Museum in Baltimore during autumn 2016, as well as examinations of brooches from early medieval English-speaking Britain of various materials and styles in the British Library study rooms in summer 2016 and autumn 2019. I found precisely this effect with the largest of the Pentney hoard Trewhiddle style disc brooches (102 mm) when tilted slightly in even ambient

interior light (British Museum, 1980, 1008.5, image available online at www.britishmuseum.org/collection/object/H_1980-1008-5).

111 Carruthers, *The experience of beauty*, p. 38.

112 *Ibid.*, p. 39. On the position that 'the doctrinal content is unremarkable ...', cf. Jorgensen, 'Introduction', pp. 1–2.

113 *The dream of the rood*, ll. 1–2; further references given parenthetically, by line number. This and following translations are mine.

114 Carruthers, *The experience of beauty*, p. 36.

115 Blaser, *The holy forest*, pp. 177–8. The opening parenthesis without a subsequent closing parenthesis is a ubiquitous typographical convention in the writing of much of the New American Poetry.

116 *Ibid.*, p. 177.

117 Tolkien, 'Monsters', p. 6.

118 Blaser, *The holy forest*, p. 177.

119 *Ibid.*

120 On *sinc*, see Tyler, *Old English*, pp. 33–4, 37.

121 I have not been able to determine whether Blaser was working from Old English, from a translation, or from memory.

122 Carruthers, *The experience of beauty*, p. 37.

123 Carruthers argues, against translations that translate *beam* or *treow* as 'cross' early in the poem, that 'the experience is sensible on its own terms, and indeed if we insist on glossing it from the start with external doctrines, we will compromise its artistic power'. See *The experience of beauty*, p. 37.

124 See *TF*, p. 115; *AT*, p. 153. The Latin *angelus* can mean messenger, and this is attested as well as a meaning of OE *engel*, used as a gloss for that word. See *DOE*, sv. *engel*, 2.

125 See Carruthers, *The experience of beauty*, p. 38.

126 My thanks to Haruko Momma for this idea over a decade ago. On this marked sense of *reordberend*, see Irvine, 'Anglo-Saxon literary theory', p. 172.

127 Pasternack, 'Stylistic disjunctions', pp. 170–1. Pasternack has it that 'formal disjunction' finds a counterpart in 'formal unity', whereas I am reading style as the composition of a *perception*—not as an abstract unity, which is precisely not a matter of aesthetics.

128 McCaffery, 'Blaser's Deleuzian folds', p. 108.

129 *Ibid.*, p. 106.

130 Blaser, *The holy forest*, p. 177.

131 Chapman, *Bussy d'Ambois*, 5.3.41–4.

132 Blaser, *The holy forest*, p. 177.

133 Liddell and Scott, *An intermediate Greek-English lexicon*, s.v. κόσμος (1), I, II, IV.

134 On heat in Dante's *Purgatorio*, see *AT*, p. 106.
135 E.g. Riddle 31, ll. 1–2. And see Remein, 'Decorate', pp. 96–9.
136 Robinson, 'Lexicography and literary criticism', p. 106. And see Greenfield, *Interpretation*, p. 95.
137 See Overing, *Language*, p. 46.
138 Overing, *'Beowulf*: a poem in our time', p. 326; and see Overing, *'Beowulf* on gender', p. 7.
139 Overing, *'Beowulf*: a poem in our time', pp. 324–5.
140 Paz, *Nonhuman voices*, pp. 34, 56.
141 All translations mine unless noted. Here, I follow Liuzza's rendering of 'æscholt ufan græg' (l. 330a) as a description of spears figured as a forest or grove. The possibility that *æscholt* (ash-grove) should be taken as an entirely lexicalized compound for 'spear' seems unlikely given the rarity of the word in the corpus (two occurrences). See Liuzza, *Beowulf*, l. 330 ('grey forest of ash'); *DOE*, s.v. *æscholt*, cf. *DOE*, s.v. *æsc*, 3.
142 Irving, *A reading*, p. 57.
143 *AOB*, p. 44. And see Overing, *'Beowulf* on gender', p. 7.
144 *AOB*, p. 42–3. Chapter 3 will address the aesthetics of variation directly.
145 *Ibid.* Brodeur is alone in insisting that the adjectives modifying these nouns are not also a part of the variation. Cf. Robinson, 'Variation', p. 29 n. 2.
146 *AOB*, p. 43.
147 Robinson notes a lack of 'general principles for distinguishing between attributive adjectives and temporarily substantivised adjectives' in such cases, finding no examples of an adjective immediately following a noun that he accepts as a separate, substantivised variation. See Robinson, 'Variation', pp. 100–3.
148 Irving, *A reading*, p. 57. My attention to this detail is also indebted to Martin Foys' conference papers 'Hearing the bell' and 'Ephemeral rings'.
149 On such personification, see Overing, *'Beowulf*: a poem in our time', p. 325.
150 Although *bitan* can mean *cut* in poetic contexts, the term also has the primary, prosaic sense of its Present Day English reflex, *bite*. The poem's tendency to confer 'a degree of interiority' on weapons lends further credence to reading the term with its literal sense here—as if the sword did not like the taste of Grendel's mother. See *DOE*, s.v. *bitan*; Overing, *'Beowulf*: a poem in our time', p. 325.
151 I follow Liuzza's translation of *gedrefed* here, which may simply mean 'disturbed' but, in the context of dark water, seems to suggest the

opacity of disturbed murky water, which is, after all, also full of boiling blood and hot gore (ll. 1422a, 1423a). See Liuzza, *Beowulf*, l. 1417; *DOE*, s.v. *gedrefed*, 1.a.i.a.

152 Klein, 'The coarser senses', p. 173.

153 *Ibid.*, pp. 113, 173–4.

154 As it does not bear on my reading here, my translation follows Kl. 4 in reading *egl' unheoru* as an asyndetic parataxis of adjectives (hideous, unpleasant), rather than taking the MS. *egl* as 'claw', as do some editors and translators (see Kl. 4, p. 175 n. 984–7). Cf. Liuzza, *Beowulf*, l. 987.

155 Saltzman, 'Community', pp. 33, 40–1.

156 Zupitza, *Ælfric's Grammatik und Glossar*, p. 7, l. 13.

157 See JH, s.v. *swég*; BT, s.v, *swég*. The word does not necessarily *pejoratively* designate noise; it *can* refer to organized music in highly ameliorated usages. E.g. *Guthlac*, ll. 1215b–1316a.

158 See Saltzman, 'Community', pp. 33–6, with analysis of this passage at p. 33.

159 Garner, 'Deaf studies', p. 22.

160 Abram, 'At home in the fens', p. 138.

161 Here I follow Saltzman's reading of *gamen* as 'joyous sounds' (cf. the abstracting definitions in Kl. 4, s.v. *gomen*). The *DOE* gives its primary definition as 'amusement, merriment, mirth; joy', and yet someone else's merriment in one's neighborhood might keep you up at night. See Saltzman, 'Community', p. 41; *DOE*, s.v. *gamen*, 1.

162 Robinson, 'Lexicography', p. 106.

163 Foys, 'A sensual philology', pp. 462–3.

164 And see 'cealde streamas' (l. 1261a) (cold streams); 'cealdum cear-siðum' (l. 2396a) (cold sorrow-journeys); 'morgenceald' (l. 3022a) (morning-cold).

165 E.g. *stenc* (smell, odor) in the Exeter book *Physiologus* poems. See *The panther*, ll. 64b–74; *The whale*, ll. 54b–58a. On the standard hierarchy of the senses in these poems, see Hoek, 'Anglo-Saxon innovation'.

166 E.g. 'heofon rece swealg' (l. 3155b) (heaven swallowed the smoke): the noun *rec*, for which 'reek' is the reflex, seems to only mean 'smoke' and not aroma, although odor is sometimes indistinguishable from steam or smoke in OE texts. See Klein, 'The coarser senses', pp. 96–7.

167 See l. 2593b: 'hreðer æðme weoll' (the chest boiled with breath).

168 Consider the verbs analyzed in Klein, 'The coarser senses', pp. 65–97.

169 Kl. 4, p. 240 n. 2288b.

170 See Kl. 4, p. 240 n. 2288b, but also Klein, '*Stonc æfter stane*'.

3

The heat of *earmsceapen* style: translatability and compound diction

The mid-century variety of critical attention to the aesthetics of poetic diction in *Beowulf* lived and died on the viability of the individual authorial mind as a category in the study of Old English poetry. This liability is perhaps nowhere more legible than in Stanley B. Greenfield's masterful 1972 volume, *The interpretation of Old English poems*. When Greenfield argued that the formulaic nature of Old English poetry does not 'militate against our praising a scop for having chosen *le mot juste*', and that the degree to which a traditional '*combination of words*' may have once been and still be appraised as 'suitable or aesthetically right',[1] he was, in part, carrying a torch for his teacher, Arthur G. Brodeur, by modifying the latter's position. Previously, Greenfield had already followed Quirk's argument that formulaic utterances are '*only* the starting point' for the study of Old English poetry in asserting that formulas 'were but counters for the Old English poet to use either conventionally ... or brilliantly and strikingly'.[2] By rescaling the units of composition to which Brodeur's insistence on individuality or originality as the primary measure of Old English poetic diction pertained, Greenfield upheld what is in effect a recoding of Brodeur's arguments that 'oral composition and communication do not, invariably, and remorselessly, constrict the poetic vocabulary and suppress individuality' and that the *Beowulf* poet's particular individuality is reflected in 'words which convey thought or feeling more freshly and vividly than the powers of other Anglo-Saxon poets ever compassed'.[3]

Greenfield's intervention was to cede to the oral-formulaicists the unit of analysis as a way to maintain Brodeur's basic orientation towards aesthetic inquiry. As Carol Braun Pasternack puts it, Greenfield wanted to be able to believe that 'some poets used formulas more artistically than others'.[4] But in extending the viability of his teacher's argument by adapting it to identify individuality on a scale commensurate with formulaic composition, Greenfield further consolidated the inquiry into diction as a question of the individuality of *choices*. The combination of formulaic utterances, measured along a spectrum of originality (with pure formulaic or metrical necessity at the other end), became 'the dictional choice itself'.[5] Even if the critiques of the author and of the subject in the latter half of the twentieth century did not render this construction of authorial choice incoherent, posed this way, the question of Old English 'poetic diction' remains cut off from readings attuned to aesthetics as a question of 'attributes of *style*, intended effects of the artefact on the perceiver'.[6]

This chapter is about compound diction in *Beowulf* and its place in what Blaser calls 'the heat of that story'. Blaser's and Spicer's translations of *Beowulf* loom large in the first part of this chapter for what they are able to tell us about alternative trajectories for Brodeur's interest in the poetic diction of the poem. As already suggested, neither Spicer's translation of *Beowulf* nor the surviving portion of Blaser's translation immediately reflect the complexity and adventurousness of their later poetics.[7] Superficially, their attention to diction may seem stifled by an (entirely reasonable) student's reliance on Klaeber's glossary. But, precisely as provisional, student translations, they register responses to Brodeur's categories within the horizon of Blaser's and Spicer's developing poetics and so also point, however indirectly, towards revisiting Brodeur's interest in the aesthetics of diction. The translations thus provide less an immediate critical frame than a catalyst for an account of the aesthetics of poetic diction in *Beowulf* in terms of the heat (in the sense of translative, sensorial processes of the poem described in the previous chapter) that Blaser ascribes to the poem. A demonstration, scaled to the lexis, of an early medieval aesthetics of fluctuation, imbalance, and unstable corporeal morphology, this chapter charts the functions of compound poetic diction in *Beowulf* in terms not of their aptness or originality, but of their place in a deforming aesthetics by which the poem's inclusions of the non-human world are permitted to impinge on the human sensorium and its vulnerable corporeal and affective morphology. We will alight on the poetic compound *earmsceapen* (ill-shaped) as a descriptive locus for the operation of these values in complexion, especially in the poem's description of the path to the Grendel-mere. In what follows, I allow myself—quite intentionally—to get bogged down in the minutiae of Old English diction in order to consider how the poem performs perceptual processes on a small scale and renders sensible a rhetorical *ductus* (path) through text.

This *earmsceapen* style coalesces largely out of a kinetic quality internal to compound lexemes that critics have sporadically hinted at since Greenfield's intervention. Roberta Frank, for example, analyzes the way the poem's use of the simplex *mere* (pool/sea) activates distinct items in the poetic and prose lexicons so that 'the word would start sparkling, flashing this way and that'.[8] Robinson's account of the appositive style of *Beowulf* implicitly contests the poem's supposedly static aesthetics, arguing that especially when we consider compounds alongside nominal periphrastic constructions, 'beneath the surface ... the diction is alive with verbal activity'.[9] Overing's account of compound diction in *Beowulf* as 'kinetic' also challenges assumptions about the poem's 'balance' of dyadic forces.[10] For Overing, this dynamism is fundamentally metonymic and occurs *between* compounds—not *internally*—but her view of 'the compound as an event, a split second of illumination' that colludes with the 'pace of the poem' in a restless, open-ended, 'dynamism' will return below, and in the next chapter.[11] Just how literally can we take the kinetic activity implied by such accounts of diction? To what extent are such characterizations mere 'poetic license', or responses to a perceptual process of the poem on the level of diction? Blaser's and Spicer's experiments in translating *Beowulf* under Brodeur's tutelage will help to phrase these questions more precisely and pragmatically.

In translation: unspooling compound words

Taken in tandem as a response to Brodeur's instruction, Blaser's and Spicer's translations—worked out, we recall, as a 'job' punctuated by their visits to the bar scene—test the claims about and taxonomies of poetic diction in *Beowulf* that Brodeur would later lay out in his monograph. In order to make those claims, Brodeur needs to 'open up' the internal workings of the poetic compound. For example, he argues (twice!) that

> [Old English] poets seem to have felt no distinction between the poetic compounds and the combinations of basic noun with limiting genitive. The two types are indeed logically identical: *yðgewinn* [lit. wavestrife]

and *yða gewinn* [lit. strife of waves] mean precisely the same thing. The first element of a compound limits or characterizes the meaning of the second, or basic element; just as the genitive in a combinatory appellation limits or characterizes the meaning of the basic noun combined with it.[12]

Brodeur also takes a firm line on what Overing would characterize much later on as a 'strict' definition of the *kenning* as opposed to the basic compound noun,[13] or what Brodeur calls, following the Old Norse poetic taxonomies, *kend heiti* (lit. characterized terms):[14]

> The qualitative difference between these kennings and such compounds and combinations as 'helm-bearer', 'wave-traverser', 'heath-stepper', 'breaker of rings' is obvious. These last, unlike kennings, express the concepts for which they stand through an identification of the referent with something which it actually *is*.[15]

A kenning, for Brodeur, differs from a *kent heiti* in that it is a particular kind of metaphor, which can be called *kenning* 'only if it contains an incongruity between the referent and the meaning of the base-word; in the kenning the limiting word is essential to the figure because without it the incongruity would make any identification impossible'.[16] I revisit this 'strict' definition and its detractors at the end of this chapter. More important for now is Brodeur's impulse to consider the inner workings of poetic diction in order to determine the extent to which they do or do not yield aesthetic effects at a larger scale—predicated on 'individuality' and *dignitas* (flexibility and restraint).[17]

As their aforementioned Old English lexicography project suggests, Blaser and Spicer came into Brodeur's classroom already invested in questions of diction, and their translations overtly signal their attempts to test their instructor's claims. The incomplete state of Blaser's translation makes it difficult to compare them point for point in all cases but even their general tendencies and accidental details are instructive. Blaser often underlines his translations of compounds, nominal periphrases, or traditional poetic collocations as if tracking the pervasiveness and patterning of formulaic expressions as well as the extent to which subtle differences in similar expressions register as equally traditional or subtly distinct. In translations of negating adverbs or adverbial phrases, he tends to flatten different degrees of emphasis, rendering almost all as if he were translating the Old English emphatic negation *neallas* (which he renders as 'not at all') and underlining the collocation (see Figure 3.1).[18] Spicer's translation signals his attention to his teacher's instruction with footnotes that specifically reference Brodeur's positions on ongoing scholarly discussions. Sean Reynolds identifies one such footnote that addresses the Old English compound *hronrád* (often translated, some scholars think problematically, as 'whale-road'), to which Spicer devotes considerable space and detail.[19] Spicer's note first records Brodeur's discussion of what would later be Caroline Brady's argument (appearing in print in 1952) that Old English nominal poetic compounds that end in *–rád* should not be misunderstood on the basis of that element's status as a false cognate with Present Day English *road*, but with respect to the related verb *rídan* (to ride).[20] Then, as Reynolds also notes, Spicer turns to points of Brodeur's instruction that anticipate, almost verbatim, his commentary on his 'strict' definition of kennings in *The art of Beowulf* (in order to identify *hronrád* as a kenning meaning 'place where the whale rides like a ship riding at anchor'):

> Kennings are periphrasis of literal term[s] for person or thing so conceived that the periphrasis contains a metaphor. This is broadest possible definition. Not every periphrasis with metaphor is a kenning. Two requirements 1) peri[phrasis] shall have a specific form—substantive with basic sense of whole + substantive in dependent relation on the first. Dependence expressed as first word of compound or by qualifying sub.[stantive] by noun in genitive (e.g. ganotes bæþ [Gannet's bath]). 2) must express a special kind of metaphor. Eg. in ON "<u>snow</u> of the crucible" = silver, steed of the billows = ship. These are kennings. Also kelp of the hillside = grass. If genitive is left out you have the wrong term. That is the essence of the kenning. Qualifying phrase makes the whole figure possible. Identification with another thing which it cannot be except in terms of a very special relation. First formulated by Heusler a short time ago.[21]

Of interest here is not whether or not *hronrád* should be read as a kenning—and in fact, the meaning of *-rád* is not an entirely settled matter even now—but Spicer's detailed interest in Brodeur's process of 'opening up' compound diction and the extent to which he was 'tracking' his teacher's approach.[22]

For Spicer, this attention crystallizes in his unusual translation of the compound word *hellrune*. In *Beowulf*, the word occurs as

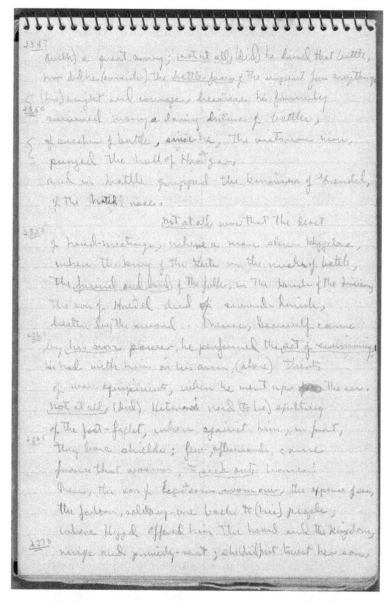

Figure 3.1 Page from Robin Blaser's translation of *Beowulf*, ll. 2347–2370.

an obscure reference to Grendel, his mother, and related creatures, but Spicer translates it with the Present Day English simplex 'witches'.[23] Spicer's copy of Klaeber's *Beowulf* would have glossed the word as 'one skilled in the mysteries of hell, demon'.[24] A more recent authoritative translation of the term gives 'whispering demons',[25] appealing to the senses of secrecy, counsel, or secret wisdom associated with the base-word *run* while preserving the gravitas of the relatively rare compound.[26] So Spicer's 'reduction' might seem to indicate an insensitivity to the effect of the internal dynamics of the word on its aesthetic function. But if Spicer's 'witches' may seem at first glance to colloquialize or even domesticate the register of this rare compound, it also comprehends the more complicated possible range of associations now suggested by word's entry in the *DOE* and so points to Spicer's own apparent lexicographical erudition. The *DOE*, which notes only eight occurrences of this compound as a weak feminine noun (plus two more as a strong feminine noun),[27] leads with its sense as a gloss on the Latin word *pythonissa* ('possessed woman', sorceress) and *pytho* (sorceress, sorcerer).[28] Under the second numerical heading, the *DOE* then cites this occurrence in *Beowulf* as having the sense of 'a demon, one knowing the mysteries of hell'.[29] What, in Spicer's rendering, might at first seem like a capricious lateral shift in denotation and downward adjustment of aesthetic register instead offers an implicit analysis of the aesthetic value that results from the interaction of multiple registers *between the constituents of the compound*—a word in prose, a word in verse, a vernacular word used to translate from a prestige language.

When we can compare them side by side, Blaser's and Spicer's translations fit together even more in the patterned divergence of their strategies for translating poetic nominal compounds. Coordinated at this level, the translations point to the linguistic conditions that allow Brodeur's 'opening up' of compound words in the first place. Consider their translations of this passage from Beowulf's report to Hygelac about the scene in Hrothgar's hall (three salient points of comparison appear in bold in Old English and each translation):

> Þær wæs gidd ond gleo;   gomela Scilding,
> felafricgende   feorran rehte
> hwilum **hildedeor**   hearpan wynne,
> **gomenwudu grette,**   hwilum gyd awræc

soð ond sarlic,   hwilum syllic spell
rehte æfter rihte   rumheort cyning (ll. 2105–2110)

There was song and mirth; the aged Scylding,
well-informed narrated from far;
at times, **the brave one in battle**, touched the delightful
harp, the **wood of mirth**, sometimes he recited a tale
true and sad, at times he told **a wonderful tale**
in accordance with right, the large-hearted king (RBB)

There was song and mirth; the old Scilding
well informed, told of far off (times);
at times the **battle valiant** touched the joy of the harp,
the **pleasure wood**, at times he told a story
true and sorrowful, at times the large hearted king
told **a strange tale rightly** (JSB)

Blaser tends to stay 'on-glossary', sticking closely to or importing directly from Klaeber's glosses without adjusting them much for the context, and, moreover, tends to expand nominal compounds into nominal periphrases. Spicer tends to render compounds in Old English as either compounds (although usually unhyphenated) or simplexes in Present Day English and to render periphrases in Old English as periphrases in Present Day English (or, as seen here, even 'reduces' a prepositional collocation to a single Present Day English adverb).

In a paradigmatic example of this relatively coordinated pattern of Spicer's use of off-glossary 'condensed' forms and Blaser's cribbing of Klaeber-derived glossary entries, Blaser modifies Klaeber's entry for the unique compound *uhtsceaða* (predawn-harmer)—an epithet for the dragon—only minutely, adjusting 'depredator at (dawn) night' to 'depredator-at-night'.[30] He simply removes the parenthetical expression (which Klaeber inserts to register the polysemy of the noun *uht*) that might have made this periphrastic gloss on a compound noun,[31] already bulky with archaism, totally unworkable. Spicer, by contrast, gives the pulpy term, 'night robber',[32] retaining the compound lexical item but laterally remapping the base-word of the compound onto a more colloquial, maybe even juvenile, register. Elsewhere, Blaser twice renders another compound epithet for the dragon, *hordweard* (lit. treasure-guard), with the periphrasis, 'guardian of the hoard' (minimally altering Klaeber's gloss, 'guardian of treasure'), giving the compound 'hoard-guardian' only for the final two occurrences of the word in the poem.[33] Opposite these, Spicer's text has, accordingly, 'hoard keeper' for the first occurrence and 'treasure guard' for the final three.[34] Even in a case in which Blaser renders a compound noun with a compound not taken directly from Klaeber's glossary, such as 'princely throne' (once) and 'princely-seat' (twice) for *bregostol*, Spicer's translation is lexically 'reduced' or 'condensed' into the simplex 'principality' (for the first occurrence) and 'throne' (for the second two).[35]

An example of this patterned response in a borderline case of compounding is particularly illustrative—namely, Blaser's and Spicer's translations of the adjective *feohleas*, formed from the noun *feoh* (property, wealth—in other contexts, cattle, livestock) and the adjective *leas* (loose, free from), the latter of which occurs both as an independent word and as one of the more productive suffixes for adjective-formation in Old English.[36] The adjective can be translated literally as 'payment-lacking', describing an offense for which the practice of making restitution with monetary compensation is insufficient or not germane. Klaeber gives two glosses for the word, the periphrastic phrase 'not to be atoned for with money' and the complex derivational adjective 'inexpiable'.[37] Blaser slightly modifies Klaeber's periphrastic gloss as 'not-to-be-atoned-for', while Spicer opts for the non-periphrastic 'unexpiable', slightly modifying one of Klaeber's glosses by swapping one derivational prefix for another.[38]

That Klaeber can offer these two glosses for *feohleas* already highlights a certain destabilizing capacity on the part of the Old English. Many technical studies of Old English compounds would exclude *feohleas* from their corpus, along with other examples of complex word-formation by affixation with bound morphemes and/or what some linguists have termed 'affixoids'—free morphemes that occur both as independent lexemes and grammaticalized affixes.[39] While it is easy to see why technical studies might exclude complex words formed with derivational affixes since these tend to behave differently within the prosodical system of Old English verse, complex words formed with ambiguously grammaticalized elements that occur both as productive affixes and as independent words present a more complicated problem for the aesthetics of diction. On the one hand, one can point out that even when such borderline lexical elements seem to activate the same semantic field regardless of whether they occur as free words or as part of complex words, their participation in derivational word-formation seems to follow individual sets of rules concerning the syntactic classes of words to which they can attach (i.e. they function in that case as a grammaticalized affix).[40] Thus, some of the most productive suffixes for adjective-formation in Old English, *-ful* (-full), *-leas* (lacking, loose), and *-lic* (-'like') (all of which appear elsewhere as semantically related independent words), can only attach to nouns.[41] On the other hand, 'in some cases, a sharp boundary is nonexistent between compounding and derivatives', and such affix-like elements in Old English may also be plotted along a 'morphological cline' describing various degrees of transition towards grammaticalization.[42]

The difficulty of translating a word like *feohleas* into Present Day English—and any aesthetic implications arising from the linguistic status of its constituents—thus stems *first* from the uncertainty of categorically locating the lexical item to be translated along a cline between poles of productive modes of word-formation within *its own* language. But that Blaser takes, more or less, Klaeber's periphrastic gloss while Spicer pulls the 'least complex' gloss (a derivational prefixed adjective) while also specifically changing the prefix without substantially changing its sense (perhaps modulating towards a more colloquial register with a nonce word formed on analogy with the more common dictionary term)[43] registers and turns on a potential for a kind of lexical instability along a spectrum of compound and complex word-formation at a scale and from a conceptual vantage that Brodeur's attention to diction probably could not consider.

The change in the derivational negating prefix from *in-* to *un-* (leaving the adjective base-word and its sense unchanged) throws into relief that neither of Klaeber's glosses, nor Blaser's or Spicer's modifications of them, track the processes of Old English word-formation or their potential aesthetic functions in the case of *feohleas*. Neither *in-* nor *un-expiable* tracks the precise nature of the word along the Old English complex/compound continuum. Instead, Spicer performs a sort of double translation, first laterally shifting the base-word from a noun (*feoh*, wealth) to a 'positive' adjective (*expiable*) that might on its own modify the antonym of the 'crime' or 'offense' implied by the negating adjective *feohleas*—*then* adding a purely grammaticalized negative prefix to restore the necessary negation.

To risk philosophizing the philological, one might rightly ask in which language each phase of this double translation occurs. It may seem a matter of speculative frivolity, but the quandary recalls structuring questions of translation theory that implicitly aestheticize these fundamental instabilities of compound diction. This coordinated unspooling and rewinding of Old English compound and complex words in Present Day English registers what I want to call *translatability*—operative already within the Old English text of *Beowulf*—quite ahead of or apart from the pragmatics of translating the poem into any other language. In gesturing to the translatability of these compounds and thus pointing to a certain kind of lexical instability within Old English poetic diction, Blaser's and Spicer's translations also point to an alternative ground on which to consider their teacher's interest in the aesthetic functions of compound words. The difficulty of translating *feohleas* out of Old English, after all, is conditioned in part by the capacity for compound words to give way to aesthetically heterogeneous rephrasings within Old English itself.

Translatability and aesthetics

That a term like 'translatability' should obtain within a text without reference to its possible translation into another language would not be news in theoretical conversations about translation. As much as the posture of deconstruction might seem to relish the chance to mark 'the untranslatable', or even the general impossibility of translation,[44] Derrida re-marks the limits of translation as both its impossibility and the horizon of pure translatability: 'the sacred text marks the limit, the pure even if inaccessible model of pure translatability, the ideal starting from which one could think, evaluate, measure the essential, that is to say, poetic, translation'.[45] This is because in the very untranslatability of the sacred text, 'in which meaning and literality are no longer discernible as they form the body of a unique, irreplaceable, and untransferable event', the promise of 'the pure translatable can announce itself, give itself, present itself, let itself be translated *as untranslatable*'.[46] This untranslatable opacity that conditions the legibility of the pure translatable points to the remarkable possibility that 'translation is experience, which one can translate or experience also: experience is translation'.[47] *Translatability* would here name not only a structuring condition or limit of translation from one language to another but also an irreducible event—which cannot be fully distinguished from the conventional, historical instances of translation between two languages—of a given language promising what language promises to do as language, both deconstructing and heralding a phenomenological horizon.

Derrida turns translation and experience towards each other because Walter Benjamin had already invoked the concept of 'intention' to characterize the 'to-be-translated'—a concept that Derrida rightly indexes to a 'scholastico-phenomenological language'[48] and thus to that same medievalism of modern phenomenology, 'borrowed from the scholastics by Brentano and Husserl', from whence the concept of *intentio* returned to the language of philosophy.[49] Properly bracketing the intended from the mode of intention, Derrida positions this 'intensive mode that renders present what is absent, that allows remoteness to approach as remoteness' with respect to that most remote '"language of truth" that is the "true language"'—a remoteness one can know but 'cannot overcome'.[50] For Derrida, translation 'is experience' and 'experience is translation' because the impossible side of translatability can only ever attain the status of an announcement or a promise—and yet, 'a promise is not nothing',[51] so this promise itself constitutes the event and the 'experience'.

Within the horizon of the Derridean critique of presence, such 'experience' is thus absolute and formal rather than sensory-affective. But what happens if we understand the intentionality of translatability, regardless of its deconstructable character, as belonging to perception rather than signification? Irrespective of its absolute genesis, the translatability of Old English compounds as an element of poetic diction to which Blaser's and Spicer's experiments point—this capacity to unspool into periphrastic constructions and to variably twist registers between components—posits a different *activity*. Old English poetic compounds (and sometimes borderline complex words) already activate nodes of inescapably stylistic, aesthetic instability that result from their marked potential for the 'intralingual' translation (or '*rewording* [within the same language]') that Roman Jakobson influentially distinguished from 'translation proper' and 'intersemiotic' translation ('transmutation').[52] To the extent that we take 'translation' and 'experience' as mutually determinative horizons, and in its heightened susceptibility to rewording (as a subspecies of translation), we might consider how to give an account of Old English compound poetic diction as a site of (the poem's) experience determined by these lexical instabilities.

The kinetics of this process already inheres in compound word-formation. While modern vocabulary for 'compound words' emphasizes a static structure, the relevant Latin grammatical traditions and their Old English counterparts accentuate a 'process of combining' within a 'combinatory view of language'.[53] For Latin-literate readers trained in grammar, compounds would have been distinguishable from simplexes as such, and may have seemed a 'less stable' or even 'less permanent' part of the lexicon.[54] The concept of the translatability of compound lexemes concerns a potential lateral movement and/ or rearrangement within Old English itself, describing the conditions of this active combinatory emphasis.

In the Old English text of *Beowulf*, this movement conditions and limns Blaser's and Spicer's patterned experiments. Blaser and Spicer do not, per se, 'prove' Brodeur's claims one way or the other, but their experiments indirectly suggest an essential modification of their teacher's obsession. It is not, after all, a question of whether the compound and the periphrasis are 'felt' differently in aesthetic or semantic terms (nor, as will become clear further below, of whether or not to hold to a 'strict' definition of the kenning). The condition of aesthetic activity lies not in the choice of one or the other but in this potential or virtual rewording, displacing the internal boundaries of the language itself and its 'poetic' registers in the movement between (and elicited by either) compound or periphrasis and underscored by fluctuating degrees of lexicalization and borderline cases along a larger 'morphological cline'. By thus disturbing the identity of the language with itself, the translatability of compounds is especially prone to being swept up by the sort of performative force that can overtake the referential functions of a language as a cresting wave of an 'experience' determined by sensorial materiality rather than absolute structure.

In his deconstruction of Jakobson's aforementioned tripartite taxonomy of translation, Derrida gestures to a similar set of displace-ments, with related effects, that crop up around the attempt to isolate and distinguish the kind of 'rewording' implied by translat-ability: by distinguishing a 'proper' form of translation and supposing that 'everyone understands what that means', Jakobson also introduces a whole order of 'inadequate translation, like metaphors, in short, of twists and turns of translation in the proper sense'. [55] Aside from casting doubt on the possibility that 'one can know in the final analysis how to determine rigorously the unity and identity of a language', the specter and range of such improper translations render determining the specific number of moves implicit in any translation only more complex and problematic.[56] (By the same stroke, it is unlikely to prove possible or productive to attempt a consistent and rigorous distinction between translatability as a condition of intra-lingual translation and as a condition of 'translation proper'; accordingly, what follows will not avoid strategic conflations of these two senses of translation and translatability.) The sometimes sentence-level linguistic complexity of Old English compounds only multiplies the likelihood of such 'twists and turns' and their potentially fluctuating phenomenological force as a kind of kinetic energy *internal* to a given lexical unit—even as the slipperiness of distinguishing the proper field of 'intralingual translation' amplifies the potential aesthetic stakes of translatability.

This 'translatability' of compound words goes a long way to suggest why the Old English corpus does not consistently record the use of compounds specifically 'as translation tools' in cases of interlingual translation *into* Old English, whether as glosses on a given Latin lemma or within larger verse texts.[57] Contrary to what one might expect, they did not appeal to translators as offering greater 'precision', but rather as offering the culturally domesticizing potential of what the compound signified as a form.[58] Even in cases in which compounds are consistently used for what Jonathan Davis-Secord calls 'direct construal' of a specific source-lexeme or for specific semantic nuance, the pattern 'is not one of creating transla-tions of the greatest adequacy but one of eliminating the resonances of the source culture and introducing elements that resonate instead with the target culture'.[59]

Jakobson already underscores that in instances of rewording, 'synonymy, as a rule, is not complete equivalence', and any simplex is also subject to rewording.[60] So it is precisely the distance between the multiple lexemes of a compound term or a periphrastic construc-tion and their mutual implied near-rephrasability which amplifies the potential aesthetic dimensions of this activity. Brodeur wanted to 'open up' the 'moving parts' of the poem's poetic diction to measure its appropriateness and originality, taking each word in its right place as the index of a stolid, unmoving 'beauty' or 'art'. In scholarship more recent than Brodeur's, the aesthetic implications of compound words in Old English poetry—legible as distinct from those of simplexes—have been understood mainly in terms of their capacity to broadly emphasize referents on the level of the sentence and larger discursive structures.[61] However, as responses to Brodeur's instruction, Blaser's and Spicer's experiments redirect attention to the moving parts of compound lexemes. It is in the incompletion, the potential for unbalanced movement in the translatability of compound words, that the poem opens itself to vectors aside from the referential function of its language and enacts a form of aesthetic activity in which translation is indeed *experience*, determined as kinetic lexical shifts that open up pores in the skin of the text.

Compounding movement

How would the translatability of compound words perceptibly condition the aesthetics of *Beowulf*? The remainder of this chapter performs an exaggeratedly close reading of Hrothgar's verbal map to and of the so-called 'Grendel-mere' to begin to answer this question.[62] It will require two 'passes' at the text. One, to consider how compound words structure it as a legible unit of the poem and set its aesthetic activity in motion, and a second, to more painstakingly 'open up' those compounds, tracking their aesthetic function as an unbalanced process of perceiving a grim non-human topography and deforming the human sensorium. Incidentally, this passage does not appear in either Blaser's or Spicer's extant translations,[63] so there is no temptation to get lost evaluating the particulars of their readings, and we are free to follow the processes to which their experiments gesture in the heat of the poem.

The poem has Hrothgar give the speech in question after his lament for his beloved Æschere, whose decapitated body has been discovered in the aftermath of the attack by Grendel's mother. Brodeur characterizes these lines as 'one of the finest passages in *Beowulf*', but not, surprisingly, as part of his discussion of compounds; rather, he musters his analysis of the passage to his quarrel with the oral-formulaicists by focusing more generally on the 'admirably chosen adjectives' (irrespective of their status as compounds or simplexes) in which, Brodeur argues, 'much of the power and terror of the description resides'.[64] Not uncharacteristically, Brodeur describes the effect of the passage in terms of balance and restraint, qualities that serve the stability of a description determined as 'symbolic rather than representational'.[65] The adjectives are admirably chosen precisely because they are 'not extravagant, nor even striking in themselves'; powerful because they are 'mostly combined with nouns' in designating features of a 'terrifying landscape' that yields a 'mood of terror'.[66] Yet, in thus granting the description any non-representational force at all, Brodeur's analysis already points to the production of a less static perceptual process.

If we tend to the compounds that—in this curious instance—Brodeur avoided, a more phenomenologically active, less symbolic, and less balanced style materializes to condition the non-representational force of Hrothgar's speech (quoted here for reference in full with compound words in bold and some periphrastic constructions underscored):

Ic þæt **londbuend**,   leode mine,
selerædende   secgan hyrde
þæt hie gesawon   swylce twegen
micle **mearcstapan**   moras healdan,
ellorgæstas.   Ðæra oðer wæs,
þæs þe hie gewislicost   gewitan meahton,
<u>idese onlicnæs</u>;   oðer **earmsceapen**
on <u>weres wæstmum</u>   **wræclastas** træd,
næfne he wæs mara   þonne ænig man oðer;
þone on **geardagum**   Grendel nemdon
foldbuende;   no hie fæder cunnon,
hwæþer him ænig wæs   ær acenned
dyrna gasta.   Hie dygel long
warigeað, **wulfhleoþu**,   windige næssas,
frecne **fengelad**,   ðær **fyrgenstream**
under <u>næssa genipu</u>   niþer gewiteð,
flod under foldan.   Nis þæt feor heonon
milgemearces   þæt se mere standeð;
ofer þæm hongiað   hrinde bearwas,
wudu wyrtum fæst   wæter **oferhelmað**.

Þær mæg nihta gehwæm   **niðwundor** seon,
fyr on flode.   No þæs frod leofað
<u>gumena bearna</u>,   þæt þone grund wite.
Ðeah þe **hæðstapa**   <u>hundum geswenced</u>,
heorot hornum trum   holtwudu sece,
feorran geflymed,   ær he feorh seleð,
aldor on ofre,   ær he in wille,
hafelan beorgan;   nis þæt heoru stow.
Þonon **yðgeblond**   up astigeð
won to wolcnum   þonne wind styreþ
laþ gewidru,   oð þæt lyft ðrysmaþ,
roderas reotað.   Nu is se ræd gelang
eft æt þe anum.   Eard git ne const,
frecne stowe,   ðær þu findan miht
sinnigne secg;   sec gif þu dyrre!
Ic þe þa fæhðe   feo leanige,
ealdgestreonum,   swa ic ær dyde,
wundengolde,[67]   gyf þu on weg cymest. (ll. 1345–1382)

I have heard the **land-dwellers**, my people,
hall-counselors say this:
that they saw two such
big **border-walkers** keeping the moors,
alien-spirits. The second of them was
—so far as they could figure with any certainty—
in the shape of a woman; the other, **wrong-shaped**,
in the <u>form of a man</u>, plodded the **exile's-track**—
except he was bigger than any other person;
this one, in **former-days**, was named Grendel
by the **earth-dwellers** (they did not know of a father,
whether before him were begotten
any cryptic spirits). That obscure land
they control: **wolf-slopes**, windy promontories,
perilous **swamp-courses**—where **mountain-streams**
disappear down underneath the <u>dusks of promontories</u>,
the torrent underground. It is not far from here
in **mile-measures** that the pool sits:
over this hangs frosted-over groves,
a wood tightly bound with roots **over-shadows** the water.
There one can—each night—see a **terror-wonder**:
fire in flood.[68] None so wise lives
among the <u>children of humanity</u> that knows this abyss.
Though the **heath-walker** <u>assaulted by hounds</u>,

the hart with sturdy horns, might seek the wood-stand,
sent long on the run—yet he gives up his life,
his existence on the bank, before he wants—in there—
to hide his head: it is not a nice place.
From there **wave-tossing** mounts up,
dark to the skies, when wind churns
ugly storms until the atmosphere chokes,
the heavens weep. Now an answer is dependent
again on you alone. You do not yet know this country/land,
the perilous place where you may find
the guilty warrior; search if you dare!
I will compensate you for this feud
with **ancient-treasure** as I did before,
entwined-gold—if you come back.

Hrothgar's verbal cartography is full of compounds, often rare or otherwise remarkable in themselves. And it is at least partly set off from the rest of the poem as what Pasternack calls a verse 'movement' (a sequence of inscribed verses that—through aural, formal patterns and sometimes manuscript cues—suggests itself as a coherently performable unit of poetry) by virtue of the aesthetic imbalances they set in motion.[69] But the critical literature has been largely unable to produce an account of these aesthetics more finely grained than Brodeur's consideration of 'horror' and 'terror'. Whether or not it can still be said that 'no passage in *Beowulf* is more famous',[70] few critics would disagree with W. W. Lawrence's assertion that it constitutes 'one of the finest pieces of description' in the corpus.[71] This claim was the template for Brodeur's aforementioned estimation,[72] and its influence left critics to debate intersecting thematic and intertextual questions instead of reconsidering the question of style.

As Frank puts it, 'the haunt of the monsters in *Beowulf* has spawned a literature of its own' around how to identify the topography in question—whether symbolic or naturalistic, inland or connected to the sea, best understood in terms of early medieval Christian intertexts or pagan Norse associations.[73] Yet a major crux of these debates hangs on a question about the aesthetic dimensions of diction—if, at first, only a simplex—specifically around the word *mere* (as mentioned above), which describes the watery abode of Grendel and his mother. As Frank inimitably explains, the critics fall into a 'saltwater school' that adheres to the 'poetic meaning' of the word or a 'freshwater school' that follows the term's prose meaning—each of which has a series of implications for how to calibrate the symbolic, naturalistic, and intertextual potential of the passage.[74] But in *Beowulf*, this word manages to consolidate what Frank refers to as a possible 'bilingualism' of sorts between Old English poetry and Old English prose, whereby the poet is able to blend 'the poetic word with its common homonym in daily life' so that 'mere' appears as both the item in the poetic lexicon and the item in the prosaic lexicon.[75] The effect is central to a major ideological project of the poem—an effort to 'underline the temporal and cultural distance between a pagan Scandinavian past and the England of his day' while simultaneously enacting a 'conquest' of that distance.[76] And yet this effect is dependent on the way this word first activates questions of *style* since, in this context, the poet 'permitted the *Beowulf* poet to sustain his epic *dignity* while letting other, more familiar associations do their work' (emphasis mine).[77] This stylistic vortex facilitated by larger linguistic conditions constitutes the refractive movement of this word as a locus of aesthetic activity.

A pattern of compound words that sets off this passage as a relatively long coherent unit of verse activates similar questions of style.[78] As Brodeur counted, about one-third of the poem's lexicon consists of compound words.[79] A more recent set of calculations by Davis-Secord figures that compounds appear on an average of every 2.17 lines in the poem, and that the average number of compounds per five lines is 2.30.[80] Here, four of the first five lines contain a compound, all in the a-verse, two of which are single-verse compounds (which draw attention to their status as compounds by requiring all the prosodical resources of that a-verse for themselves).[81] These compounds interact with the kind of first-person statement of oral learning that so often initiates a prologue and announces lyric performance in Old English verse ('Ic þæt londbuend/... secgan hyrde' [I have heard the land-dwellers/ ... say this]),[82] reenacting in miniature the invocation of communal knowledge that famously opens the entire poem ('Hwæt, we Gar-dena ... þrym gefrunon').

Two similar clusters of compounds or periphrastic constructions subsequently appear, then compounds appear more sparsely for a few lines before Hrothgar's example of the hunted deer. A differently focused performance of the passage might conceivably break the movement there, or at least register a subtly formal shift, since the concessive clause 'Ðeah þe hæðstapa hundum geswenced' (l. 1368) (though the heath-walker, assaulted by hounds) could be performed as signaling the prologue to a formal pattern of gnomic verse. This sense might even be reinforced by the extraprosodical repetition of interdental fricatives (*Ðeah þe*), the continuation of the prosodical alliteration on *h* in the following pair of verses, and the introduction of the relatively less common Sievers D2 type verse (//x\) in the a-verse 'heorot hornum trum' (l. 1369a) (the hart with sturdy horns). Such disturbances of aural and prosodical patterns often announce the boundary of a movement.[83] But an unbalanced pattern of compounds also traverses this narrowing of topical focus and its alternative stopping-point. The dense clusters of compounds gradually become sparser, with the last cluster straddling this very boundary (two compounds and two periphrastic constructions in just three lines). There is then only one more—this time isolated—compound (*yðgeblond*, wave-tossing) before the final two lines of the speech are both punctuated by a whole-verse compound in the first half-line of each pair of verses.

These clusters of compounds and periphrastic constructions yield a dynamic and asymmetrical pattern that structures the movement's rhetorical *ductus* and the material of its heat. The concept of *ductus* quietly governs the aesthetics of this verse-sequence especially because, as Carruthers notes, '*ductus* insists on movement, the con*duct* of a thinking mind on its *way* through a composition'.[84] Here, as nodes or relays of this movement, these clusters chart an uneven, careening *iter* (journey). The compounds thus mark the activity of the verse, the energy by which it includes the human sensorium in the composition. The directional sense that inheres in the *ductus* as an articulation of *intentio,* especially as a term of perception and cognition, links it closely to the common function of a *ductus* as a guide towards a *skopos*, an aim or target resulting from the totality of the *ductus*.[85] Within this verse-sequence, which renders the quality of its *ductus*-as-itinerary explicit to the extent that it provides directions to the mere, the *iter* itself seems to take precedence over any particular goal (as in the colloquial platitude, *the journey is the experience*) while also indexing the poem's effort to perceive this non-human world. This is not the say that the *ductus* or the aesthetic qualities of its movement are coextensive with or necessarily subordinated to the representational description of the path to the mere. As an articulation of the text's *intentio*, the *ductus* propels and modulates the human sensorium through the composition itself.[86] The *ductus* is the path of the composition rendering its perceptual functions sensible. The *movement* of the verse-sequence as articulated by compound clusters registers the active experience of the text—that is, 'the ability to intend and thus affect those intently experiencing it'.[87] If we open up the *translatability* of the individual compounds that articulate the shape of this perceptual movement, we find, in the context of this terror-ridden itinerary, a series of unbalanced movements, powerful in force, that translate an invisible complexion of anxiety, tactility, and mutable corporeality—rendering a non-human topography legible to the human sensorium in a process of sensory de-forming.

Compounding instability

Individually, these compound words set in motion the aesthetics of what might otherwise seem stable lexical positions. Take the very famous nominal compound *mearcstapa*, or 'border-walker'. The word is attested uniquely in *Beowulf* (also at l. 103), although -*stapa* (stepper, walker) is attested as a base-word productive of a handful of other (mostly poetic, rare) compounds.[88] The word might be rephrased as 'walker/stalker of the border', or expanded again to 'one who walks on the border', but the nature of the prepositional relationship just as easily suggests 'one who walks at the border', 'one who walks to the border', or even 'one who walks over the border'. These polysemic implications are of course hermeneutically suggestive. But as an index of translatability, these potential rephrasings also generate an uncertain kinesthetic field. Far from offering precisely the *mot juste*, these potential rephrasings render not only a range of potential meanings but also an unstable aesthetic value: a kind of flickering or twisting of style at this lexical position of the poem.

Precisely why we should understand this lexical movement as a perceptual function of the poem may not yet be clear; nor, of course, would this much be exclusive to *this* compound word or *this*

verse-movement. Why is this aspect of *mearcstapa* not sufficiently
described by Robinson's crucial account of the poem's 'appositive
style', which resolves any 'verbal activity' of the juxtaposed terms
in an exercise in Christian meaning-making?[89] Robinson argues that
an implicit early medieval Christian 'context' will always ensure a
final resolution of any polysemy, and so too a transcendence of any
'verbal movement' on the level of diction (the old dichotomy of the
spirit [meaning] superseding the body [aesthetics]).[90] To the extent
that such readings reopen Brodeur's impulse to 'open up' compound
words, they also efface the question of style as it is posed here,
resolving the 'syntactic openness' of compound diction on the level
of semiotics or even hermeneutics. Yet, the structural position of a
reader-as-performer within the textual conditions of Old English
verse cannot guarantee a resolution of such verbal activity so 'singular
and specific' as a stable semantic value,[91] much less subordinate
such stylistic momentum to meaning without remainder. It is thus
an implied aesthetic activity *within the context* of these other
compounds that seems to keep the constituent parts of *mearcstapa*
in motion.

Two of the other three compounds within the first five lines of this
movement are also nominal compounds with a noun-noun structure
and a limiting-word whose conventional referents include salient
spatial, geographical, or otherwise locative dimensions. In the case
of *mearcstapa* as well as *londbuend* (land-dweller/cultivator) and
selerædende (hall-counselor/speaker), the base-word (for the latter
two, a nominalized participle; for the former, a weak noun also
corresponding to a verb) is launched into activity *within*, or *on*, or
in, or *around*, or *at*, etc., with respect to the spatial dimensions of
the limiting-word's referent. The word's rephrasability thus yields
a whole matrix of prepositional vectors along which the base-word
might follow in its particularization against the limiting-word.

The compound *ellorgæstas* (alien/foreign-spirits/intelligences), an
adjective-noun compound noun, disrupts this nascent pattern. Rather
than stabilizing the descriptive force of the passage, the adjective
lends not only a syntactic complexity but also an entire narrative
structure that does less to describe than to enact a movement between
the multipotent prepositional force of the other compounds. The
gæstas (spirits/intelligences) that are *ellor* (foreign/alien) only appear
so in the context of the implied before and after of some movement

from there to here, of culturally coded travel and/or migration.
Especially since *ellorgæstas* occurs as a variation apposite *mearcstapa*,
and in the context of these other compounds that suggest spatial
relations within a passage replete with a cartographic force and an
anxiety about enforcing territory, the motion implied by the referential
function of *ellorgæstas* thus reframes the translatability of *mearcstapa*.
Disrupting an emergent pattern of noun-noun compounds, the internal
dynamics of *ellorgæstas* extend the prepositional range regulating
the internal dynamics of *mearcstapa*—reinjecting a sense of movement
backwards into the compound cluster.

This mutually deforming interaction between *mearcstapa* and
ellorgæstas as epithets for Grendel and his mother then moves as
a destabilizing counterforce to that of *londbuend* (lit. land-dweller)
and *seleræden de* (lit. hall-speaker/counselor) as epithets for Hrothgar's
subjects. While *londbuend* occurs around twenty-three times in the
surviving corpus (in poetic texts and a number of glosses, with
evidence of a range of poetic, prosaic, and learned registers), *selerædende* is much more rare, with only three occurrences—two in
Beowulf and the other (in *Andreas*) likely borrowed from its use in
Beowulf.[92] *Londbuend* occurs in earlier glosses as a translation of
agricola, with the prosaic sense of 'cultivator of the land' or simply
'farmer'.[93] However, in keeping with Frank's sense of the 'separate
diction of poetry and prose' in Old English, the poetic sense (occurring
in six poems in addition to *Beowulf*) is more generalized, suggesting
something more along the lines of a dweller *of* the land—an inhabitant
of a particular region.[94] *Seleræden de*, on the other hand, would
have fit Brodeur's narrative that the *Beowulf* poet 'was himself
responsible for the creation of many of his compounds', even if the
critic could not strictly count the word among the 148 base-words
that form 'more compounds peculiar to *Beowulf* than to any other
single poem' in the corpus.[95] Even if the word also occurred in other,
no longer extant texts, it is not unlikely to have registered some
degree of strangeness here.

This distinct aesthetic force that issues from the intersection of these
two unbalanced vectors then calls attention to the possibility that,
contrary to one likely initial reading, *londbuend* and *seleræden de* are
neither rough formulaic equivalents nor strictly referent-identical variations apposite *leode mine* (my people). By emphasizing the contrasting
semantic range of these compounds, the poem subtly differentiates

the *londbuend* from the all-encompassing *leode mine*, pointing away
from an elevated usage back to the more narrow, prosaic sense of
londbuend—as cultivator/settler of the land, or farmer—and destabilizing the stylistic value at that lexical position. The next chapter will
address Brodeur's attempt to define variation in terms of exact 'identity
of reference'.[96] But, however these semantic potentialities are or are
not to be resolved, they harbor an implicit aesthetic function by
referring to a range of possible spatial relationships while simultaneously destabilizing the specific register of the poem at this lexical
position.

Moreover, the lexical energy along the axis between *londbuend*
and *selerædende* spills over into that between *mearcstapa* and
ellorgæstas, this latter pair repeating not the pattern of the former's
syntax or prosody but the overall placement of compounds within
the long line. In each, the first compound occurs as the final lexeme
of an a-verse and the second compound occurs as a whole-verse
compound occupying the entirety of the a-verse in the following
line. These whole-verse compounds evince an aesthetic link that
traverses the pairs of words for Hrothgar's subjects and for Grendel
and his mother even as the final whole-verse compound of these
two pairs (*ellorgæstas*) disrupts any symmetry by breaking the string
of noun-noun compounds. By destabilizing what might have been
a solid wall of *dignitas* built up by a marked poetic lexicon, the
varied composition, placement, and register of the compounds set
off a series of swirling oscillations of lexical kinesthesia both within
and between individual compounds—as both individual components
and entire lexical positions flash between various combinations of
stylistic values.

But which values? How can this abstracted 'translatability' and
its resulting 'lexical movement' interface with concrete sensory-
affective phenomena? At this point in the verse-movement, the
physical sensorium has been explicitly invoked twice, in terms of
aural and visual perception ('Ic þæt londbuend ... secgan hyrde', I
have heard those land-dwellers say this; 'hie gesawon ... micle
mearcstapan', they saw or beheld ... big border-crossers). In an
astonishingly instructive, if unfortunately patronizing and certainly
exaggerated comment on the sensorium of the poem's description
of the mere from 1929, J. R. Hulbert claims that 'the poet does not
visualize the scene because he was not accustomed to visualizing

anything ... there is not in the entire poem a piece of description that appeals to the visual sense'.[97] And against the backdrop of an ideological privileging of the visual in the early medieval hierarchy of the senses, it is here a vibratory, tactile, morphological, and kinesthetic gesture—either obscuring or largely ignoring vision—that the poem performs by means of an unbalanced, jittery, lexical movement given back in particular spatial terms.

Deforming style

Subsequent compounds not only continue this kinetic lexical activity but also provide the reader with an aesthetic vocabulary for it. Thus, the next cluster continues the emphasis on references to movement and spatiality with words whose gravity would again seem to summon the *dignitas* of the poetic lexicon: *earmsceapen, wræclastas, geardagum, foldbuende,* and the periphrases *idese onlicnæs* and *weres wæstmum.*[98] *Wræclast* (exile-track) is a relatively rare word (eight occurrences as a noun, all in poetry) and while *foldbuend* (earth-dweller) is much more common (ca. eighteen occurrences), it survives exclusively in verse.[99] The noun *geardagas* (former-days) is even more common (twenty-four occurrences), probably acceding to a high degree of lexicalization, but again is found mostly in poetic texts.[100]

But it is the compound *earmsceapen* (lit. wretched-shaped, miserable-shaped, poor-shaped)—an adjective formed from the noun *earm* (wretched, miserable, impoverished) and the past participle of the verb *scyppan* (to create, form)—that both destabilizes and provides a descriptor for this aesthetic trajectory. The bulk of the word's attestations is found in explicitly religious texts (a mixture of verse and homily), where the word, often used of devils, means 'miserable' in the specific pejorative sense of 'vile' or 'damned' (as a moral or theological judgment).[101] The *DOE* even cites this very occurrence for this last sense, and this religious register resonates with the poem's association of Grendel and his mother with 'Caines cynne' (the race of Cain) (l. 107), as well as with the ameliorated sense of 'pitiable'.[102] A particular range of socially coded affects also adhere to and presumably shape these perceptual patterns—as registered by the constituent element *earm* in its more common simplex adjectival form (ca. 650 occurrences, mostly prose), where it describes the low, base, or precarious, in terms of poverty as well as social and moral status.[103]

The sense of creating, making, or forming that inheres in *-sceapen* resonates with the senses of physical morphology and destabilized aesthetic movements in the other compounds and periphrases, including the morphological nebulousness with which Grendel and his mother are characterized—as in *on weres wæstmum* (in the shape of a man) and *idese onlicnæs* (in the shape of a woman).[104] On analogy with the verb *forscyppan* (which can mean 'to transform'), the connotations of the component *-sceapen* may suggest a sense not only of shape or making but also of physical metamorphosis.[105] Moreover, as an independent verb, *scyppan* is explicitly associated with the most salient vocabulary of the period for the process of word-compounding and the related concepts of shaping, composing, and joining that link Old English and relevant Latin traditions of grammar and rhetoric—as in Ælfric's much remarked-on translation of Latin *compositum* (as opposed to *simplex* in medieval grammars) with Old English *gefeged* (put-together, joined, composed, built), and *figura* (here in the sense of forming or making) with *gefegednes* (joinedness, form, compounding).[106] As far as grammatical treatises might seem from this vernacular poetic description of Grendel, for an audience trained in grammar, *-sceapen* links the compound of which it is a constituent to ways of talking about the process of word-compounding as such.

Within this verse-movement in which compounds are already doing important stylistic work, *earmsceapen* is thus implicitly marked as a descriptor for the de-forming stylistic effects generated specifically by the inner dynamics (their put-together-ness) of compounds as a distinct lexical category at this point in the poem. The style is *earmsceapen*, ill-shaped. This is not to say that the verses are in any way defective or incomplete, but that their lexical energies attempt to translate an *earm* sensory-affective reality into a poetic lexicon. The lines yield (in classical terms) neither unadulterated dignity, disgust, nor even the balance and potential legibility of a mixed style, but a substantialized feeling of dynamic de-formation—of an imbalanced corporeality, of a sensorium whose corporeal locus is itself unstable.

If we follow the generally accepted emendation that identifies *earmsceapen* in a corrupt passage about the thief in the dragon-barrow (likely describing the thief) (l. 2229a), we may (stopping short of a reconstruction of the passage unambiguously indicating that the dragon is a transformed human)[107] associate *earmsceapen* with the dragon as a shape-unstable body impinging on and reshaping vulnerable human sensoriality. As a function of the poem's ecopoetical perception of a world whose multisensoriality exceeds the human sensorium—or at least a hierarchy of separated senses—the kinetics of the *ductus* deform not only what the body senses but the very corporeal contours of the sensorium.

The ensuing cluster of famous geographical compounds, which underscore the advent of a more descriptive mode, continue to deform this perceptual process with the instability of the spaces that Grendel and his mother *warigeað* (control, occupy): *wulfhleoþu, fengelad, fyrgenstream, milgemearces, oferhelmað, niðwundor*. The hapax-legomenon *wulfhleoþu* maintains the predominance of noun-noun nominal compounds in this passage, but with a subtle recalibration of the direction of possible spatial relationships implied by the word. In this case, the base-word posits a space that is modified or possessed by, characterized by, or perhaps belonging to the referent of the limiting-word. Although not particularly common as an individual noun (ca. fifteen occurrences), the base-word *hliþ*—as in Frank's analysis of the word *mere*—could mean one thing in verse and something else in prose, and here the poem seems to draw on the disjunction, however subtle, between the distinct registers in these separate lexicons. While the poetic term refers to *dignitas*-deserving slopes and mountains of immense size, its function in charters and boundary clauses is restricted to the more quotidian and less dread-associated sense of a mere hillside (i.e. as real estate).[108] Usually a verse context would not render this legal sense salient but, as mentioned above, this whole verse-movement compositionally alludes to the kind of verbal maps generated by Old English boundary clauses.[109] Moreover, the custodial and proprietary senses of *warian* (to guard, occupy, possess, etc.)—the verb that governs Grendel and his mother's relationship to the *wulfhleoþu*—educe the sense of *hliþ* within a lexicon of legal prose. It is also worth noting, in this regard, that when Beowulf does enter this landscape, he moves 'ofer harne stan' (over/past the gray stone) (l. 1415b). This type of landscape feature, among several others, is similarly described in a number of Old English charter boundary clauses even as the phrase additionally echoes the terrifying, otherworldly (and thus un-ownable) theological connotations of 'sumne harne stan' (a certain gray stone) reportedly seen in Blickling Homily XVI—where the stone is beset by devils and the bound souls of the damned, as well as cliffs, icicles, monsters, and wolves (a parallel that may ultimately derive from independent influence on *Beowulf* and the homily by a version of the *Visio S. Pauli* similar to an extant redaction of likely Irish origin).[110]

Referentially, the intensity of the passage still suggests an attempt to lend poetic dignity to a topography that is at once legally defined and otherworldly, a 'cliff where wolves lurked, feeding upon animal and human carcasses',[111] or less literally, a landscape that might itself kill, or where killing occurs. But, combined with *wulfhleoþu*'s probable rarity, the variable association of *hliþ* with the legal and homiletic terminologies of the prose lexicon anxiously twists *part* of the word between multiple registers. Similar to Frank's characterization of *mere* as summoning otherwise distinct prose and poetic functions, in this instance of *wulfhleoþu* an invisible movement tugs unevenly at the word. However, it catches only one of the two elements of the compound, deforming or disarticulating the unity of the particular aesthetic value at this lexical position of the verse.

At stake here is not specific semantic content or even semantic complexity (i.e. what *wulfhleoþu* means), but *what the poem is doing to its aesthetics at a given position on the scale of compound lexemes*. Nervous—now furtive, now frantic—traversing unbalanced paths, the *ductus* is here too erratic to rest at a well-advised degree of *varietas*. And as this kinetic, deforming style accrues, the referential functions of two other words from this cluster of geographical compounds—*fengelad* (fen-paths, swamp-courses) and *fyrgenstream* (mountain-streams)—begin to suggest an even more concrete shape or space with which to describe this aesthetic activity.

The hapax-legomenon *fengelad* is another word that Brodeur added to his counts, since *fen-* survives as a limiting term only in four compounds in *Beowulf* and in one other compound occurring in two other poems.[112] And *fyrgen-* appears in Brodeur's list of limiting words that form 'more compounds peculiar to *Beowulf* than compounds peculiar to any other poem'.[113] *Fengelad* (often taken as 'paths through a fen', although I favor reading it as the courses or currents of the fen itself),[114] which traces the swampy lowlands near the mere, is constructed of a noun referencing a body of water as its limiting-word and a base-word with a more strictly topographical or cartographical semantic range. *Fyrgenstream*—which occurs only seven times, all in poetry—leaps from these low elevations to mark out the ultimate sources of those *fengelad*, and simultaneously reverses the arrangement of its constituent elements with respect to their watery or terrestrial referential ranges (water-land vs. land-water)—but with a destabilizing twist. Not all critics would count *fyrgenstream* as a compound along with Brodeur, even though it seems to function like one here, since *fyrgen-* does not survive as an independent noun and may be closer along the 'morphological cline' to an affix or an archaic noun that only appears in fully lexicalized poetic compounds.[115] Whether the word would have been felt as a compound, a lexicalized compound, an affixed word, or an especially poetic example of any of these, this quality of the element *fyrgen-* knocks askew the otherwise symmetrical reversal of referential targets in the components of *fengelad* and *fyrgenstream*. These cross-currents, accelerated by the gravity of the words' rarity and their semantic range, suggest a dizzying kinesthesia. And this plicating destabilization of symmetry focuses and unleashes the unstable flow of the *ductus* that issues from the surrounding compounds into a volatile, proprioceptively overwhelming, hydraulic energy.

This landscape of the non-human described in Hrothgar's ensuing speech, like the *earmsceapen* and *mara* (bigger) body of Grendel, helps concretize these dynamics: terrifyingly outside the human world, ably traversed by the seemingly languageless 'land-fish' Grendel and his mother,[116] whose bodies (as the inhabitants of Heorot perceive them), if not 'impaired', embody the aesthetics of the *unhælu* (un-whole/un-healthy/un-holy), whatever 'superability' they may possess.[117] This *deogol* (obscure, dark, secret) land of unseen, unknowable topography may render vision irrelevant while also exceeding and indeed threatening the sensorium of the supposedly abled body. As a phenomenological translator, amplifier, and inhibitor, here an *earmsceapen* style reshapes the experience of vulnerable corporeality, modulating its experience of mobility and convoluting the distinctions between assistance, extension, and impairment.

Unbalanced movement and affective process

Read as a perceptual process of the poem, these energies adhere to specific discourses of Old English vernacular cognitive and affective models. *Earmsceapen* style addresses itself to a medieval construction of the human body that is, as Carruthers reminds us, 'not a waterproof sack, but permeable to influences of all sorts of agents'.[118] We can further thicken our lexicon for sensory-affective complexion in *Beowulf* with a contemporaneous model of the emotions that resonates with the surging and deforming energy of this passage—namely, the cardiocentric, hydraulic model of emotional and cognitive experience that seems to permeate the vernacular psychology of Old English verse. As Leslie Lockett explains, in this model, experiences of the 'cardiocentric containment of the mind' result in the 'correlation of intense mental events with increased heat and pressure'—while calmer states correlate with 'mental roominess' as 'universally beneficial' (although both mental heating and cooling can be associated with both positive and negative states).[119]

In the analogy of the hydraulic model, 'when a thought or emotion transfers its energy to the container [mind/emotions/chest] and its contents, they too become hot, and they begin to seethe and expand'.[120] These processes can result from the contents of the (abstracted) mind, the (abstracted) mind itself, or the physiological seat of the mind in the chest.[121] It is particularly important here that mental 'seething and boiling' can lead to 'spatial constriction in the chest cavity' and so to 'intensely negative emotion or thought'— or even 'impaired' rational, verbal, and moral faculties.[122] As Lockett points out, direct descriptions of human mental and emotional states elsewhere in *Beowulf* are not unmarked by this vocabulary. [123]

How would this vocabulary for human corporeal experiences pertain to the aesthetic activity of compound words? Old English verse routinely invokes the hydraulic model in descriptions of objects other than the human psyche, and '*without* naming a specific thought or emotion'.[124] Here, the question concerns whether this analogy pertains not only to objects of representation but also to the perceptual functions of the poems themselves. In the case of the verse-movement in question, the currents of lexical energy generated by compound words have already been associated with a hydraulic force. After associating this *earmsceapen* lexical activity with surging hydraulic energies, the more explicitly descriptive functions of the poem additionally calibrate it in terms of the constriction of fluid and heat symptomatic of distressed and impaired cognitive and affective processes.[125]

For example, the *fyrgenstream* (mountain-streams) do not soar freely from the roomy heights, but,

under næssa genipu   niþer gewiteð,
flod under foldan. (ll. 1360–1361a)

disappear down underneath the dusks of promontories,
the torrent underground.

After so many prepositional aporias latent within the translatability of compound words, this repetition of the unambiguous preposition *under* is telling. Here, the density of compound words dissipates, and prepositions take up the slack. Shadowed and invisible under-spaces constrain the force of the mountain-streams, serving as an emblem for the style of the passage, just as prepositions replace and constrain the flow of compound diction. The genitive periphrasis *næssa genipu* (darkness of headlands) might release its own measure of translatable energy into the style of the passage if it were not immediately swallowed by the directional adverb *niþer*. *Niþer* is close enough in sense and even function to 'under' so as to draw out a lateral movement between the preposition and the adverb that ironically constrains the churning, abyssal 'dusks of promontories' as well as attenuating the energy of preceding compound words and further cueing the reader to expect unseen or invisible sensory complexions.

Subsequent prepositions further hijack the lexical kinetics of compound words in a disorienting play of over and under that both heats and constrains the *ductus:*

Nis þæt feor heonon
milgemearces   þæt se mere standeð;
ofer þæm hongiað   hrinde bearwas,
wudu wyrtum fæst   wæter oferhelmað.
Þær mæg nihta gehwæm   niðwundor seon,
fyr on flode. (ll. 1361b–1366a)

It is not far from here
in mile-measures that the pool sits:
over this hangs frosted-over groves,
a wood tightly bound with roots over-shadows the water.
There one can—each night—see a terror-wonder:
fire in the water.

Now the position and shape of the lexical style as it is caught up in the descriptive function of the poem is finally locatable, rendered with explicit prepositions—it is *þær*. But in this place, the compound with perhaps the most lexical energy yet—the hapax-legomenon *niðwundor* (terror-wonder, harm-wonder, violent-wonder)—is disturbingly constrained. Hemmed in by the prepositions of representational description, the *niðwundor* erupts as paradoxical heat: *fyr on flode* (fire in the water)—a pool of constrained, paradoxically burning fluid, the perfect emblem for the perceptual activity of these verses.[126]

The final description of the 'mere' in this movement further elaborates this index of aesthetically unstable heat with yet another emblematic compound:

> Þonon yðgeblond   up astigeð
> won to wolcnum   þonne wind styreþ
> laþ gewidru,   oð þæt lyft ðrysmaþ,
> roderas reotað. (ll. 1373–1376a)

> From there wave-tossing mounts up,
> dark to the skies, when wind churns
> ugly storms until the atmosphere chokes,
> the heavens weep.

Here, *yðgeblond* (wave-tossing, wave-strife), a compound unique to *Beowulf,* enacts a range of prepositional instability that recalls the compounds at the beginning of the movement. As an independent noun, the base-word, *gebland* (which itself occurs only twice, in poetry),[127] refers primarily to mixing or mingling—but not in the sense of the moderation or balance that characterizes a classically defined 'mixed style'. In fact, its related verbal form *geblandan* can mean to mix in the sense of tingeing or infecting, and the past participle form *geblanden*, which occurs eighteen times, frequently in poetry (enough, apparently, to warrant its own entry in the *DOE*), often means 'corrupted' (or even, in prose, 'infected', i.e. mixed specifically with infection or poison) and, more importantly, 'stirred up, agitated, disturbed'.[128]

Descriptions of affective and cognitive disturbances under the rubric of the cardiocentric hydraulic model customarily rely on the verbs *weallan* (to seethe, boil, well up, bubble up) and *belgan* (to swell up).[129] But *geblandan* is also attested in the description of hellish weather states that can be directly linked to the vocabulary of the cardiocentric hydraulic model. For example, in the Old English *Exodus*, when the Egyptians are drowned in the Red Sea, '[w]æs seo hæwene lyft heolfre *geblanden*/ brim berstende blodegesan hweop,/ sæmanna sið' (the gray-blue sky was stirred up with gore,/ the erupting (sea)surge threatened with blood-terror/ the path of the sea-farers).[130] It then becomes clear that this hydraulic distress also evokes cognitive-affective experience when these gory waters are set in contrast to God, who 'mod gerymde' (made his mind clear; lit. made it expansive/ roomy).[131] Elsewhere, *Beowulf* links the turbid mere explicitly to the verb *weallan* (to seethe, boil, well up, bubble up): 'flod blode weol ... hatan heolfre' (the water boiled over with blood ... with hot gore) (ll. 1422–1423a).[132] One might take this whole construction as an intralingual translation of *yðgeblond*, rephrasing the word as narrative and taking the measure of the perceptual style it translates into the poem.

Under pressure, the aesthetic heat of these compound words is deforming and pressurizing of both the poem and the human sensorium. In instances in which the words *wylm* or *weallan* serve to mark disturbing or even disease-like affects within the Old English corpus, they often occur along with the verb *astigan* (to go up, mount up, rise—in medical contexts, to spread), as here, 'yðgeblond up astigeð' (wave-tossing mounts upwards).[133] The verbal map to the mere and the mere itself are transformed from inert 'setting' into processes that are included in the poem's perceptual activity that impinge on human sensory-affective complexion. The already over-hung mere swells up; the sky meets it, not in a moderated mixture, but a deforming, choking space. The weeping heavens might evoke a range of affective states, and non-symmetrical clusters of compounds might yield a variety of kinetic aesthetic effects, but the aesthetic quality finally emblematized in the bulge of hot and tormenting/tormented air, water, and paradoxical fire is not in doubt; the perceptual 'gewidru' (storms) are 'laþ' (ugly).

From here, the verse-sequence levels out. Hrothgar's speech returns to the performance of a reassuring boast. The final compounds that mark the end of this particular movement of the *ductus* (*ealdgestreonum*, ancient-treasure; *wundengolde*, entwined-gold) return a more stable aesthetic energy to the poem along with their focus on value in the human world. Hrothgar's traditional heroic speech-act punctuates the movement like a coda, and the potential translatability of these last two noun-noun compounds is diverted from aesthetic into referential force.

Translatability, rumination, and a final note on the kenning

One might object that, ironically, none of this is really perceptible without the elaborate, recursive scaffolding of this chapter. Even without positing a traditionally defined oral-formulaic scene, it is not difficult to imagine, in the moment of an aural encounter with an oral performance of the poem in almost any context, that—as Overing argues—the *speed* of the poem might proscribe the kind of excruciatingly slow, 'stock taking' reading in which I have been engaged.[134]

That, *in the moment of aural reception*, the 'reader' is caught in the referential web of 'kinetic signs' built out of the metonymic force of the 'epithet and its impact' (which, as metonymic, moves externally to the compound word)[135]—this is, I think, quite right. However, interrelated early medieval monastic practices of mnemonics, reading, and listening also enabled—and sometimes accelerated—not only meditative and reflective but even recursive re-compositional engagements with texts. The practice of *ruminatio*, as Carruthers analyzes it, constitutes perhaps the most salient of those germane to Old English vernacular poetry:

> The ruminant image is basic to understanding what was involved in *memoria* as well as *meditatio* … *Ruminatio* is an image of regurgitation, quite literally intended: the memory is a stomach, the stored texts are the sweet-smelling cud originally drawn from the gardens of books (or lecture), they are chewed on the palate.[136]

Bede's mythic primal scene of vernacular English religious poetry, which describes Cædmon 'ruminating as if a clean animal' (quasi mundum animal ruminendo) in order to compose his verses, underscores the extent to which this procedure is inextricable from embodied sensory-affective experience and is a particularly apt frame in which to imagine monastic experiences of the aesthetics of vernacular poesis in early medieval England.[137] Such reading results in the (re)composition of aesthetic mixtures, conceptualized by default both as larger and more indefinite tactile corporeal sensations (regurgitation) and as taste and smell. And while one presumably imagines the point of such regurgitation arises in bringing back up only the pleasant-tasting things, it is hard not to imagine its potential for processing and reprocessing the distressing.

The manuscript context of Old English poetry and its syntactic composition may lend themselves to ruminative practice on larger scales of composition, and certainly do not inhibit it on the level of the lexeme. Pasternack's construction of the reader of Old English verse as a performer of the poem who must determine the poem's boundaries as part of its performance is partly conditioned on the relatively sparse formatting of compositional units in Old English verse manuscripts.[138] Operating within this framework, the system of traditional expression paradoxically enables the reader 'to break free from the potential linearity of the text'.[139] There is probably less 'openness' in Old English verse manuscripts on the clausal level, since, as Daniel Donoghue argues, Old English '[v]erse syntax complements [manuscript] pointing and other visual clues to a degree that it obviates the need for a fully elaborated system [of punctuation]' (and it cannot be true that sparse punctuation prevented silent reading, even if the slower pace of subvocalization may have been preferable for facilitating *ruminatio*).[140] But, the intense familiarity with verse syntax required to efficiently construe such texts would only have supported the mnemotechnical aspect of *ruminatio*, and the sparseness of punctuation would not have inhibited it. In the longer history of punctuation in western Europe, at times some monastic communities omitted frequent punctuation specifically to facilitate ruminative meditation.[141] Can we imagine a monastic reader similarly taking sparse punctuation in a vernacular verse manuscript—even if its genesis lay elsewhere—as an opportunity for meditative reading and ruminative breaks with linearity on the level of the lexis? We know, given the prosodical behavior of Old English compounds, that Old English speakers did not hear the components of compounds as separate words, but scribes did not consistently write compounds as single words or leave a space between components, and early medieval audiences of Old English poems did indeed process and feel compounds as different from simplexes—in more learned contexts, probably even after a given compound had fully lexicalized.[142]

As Carruthers argues, ruminative reading practices could reach more intense sensory-affective thresholds as well—and did not yield only quiet repose.[143] The energy inherent in what Overing identifies as the 'insistent pace' of the poem is thus not contraindicated in a re-compositionally recursive encounter with the internal structure of compound words. We might accordingly consider rumination an instrument not only of spiritualizing meditation but also of deeply corporeal sensory experience—an amplifier for a poetics of heat.

By this account, the old debates about whether to apply a 'strict' or 'loose' definition to the kenning do not necessarily impinge on how we comprehend the aesthetics of compound diction. And the question of the kenning in general emerges as a kind of epilogue to the aesthetic function of compounds in *Beowulf*. Brodeur's insistence on differentiating kennings and *kend heiti* was certainly a major motivation for his 'opening up' of the mechanics of compound poetic diction. But behind Brodeur's investment in this distinction lies the old effort to prize a poetics of balance, symmetry, and restraint. In its most extreme forms, Brodeur argues, the Old Norse kenning 'pleases *only* as a riddle pleases';[144] it involves a 'strained metaphor' and amounts to an experience which he refrains from describing as aesthetic: 'an intellectual exercise not unlike that required by a riddle' (a characterization, one might add, which is also unfair to riddles).[145] By contrast, when the more restrained Old English poets do use kennings, they are 'simpler and more transparent'.[146] As much as Brodeur may admire and enjoy the complexity of the Old Norse kenning, he exploits it as a subtly more excessive (and perhaps even a little juvenile) foil for the compound diction of *Beowulf*: 'Old English poets did not share the fondness of the skalds for mystification; and they carried variation to lengths undreamed of by Norse poets'.[147]

In any case, the so-called 'pure kenning is relatively rare in OE poetic diction'.[148] And, as Brodeur's formulation itself suggests, the distinction concerns the logic of a given word's referential process. What I have called the translatability of a given compound word depends primarily on the aesthetic forces prone to spilling out of the word in a given textual environment. Overing's deconstruction of the 'strict' definition places kennings and *kend heiti* along 'a spectrum of gradations in the dominance of external reference', with the metaphorical kennings at one pole and the metonymical compounds at the other.[149] By this reckoning, the difference between kenning and characterized term is only 'a question of degree', governed, in the last analysis, by a metonymic mode.[150] Different positions along this spectrum may involve deeper wrinkles than others in their semiotic relations or hermeneutic requirements, but these would not yield a categorical difference in the translatability of a given term.[151]

Bound to a unidimensional aesthetic axis by his investments in originality and organic unity, Brodeur phrased even the faults of *Beowulf* as 'an excess of beauty'—despite his continual preoccupation with 'terror' and 'the effects of horror' throughout the poem.[152] Set within the context of their translations of *Beowulf* as, in turn, the site of a translation between Brodeur's seminar and their revisions of Pound's medievalism in the search for a poetics of moving energies, Blaser's and Spicer's encounter with Brodeur's interest in the poem's diction points us towards an open range of particularized aesthetic qualities with non-representational functions that reshape corporeal sensory-affective processes. In Hrothgar's verbal map, compounds and compound clusters generate a dis-easing sensory-affective movement, deforming the experience of human corporeality so as to include within it a *niðwundor* imperceptible to the hierarchized sensorium.

While these aesthetic manifestations are driven by the intra-translative capacities of compound words, their larger effects mark the poem's unstable aesthetics as a fundamentally translative process. These compounds function as nodes of the poem perceiving, rendered perceptible as lexical movement. Within the frame of translatability, this process recalls that it is the impossibility of interpreting aesthetic information semantically which leads Haroldo de Campos to posit translation as a process not of carrying-across but of re-crystallization. As I noted earlier on and in a different context, he argues that the texts 'will be different in languages, but like isomorphic bodies, they will crystallize within the same system'.[153] While de Campos posits this formulation as a mode of 'interlingual' translation, I would suggest that it also inheres in the aesthetic functions of compound words in Old English verse. As de Campos argues: '[t]he more intricate a text is, the more seducing it is to "re-create" it. Of course, in a translation of this type, not only the signified but also the sign is translated, that is, the sign's tangible self, its very material self'.[154] Ahead of any thought of translating *Beowulf* out of Old English, the translatability of compound diction constitutes this 'tangible self' of the sign and the site of its mutually deforming entanglement with vulnerable, sensing, human corporeality. It heralds the fundamentally recrystallizing, translative orientation of the poem's relation to whatever may be indifferent to representational aesthetics, or even, simply, 'not language'. In the heat of *Beowulf*, what the deformed sensorium senses is not a distortion, but aesthetics.

Notes

1   Greenfield, *Interpretation*, pp. 31, 34.
2   Greenfield, 'Grendel's approach', p. 283, citing Quirk, 'Poetic language', p. 171.
3   *AOB*, pp. 37–8.
4   Pasternack, *Textuality*, p. 6.
5   Greenfield, *Interpretation*, p. 33.
6   Carruthers, *The experience of beauty*, pp. 14–15.
7   Reynolds, 'Afterword', p. 3; and see Hadbawnik, 'Introduction: "*Beowulf* is a hoax"', p. 3.
8   Frank, '"Mere" and "sund"', p. 156.
9   Robinson, *Beowulf and the appositive style*, p. 17.
10 Overing, *Language*, pp. 36, 34.
11 *Ibid.*, pp. 16, 22–3.
12 *AOB*, pp. 14–15 and at p. 248.
13 See, Overing, *Language*, p. 14.
14 See *AOB*, pp. 248–53.
15 *Ibid.*, p. 250.
16 *Ibid.*, p. 251.
17 *Ibid.*, p. 220.
18 Consider the following examples, given first in Old English with a diplomatic translation: 'no ðær aht cwices/ lað lyftfloga læfan wolde' (ll. 2314b–2315) (the loathsome air-flier would not leave anything there alive); 'no he him þa sæcce ondred' (l. 2347b) (he did not fear his [the dragon's] attack); 'No þæt læsest wæs/ hondgemota' (l. 2354b–2355a) (That was not the least of hand-meetings); 'no þon lange wæs/ feorh æþelingas flæsce bewunden' (ll. 2423b–2424) (not for long was/ the life of the nobleman wrapped with flesh); and 'Nealles Hetware hremge þorfton/ feðewiges...' (ll. 2363–2364a) (Not at all did the Hetware need exulting/ in the foot-fight). For each of the negating particles above, Blaser gives 'not at all'; e.g. 'not at all, there (would) the hostile air-leave anything of the living'; 'not at all did he dread that battle', etc. (RBB).

19 Reynolds, 'Afterword', p. 31.
20 Brady, 'The Old English nominal compounds'. Spicer's note reflects that Brodeur made this same argument, citing the same sources: 'Kl. [aeber] says kenning. Br.[odeur] says all poetic meanings are re— doesn't mean whale-road. Hist of iterated motion. In Genesis Old Eng Lit—Baugh—Kemp [Malone]—used for swinging or chains Malone points out in footnote when Satan bound. Here that rád never means road means swinging of the in O.E. and not until Shake[speare]. waves. "Where the whale Rád means rhtymic motion. moves over the swinging Rád=going on horseback, waves"' (*sic,* JSB). Cf. Brady, 'The Old English nominal compounds', pp. 556–8.
21 JSB. The note continues on from here. The language anticipates *AOB* at pp. 249–50, 253. Brodeur also gives the examples of '"snow of the crucible" for "silver"' (p. 249); '*hliðar þang*, "tang of the hillside," for grass or brush' (p. 250).
22 On *-rad* in this case, see Kl. 4, glossary, s.v. *hron-rad*, which cites Brady, but glosses the term as 'whale-ROAD'. And see *DOE*, s.v. *hran-rád*.
23 JSB; cf. Kl. 3, ll. 162–163. Kl. 4 reads the same at these lines.
24 Kl. 3, glossary, s.v. hel-rúne.
25 Liuzza, *Beowulf*, ll. 162–163.
26 BT, s.v. *rún*: the primary sense is given as 'whisper', in the literal sense of 'speech not meant to be overheard', and the more figurative 'counsel', followed by increasingly abstracted senses ('mystery', 'secret') before shifting to the sense of 'secret writing' following accordingly. JH gives similar senses in a different order of precedence (JH, sv. *rúnian*).
27 *DOE*, sv. *hell-rún, helle-rún*.
28 *DOE*, sv. *hell-rún, helle-rún*, 1, 1.a.
29 *DOE*, sv. *hell-rún, helle-rún*, 2.
30 Kl. 3, l. 2271, and sv. *uht-sceaða*; RBB.
31 In some contexts, *uht* refers specifically to the period before dawn, or 'predawn'. See BT, s.v. úht.
32 JSB.
33 RBB; cf. Kl. 3, ll. 2293b, 2302b, and glossary, s.v. *hord-weard*. This word also occurs twice in *Beowulf* as an epithet for 'king,' but outside of the extant overlapping lines of Blaser's and Spicer's translations.
34 JSB.
35 Kl. 3, ll. 2196a, 2370a, 2389a; JSB. Klaeber gives 'princely seat, throne, principality'. Perhaps ironically, here Spicer's renderings—both of them—are exactly 'on-glossary'. For the former, Spicer selects the simplex available in the glossary that indicates the domain of a *prince*,

or an office of power under a sovereign (to differentiate from the use of this compound to refer to a completely sovereign kingship, for which Spicer reserves the glossary term, *throne*).

36 See Quirk and Wrenn, *An Old English grammar*, §165.
37 Kl. 3, l. 2441a, and glossary, s.v. *feoh-léas*.
38 JSB.
39 See Davis-Secord, *Joinings*, pp. 32–3.
40 E.g. *Ibid.*, p. 35.
41 See Quirk and Wrenn, *An Old English grammar*, §165.
42 Kim, 'Demarcation of compounding', pp. 421, 438–9.
43 *The American heritage dictionary*, as a measure of usage in present day North American English, records an entry for *inexpiable*, but not *unpexiable*. The *OED* follows the same pattern.
44 Derrida casts his reading of the Biblical narrative of the tower of Babel alongside the logic of Benjamin's 'Task of the translator' and the well-worn deconstructive concept of the impossible double-bind in which 'translation becomes the law, duty, and debt, but the debt one can no longer discharge' ('Des Tours de Babel', 201, 199). It is the name of God in particular, as both proper name and common noun, that prompts translation's 'necessity *as* impossibility' (197).
45 *Ibid.*, p. 223.
46 *Ibid.*
47 *Ibid.*
48 *Ibid.*, p. 222.
49 *Ibid.*, p. 221.
50 *Ibid.*, p. 223.
51 *Ibid.*, p. 213.
52 Jakobson, 'On linguistic aspects of translation', p. 139.
53 Chapman, 'Composing and joining', pp. 47–8, 51.
54 *Ibid.*, p. 54.
55 Derrida, 'Des tours de Babel', pp. 198–9.
56 *Ibid.*
57 Davis-Secord, *Joinings*, p. 38.
58 On 'domesticizing', see Venuti, 'Translation as cultural politics'.
59 Davis-Secord, *Joinings*, p. 52.
60 Jakobson, 'On linguistic aspects of translation', p. 139.
61 Davis-Secord, *Joinings*, p. 96. I see my argument as complementary to that of Davis-Secord, who identifies effects 'less on semantic complexity' than on the complexity of word-formation and Jakobson's 'poetic function' of language (see pp. 71–83).
62 See Howe, *Writing the map*, pp. 67–9, which discusses the actual *journey* to the mere in relation to boundary-clauses.

63   Only Blaser's translation of the last phase of the poem survives. Spicer's translation has a lacuna of several hundred lines in the middle of the poem.

64   *AOB*, p. 25.

65   *Ibid.*, p. 26.

66   *Ibid.*, p. 25.

67   Here I follow Kiernan's emendation of MS *wun / dini* or *–dmi.* Kl. 4 has wund*nan* (l. 1382a). See Kiernan, *Electronic Beowulf.* I follow this reading to accentuate the possibilities of reading compound words in this passage, on the grounds that the 'irregularity of word division and the common division of Old English compounds in manuscripts' likely yields 'morpheme or constituent based rather than whole word processing' (Davis-Secord, *Joinings*, pp. 43–4).

68   This preposition is conventionally translated as *on* (e.g. Liuzza, *Beowulf*, l. 1366), but I follow the suggestion of Christopher Abram, who reads the half-line as riddling on the seeming impossibility of fire *in* water See Abram, 'New light', pp. 199, 201, 208–9. Abram in turn draws on Russom, 'At the center of *Beowulf*', p. 234.

69   Pasternack, *Textuality*, pp. 8–11, 147. This terminology arises as a way to describe units of inscribed text within 'verse sequences that *act as* poems when certain conditions suggest their coherence' (p. 147).

70   Frey, 'Lyric in epic', p. 296.

71   Lawrence, *Beowulf and epic tradition*, p. 183.

72   E.g. *AOB*, p. 95.

73   Frank, '"Mere" and "sund"', p. 154. Frank's summary of the relevant literature supplants the need for an extensive list here (see pp. 154–6). Malone is usually credited with establishing the association of the mere with contemporary descriptions of hell. See 'Grendel and his abode', p. 306. On navigating debates about Christian and Norse associations, see Abram, 'New light'.

74   Frank, '"Mere" and "sund"', p. 154.

75   *Ibid.*, pp. 154, 157.

76   *Ibid.*, pp. 164–5, and see p. 159.

77   *Ibid.*, p.157.

78   Pasternack, *Textuality*, pp. 11–12, 29–30, 147. Pasternack suggests that such movements 'for the most part range in length from ten to twenty-five pairs of verses' (p. 11), although longer sequences are possible (p. 166).

79   *AOB*, p. 7.

80   Davis-Secord, *Joinings*, pp. 85 n. 51, 176 n. 34.

81   Davis-Secord uses the given figures as a means 'to confirm the statistical significance of compound clusters within their textual contexts and

ensuring that I am not simply going with my "gut"' (*Joinings*, p. 176). The cluster of compounds I identify above would *not* be statistically significant in Davis-Secord's study (which requires clusters of five or more) (p. 176 n. 34). In the context of my analysis, an 'objective' test is not necessary to identify thresholds of *aesthetic activity* in the poem, which can be measured, occasionally, by the 'gut'.

82 Pasternack, *Textuality*, pp. 137, 151.

83 *Ibid.*, p. 125, and see p. 124. It is also worth noting that repeated sequences of Sievers type C-A-C verses from 1357b to 1376a (*Hie dygel lond* to *roderas reotað*) may articulate a distinct 'lyric' passage within the larger sequence. See Frey, 'Lyric in epic'.

84 Carruthers, *The craft of thought*, p. 77. Italics in original.

85 *Ibid.*, p. 79.

86 My thanks to an anonymous manuscript reader for encouraging me to clarify this point.

87 Carruthers, *The experience of beauty*, p. 54.

88 Searches of the *DOE Web Corpus* for *stapa* and declensional forms return the most complete information here, but Riebel's 1963 dissertation, 'A grammatical index', organised by base-word, proved a useful tool for orienting my initial inquiries into the distribution of compounds and particular base-words within the poetic corpus.

89 Robinson, *Beowulf and the appositive style*, pp. 17, 58–9.

90 *Ibid.*

91 Pasternack, *Textuality*, p. 24–5 n. 91; see also pp. 21–6.

92 The literature documenting the relationship of *Andreas* to *Beowulf* is vast. E.g. Riedinger, 'The formulaic relationship'; for more recent work, see Dumistrescu, '*Beowulf* and *Andreas*'.

93 E.g. in John 15:2 of the Lindisfarne Gospels: '*Ego sum uitis uera et pater meus agricola est* / ic am wintreo soð & fæder min londbuend is'. See Skeat, *The Holy Gospels*, p. 137.

94 JH, s.v. *landbuend*, has 'inhabitant, native' as its primary sense; Kl. 4, sv. *land-buend*, has 'land-dweller, earth-dweller'; and Wrenn and Bolton gloss it as 'dweller on the earth; inhabitant' (see Wrenn, *Beowulf*, glossary, s.v. land-buend). In *Widsith* the term is so general as to mean 'people': 'se biþ leofast londbuendum/ se þe him god syleð gumena rice/ to gehealdenne, þenden he her leofað' (*Widsith*, ASPR 3, ll. 132–134) (he is most dear to *land-dwellers*—/he to whom God gives rule over men/ to preserve while he lives here) (trans. mine).

95 *AOB*, p. 9.

96 See *AOB*, p. 279; Greenfield, *Interpretation*, pp. 64–9.

97 Hulbert, 'A note on the psychology of the *Beowulf* poet', p. 192.

98 These are inflected forms of these words as they appear in the passage.

99 Here I rely on the *DOE* and a fragmentary search of the *DOE Web Corpus* for 'wræcla' and 'wrecla' to cover variant spellings. A verbal form of *wræclast*, *wræclastian* (meaning, to walk the exile's path), is attested in two glosses. See also *DOE*, s.v. *fold-buend*.

100 See *DOE*, s.v,. *gear-dagas*.

101 *DOE*, s.v. *earm-sceapen*. Wulfstan, for example, uses the word to describe the anti-christ. See *The homilies of Wulfstan*, pp. 185–91.

102 *DOE*, s.v. *earm-sceapen*.

103 See *DOE*, s.v. *earm* adj., A.4, B.

104 But see, in favor of 'wretched', Stanley, '"A very land-fish"', pp. 85–6.

105 Braeger, 'Connotations of (*earm*)*sceapen*', p. 328.

106 See Chapman, 'Composing and joining', pp. 42–7; Davis-Secord, *Joinings*, pp. 9–11.

107 See Braeger, 'Connotations of (*earm*)*sceapen*', p. 327; Tripp, *More about the fight with the dragon*, p. 423. Tripp and Braeger restore the manuscript reading very differently than Kl. 4, based on evidence that *sceapen* occurs in the b-verse of both ll. 2228 and 2229. But see Kiernan, *Beowulf and the Beowulf manuscript*, pp. 228–40, and *Electronic Beowulf*, conjectural restoration notes, MS 179v, https://ebeowulf.uky.edu/ebeo4.0/CD/o/179v/179v-all.htm#179v1d.

108 *DOE*, s.v. *hliþ*.

109 See Howe, *Writing the map*, pp. 25–36.

110 See *DOE*, s.v. *hár*, 2.g.i.a. My thanks to an anonymous reader for pointing to its occurrence in boundary clauses. And see Howe's analysis of ll. 1402b–1417a, which does not mention the gray stone but notes that the list of topographical features in the passage similar to those of boundary clauses is used to 'radically dissimilar' effect (*Writing the map*, pp. 68–9). My thanks to another anonymous reader for reminding me of the *Visio S. Pauli* analogue. See Kl. 4, p. 203 n. 1415, appendix A§6; Wright, *The Irish tradition*, pp. 111, 117–36. On the reference to a Christian hell not exhausting the context of the scene, see Abram, 'New light', pp. 199–200.

111 Eliason, 'Wulfhliþ'. And see *DOE*, s.v. *hliþ*.

112 *AOB*, p. 270. Brodeur characterizes these non-*Beowulf*ian compounds with *fen-* as 'distinctly unpoetic' (e.g. *fenyce* (fen-frog? fen-turtle?), Riddle 40, l. 71).

113 *AOB*, p. 270.

114 I am in the minority. See Cronan, 'Old English *gelad*'; Gelling, 'The landscape of *Beowulf*', pp. 10–11. The *DOE* and Kl. 4 both suggest a path through a fen, but observe here the inclusion of the *ge-* particle and its alliterative link with *fyrgenstream*, which definitely names a kind of water-course.

115 The *DOE* classifies it as a 'nominal affix'. See, *DOE*, sv. *fyrgen-*.

116 Stanley, 'A very land-fish', pp. 86, 92.

117 Wallace, 'Grendel and Goliath', pp. 107–9.

118 Carruthers, *The experience of beauty*, pp. 33, 45, 47.

119 Lockett, *Anglo-Saxon psychologies*, pp, 54, 68–70.

120 *Ibid.*, p. 63.

121 *Ibid.*

122 *Ibid.*, pp. 59–60; on constriction, pp. 73–7; on impairment, pp. 4, 68 78, 101.

123 *Ibid.*, pp. 68 (Kl. 4 ll. 282, 2066); 72 (l. 278).

124 *Ibid.*, pp. 66–7.

125 *Ibid.*, p. 73.

126 But see Abram, 'New light', which reads this phrase as a riddle for treasure.

127 See *DOE*, sv. *gebland*. As a simplex, without the *ge-* intensifier, the word *bland* is also attested, with nearly the same sense, but only once. See *DOE*, sv. *bland*.

128 See *DOE*, sv. *geblandan* (and see the similar entry for *blandan*); and sv. *geblanden*, 2, 4.

129 See Lockett, *Anglo-Saxon psychologies*, p. 59.

130 *Exodus*, ll. 477–479a.

131 *Ibid.*, l. 480b. Here I retain the MS reading, which Liuzza gives as 'revealed his fury'. I take the phrase as a literal expression of the hydraulic model—making the *mod* plain or clear by making it roomy—invoked here as an ironic understatement that has the figurative sense of Liuzza's translation but does not lose the reference to a physiological state. Krapp emends to *modge rymde*. See *ASPR* 1, p. 214 n. 480; Liuzza, *Old English*, p. 131.

132 Lockett would disambiguate the use of *weallan* and *wylm* in descriptions of sea-water from occurrences with psychological connotations—especially in *Beowulf* (*Anglo-Saxon psychologies*, p. 59). However, especially given the double register of the word *mere* at this point in the poem, I would suggest that here *weol* serves *both* in representational description of water and as marker of an affective process.

133 E.g. *Genesis*, l. 980b. On this, see Lockett, *Anglo-Saxon psychologies*, p. 61. And see *DOE*, s.v. *astigan*. N.B., in some contexts, the word may also mean 'to descend'.

134 Overing, *Language*, p. 15.

135 *Ibid.*, pp. 65, 16, 10.

136 Carruthers, *The book of memory*, p. 206.

137 Bede, *Historiae ecclesiastica*, p. 24. See Carruthers' analysis, *The book of memory*, pp. 206–7.

138 Pasternack, *Textuality*, pp. 10–11.

139 *Ibid.*, p. 88.

140 Donogue, *How the Anglo-Saxons read their poems*, pp. 126, 36.

141 Parkes, *Pause*, 13–18; and see Pasternack, *Textuality*, pp. 9–10.

142 Chapman, 'Composing and joining', pp. 51, 54; Davis-Secord, *Joinings*, pp. 42–5; Donogue, *How the Anglo-Saxons read their poems*, pp. 134–5.

143 Carruthers, *The craft of thought*, pp. 104–5.

144 *AOB*, p. 249, italics mine.

145 *Ibid.*, p. 253.

146 *Ibid.*, p. 250.

147 *Ibid.*, p. 252.

148 Gardner, 'The Old English kenning', p. 115.

149 Overing, *Language*, p. 19.

150 *Ibid.*, p. 20.

151 Despite commonplaces about the kenning in Old English poetry, it can be argued that at least the OE circumlocutory genitival phrase may often reflect the influence of medieval Latin models. See Gardner, 'The Old English kenning', pp. 115–17. Cf. Calder, 'The study of style', pp. 39–42.

152 *AOB*, pp. 239, 202.

153 De Campos, 'Translation as creation and criticism', p. 315.

154 *Ibid.*

4

'Real cliffs': variation and lexical kinetics

Especially because of the symbiotic relationship between compounding and substitution in Old English poetic appellations,[1] the rhetorical figure of *variation* preoccupies the mid-century interest in the aesthetics of Old English verse as a natural extension of the poem's composition on the level of the compound word. Brodeur certainly lavished no less attention on the figure—including his study of 'The limits of variation' alongside the appendices on compound diction in *The art of Beowulf*, and arguing in his chapter devoted to the subject that

> Variation is indeed the chief characteristic of the poetic mode of expression; the poetic appellations, however striking in themselves, and however often they may serve as pure substitutions, find their most effective use as the materials of variation or variation-like structures.[2]

Variation, for Brodeur, is thus the pattern to which the judicious use of individual elements of poetic diction—especially compounds—accede on an incrementally larger scale of the poem. In these claims, Brodeur was on less contentious ground than in his attempt to assert originality on the level of individual words and was able to appeal to the authority of Klaeber, whose comments on variation in *Beowulf* stand out from his dissatisfaction with the aesthetics of the poem's larger structures: '[a]s regards the handling of the sentence, by far the most important rhetorical figure, in fact, the very soul of the Old English poetical style, is of course the device of "variation", which may be studied to perfection in the *Beowulf*'.[3] For Klaeber, too, compound poetic diction and variation operate in tandem, in 'an organic relationship between the rhetorical characteristics and certain narrower linguistic facts'.[4] Yet, as we will see, as a direct corollary to the investment in originality and the possibility of precise (as opposed to broadly 'formulaic') meaning in Old English poetic diction, the debates about variation shaped by Brodeur and his followers struggled to reconcile an interest in the stylistic functions of variation with an anxiety about its potential to produce referential redundancy, and even subsequent critical interventions unconcerned with redundancy tend to read variation as a semantic rather than aesthetic phenomenon.

Curiously, for all Brodeur's attention to variation, the extant portions of Blaser's and Spicer's *Beowulf*-related papers do not preserve a sustained attention, or assignments related to variation. Nor, aside from the tendency of translations of Old English poetry as class-preparation to proceed half-line by half-line, can I find any special attention to variation in the language of their translations. This does not mean, however, that their poetics, marked as they are by the heat of *Beowulf*, are not positioned to help describe the function of variation within the translative perceptual aesthetics elaborated in the previous chapters. As I explore below, Blaser's and Spicer's work implicitly responds to a strain of radical modernism that, for very different reasons, was equally anxious about lexical redundancy. In Spicer's engagement with Old English verse in his early lyrics, and in his later, more robust theorizations of poetic diction, he experiments with the non-representational functions of lexical economy and a reactivation of the aesthetic functions of reference in ways that, I would argue, both respond to and help reframe the non-representational dimensions of variation in Old English verse. Especially because these experiments play out in poems that are both topically and perceptually preoccupied with an ecopoetics of the ocean and the shore (a common Spicerian subject), I read them as generating a comparative critical frame for the two major sea-crossings of *Beowulf*—passages emblematic for twentieth-century debates about variation as well as old and ongoing arguments about how to measure the nature of the poem's relationship to a larger oceanic and littoral geography.

This chapter thus offers an account of variation in *Beowulf* that implicitly builds on the kinetic activity of compound words within a ruminative encounter with the poem as discussed in the previous chapter, extending the analysis of the collective aesthetic effects of individual lexical positions along a rhetorical *ductus* to the interaction of words as part of a larger rhetorical unit. While individual compounds were found to deform the style of the poem at particular positions in order to reshape the contours of the human sensorium into contact with the non-human world, Spicer's experiments in redundancy and poetic diction help point towards readings of variation in the sea-crossings of *Beowulf* as a permutational, recombinatory lexical kinetics that render poetic diction simultaneously more adhesive and more porous to an unassimilable Outside. Although critics often dismiss the 'reality' of the seas and shores of *Beowulf* within an assumed representational horizon, I track the place of variation in a kind of restylization of the referential functions of poetic diction, exploring it as a perceptual process that sweeps some measure of physical geography into the heat of the poem. Before turning to the sea-crossings, the chapter thus retheorizes the aesthetics of variation in two phases: first, by deconstructing the effect of a long-lived anxiety about redundancy in Old English poetry within the still influential mid-century and later twentieth-century discourses about variation, tracing how interest in the semantic functions of variation came to eclipse questions about style; second, by tracing the stylistic dynamics of redundancy and lexical permutation in Spicer's corpus.

Redundancy-anxiety: theorizing variation in Old English poetry

The tendency to variation in Old English poetry was not always so uniformly praised, earning detractors, according to Fred C. Robinson, as early as John Milton.[5] Among the negative appraisals of Old English verse in the late eighteenth and early nineteenth centuries that, as Calder chronicles, 'disappeared slowly' are those that dismiss the style of Old English poetry within a racializing 'evolutionary view of poetry'.[6] Sharon Turner's racist, colonialist Anglo-Saxonism, for example, paradoxically identifies one of the 'barbarous' elements of Old English poetry in 'that redundant repetition of phrases, which, though it added little to the meaning of the poet's lay, was yet the emphatic effusion of his heart'.[7]

According to Robinson, it is Richard Heinzel, in 1875, who first identifies variation as such in Old English poetry, adapting a word developed by post-classical Latin writers and deploying it as a technical rhetorical term (and not in a loose analogy with musical form, as some earlier scholars attempted to explain it).[8] Subsequent scholars adopted Heinzel's 'vague' definition of variation,[9] but Walther Paetzel's 1913 study, with its more systematic definition, 'remains the foundation for all modern investigations'.[10] Calder helpfully characterizes and translates Paetzel's guiding criteria:

> Variation occurs when a concept, already sufficiently characterized for understanding, is brought to the attention of the listener or reader once again, often with interruption of the syntactic context. The main characteristics of variation are 1) conceptual repetition, 2) looseness of relation to the syntax of the sentence, and 3) rare occurrence in prose.[11]

Crucially, Paetzel also considers variation on multiple syntactic scales: the individual word, the sentence or clause, and sub-clausal word groups.[12]

Brodeur offers the most salient attempt to loosen Paetzel's criteria,[13] arguing that Paetzel's work 'seems to me to lay somewhat too much stress upon form rather than content',[14] and that 'identity of meaning … is more essential to variation than identity of structure'.[15] Brodeur wants to distinguish between syntax and figure, 'between variation and parallelism':

> I should prefer to define variation as a double or multiple statement of the same concept or idea in different words, with a more or less perceptible shift in stress: one member of a variation may state the thought either more generally or more specifically than the other; or the second member, while restating essentially the same concept or idea, may do so in a manner which emphasises a somewhat different aspect of it. When the members of a variation possess the same grammatical structure, they constitute a parallelism as well as a variation; but not all variations are parallelisms, nor are all parallelisms variations.[16]

Brodeur classifies examples of what other scholars consider to be variation, but in which he does not detect identity of reference, as 'parallelism without variation'[17]—amounting to merely enumeration or progression.[18] Robinson's dissertation (which remains among the only extended, stand-alone, systematic treatments of variation as such in English) argues that Brodeur mischaracterizes Paetzel's distinctions (wherein parallelism and variation are, according to Robinson, also problematically opposed) and that accepting variation without syntactic parallelism yields examples 'undistinguished as stylistic devices'.[19]

Following the more lasting interventions of deconstruction, the possibility of maintaining a critically viable concept of 'identity of reference'[20] (which posits at once an entire implicit ontology of the parts and wholes of 'present' referents, as well as the unicity and verifiable directionality of multiple, contemporaneous signs) is at best a dubious proposition—functional perhaps as a heuristic, but not as a generalizable critical structure. Even in a conventional sense, as Robinson modestly notes, 'common reference is at times a subtle matter', especially among word groups, where it is often difficult to distinguish whether two consecutive constructions describe a single action twice, distinct stages of a single action, or even sequential but distinct actions.[21]

Robinson's response is thus an admittedly 'somewhat narrow' definition, 'a respectful modification of that proposed by Walther Paetzel':

> 'syntactically parallel words or word-groups which share a common referent, and which occur within a single clause (or, in the instance of sentence variation, within contiguous clauses)'. Simply stated, I regard variation as apposition (Sweet's old term), if apposition be extended to include restatements of adjectives, verbs, and phrases, as well as of nouns and pronouns.[22]

Although unable to part entirely with the concept of 'identity of reference', the definition reduces its relative weight, taking syntax as its primary criteria and excluding stylistic structures that share 'fundamental characteristics' with variation for the sake of taxonomic functionality: 'there are some common features shared by stylistic devices which bear different names'.[23] Other scholars tacitly adopt, or advocate on behalf of, more narrow or loose definitions (R. F. Leslie goes so far as the category of 'conceptual variation')[24] and engage the question of how to understand variation within the frameworks that developed out of oral-formulaicist interventions.[25]

In any case, the apparent redundancy of variation that dissatisfied early critics seems to attain a convoluted reversal of fortunes—in differing ways—in Brodeur's and Robinson's work. Brodeur's 'identity of reference' as the criteria for the 'chief characteristic of the poetic mode of expression' implicitly elevates the redundant even as he warns that variation 'could be a dangerous instrument in the hands of an inferior poet', with 'an effect of sheer redundancy' the leading result of its mishandling.[26] By contrast, in emphasizing syntax rather than semantics in his definition of variation (apposition vs. identity of reference) Robinson's early work on variation seems entirely indifferent to its potential redundancy. Robinson thus emphasizes that variation can 'clarify' a term or 'translate' an obscure or enigmatic compound with a common one, or 'increase flexibility of poetic vocabulary' by relying on the associative powers of apposition to contextualize compound words into alternately metaphorical or literal usages.[27] But just as easily, and without Brodeur's caveats, he pays special attention to the structural and rhetorical functions of variation that embrace its repetitive quality—including those hinted at in Brodeur's brief references to its function with respect to emphasis, pace, transition, and structure (more on these below).[28] In addition to marking structural or rhetorical boundaries,[29] variation can anticipate a subsequent narrative shift or, as Robinson later rephrases it, 'effect a swift rhetorical transition without the interrupting mechanics of hypotactic linkage'.[30] In his most innovative argument about variation, and the one in which the semantic dimensions of the device are least germane and redundancy most acceptable, Robinson argues that it can 'heighten syntactical suspense' or underscore periodic structure even when it does not increase suspense: 'in such instances, the referent of the variation may be of secondary importance'.[31] In a later article, Robinson goes so far as to argue against the tacit assumption that Old English verse 'may not repeat a major word in the two parts of a variation', which leads most editors to emend instances of such 'spoiled variations' that include exact repetition of a key term in their manuscript witness.[32]

So some of the stylistic effects of variation enumerated in the second half of the twentieth century are perfectly commensurate with absolute lexical repetition and, by his own definition of the figure, Brodeur had to evince some comfort with a certain degree of redundant reference. However, crucial examples of variation, which depend upon the exploitation of a nearly, but not completely, overlapping mode of synonymy, left Brodeur and his followers still furtively nervous about redundancy. For Brodeur, '[v]ariation restrains the pace of Old English poetic narrative, gives to dialogue or monologue its leisurely or stately character, raises into high relief those concepts which the poet wishes to emphasize, and permits him to exhibit the object of his thought in all its aspects'.[33] Further functions, commensurate with what Robinson later rehearses, include its use to mark narrative transitions and to clarify a more general term with a more specific one.[34] Variation also serves representational verisimilitude, emphasizing and expanding 'representation of a dramatically significant emotion', capturing 'the complexity of human relationships', marking 'the dominant mood'—and, by repeatedly emphasizing the 'impelling emotions' of characters, lending a 'close dramatic texture' to the organic unity of the poem.[35] The effects of variation on pacing, rhetorical structuring (e.g. marking transitions), and even this role in mimesis can depend on conventional synonymy; but clarification, tonal modulation, or multi-aspectual thought all depend upon at least a *partial* non-identity of reference. Thus, Brodeur attempts to distinguish a less artful category of 'variations which have no other function than that of an ornament of style' (a statement that harbors constricted assumptions about ornament and style),[36] and ends up with his somewhat tortuous definition of variation (cited above) as restatements that emphasize different aspects of the same referent.[37] In not quite knowing what to do with the possibility or the impossibility of redundancy (since he needs variation to be determined by both) the convolutions of Brodeur's definition implicitly sprout a whole theory of the sign and of semantics, distinguishing the sign's relationship to a referent from a supplementary 'aspectual' function.

In a study of 'The synonyms for "sea" in *Beowulf*', Brady expresses a more direct anxiety about synonymy, emphasizing that only a small number of words in her inventory of the poem's references to the sea occur 'as or with variation':

> this poet does not use all of the 40 terms as synonyms, with the general sense of 'sea'.
> By 'synonyms' I mean alternative words and locutions which have the same or a sufficiently similar referent; although, themselves

having different semantic ranges, they may express different subjective apprehensions of the referent, different attitudes towards it, and thus, within the limits set by the context, emphasize different aspects of it. According to this definition, it does not follow that all terms *pertaining to* the sea 'mean "sea"'.[38]

Attempting to shore up Brodeur's argument for the originality of the *Beowulf* poet's poetic diction, Brady seems to want to hedge her bets against redundancy: to say both that since these words do not occur in variations, they are not synonyms, and that even if they were synonyms, this would not be a problem, since synonymy is not, after all, total semantic coincidence. Bonjour goes further in a 1955 note on Brady's article, taking 'two pairs of parallel sea terms' drawn from Brady's argument in order 'to submit further reasons that the poet used them discriminately'.[39]

Citing Brodeur's definition of variation as his reference point,[40] Stanley B. Greenfield delineates perhaps the loosest approach of that period—perhaps ironically, one in which the very possibility of redundancy in variation seems to disappear. He readily admits, on the one hand, that '[i]dentity of reference is particularly difficult with actions or states of mind, but even with identifiable objects it is not always easy to be sure', and affirms that 'some kind of parallelism is necessary for effective recognition [of variation] by listener or reader' (while additionally noting the extent to which hypotaxis in Old English poetry can make it difficult to distinguish appositive and subordinate relationships between clauses).[41] Yet, for Greenfield, this parallelism need only accede to the point where 'implications of the form can be measured on the pulse, so to speak', and so allows for the possibility of a rhetorically marked 'appositive substitute' to strict grammatical parallelism.[42] Greenfield thus considers, but marks as outside his 'central conception of variation', both 'clausal variation without exact parallelism' and Leslie's 'conceptual variation'.[43] In teasing out the implications of the notion that 'the components of a variation conventionally show the same referent under different aspects or with different attributions', he goes so far as to suggest that variation has the capacity to represent 'a *combination* of series and variation'.[44] Taking *Beowulf*'s narration of the approach to Denmark by sea as an example, Greenfield argues that variation functions representationally to suggest a 'logical order of perception of the same elements of the landscape as the sailors reach their destination', so that, as a function of variation, 'a sense of movement is created, a shift in perspective obtained, without explicit statement or the employment of other syntactic means'.[45]

Where Brodeur implicitly splits up the sign-function of individual components of a variation into basic reference and a supplemental 'aspectual' dimension, Greenfield, by degrees, plays out this logic further. The vital effects of variation, for Greenfield, concern those that 'enlarge the world of meaning of a poem'.[46] So, while the repeated references of a variation may approach absolute referential redundancy, the non-identity of meaning, however slight, ensures that the repetitions of references to the same referent may retain non-redundant *semantic* and *narrative* functions within the horizon of a representational poetics and an overall 'organic unity'. Greenfield then dismisses the 'allegations' of the structural and rhetorical functions of variation (despite admitting that they are 'worth further investigation'),[47] with the result that, paradoxically, his looser criteria for identifying variation yield a much narrower account of its capacities.

As with the mid-century discussion of Old English poetic diction, the oral-formulaic approach to Old English poetry at mid-century also limns the place of redundancy in the discussions of variation by Brodeur and his followers. Brodeur could hold up variation as the shining prize of his project because the device was at first, as O'Brien O'Keeffe puts it, 'something of an embarrassment' to oral-formulaic approaches in its contempt for Homeric-style 'thrift'.[48] The oral-formulaic approach swiftly rebranded the device as formulaic in character and a matter of prosodical exigency outweighing 'thrift'—with the 'reduction of meaning' that attends a strictly orthodox approach to the formula in tow[49] (and in any case, there is a contradiction in claiming the unthrifty-ness of variation in favor of Brodeur's thesis, since variation is only unthrifty if it is redundant). Greenfield admits that 'in an orally based mode of poetry, variation may often be its own justification', but only as the backdrop against which more original variations can stand out: '[i]n interpreting variations, the critic must weigh thematic probabilities against the purely stylistic need or pleasure *per se* afforded by the variation'.[50] A given variation deserves critical bandwidth only when, in Brady's terms, the 'poet is no artificer mechanically piling up synonyms',[51]

where that subtle difference of reference and 'aspect' militates against
total lexical redundancy—leaving the aesthetic functions of variation
subsumed by its semantic functions within an ultimately representational poetics.

Despite its usual categorization as a device of style, variation
more easily tends towards resolutions of a hermeneutic rather than
an aesthetic critical horizon—even when redundancy is not a concern.
Robinson's *Beowulf and the appositive style*, which directs his earlier
interest in variation and apposition towards interpreting the poem's
juxtaposition of 'present [Christian] time confronting past [pagan]
time',[52] takes variation and apposition as continuous categories of
a style 'intimately cooperative with the tone and theme of the poem'.[53]
Reciting Tolkien's claim that a macrostructure of opposed, balanced
terms saturates every scale of the poem, Robinson phrases apposition
as the principle of an integrated structural/stylistic continuum along
which grammatically parallel 'variations' are merely one point. The
implications of this continuum are primarily *hermeneutic*:

> From the smallest element of micro-structure—the compounds, the
> grammatical appositions, the metrical line with its apposed hemistichs—
> to the comprehensive arc of the macrostructure, the poem seems built
> on apposed segments. *And the collocation of the segments usually
> implies a tacit meaning.* [italics mine][54]

Even in the sense of grammatically apposed words, Robinson situates
the device as above all else a semantic, even theological, interpretive
problem that stems from the (ambiguous, non-redundant) apposition
of 'the pagan and Christian senses of words' (which Robinson sees
as necessarily resolving in an early insular Christian synthesis).[55]
All of the rhetorical functions stand, but it is as if transcending
them that '[b]eyond these effects, however, apposition functions in
various ways to remind the poem's audience of the multiple levels
of meaning present in the words that make up the traditional Old
English diction as it was adapted by the poet of *Beowulf*.'[56]

This is all to say that approaches to style which insist on the
possibility of precision or originality (and attendant ambiguity) of
meaning in Old English poetic diction ironically desensitize themselves to a wider range of the stylistic effects of variation. And yet
Greenfield also describes the work of variation as 'like a jeweler,
turning the several facets of his gem to the light so that each may

sparkle in its turn'.[57] The claim is curious in that, while it certainly highlights the representational functions of variation (a mimesis of multiperspectival experience), it also implies the inescapability of its aesthetic horizon, imagining a poetics of ornamentation that does not represent so much as make an ornament of its object—much as the Old English Exeter Book riddles do when they declare that 'Is þes middangeard missenlicum/ wisum gewlitegad, wrættum gefrætwad' (this middle-earth is in variety/ of ways made-radiant, decorated with ornaments).[58]

On the one hand, an acceptance of redundancy in variation—or at least a deprioritizing of semantic precision—throws its rhetorical functions into relief. If, on the other hand, a sensitivity to the impossibility of totally saturated synonymy alerts us to the semantic and thematic functions of variation, these need not be automatically subsumed within a horizon of representational poetics or a purported organic unity. Rather, Greenfield's 'jeweler', while likely intended as a figure for the individuality of the artist, also hints at another possibility—one that Spicer's experiments in poetic diction will help clarify: the aesthetic horizon that inheres in *the performative force of the semantic functions* of variation, especially as conditioned by the (im)possibility of redundancy.

Spicer's barnacles and the 'Lowghost': de-sacralizing poetic diction

As suggested above, an anxiety about redundancy hung over the mid-century English-language poetry avant-garde, too—not, unsurprisingly, out of a debate about how to taxonomize a rhetorical device or a desire for organic unity, but out of a desire for a concept of poetic diction commensurate to a non-representational poetics. Ezra Pound's perhaps most famous injunction, cited in the *Imagiste* manifesto, to 'use absolutely no word that does not contribute to the presentation', goes hand in hand with a definition of the 'Image' wrested from mere description as 'an intellectual and emotional complex in an instant of time'.[59] This definition finds its apotheosis in the 'Vorticism' that Peter Nicholls characterizes as Pound's effort at an 'identification of the modern with the non-mimetic', and which, Pound insists, 'MAKES NO PICTURE'.[60] Pound explains that the intensified 'Image' of Vorticism is 'not an idea. It is a radiant node or cluster; it is ... a VORTEX, from which, and through which, and into which, ideas are constantly rushing'.[61] More immediate to Spicer's orbit, in positing the poem as a 'high-energy construct, and at all points, an energy-discharge', Charles Olson's landmark essay on 'Projective verse' (which would appear by 1950) also expounds the necessity of an efficiency in which the poet must 'USE USE USE the process at all points', and in which 'the descriptive functions generally have to be watched, every second ... because of their easiness, and thus their drain on the energy which composition by field allows into a poem'.[62] For '[a]ny slackness takes off attention ... from the *push* of the line'.[63] Once the possibility of poesis as a non-representational force is conceptualized as sensory-affective and/ or sexual *energy*, especially under the shadow of Pound's masculinist ideology, redundancy becomes a liability—a lapse into mere descrip- tion, weakness, laziness, or the 'observation' that Olson thinks is 'previous to the act of the poem'.[64]

An abiding preoccupation of Spicer's corpus, seemingly informed by his study of Old English poetic diction, responds to this anxiety by directly experimenting with the dynamics of redundancy and repetitiveness in variation—especially in its relationship to compound nouns. This interest in redundancy appears in a crucial early poem and seems to persist, in modulated forms, during and after Spicer's famous self-thematized rupture (realized in his 1957 works *After Lorca* and *Admonitions*) between his early lyrics and later serial poems.[65] Among Spicer's earliest complete poems that move beyond his juvenilia, 'A portrait of the artist as a young landscape' consists of a sequence with a teasing thirteen-line prologue that elegizes the eroding sites (literal and metaphorical) of major western literary encounters with the sea ('for only water now/ Stands once where Arnold stood, or Lear or Sappho stood'), followed by three sections identified with an ocean and a poet: 'I. The Indian Ocean: Rimbaud', 'II: The Atlantic Ocean: Hart Crane', 'III: The Pacific Ocean' (this last mentions Ben Jonson but is tacitly that of the Californian, Spicer himself).[66] As Daniel Katz points out, these titles first appear in Spicer's typescript for the poem, where they cancel and replace those that were previously inserted into the most complete holograph version: 'I: Mind as present perception', 'II: Mind as past perception', and 'III: Mind as potential perception'.[67] This change marks a shift from using 'the "ocean" in its ideality to map the different aspects of the poet's own "mind"' to using 'different *particular* oceans to map the poet himself in relation to other poets'.[68] But it also suggests an attempt to displace the representational expression of perceptual experience by exteriorizing and performing the processes of perception in the accidents of the poem's relationship to particular oceans.

Each of the main sections of the poem contains an extended variation made up of mostly compound nouns, with or without modifiers, along with some clausal-level 'variation-like' repetitions. The variation in Part II—a series of vocatives in a supplicatory or imperative utterance—concludes its respective section, addressing both an ocean 'in the mind' which is 'the deep-end of dreaming' and a real ocean where 'There are stacks/ Of broken sailors, sweet and harvested':

> Harvesting angel, out of these pleasures
> Out of the kelp-fields and the sea-brambles
> Tide-weaver, hunter and planter,
> Harvesting angel, paradise-keeper
> Harvesting dolphin-angel, coffin-lover
> Keep safe his sleeping bones.[69]

The variations in Part III are followed only by a brief rhyming coda before the end of the entire poem. Also a series of vocatives, these address 'a sea/ Of real appearance', and reference a joke from earlier in the section about the sort of sea 'Dr. [Ben] Johnson [*sic*] would have stamped his goutish leg upon', in the style of his famous 'appeal to the stone' meant to refute George Berkeley's idealism (an allusion that unspools an implicit pun, positioning the poetics of Spicer's own 'Berkeley Renaissance' on very slippery shores indeed):

> The sun becomes a nest of singing birds and he is gone
> The painted sea is gone.
> Gout-ridden angel, out of these terrors,
> Out of the mind's infidelity and the heart's horror
> Deliver my natural body.
> Gout-ridden angel, slayer of oceans
> Gout-ridden common-angel, keeper of virtue,
> Deliver my natural body.[70]

Variations comprised of apposing vocatives may feel relatively unmarked in themselves (piling up one right after the other, or, if beginning the subsequent contiguous clause or sentence, occupying the same (first) position otherwise occupied by a subject). And variations in vocative expressions are indeed common in Old English poetry.[71] But these variations are especially heavy, and in both cases, both the reality of the ocean they address and the poem's performative relationship to that ocean seem up for grabs.

This is a good point to introduce the technical terms that Robinson influentially codified to distinguish the parts of a variation: the total construction is called the *variation*, its parts are called *components*, the initial component (whether an individual term, noun-phrase, clause, or sentence) is called the *variatum*, and any subsequent component is called a *varians*.[72] The variation in the first passage consists of seven components, one of which is an exact repetition (conservatively counting 'hunter and planter' as one component). The variation of the second passage, taken as a larger looser construction, consists of six components (including 'the sun'). Both variations foreground the repetitiveness of variation—for example, in composing a varians by repeating the adjective in the variatum exactly while repeating the noun in the variatum as an element of a new compound noun ('Harvesting angel'/'Harvesting dolphin-angel', 'Gout-ridden angel'/'Gout-ridden common-angel').

Moreover, in Spicer's drafts, these variations fluctuate in the number and repetition of/within their components. The earliest draft of section II (and the earliest draft of any part of the poem) is out of order, in pencil, and at times overwritten with corrections in blue pencil, on the front and back of an envelope addressed to Spicer's friend Gene Wahl, at Big Sur. Here, Spicer alters 'Harvesting serpent-angel' to the 'Harvesting dolphin-angel', which remains in all subsequent drafts (Figure 4.1).[73] Initially, this component is even longer, enjambed with another adjective on the previous line: 'paradise-keeping/ Harvesting serpent-angel'. Spicer subsequently overwrites 'paradise-keeping' with 'paradise-keeper', turning the modifier into a noun (and thus a component in its own right), and extending the variation. This revision too appears in the final typescript and established text, but the next two subsequent holograph drafts revert to 'paradise-keeping'. And, the component in the position of 'coffin-lover' in the final version goes through two revisions: 'ocean-lover' replaces the first draft's 'tireless/ sword-bearer' in the second and third drafts, and it is changed to 'coffin-lover' only in

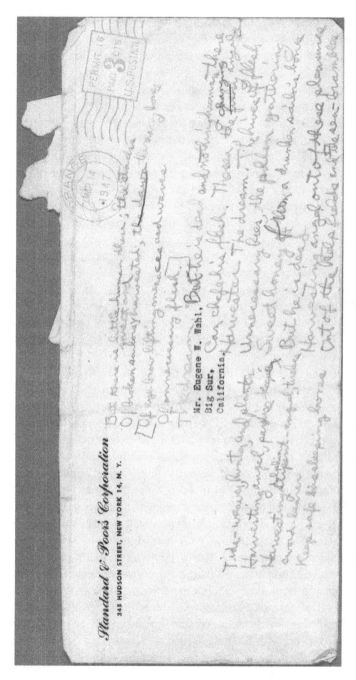

Figure 4.1 Draft of Jack Spicer's 'Portrait of the artist as a young landscape' (1947).

a handwritten correction to the typescript. In the final section of the poem, 'slayer of oceans' replaces what in the first draft were two separate components—'land-guardian, sea-fighter'—the first of which is written in the space of another rejected, partially erased and overwritten compound (possibly, 'Terror-keeper').

Perhaps most intriguing, however, are the word-variations and the looser, variation-like repetitions in the first numbered section of the poem, which is worth quoting in full:

> I watched and saw a sailor floating in that sea
> And melt before he drowned.
> Asleep and fragrant as that sleep, he seemed
> To draw the sun within his flesh and melt. He seemed
> To draw the fire from that angel and to melt. Now he is dead.
> To melt is not to drown but is enough
> To shear the body of its flesh; the sea
> Is meant for drowning, but when God is short
> Of waters for his purpose then the sea
> Becomes a pool of fire; angels ride
> Astride their flamy waves
> Pale as desire
> Terrible angel, out of that fire
> Out of the beach-bones, melted like butter
> Out of the blazing waves, the hot tide
> Terrible angel, sea-monster
> Terrible fish-like angel, fire breather
> Source of the burning ocean.[74]

Grammatically, the opening declaration that 'I watched and saw' is enumerative or accretive in force (and one can make plenty of functional distinctions between the overlapping vernacular semantic ranges of 'watch' and 'see'), but from the first it as good as announces a lexical economy that more austere poems might avoid. It is then increasingly unclear whether the first three sentences, taken together or in smaller segments, operate in a loosely variational, accretive, or enumerative relationship. However, if read with a riddle-like metaphorical quality (taking 'angel' as an epithet for 'sun') they constitute a relatively precise sentence-level variation. We can take this riddling reading as even more likely, since 'to draw the sun within his flesh' is hardly a conventionally literal description, and the whole cast of these lines is enigmatic (how exactly does one

watch a 'sailor' melt?). The vocative variations with clearer grammatical apposition at the end of the section—and which exhibit the
same patterns as those in the latter two sections discussed above—also
lend credence to reading these sentences as at least 'variation-like'.
But these vocatives address an 'angel', possibly the sun or the sea
itself—either literally burning or lit by the sun in a way that resembles
burning—which thus may or may not be differentiated from the
sailor seen to melt into the sea.

Even more intriguing, one of the Old English Exeter Book riddles
seems to supply a likely source-text—or, at very least, an extremely
uncanny analog—that helps make sense of these lines as riddling
variation. Traditionally 'solved' as an iceberg or an icefloe, the riddle
figures a threatening creature and constitutes its solution as a woman
Viking warrior who travels or sails after a wave and whose mother
is paradoxically its daughter grown up and pregnant (since waves
may become ice, and ice become waves—playing with the 'mother-
daughter' motif common to many riddling traditions)[75]:

Wiht cwom æfter wege   wrætlicu liþan,
cymlic from ceole   cleopode to londe,
hlinsade hlude;   hleahtor wæs gryrelic,
egesful on earde,   ecge wæron scearpe.
Wæs hio hetegrim,   hilde to sæne,
biter beadoweorca;   bordweallas grof,
heardhiþende.   Heterune bond,
sægde searocræftig   ymb hyre sylfre gesceaft:
'Is min modor   mægða cynnes
þæs deorestan,   þæt is dohtor min
eacen up liden,   swa þæt is ældum cuþ,
firum on folce,   þæt seo on foldan sceal
on ealra londa gehwam   lissum stondan.'[76]

An ornament-like creature came after the wave, sailing,
the lovely one called out from ship to land,
loudsounded loudly; the laughter was violent,
dreadful on the earth, the edges were sharp.
She was malice-cruel: sluggish to battle
[but?] bitter in war-tasks; [she] carved [ship-]board-walls,
the hard-plundering one. She bound up a secret of malice [*lit.* hate-rune],
the trick-skilled one spoke about her own creation:
'My mother is of the most noble
of women-kind; that is my daughter

grown up pregnant; so it is known to men,
to persons among the people, that she shall, on the ground
of each and every land, stand mercifully.'

Spicer's heavily iambic poem (it does not, like so many of the Old-Englishisms of twentieth-century poetry, rely on prosody as a signal of its indebtedness) is not a direct crib of the riddle. The elements Spicer adds to the poem—angels, fire, etc.—convolute the relation between the two poems to the point that the Old English poem can help make sense of Spicer's poem even as Spicer's poem obscures any representational relationship with its source. The Old English riddle does not mark the initial speaker with a first-person subject pronoun, but Spicer's 'I watched and saw' invokes the 'ic geseah' or 'ic seah' (I beheld/saw ...) formula that opens a number of the Exeter riddles (occurring no less than twenty-three times in the surviving sequence). Spicer's poem is not itself a unitary riddle with a 'solution', but replete with riddling. The poem reverses the polarity of the obscure and the overt in the Old English poem (e.g. including multiple references to melting as enigmatic description) and distributes the creature on the wave of the Old English poem between the figures of the sailor and angel—so all the elements of riddle, hidden or overt, are rearranged into a newly enigmatic utterance.

The threatening angel addressed by Spicer's vocative variations is legible as an allusion to the riddle's paradoxically 'cymlic' (lovely) and 'hetegrim' (malice-cruel) creature, itself described in appositions whose variational or enumerative force is not transparently clear. Spicer's 'angel' is both differentiated from the waves themselves yet enigmatically remains the '[s]ource of the burning ocean', echoing the mother-daughter motif without totally remapping the paradox. In Spicer's earliest draft of this section, the sailor who melts in the paradoxically burning ocean is more explicitly like the iceberg of the riddle. In that draft, Spicer follows 'when God is short/ Of waters for his purpose, then the sea/ becomes a pool of fire' with 'bodies melt/ Upon its flame tide; Bodies melt/ Become the substance of their tidal pyre'. Taken as an allusion to the riddle, or even to Old English riddle-poetics in general, the repetitions about the melting sailor thus make sense as a variation. This recognition not only punningly underscores the poem's overall preoccupation with a 'source' (of the burning ocean/of the poem) but also with the degrees of redundancy in its variation as a possibility the poem takes from Old English verse.

The aforementioned earliest draft of the poem dates to either spring or autumn of 1947 during a trip Spicer took to Big Sur—predating his work in Brodeur's *Beowulf* seminar (although not his exposure to Old English) by at least a year (Figure 4.1).[77] So Spicer's variations may not register a direct response to Brodeur's insistence on 'identity of reference'. Nonetheless, they provide a mid-century ground for an account of variation, and the status of poetic diction within it, that responds to its variation's potential redundancy irrespective of the mid-century debates that eventually obscured the question of its aesthetic function. Specifically, Spicer's poem described above is useful in an effort to revisit Brodeur's investment in variation from the vantage of a non-representational poetics because it demonstrates a stylistic dimension of variation that suppresses neither its redundancy nor its semantic complexity and instead mobilizes the semantic and referential problems inherent in the partial redundancies of variation *as aesthetic functions*. The permutational and lexically accretive dynamics that compose the variations and variation-like structures are crucial to these mobilizations—varying sentences with partially overlapping repetitions or using appositive compound words with compounds that have the same base-element, or which repeat a word but add modifiers to it. These partial redundancies thus especially underscore the potential for the 'translatability' of each compound word to contribute to the aesthetics of variation—as if the variations of Spicer's poem perform a preemptive, rephrasing, (pre-digestive?) *ruminatio* with the compound words of the sort I describe in the previous chapter, breaking up compounds, recycling elements, and repurposing their referential functions into a quality of style.

As a vernacular verse-style, riddles were an abiding interest for Spicer, from the medieval to Lewis Carroll,[78] and at least two of his own riddles survive in his papers, probably penned the same year as this poem.[79] The riddling qualities of the poem above have already rendered the literal or figurative status of the variations' referents as at best obscure, if not intractably paradoxical. So it is not the case that repetitions have completely suppressed the semantic fluctuations within the variations, nor that their dance with redundancy and its subtle, implicit shifts of 'aspect' have suppressed the stylistic functions of the same. Rather, the referential and larger representational functions are variously rendered less salient in the overall rhetorical force of the poem or even redeployed as the scaffolding for these permutational lexical kinetics that combine translatability and partial redundancy. This is not a simple reversal of post-medieval western instrumentalizations of style (by meaning) so much as a feedback loop in which semantic functions become reinstrumentalized as perceptible aesthetic qualities. One could not claim very convincingly that these variations are not at all mimetic of the 'melting' undergone by a represented object (nor that these aesthetic qualities do not co-inhere at all with these representational functions). However, the permutational and accretive qualities of the variations coalesce as a *ductus*. Again governed by lexical movement, but no longer restricted to particular lexical positions, it interacts with syntax and prosody to trace a stuttering, heterogeneously referential, non-continuous, and recursive path through the poem—as if some Outside quality of the Ocean, unassimilable to the poem's representational capacities, has been taken into the poem.

In this way, variation becomes a mode of the poem's radical porosity—a crucial dimension of Spicer's early poetics in the context of its broader medievalism and its phenomenology, as well as a key feature in the recurrence of poems about sea and coast across Spicer's corpus (a function of a more general Californian regionalism).[80] As Katz explains, 'oceanic or fluvial imagery' in the early work often summons the later medieval trope of the human body as geographical microcosm that Spicer had studied in John Donne's poetics, and out of which a model of the poem emerges that incompletely and unevenly overlaps and interpenetrates with human corporeality.[81] Other early poems also rely on descriptions of sea infiltrating shore to representationally figure this interpenetrating and erosive porosity more explicitly.[82] And the motif lingers in Spicer's poetics, as in the second draft of a fragment from Spicer's Boston notebooks in which '[t]he waves are dark and hungry and as cruel/ As Little orphans. They cling with baby teeth to things'.[83] Here, too, poetic diction is porous and vulnerable to the sea, subject to irreverent arrangement and mastication by 'wild birds following the ships for their leavings/ Cawing at the dead sounds, snatching/ Each gutted word thrown

in their wake'—gutted, because, when asked for an appropriate
metaphor for the words, the poem opts for disemboweled bivalves:

> Roses? A clam's gut is more appropriate.
> Slimy and unyielding, you have to pull it
> Like a word in the throat
> Out of its own asshole.[84]

It is precisely the inelegance of the word and its arrangement—
scattered or clumped by the accidents of the sea, heavy with scent
and taste—as the undignified guts of shucked (if anatomically
inaccurate) mollusks, by which the poem, chewed up by the waves,
renders the ocean perceptible. We can already glimpse the Spicer
who, as Katz observes, resolutely rejects the 'mythological eco-poetics'
of many of his contemporaries, since (following one of Spicer's most
famous later poems), 'the crashing ocean speaks to us precisely
because it "means/ Nothing"'.[85] Instead, the ecopoetics and the
sensology in this poem—and, more acutely, in the *ductus* that issues
from the variations in 'Portrait'—lie not in any mode of positive
connection or comprehension, but in allowing the ocean into the
poem and rendering it perceptible to the human sensorium as a
kind of fragment of a foreign body, an indigestible registered by the
permutational lexical kinetics.

Apposition becomes less salient in Spicer's later work,[86] but Spicer's
first book, *After Lorca* (1957), more directly negotiates a modernist
redundancy-anxiety by radicalizing this irreverence for poetic diction.
Usually cited as a first flowering of Spicer's theory of the 'serial
poem', which heralds what Spicer himself considered his mature
work,[87] the book is composed of translations of the poetry of Federico
García Lorca both with and without highly unconventional interventions by Spicer (including entirely 'fictive' new poems and a fictive
preface attributed to Lorca himself),[88] and structured by six letters
addressed to Lorca. These letters unfold Spicer's theory of 'co-
respondence'—a poetics of translation and disclosure, rejecting
representation but still insisting on a dialogic, spectral concept of
tradition.[89] The second letter is prompted by a problem facing the
translator (and Spicer's cheeky solution) but it quickly moves on to
an anxiety about lexical economy:

> When I translate one of your poems and I come across words I do
> not understand, I always guess at their meanings. I am inevitably

right. A really perfect poem (no one has yet written one) could be perfectly translated by a person who did not know one word of the language it was written in. A really perfect poem has an infinitely small vocabulary.

It is very difficult. We want to transfer the immediate object, the immediate emotion to the poem—and yet the immediate always has hundreds of its own words clinging to it, short-lived and tenacious as barnacles. And it is wrong to scrape them off and substitute others. A poet is a time mechanic not an embalmer. The words around the immediate shrivel and decay like flesh around the body. No mummy-sheet of tradition can be used to stop the process. Objects, words must be led across time not preserved against it.

I yell 'Shit' down a cliff at an ocean. Even in my lifetime the immediacy of that word will fade. It will be dead as 'Alas'. But if I put the real cliff and the real ocean into the poem, the word 'Shit' will ride along with them, travel the time-machine until cliffs and oceans disappear.

Most of my friends like words too well. They set them under the blinding light of the poem and try to extract every possible connotation from each of them, every temporary pun, every direct or indirect connection—as if a word could become an object by mere addition of consequences. Others pick up words from the street, from their bars, from their offices and display them proudly in their poems as if they were shouting, 'See what I have collected from the American language. Look at my butterflies, my stamps, my old shoes!' What does one do with all this crap?

Words are what sticks to the real. We use them to push the real, to drag the real into the poem. They are what we hold on with, nothing else. They are as valuable in themselves as rope with nothing to be tied to.

I repeat—the perfect poem has an infinitely small vocabulary.[90]

Perhaps because the expressed desire to 'put the real cliff and the real ocean into the poem' speaks so well to the problems spelled out more fully in the following letter—in which Spicer so famously declares, 'I would like to make poems out of real objects', and which he selected as a formal 'statement on poetics' for Donald Allen's influential *New American poetry* anthology—it is seldom noticed that this letter can be read as a small treatise on poetic diction as such.[91] However, having suggested in the first letter the distinction that '[p]rose invents—poetry discloses',[92] and in light of the desire to get 'the real ocean' into the poem, the possibility of a poetic diction becomes at once a necessity and something of an embarrassment for both translator and 'original' poet.

The 'barnacle' words that inevitably multiply and accrete to the lexical economy of the poem beyond the asymptotic limit of an 'infinitely small vocabulary' are not without aesthetic implications. Clinging in the 'hundreds', the arthropods are small, common, inedible, given to unpleasant stench. They cluster and clump. Their impermanence is a major concern—both the instability of the logic of reference and the fact of historical language change itself—hence the centrality of the 'time-mechanic' to this letter.[93] Other problems lie in the temptation to fetishize meaning and mistake reference for an entanglement with reality ('to extract every possible connotation ...'), or to entertain a faux-gentile curatorial—or armchair anthropological—impulse that reduces words to the status of specimens and the philologist to the status of dilettante ('See what I have collected ...'). Each of these possibilities keys what Katz calls the 'adhesive' quality of the 'barnacle-words' to cluttering, garish effects that obscure the disclosive function of the poem—the poem that ostensibly would distinguish its vocabulary from that of prose. To the extent that the attempt to put 'the real ocean' into the poem takes its rejection of representation seriously, the words that constitute the conventional experience of 'poetry' are, paradoxically, at best accidental to the poem: redundancies, if not liabilities—'impermanent impurities', as Katz puts it.[94]

Yet, as a response to a multiplying, accretive lexical economy that issues from the adhesive properties of words, Spicer emphatically rejects the Eliotic effort to 'purify the dialect of the tribe',[95] along with the Eliotic 'mummy-sheet of tradition'.[96] To purify the poem of inelegant lexical clumps, like the religious acolyte or the priestly embalmer mummifying the sacred body or cleansing the cultic object so as to render it sacred (in the sense of 'forfeit to the divine', 'set apart' from the world), would equally obstruct the poem's porosity. A poem drawn from a vocabulary set apart from all worldly impurities could not possibly include a real ocean. Rather, Spicer implicitly posits a de-sacralized concept of poetic diction (a kind of poetic diction under erasure), in which the words of a poem are distinguished precisely by *not* setting them apart. Later on, Spicer will render this de-sacralization of the lexis more explicitly in 'A textbook of poetry', a serial poem from *The heads of the town up to the aether* (1960), where he coins the pun 'Lowghost' (on the Christian sense of *Logos*). The pun is a gesture to be understood with another pun, as 'not a play on words but a play between words, meaning come down to hang on a little cross for a while' (playing on the literal sense of 'metaphor' as to carry across).[97] Such words are more like specters subjected to and at the mercy of worldliness than the incarnation of the sacred. The only way in which the poem becomes 'part of and penetrated by the real'[98] is paradoxically to purposefully *not* select the 'appropriate' words for the poem.[99] The words are 'as valuable in themselves as rope with nothing to be tied to' and thus, astonishingly, accidental to the primary movement of the poem.

The ideal poem still ultimately has an 'infinitely small' vocabulary—but only because a properly poetic vocabulary cannot be distinguished from any other vocabulary, just as a given lexical economy could not be properly poetic or unpoetic. What distinguishes a poem is the extent to which the poem is porous to what is not the poem—including (in a dialectical reversal of 'organic unity' or 'individuality') the vocabulary which is not the vocabulary of the poem. The words of the poem, their 'efficiency' or arrangement, do not *themselves* (connotations, registers, etc., all included) constitute the poem's aesthetics but, by virtue of their adhesive force, their inclusion and arrangement may point to the shape and movement of the poem's porosity to the real—whether emotion or ocean.

Variation, permutation, and lexical movement: the 'real ocean' in *Beowulf*

In finally returning to the aesthetics of variation in *Beowulf*, Spicer's propensity to regionalism (and especially a Californian coastal geography) in these experiments in apposition and the economy of poetic diction has a kind of useful, if incidental felicity. Apposite Spicer's West Coast 'real cliff' and 'real ocean', and his variations on the waves penned at Big Sur, we find the Scandinavian seas and shores in the two sea-voyages of the main narrative in *Beowulf*—of Beowulf and his men traveling to Denmark, and their return voyage to Geatland. These passages are key to mid-century debates about variation, and because they will also allow us to contest conventional assumptions about the relationship of the poem's aesthetics to physical geography, they provide a compelling point of comparison to Spicer's experiments in variation. Rereading these passages with Spicer's experiments as a comparative horizon generates an account of the aesthetic functions of variation unburdened by either redundancy-anxiety or leaps to resolve questions of style on the level of meaning. The aesthetic functions of lexical accretions, partial redundancies, and permutational recombinations of compound words will recalibrate how we understand the contested status of the 'reality' of the often-debated sea and sea-cliffs featured in these two passages within a non-representational horizon and an ecopoetical trajectory.

Like Spicer's corpus, the literary world of *Beowulf,* and indeed almost every type of extant Old English writing, is interpenetrated with references to the sea.[100] Heide Estes explains that in Old English narrative, the sea 'is not simply a static stage for human actions, but a very strong presence, interacting with, influencing, and affecting the human characters'.[101] And, as Kelley M. Wickham-Crowley contends, in artefacts of the Old English period, 'the mutability of the "edge" between land and water … fits a way of thinking that considered land-water intersections as a habit of perception or vision'.[102]

Traditionally, however, critics have been highly circumspect about how to understand the 'reality' of the littoral geographies and oceanographies of *Beowulf*. Unconvinced by earlier philologist Gregor Sarrazin's claim to recognize the poem's geography of Denmark in present-day Lejre and environs,[103] Klaeber doubts that the poet 'had a clear knowledge of Northern geography', and considers the poem's 'topographical hints', especially the 'sea-cliffs', as merely 'part of a conventional description based on notions of English scenery'.[104] Although the editors of the most recent edition of Klaeber's *Beowulf* draw on archaeological excavations of three large halls at Lejre in order to keep open hypotheses about the poem's relation to geography,[105] they reaffirm Klaeber's assumptions about seas and headlands.[106] Estes, whose ecological reading does take seriously a different sense of the 'reality' of *Beowulf*'s seas, agrees that, in terms of reference, 'the sea depicted here is the imagined sea of the author and/or scribe of *Beowulf* rather than the observed sea of any actual traveler'.[107]

Closer to home for Brodeur and his students, oral-formulaic critics took up the repetitive parallelism within and between the sea-crossings in terms of formulaic type-scenes or themes in which the 'reality' of the sea and the mode of reference to it is implicitly that of traditional expression.[108] Robinson argues along different lines that in the variations of *Beowulf* that describe the natural world, coastlines included, 'it is the typical rather than the picturesque detail which is usually emphasized'.[109] In these readings, under the assumption of a representational horizon, the stylization of the sea and cliffs proscribes their reality from entering the poem.

And yet, Marijane Osborn and Gillian R. Overing explore the sea-voyage passages through 'a suspicion, and then a conviction, that "real" things mattered [in *Beowulf*], held their own and their own existence—that the *Beowulf* poet, for example ... knew in some measure of the visual reality of which he wrote'.[110] The record and analysis of their 'reinvention' of Beowulf's voyage to Heorot (and Osborn's reinvention of the voyage back)—not as a 'replica' voyage but as a 'speculative, imaginative, and fictional enterprise'[111]—left the two scholars with the conviction that the sea-crossings are not indifferent to a real sea with 'a route that may actually be traversed'.[112] Osborn and Overing thus position their 'reinvention' as a reversal of Klaeber's position claims about *Beowulf*'s seas and shores, affirming 'the poet's practical understanding of what he was talking about'.[113]

Addressing the text of the sea-crossing passages themselves, Osborn and Overing variously describe the narrative of the voyage *to* Heorot as among the most 'beautiful' and the most 'exciting' of the poem.[114] Narratively, the first passage follows directly from Beowulf's resolution to come to Hrothgar's aid, and the return voyage follows the return to the ship after Beowulf's parting embrace with Hrothgar. In these contexts, they offer, as Edward B. Irving notes, a tonal contrast to the 'disturbing suggestions' of the passages that they follow[115]—even as critics note their superfluity to the main narrative.[116] Both passages are replete with variations, and with 'sea-lexemes' and 'shore-lexemes'—either as nouns for sea or shore, or as components of compound nouns or adjectives for sea-related things (like weather). To better exhibit the resemblance and likely formulaic qualities of the passages, I provide them both here (with 'sea-lexemes' in bold and 'shore-lexemes' underlined):

Fiftyna sum
sund<u>wudu</u> sohte;   secg wisade,

lagucræftig mon   landgemyrcu.
Fyrst forð gewat;   **flota** wæs on **yðum,**
bat under beorge.   Beornas gearwe
on stefn stigon.   **Streamas** wundon,
sund wið sande.   Secgas bæron
on bearm nacan   beorhte frætwe,
guðsearo geatolic;   guman ut scufon,
weras on wilsið   wudu bundenne.
Gewat þa ofer **wægholm   winde** gefysed
flota famiheals   fugle gelicost,
oð þæt ymb antid   oþres dogores
wundenstefna   gewaden hæfde,
þæt ða liðende   land gesawon,
brimclifu blican,   beorgas steape,
side **sæ**næssas;   þa wæs **sund** liden,
eoletes æt ende.   Þanon up hraðe
Wedera leode   on wang stigon,
sæwudu sældon,   syrcan hrysedon,
guðgewædo;   Gode þancedon
þæs þe him y**þ**lade   eaðe wurdon. (ll. 207b–228)

                    A certain one of the fifteen (men)
sought the **swim**-wood; a man explained—
a **sea**-smart man—the land-marks.
The moment passed on; the **floater** was on the **waves,**
the boat under the cliff. Men eagerly
sprang up on the prow. **Currents** encoiled,
the **deep** against the gravel. Men carried
shining ornaments into the bosom of the ship,
splendid war-gear. The warriors pushed out,
men on the desired-path in the bound-up wood.
Went then over the **wave-swell,** pushed by **wind,**
the **foamy**-necked **floater,** most like a bird,
until that time on the second day
the coil-prowed (ship) had advanced
so that those sailors beheld land:
surf-cliffs flashing, steep heights,
wide **sea**-promontories; then the **deep** was
traversed, the crossing at an end. Thence hastily up,
the people of the Weders sprang onto the plains,
moored the **sea**-wood, rattled (their) mail shirts,
war-garments; gave thanks to God
that the **wave-paths** became smooth for them.[117]

Þa wæs on <u>sande</u>   sægeap naca
hladen herewædum,   hringedstefna
mearum ond maðmum;   mæst hlifade
ofer Hroðgares   hordgestreonum.
He þæm batwearde   bunden golde
swurd gesealde,   þæt he syðþan wæs
on meodubence   maþme þy weorþra,
yrfelafe.   Gewat him on naca
drefan deop **wæter**,   Dena <u>land</u> ofgeaf.
Þa wæs be mæste   merehrægla sum,
segl sale fæste;   sundwudu þunede;
no þær **wegflotan**   **wind** ofer **yðum**
siðes getwæfde;   sægenga for,
fleat **famigheals**   forð ofer **yðe**,
bundenstefna   ofer **brimstreamas**,
þæt hie Geata <u>clifu</u>   ongitan meahton,
cuþe <u>næssas</u>;   ceol up geþrang,
lyftgeswenced   on <u>lande</u> stod.
Hreþe wæs æt **holme**   hyðweard geara
se þe ær lange tid   leofra manna
fus æt **faroðe**   feor wlatode;
sælde to <u>sande</u>   sidfæþme scip
oncerbendum fæst,   þy læs hym **yþa** ðrym
wudu wynsuman   forwrecan meahte. (ll. 1896–1919)

Then the **sea-vaulted** vessel was on the <u>gravel</u> (shore)
bloated with battle-garments, the ring-prowed (ship)
with horses and treasures. The mast soared
over Hrothgar's hoard-treasures.
He (Beowulf), to that boat-guard, gave a sword
wound with gold, that he, afterwards, was
more esteemed on the mead-bench by that treasure,
that heirloom. They went out on the ship
to churn the **deep water**, shoved off the land of the Danes.
Then was by the mast, a certain sea-garment,
a sail fastened with rope; the sea-wood groaned;
not at all did **wind** over **waves** detach the **swell-floater**
from the path; the sea-goer traveled,
foamy-throated (ship) floated forward across the **waves**,
the curled-prow over the **whitecap-currents**,
until they could reach the <u>cliffs</u> of the Geats,
known <u>headlands</u>. The ship pushed on up,
wind-thrust, rested on <u>land</u>.

> Hurriedly, the **harbour**-guard was ready at the **billowing water**,
> he that for a long time before, for the dear man,
> frequently at the <u>shallows</u>, gazed out far;
> he moored the wide-bosomed ship to the <u>gravel shore</u>
> firm with anchor-ropes, lest the force of the **waves**
> might crash away the most pleasant wooden vessel.

As Kinshiro Oshitari argues, the striking parallels and repetitions between the two passages, including two of only three surviving occurrences of *famigheals* (foamy-necked, as adjective and substantive adjective),[118] underscore their function as a structural frame for the events of the poem set at Heorot,[119] and, more to our purposes, give 'the impression of isolation of land surrounded by the sea'.[120] And indeed, both passages are brimming with lexical elements that refer to or conventionally modify references to the sea, as well as shoreline.

Focusing only on the 'sea-lexemes', the first passage includes a total of sixteen such elements, seven of which occur as nominal simplexes, six as the limiting-element of a nominal compound, one as the limiting-element of an adjectival compound, and two (previously uncounted) which combine into the base and limiting-element of a single nominal compound (*wægholm*). The passage comprising the voyage back includes a total of nineteen such elements, seven that occur as nominal simplexes, one as an adjectival simplex, four as the limiting-element of a nominal compound, and two as the limiting-element of an adjectival compound (including the participial *lyft-geswenced*), and two pairs which each constitute a nominal compound (*wegflotan, brimstreamas*). Lexical elements related to sea, sea-weather, and shore topography repeat within and between both passages—whether as variously declined simplexes or as an element of a compound: *sund/sund-* (three times in the first passage, once in the second), *yþ/yþ-* (twice in the first passage, three times in the second), *flota* (twice in the first passage), *stream/-stream* (once in each passage), *weg-* (once in each passage), *holm/-holm* (once in each passage), *wind* (once in each passage), *famig-* (once in each passage), *brim-* (once in each passage), *sæ-* (twice in the first passage, twice in the second), *land/land-* (twice in the first passage, twice in the second), *sand* (once in the first passage, twice in the second), *clif/-clif* (once in each passage), *næss* (once in each passage).

With this surfeit of sea- and shore-lexemes, the description of the voyage to Heorot in particular took on the aspect of a cause célèbre in the study of variation at mid-century. For Brodeur, the moment in which the sailors 'land gesawon/ brimclifu blican, beorgas steape/ side sænæssas' (ll. 221b–223a) (beheld land:/ surf-cliffs flashing, steep heights,/ wide sea-promontories) is the perfect emblem of the limits of variation as defined by his sense of 'identity of reference': since Brodeur takes the noun phrases as 'enumerating the various features of the Danish coastline' and lacking a common referent, he classifies the construction as 'parallelism without variation'.[121] Disagreeing with Brodeur, Robinson takes the construction as 'a four-part variation in which the general term *land* is varied by three more precise terms of "land fronting sea"', adding that 'they suggest different aspects of the same referent', especially as 'the poet's usual procedure in describing the approach of voyagers to land is to supply a variation for the shoreline'.[122] Greenfield in turn, as already noted, pushes the mimetic implications of Robinson's claim further, taking the construction as 'a *combination* of series and variation … a logical order of perception of the *same* elements of the landscape'.[123] Later in the century, Osborn and Overing record experiencing an entirely different, procedural mode of reference in the construction, reporting that in their 'reinvention' of the voyage, 'these landmarks appear in just this order so spectacularly that one wonders whether the poet did not know something about this approach, either personally or by hearsay', and suggesting that the construction may bear the traces of an abbreviated 'verbal sea chart' of the sort necessary to early medieval sailors for coastal navigation and tricky landfalls.[124]

Yet, aside from the variation of 'streamas' (currents) with 'sund' (the deep) in the first passage (ll. 212b–213a), along with the references to the Danish cliffs noted above and the variation of 'Geata clifu' (cliffs of the Geats) with 'cuþe næssas' (known promontories) (ll. 1911a–1912a), the sea- and shore-lexemes do not constitute the bulk of the variations in these otherwise variation-rich passages—nor are the sea or the shore, despite the thalassocentric and littoralocentric lexicon of these voyages, even the main objects of representation. The passages are not at first glance 'porous' to the world in their openness to a nonpoetic lexicon. Rather, they accrete around conventionally poetic variations that take elements of the human heroic world as their objects of representation. The variation of 'beorhte frætwe/ guðsearo geatolic' (ll. 214b–215a) (shining ornaments/ splendid war-gear), for example, describes the armor and gear that will intimidate the harbor guard on the arrival in Denmark, and the variation of 'syrcan' (mail shirts) and 'guðgewædo' (battle-garments) literally sounds the end of the voyage with reference to what the warriors conspicuously rattle (*hrissan*) as they exit the boat (ll. 226b–228a). Robinson cites the variation of 'guman' (warriors/men) with 'weras' (men) (ll. 215b–216a) as one of the more rare instances in which variations are constituted by 'mere synonyms'[125]—and even if we take the varians in this construction as constituted by the entire noun-phrase 'weras on wilsið wudu bundenne' (l. 216) (men on the desired-path in the bound-up wood), the additive component situates the men in a high-status vessel on a heroic endeavour. Rather than lavish any variation on the location of the ship 'on sande' (on the gravel) or the water it soon enters during the return voyage, the variation that launches the voyage describes the sword Beowulf gives to the boat-guard as 'maþme' (treasure) and as an 'yrfelafe' (heirloom) (ll. 1902b–1903a).

Moreover, sea-lexemes that do occur in variations are, most of the time, subordinated either as limiting words in compounds or with phrases modifying the ship as an element of a heroic human action for which the sea is seemingly but background. Perhaps most obviously here, we can cite the variation describing the boat awaiting Beowulf and his men on the journey out: 'flota wæs on yðum,/ bat under beorge' (ll. 210b–211a) (the floater was on the waves,/ boat under the cliff)—another variation whose status is contested at mid-century. Brodeur and Robinson only consider 'flota .../ bat' (floater .../ boat) as a variation, but Greenfield considers the prepositional phrases as 'referring to the same location' and another instance of 'the implication of movement in variation ... channeled into a changing perspective'.[126] In either case, the representational energy of the passage lies in the grammatical subject of both components, *flota* (floater) and *bat* (boat, ship).

This phenomenon is more subtle on the level of sea-lexemes serving as elements of compounds that constitute components of variations. In the first voyage, for example, *lagu-* (sea-) only occurs as a limiting-element in the variation 'secg .../ lagucræftig mon' (ll. 208b–209a) (man .../ sea-smart man), not contributing in any way to a representation of the sea but specifying the (navigational) nature of the specialized knowledge that defines this person. In the second voyage, *sæ-* modifies the spaciously curved shape of the ship in a variation that highlights the ship's status (defined by a substantive reference to its ornate prow, and loaded up with treasure and wealth): 'sægeap naca/ hladen herewædum, hringedstefna/ mearum ond maðmum' (ll. 1896b–1898a) (sea-vaulted vessel/ bloated with battle-garments, ring-prowed ship/ with horses and treasures).[127]

Even in the most 'sea-full' variation describing the ship—a more rare instance of sentence-level variation—the representational economy favors the 'easy effortless power' of heroic action that Irving finds in the sea-voyages: 'sægenga for,/ fleat famigheals forð ofer yðe' (ll. 1908b–1909) (the sea-goer traveled,/ the foamy-necked [ship] floated forward across the waves).[128] If we append the following line, 'bundenstefna ofer brimstreamas' (l. 1910) (the curled-prow over the white-cap currents), to these in a looser variation-like construction, the ostensible object of representation in the total construction remains, as Irving puts it, something 'emphatically done to sea'.[129] On the level of the variation, the conventional referential target of the lexeme '*sæ*' is lost to the 'going' of the ship, just as the waves and even the choppy *brimstreamas* (white-cap currents, surge-streams) are relegated to serve as indicators of the 'rapidity of the journey, and the feeling of human control'.[130]

Despite the density of sea-lexemes in these passages about sea-crossings, the representational functions of these famous variations give us a sea that is either a backdrop for human heroic action or, as Hugh Magennis characterizes it, 'an ever-present feature of the setting', but only within 'the completeness of the poem's subjection of physical reality to the expression of mood'.[131] Although Peter Clemoes does not take the sea in *Beowulf* as a purely passive 'setting' (and, in distinction to Greenfield, argues that the passage lacks a particularized perspective), his characterization of the representational economy of the journey to Heorot is also particularly telling: '[t]his journey is not a traveling through space objectively conceived … it is a qualitative development by which the uncomplicated action of the ship is replaced by, issues in, makes directly possible, another, fuller, more significant action by the men.'[132]

Yet the lexical economy of the sea-voyage narratives is not so neatly teleological and totalized as to transparently sublimate into

a simple heroic object. Despite Clemoes' conception of the voyage
to Heorot as expressing heroic characterization in action, the sea-
lexemes seem to force him to cede some ground to the sea, acknowl-
edging that 'the interaction of the boat and sea is what matters':[133]

> That this interaction is organic is borne out by the vocabulary: the
> sea is at first waves, then currents with depth, and finally a *wægholm*,
> a whole sea of waves; the boat changes from a utilitarian thing of
> specific parts, a prow and a hold, to a whole object designed to
> withstand the sea, *wudu bundenne*, and finally becomes a thing of
> pure movement, a foamy-necked floater like a bird. Both boat and
> sea undergo development within their distinctive beings.[134]

Clemoes offers this as evidence that the poem is primarily interested
in representing the 'inner principles' of things.[135] But it also seems
to suggest that the accretions of sea-lexemes adhering to the variations
of the passage lend to it an aesthetic quality (movement)—and that
this quality depends on and overtakes the subordination of the
sea-lexemes within the conventional representational logic of the
passage, eventually destabilizing the very referential identity of its
most salient objects of representation.

Indeed, as John Niles writes in comparing the style of this passage
to insular styles of early medieval metalwork, '[t]here is no point
of stasis, such as is required with set literary descriptions'.[136] Overing
attributes this dynamism in the description of the voyage to Heorot
in large part to the 'speed and intensity' generated by the metonymic
mode of juxtaposed compound terms.[137] I would argue that in tandem
with this quality of metonymy-driven 'pace',[138] in both sea-crossing
passages, the sea-lexeme encrusted variations do not univocally direct
the energy of their 'dynamism' towards representation. Just as the
partial redundancy of the variations throws their referential teleology
into play, it also allows the repetition of sea-lexemes, regardless of
their grammatical function, to surface in a surfeit of references to
the sea, and for those *references* to take on an aesthetic function.
Under these conditions, we can no longer assume that we can account
for or assess the 'reality' of references to the sea in these passages
entirely within a representational horizon.

Taking up some of the slack, a permutational lexical movement
traverses the variations. Recall the clumps of proximate sea-lexemes
in the description of the return voyage. The element *sæ-* (sea-)

occurs first subordinated to its function as limiting term within the compound *sægeap* (sea-vaulted, sea-curved), itself in turn only a modifier of *naca* (ship) and thus part of the variatum for which *hringedstefna* (ring-prowed [thing]) is the varians. In the full long-line 'Þa wæs on sande sægeap naca' (then the sea-curved ship was on the gravel shore), the alliteration skips the first stress. This is a completely normal possibility of Old English prosody—but here it subtly lends extra emphasis to the juxtaposition of *sande* (sand) with the element *sæ-* as alliterating elements of the line. The alliteration on 'sande' and 'sæ-' breaks up or at least softens the syntactic subordination of limiting-element to base-word, the two lexemes doubly entangled in their sonic contiguity and their semantic fields as sea- and shore-lexemes, separated only by one un-stressed syllable. As a synecdoche for ship, the substantive adjective *hringedstefna* (ring-prowed) ostensibly follows the general pattern of referentially 'clarifying' variations.[139] However, as the energy of the prosodical coupling of sea- and shore-lexemes tumbles over the enjambment with the following line, it crashes into the base-word of the varians, *hringed-* (curled, ringed), as an element that might aptly—if not conventionally—suggest the curling movements of water and gravel or sand at the shore. As another way to read this in light of the translatability of the previous chapter and Spicer's experiments with variation, we might say that the partial redundancy of the variations thus further launches the kinetics of the compounds by underscoring their potential for not only rephrasing but also permutational recombination. Even if only briefly, this tumbling together of a simplex and elements from different compounds cuts across the variation, briefly severing *hringed-* from its base-word. This brief reframing of *hringed-* as part of an accretion of sea- and shore-lexemes additionally underscores that the synecdoche *hringedstefna* does not share the same literal referent as *naca*. As this recognition weakens the possibility of any 'identity of reference', it allows the aesthetic implications of the interactions of sea- and shore-lexemes—these lexical kinetics—a chance to overtake the representation of the ship in directing the *ductus*.

As subsequent elements of compounds that, taken on their own, would register as references to sea or shore then accrete in clusters throughout the passage, the verse invites further lexical permutations that cut across the variations. And since sea-lexemes otherwise subordinated to their function as the base-words of compounds generally occur as the first element of the compound, the prosody of Old English verse tends to emphasize and aurally link those elements when such a compound occurs in a stressed position. In this way, the passage surges with pulsing lexical elements associated with seascape topography and the morphology of bodies of water, overwhelming the reader with instances of these elements as if they were, if only briefly, their own lexical 'free-agents', available to participate in a kind of recombinatory and permutational movement similar to—if less concentrated than—the partially overlapping vocative variations of Spicer's early sea-poem. As a *ductus*, this hiving lexical motion draws attention to the sea and away from the ostensible objects of representation, breaking up the components of variations, repurposing their referential functions, and scrambling and scuffing the laminar flow of the poem's representational process.

We are thus invited to hear the *weg* (wave) of *wegflota* (wave-floater) crashing as the very *wind ofer yðum* (wind over the waves); the *bunden* (bound, wound, coiled) in *bundenstefna* (coiled-prow) recombined with *brimstreamas* (surf-streams), to modify the *brimstreamas*, not unnaturalistically, as coiled or winding surge-streams. And similar dynamics play out in the passage describing the voyage out as well—as in the interactions between and the sheer density of the sea- and shore-lexemes in the alliterating compounds, *lagucræftig* (water-smart) and *landgemyrcu* (land-marks), so near to the variation that begins, 'flota wæs on yðum' (the floater/ship was on the waves'), in the b-verse of the subsequent line. In these two passages, as the mass and spread of sea- and shore-lexemes are caught up in the dynamics of variation (and the attendant effects of *both* redundancy and subtle shifts of meaning this makes available), a ruminative, permutational movement generates vibrating lexical fragments, clumps, and piles that cannot help but mark the poem's porosity or adhesion to the sea even as it is decidedly representing something else. The impossibility of redundancy that conditions and is forbidden by variation thus activates non-representational functions of even the referential dimensions of poetic diction.

In his post-war avant-garde, Spicer was able to dream of a purely de-sacralized poetic diction that would allow his poem to translate an unassimilable Outside—an Ocean—by allowing it to enter and disrupt the poem. Given that Old English poetic diction is largely defined by its status as a specialized (set apart) lexicon, the vocabulary of *Beowulf* must collude with the aesthetic habits of rhetorical and syntactic patterns—here, permutational movements—for its worldly porosity. Instead of allowing variation or any play with redundancy to facilitate the inclusion of words that are 'not the vocabulary of the poem', these passages of *Beowulf* rely on variation, compound words, and partial repetition (in combination with prosodical syntax) to launch a set of kinetic, lexically ruminative permutations that would constitute those words that are not the vocabulary of the poem and generate the *ductus* that renders their inclusion—and the poem's porosity—sensible.

This suggestion simultaneously radicalizes and de-ocularcentrizes Blomfield's influential notion from the late 1930s that in instances of variation, the *Beowulf* poet 'sees with the poet's eye which splits and recombines the elements of everyday perceptions'—with the emphasis here on the kinetics of *splits and recombines* as a perceptible quality of the poem's aesthetics, borne out in the interaction of compound diction and variation.[140] Here, one might conceive of the poem's perceptual style in terms an aesthetics of such a smashing apart and recombining—not of already congealed percepts, but of *lexemes*.[141] Citing Blomfield's remark, Niles suggests that, 'rather than speak of the "lack of realism" of the poetry of this period, one might better speak of its possession of a set of conventions that permit it to express unerringly what it considers most important ... these matters do not have to do with the outward appearance of people or things, or with their external relations, but with their ethical or spiritual significance'.[142] While this is quite correct in many cases, in the leap from representational realism to stylized expressions of spiritual significance we miss the possibility that the verse remains interested in a physical reality it does not directly express—that the poem, *precisely as a stylization*, may yet render perceptible to its readers a 'reality' that it does not announce or privilege in the terms that govern its representational or expressive economy.

One might tentatively suggest that these permutational inclusions register an ill-defined but nonetheless intense 'reality' of the sea exerting a force on the poem's variations, dislodging them from positions saturated by representational *dignitas* and scuffing them like little patches of poetic Velcro, leaving behind accretions of diction that are, like Spicer's 'Lowghosts' and 'barnacles', aesthetically adhesive to elements of the physical world they do not represent. What was for Brodeur and his followers only the possibility of more or less original, more or less artful, more or less redundant references to a static representational 'setting' thus emerges as an invisible movement of sea and shore indirectly disturbing the representational processes of the poem. Even in *Beowulf*, as Spicer learned, words are all we have to hold on with. But this does not mean that the most adhesive or worldly quality of words is found in representation. Whether or not one can or cannot imagine the sea and sea-cliffs of *Beowulf* as a particular 'real' ocean or sea-cliff, it does not mean that the reality of the ocean and the cliff are not the Lowghosts haunting the aesthetics of the poem.

Notes

1 *AOB*, p. 253.
2 *Ibid.*, Appendix C, pp. 271–83, and p. 39.
3 Kl. 3, p. lxv, quoted in *AOB*, p. 39. The same sentiment is repeated in Kl. 4, p. cxviii.
4 Kl. 3, p. lxv.
5 Robinson, 'Two aspects', p. 128.
6 Calder, 'The study of style', p. 9.
7 Turner, *History of the Anglo-Saxons*, pp. 264, 270–1, quoted in Calder, 'The study of style', pp. 8–9. Robinson notes similar comments by John J. Conybeare. See Robinson, 'Two aspects', p. 128 n. 4. On race and colonialism in Turner's writings, see Ellard, *Anglo-Saxon(ist) pasts,* pp. 61–100; Young, 'Whiteness and time', p. 44.
8 Robinson, 'Two aspects', pp. 128–9, citing Heinzel, *Über den Stil der altergermanischen Poesie*, pp. 3–9, 49. A slightly more detailed version of this analysis can be found in Robinson, 'Variation', pp. 1–3. And see Calder, 'The study of style', pp. 16–17.
9 Robinson, 'Two aspects', p. 129; and see Robinson, 'Variation', pp. 1–4 for further detail.
10 Robinson, 'Two aspects', p. 129; Calder, 'The study of style', p. 35.
11 Calder, 'The study of style', pp. 36–7; the enumerated list is loosely translated from Paetzel, *Die Variationen*, p. 4.
12 Robinson, 'Variation', p. 5; citing Paetzel, *Die Variationen*, pp. 12–23.
13 On the relative importance given to Brodeur's argument, see e.g. O'Brien O'Keeffe, 'Diction', pp. 96–7; Greenfield, *Interpretation*, pp. 64–5; Calder, 'The study of style', pp. 36–7; Robinson, 'Variation', pp. 8–10.

14 *AOB*, p. 272.
15 *Ibid.*, p. 274.
16 *Ibid.*, p. 40.
17 *Ibid.*, p. 274.
18 *Ibid.*, p. 41.
19 Robinson, 'Variation', p. 25 n. 49. Robinson also finds the same problem in definitions that do not limit the components of variation to occurring within a single clause, or adjacent clauses when on the level of the sentence—because 'they would not be apprehended as a restatement' (p. 21 n. 43).
20 *AOB*, p. 279.
21 Robinson, 'Variation', p. 20.
22 Robinson, "Two aspects', p. 129. And see Robinson, 'Variation', pp. 5–6, 12–15; Robinson, *Beowulf and the appositive style*, p. 3. Robinson's modifications, unmarked in the statement quoted here, make Paetzel's definition more strict, while loosening restrictions that Robinson finds arbitrary or contradictory. This includes making the role of apposition more unshakable and ruling out Paetzel's exclusions of 'explanatory appositions', 'recurring epithets', and 'pronominal variation' (pronoun + appositive).
23 Robinson, 'Two aspects', pp. 129–30.
24 Leslie, 'Analysis of stylistic devices', pp. 258–9.
25 Primary to what follows, see Greenfield, 'Beowulf" 207b–228'; Greenfield, *Interpretation*, pp. 60–5; Quirk 'Poetic language', p. 158; Brady, 'The synonyms for "sea" in *Beowulf*', pp. 22–32; Harris, 'Techniques of pacing'. For an overview of the late twentieth century, see O'Brien O'Keeffe, 'Diction', pp. 94–8. See also (a non-exhaustive list): Shaar, 'On a new theory'; Malone, 'Variation in *Widsith*'; Taylor, 'Themes of death'; Bolton, '"Variation" in *The battle of* Brunanburh'; Whallon, 'The diction of *Beowulf*', 'Formulas for heroes'; Fry, 'Variation and economy'; Ramey, 'Variation and the poetics of oral performance'.
26 *AOB* p. 279, p. 39.
27 Robinson, 'Variation', pp. 137–9, 153. Aspects of Robinson's dissertation are superseded by his later essay ('Two aspects') and his monograph, *The appositive style in Beowulf*. However, it was long taken as an unavoidable contributor to the debate in its moment, e.g., Greenfield, *Interpretation*, pp. 64, 68–9, 73–4, 78–9, 83. And see Osborn, '"Verbal sea charts"', p. 443.
28 Robinson, 'Variation', pp. 140–1, 144, 145, 147.
29 This observation is anticipated in Bartlett, *The larger rhetorical patterns*, pp. 9–48. Robinson admits as much (see 'Variation', p. 145 n. 32). It is also reaffirmed much later in concept by Pasternack, who

cites his dissertation but disagrees with his examples. See Pasternack, *Textuality*, pp. 134–5, and 134–5 n. 35; see also pp. 121, 184.

30 Robinson, 'Two aspects', p. 130. See Robinson, 'Variation', pp. 147–51. All of these possibilities for variation are rehearsed again in Robinson, *Beowulf and the appositive style*, pp. 60–1.

31 Robinson, 'Variation', p. 142.

32 Robinson, 'Two aspects', pp. 138–42.

33 *AOB*, p. 39.

34 *Ibid.*, pp. 61, 273.

35 *Ibid.*, pp. 52, 69, 221.

36 *Ibid.*, p. 68.

37 *Ibid.*, p. 272.

38 Brady, 'The synonyms for "sea" in *Beowulf*', p. 32. Italics in original. Oshitari counts thirty-one 'sea words'. On the difficulty of getting a precise count of references to the sea in *Beowulf*, see Oshitari, 'The sea in *Beowulf*', p. 4.

39 Bonjour, *Twelve Beowulf papers*, pp. 116, 119.

40 Greenfield, *Interpretation*, p. 64, citing *AOB*, p. 40.

41 Greenfield, *Interpretation*, p. 64.

42 *Ibid.*

43 *Ibid.*, pp. 78–9.

44 Greenfield, '"Beowulf" 207b–228', p. 88.

45 Greenfield, *Interpretation*, pp. 68–9. Robinson later affirms these possibilities. See Robinson, 'Variation', p. 130.

46 Greenfield, *Interpretation*, p. 83.

47 *Ibid.*

48 O'Brien O'Keeffe, 'Diction', pp. 97, 100.

49 *Ibid.*, and see Lord, *Singer of tales*, pp. 30, 65–7.

50 Greenfield, *Interpretation*, p. 83.

51 Brady, 'The synonyms for "sea" in *Beowulf*', p. 44.

52 Robinson, *Beowulf and the appositive style*, p. 27.

53 *Ibid.*, pp. 24–5, 5–6.

54 *Ibid.*, pp. 24–5. Note that Tolkien's effort to relate macro-structure to the structure of the long line was neither totally novel nor met with universal acceptance. See Calder, 'The study of style', p. 17, on Heinzel's effort. And see Sisam, *Structure*, p. 21, citing van Meurs, '*Beowulf* and literary criticism'.

55 Robinson, *Beowulf and the appositive style*, p. 81; but see Pasternack, *Textuality*, pp. 24–6 and 24–5 n. 91.

56 Robinson, *Beowulf and the appositive style*, pp. 60–1.

57 Greenfield, *Interpretation*, p. 82.

58 See Remein, 'Decorate', pp. 96–9.

59 Pound, *Early writings*, pp. 209–10; Pound, *Literary essays*, p. 4.
60 Nicholls, *Modernisms*, p. 171; Pound, *Early writings*, p. 288.
61 Pound, *Early writings*, pp. 285, 289.
62 Olson, 'Projective verse', pp. 240, 243.
63 *Ibid.*, p. 243.
64 *Ibid.*
65 On negotiating this rupture, see Katz, *The poetry*, pp. 19–22, 54–5, 63.
66 *MV*, pp. 6–10.
67 Katz, *The poetry*, p. 24. See JSB, Box 6, folder 32.
68 Katz, *The poetry*. This shift is further underscored by a growing disdain for naive application of the pathetic fallacy (à la Matthew Arnold) in the earliest working titles in the manuscripts: 'A portrait of the artist as a young beach', 'Dover Beach – 1947', and 'Dover bitch' (JSP, Box 6, folder 32).
69 *MV*, p. 8.
70 *Ibid.*, pp. 9–10.
71 Robinson, 'Variation', p. 102.
72 *Ibid.*, pp. 16–17; the terms were subsequently taken up in Calder, 'The study of style', p. 37, and Greenfield, *Interpretation*, p. 65.
73 Following references to the drafts of this poem refer to JSP, Box 6, folders 32 and 43.
74 *MV*, p. 7.
75 On the 'mother-daughter' riddle motif and this riddle, see Tupper, *The riddles of the Exeter Book*, pp. 147–8.
76 Riddle 33.
77 The envelope on which Spicer wrote the draft is addressed to Spicer's friend, 'Big' Gene Wahl, at a Big Sur address, postmarked March 13, 1947 (JSP, Box 6, folder 43). Spicer took a trip to Big Sur in spring or autumn of 1947 (or both? See *PBLG*, p. 21; but see 'Chronology' in *MV*, p. 49). Another manuscript of the poem includes a note that mentions meeting folklorist Jaime de Angulo—an event that did occur on that trip—while asking a friend (probably Duncan) to type and comment on the poem (see 'Chronology' in *MV*, p. 249; JSP, Box 6, folder 32). I have not been able to locate any of Spicer's academic records at UC Berkeley *prior* to the start of his MA degree in autumn 1947, but given Spicer's and Blaser's OE lexicography project, it is difficult to believe that he had no prior exposure to Old English literature (possibly with Brodeur). In September of 1947, Spicer was enrolled in Kantorowicz's History 152a-b or 151a-b (the handwriting is unclear), which correlates with the course descriptions and lecture notes for Kantorowicz's courses on 'English constitutional history I-II,

or 'Medieval England' (Spicer's undated notebooks might correlate with either, but the dates on Kantorowicz's notes suggest the former). These include lectures on Roman Britain, the *Chronicle* in Old English, Bede, Gildas, OE period Charters, the laws of Kentish Kings, the Laws of Ine, and a number of extended exhortations on historiography (see Kantorowicz, Lecture notes).

78 *PBLG*, pp. 2, 57, 113, 137, 189, 207; *House*, p. 50; Spicer, 'Book of Gawain', in *MV*, p. 331.

79 The pieces register generically as pure riddle and were catalogued as such by Kevin Killian in Spicer's papers at the Bancroft. In an extended correspondence on them in 2013, Killian and I reached no 'solution' to either. Katz dates them to 1947. See Spicer, *Be brave*, p. 33.

80 *House*, pp. 199–206; and see Katz, *The poetry*, pp. 163–4.

81 Katz, *The poetry*, pp. 24–5.

82 *Ibid*. Katz mentions 'On falling into your eyes' (*Be brave*, p. 51) and an untitled poem beginning, 'Any fool can get into an ocean' (*MV*, p. 23), to which I would add 'At Slim Gordon's' (*Be brave*, p. 9) and 'At point Sur' (which includes yet another variation naming ocean waves) (JSP Box 5, folder 17). This last poem remains unpublished.

83 Spicer, *Be brave*, pp. 96–7. The unfinished poem contains an anti-Semitic line which renders it not worth rehearsing in full; but it was planned to have four sections like the earlier 'Portrait': '1. The Waves', '2. The Red Sea', '3. Song for Hart Crane', '4. The Pacific'. Only the first section was finished and is printed as an individual poem in *Be brave*. JSP, Box 8, folder 1. I am grateful that Kevin Killian discussed Spicer's trail of sea-poems with me in winter 2013. And see Katz's note in *Be brave*, p. 329.

84 Spicer, *Be brave*, p. 97.

85 Katz, *The poetry*, p. 5, citing *MV*, p. 373.

86 An intriguing vocative variation is preserved in what I believe to be the drafts of his well-known poem, 'A poem to the reader of the poem', from the Boston period: 'Translator/ Wet dreamer/ Wrestler/ with other people's angels'. It appears in a notebook as a fragment preceding a partial draft of the poem. JSP, Box 8, folder 4. See Spicer, *Be brave*, p. 98.

87 Most critics take Spicer's division of his work as a meaningful shift, but there is disagreement about how to negotiate it. My sympathies here lie largely with Katz, *The poetry*, pp. 8–9, 20–1, 53. But see Snediker, 'Prodigal son', p. 503; Snediker, *Queer optimism*, pp. 146–52.

88 Chamberlain, Katz, and Hadbawnik make convincing arguments that the book performs a serious theory of translation. See Chamberlain, 'Ghostwriting the text'; Hadbawnik, 'Time mechanics', pp. 272–4;

Katz, *The poetry*, pp. 53–4, 56, 58, 74 n. 5. For a traditional crib of the poems against the source-texts see Eshleman, 'The Lorca working'.

89 See Katz, *The poetry*, pp. 56–9; Hadbawnik, 'Time mechanics', pp. 272–4.

90 *MV*, pp. 122–3.

91 *Ibid.*, p. 133; and see Allen, *The new American poetry*, pp. 413–14.

92 *MV*, p. 111.

93 See Katz, *The poetry*, p. 56; Hadbawnik, 'Time mechanics', pp. 273–4. Spicer articulates this impermanence more specifically in terms of linguistic variation and Poundian translation in rejected drafts preserved in his *Lorca* notebooks. Asking whether Chaucer would be more legible to Present Day English speakers if Middle English were written in ideograms(!), he writes 'It is not merely that the voice, the personal gets in the way of the poem. This is bad enough. But worse, the sounds of the language change year by year and mile by mile from the speaker' (JSP, Box 9, folder 4).

94 Katz, *The poetry*, p. 56.

95 The phrase is from 'Little Gidding'. See Eliot, *Collected poems*, p. 204.

96 On 'tradition' here, see Katz, *The poetry*, pp. 56–7; Hadbawnik, 'Time mechanics', pp. 273–6 and 'Jack Spicer and the English department'; Holt, 'Spicer's poetic correspondence', pp. 39, 45, 49–64.

97 *MV*, p. 308. On the 'Lowghost' in Spicer's translation practice and interest in Old English, see Reynolds, 'Afterword', pp. 33–7.

98 Katz, *The poetry*, p. 56.

99 *After Lorca* is generally considered to predate Spicer's full-blown poetics of dictation; this aspect of the book especially contributes to its 'proto-poetics of dictation' (see Katz, *The poetry*, p. 53).

100 Sobecki, *The sea and medieval English literature*, p. 43.

101 Estes, *Anglo-Saxon literary landscapes*, pp. 35–6.

102 Wickham-Crowley, 'Living on the *ecg*', p. 85.

103 Kl. 3, p. xxxvii, citing Sarrazin, *Beowulf-Studien*, p. 4 and following.

104 Kl. 3, p. xlvii.

105 Kl. 4, p. lviii. And see Niles (et al.), *Beowulf and Lejre*.

106 Kl. 4, pp. lvxi–lvxii. Notably, discussions of topography in Klaeber's introduction and its latest revision are conducted under 'The historical elements' and 'The world of the humans' rather than a consideration of the poem's geographies as such.

107 Estes, *Anglo-Saxon literary landscapes*, p. 43.

108 E.g. Clarke, 'The traveler recognizes his goal', pp. 655–6; Diamond, 'Theme as ornament', pp. 465–6; Ramsey, 'The sea voyages', pp. 53–4, 59; Crowne, 'The hero on the beach'; Renoir, 'Oral formulaic rhetoric' p. 105; Irving, *A reading* pp. 47–8.

109 Robinson, 'Variation', p. 81.
110 Overing and Osborn, *Landscape of desire*, p. xv. And see Osborn, '"Verbal sea charts"'; Overing, 'Reinventing'.
111 Overing and Osborn, *Landscape of desire*, pp. 1–2.
112 *Ibid.*, p. 14.
113 *Ibid.*, pp. 13
114 The latter description appears in Overing and Osborn, *Landscape of desire*, p. 13; and Overing, 'Reinventing', p. 35. The former is attributed to Overing ('Reinventing') by Osborn in '"Verbal sea charts"', p. 443, but I cannot locate the precise quotation and I suspect it is a paraphrase of Overing.
115 Irving, *A reading*, p. 48.
116 E.g. Ramsey, 'The sea voyages', p. 57. But the best expression of this point I have found is in an unpublished dissertation on sea-imagery in the poem that disagrees with Ramsey: 'each [passage] devotes much description to the events, which do not seem to have much to do with the poem's story of monsters and national politics. All that is strictly necessary to the story is to mention that Beowulf and company crossed the sea, and that would need only a line or two' (Smith, 'Seafaring imagery in Old English poetry', p. 229).
117 I follow Brady in taking *sund* as related to its sense as *swimming* ('water one can swim across'), and referring to *deep* water, translating as consistently as is reasonable. In the case of *sund wið sande*, as Brady argues, *sund* seems to refer to shallow 'water of the sea', but the alliterative pair is suggestive of a contrast. I follow Brady in taking *brim* and *holm* as referring to rising motions of the open sea. One may be legitimately circumspect about translating *flota* with 'floater', but it is conventional in standard translations and it is supported by the likely relationship of the noun to the verbs *fleotan* and *flotian*. See Brady, 'The synonyms for "sea" in *Beowulf*', pp. 32–4; *DOE*, s.v. *flota* (cf. s.v,. *flot*). Also useful here is Strite, 'Old English sea-terms', which compiles lexicography on OE sea-terms prior to 1970. For the crux in l. 224a, *eoletes* (otherwise unrecorded), I follow conventional translations and the notes of Kl. 4, p. 132 n. 224.
118 The third occurrence, in *Andreas*, likely derives from these two in *Beowulf*. E.g. Riedinger, 'The formulaic relationship', p. 302.
119 The passages fit neatly into conventional schemas of 'envelope' structure in the poem, e.g. Hieatt, 'Envelope patterns', p. 260. But see Niles, 'Ring composition', p. 925.
120 Oshitari, 'The sea in *Beowulf*', p. 15.
121 *AOB*, p. 274.
122 Robinson, 'Variation', p. 82 n. 98.

123 Greenfield, '"Beowulf" 207b–228', pp. 88–9.
124 Overing and Osborn, *Landscape of desire*, p. 11. See also Osborn, '"Verbal sea charts"', pp. 444–5, 451–2; Overing, 'Reinventing', p. 32. Osborn is clear that poet does *not* intend 'to represent an actual verbal sea chart' but the passage may be 'based on … a trace of what is probably the most functional genre of oral composition in *Beowulf*' ('"Verbal sea charts"', pp. 451–5).
125 Robinson, 'Variation', p. 185.
126 *AOB*, p. 274; Robinson, 'Variation', pp. 9–10, and 9–10 n. 15, 62, 146 n. 36; Greenfield, *Interpretation*, pp. 73–4. And see Greenfield, '"Beowulf" 207b–228', pp. 89 and 89 n. 10.
127 Robinson only counts the references to the ship as part of variation defined by strict parallelism, but only the slightest loosening allows either that the apposite *herewædum* and *mearum ond maðmum* participate in a crossed or second variation. See Robinson, 'Variation', p. 62.
128 Irving, *A reading*, pp. 48–9.
129 *Ibid.*, p. 49. Robinson includes ll. 1908–1909 as a sentence-variation, and so presumably excludes l. 1910 because, lacking an expressed verb, it cannot be construed as precisely parallel. See Robinson, 'Variation', p. 91. One might conceivably also construe *bundenstefna* as separate, 'crossed' variation with *famigheals* and *sægenga*, and the same for the prepositional phrases, maintaining the sentence level variation as an overlapping but separate construction. Greenfield opens his chapter on variation with these lines but his position is less clear. See Greenfield, *Interpretation*, p. 62.
130 Clarke, 'The traveler recognizes his goal', p. 657.
131 Magennis, *Images of community*, pp. 121, 142–3.
132 Clemoes, 'Action in Beowulf', 148, 157–8.
133 *Ibid.*, p. 158.
134 *Ibid.*, p. 152.
135 *Ibid.*, p. 148.
136 Niles, 'Introduction: negotiating', p. 5.
137 Overing, *Language*, pp. 22–4. Overing takes care to note that 'variation, parataxis, and alliteration' also play important roles here (p. 23).
138 *Ibid.*, p. 22.
139 Robinson, 'Two aspects', p. 1.
140 Blomfield, 'The style and structure', p. 402.
141 I thank Michael Sells for suggesting the related phrase 'smashing lexemes'. I use *lexemes*, and not *words*, advisedly, to include the elements of compounds both as elements and simplexes.
142 Niles, *Beowulf: the poem and its tradition*, p. 167.

5

Narrating heat in a hot world

> What I recognize to be living—living in the immediate sense—is what
> I recognize as being hot.
>
> Gaston Bachelard[1]

Figures for stasis

While Brodeur's approach to the aesthetics of *Beowulf* on smaller
scales of composition fell by the wayside, studies calibrated to the
scale of structure and narrative—at times conflating these two
categories—have persisted into the present, continuing Brodeur's
exploration of the poem in terms of 'the harmonious interplay of
main action and subplot [which] reaches a perfect fusion in the final
scenes'.[2] Such accounts tend to continue or even more deeply entrench
Tolkien's influential account of the poem as 'essentially a balance,
an opposition of ends and beginnings', resulting in a 'simple and
static structure, solid and strong'.[3] Although the isolation of a two-part
structure proved less important, and was often rejected during the
next few decades, critics would go on to posit a number of permutations of this diagnosis of stasis and/or symmetry in tandem with
accounts of the poem's structural unity.

John Leyerle's still influential account of the poem's narrative as
'a complex, tightly-knotted lacertine interlace' is so organically
integrated that, for Leyerle, '[t]here are no digressions in *Beowulf*'.[4]
Models of related integrative chiastic narrative structures proliferated
in the 1960s and 1970s, adapting Adeline Courtney Bartlett's earlier
identification of 'envelope patterns' to the scale of the entire poem.[5]
John D. Niles specifically identified his account of 'ring composition'

as a sub-type of interlace structure.[6] Overlapping these efforts, some critics continue to hunt for underlying numerical or even arithmetical or geometrical patterns underlying the poem's structure.[7] Among these, Robert D. Stevick modifies the carpet-page analogy, demoting 'interlace' from a structural principle to the matter or content to be fitted into the form or structure: 'essentially filler ornament which lends itself to being poured (so to speak) into ... an area of almost any shape'.[8] As John M. Hill clarifies, Stevick's work 'lays out a groundwork of proportional or else modular design' to be completed by 'filling in the space'.[9] Stevick's 'criteria' for evaluating the aesthetics of *Beowulf* thus depend on identifying 'divisions that embody one or two key ratios'.[10]

Without meaning to impugn the usefulness of these last propositions, it would not do to pass over the irony here without comment: that what is perhaps the longest surviving thread of Tolkien's rejection of Classical aesthetics on the level of narrative structure should return in the end to concepts of 'proportion' that 'owe something to Classical thought about form and universal order'.[11] This attention to ratio or proportion throws into relief a set of commonalities underlying these otherwise varied approaches: 1) a comprehension of aesthetics on the level of narrative structure as an abstracted, if not always mathematical, structure, set apart from, if not transcendent of, a sensory-affective world; 2) an attendant tacit consent to accounts of the poem's stasis, stability, and balance (whether as symmetry or as moderation); and 3) a continued inscription of aesthetics on the level of narrative structure within a reduced 'form vs. content' dyad. While chiastic models might seem to imply some degree of back and forth movement, they still outline a closed system. Thus, Niles, who rightly argues that 'one cannot conceive of structural phenomena in literature that are devoid of aesthetic implications',[12] echoes Tolkien's rhetoric in his description of a ring-structured *Beowulf* that comes 'to a gradual close, so that the work as a whole has the solidity and grace of a well-planned piece of architecture'.[13]

It is not insensible that if a strand of the mid-century attention to *Beowulf*'s aesthetics should survive so long—even with such a twist—it would do so as an interest in narrative structure. After all, the critical investment in chiastic structures, and even the fixation on the poem's 'unity', both predate Tolkien.[14] Moreover, while oral-formulaic approaches seemed to radically undercut 'modern' approaches to smaller rhetorical units, they put less direct pressure on attention to narrative. The emphasis on isolating formulaic narratives and traditional 'type-scenes', along with, perhaps, the anthropological and folkloric orientation of the Lord and Parry project, made them compatible with structuralist narratology.[15] If the advent of structuralism to literary studies rendered Brodeur's approach to diction less tenable, it also made attention to *generalized* (and thus, 'traditional', rather than 'original') narrative structure more viable. So during a period of Old English studies otherwise characterized by resistance to literary theory, Russian formalism significantly shaped the study of *Beowulf*'s narrative structure.[16] The predilection of structuralism to posit dyads—for example, Todorov's reduction of the elements of narrative to only 'transformation' and 'succession'—similarly posed no threat to the studies of chiastic structure,[17] and, read recklessly, Shklovsky's distinction of *syuzhet* and *fabula* (or, respectively, the plot—or order of events as presented in a text—and the raw 'material for plot formation')[18] might seem to endorse a scheme in which a pre-existing *story* might be simply plotted into a given form.

Without meaning to suggest that these critical moves do not comprehend *Beowulf* in interesting ways, we can surmise that they are not calibrated to grasp the poem's non-representational aesthetics. They do not ask how the poem enfolds the human sensorium in its perceptual processes on the scale of narrative structure. This final chapter thus takes on the aesthetic implications of what Blaser called 'the heat of that story' in terms of the experience of the 'story'. This analysis of narrative aesthetics will not identify a structure in perfect continuity with the aesthetic functions of diction and variation described in previous chapters. In Brodeur's assumption of an integrative organic unity, or later models of envelope or interlace, one can draw a continuous (if not always perfectly straight) line from diction through variation to structure: variation 'could give unity to a scene, even to a sequence of scenes ... transferred from phrasal to structural use, it could establish a structural unity through the poem as a whole'.[19] In contrast, by experimenting with the possibility that Blaser's and Spicer's later poetics of serial composition are, in part, informed by their work with *Beowulf* and Brodeur's approach to the poem, this chapter traces a narrative style characterized by a discontinuity with itself and an indifference to its remainderless integration with smaller units of composition. While the logic of these aesthetics will be congruent with the processes of 'inclusions' that constitute the heat of *Beowulf* on smaller scales of composition, on the level of narrative structure such inclusions will depend less on lexical movement than on a kind of spacing that interrupts the activity of the poem and breaches the narrative *ductus*.

As Hadbawnik argues, 'the germ of Spicer's approach to the serial poem' can be linked in part to Brodeur's interest in the famously 'fragmented approach' of *Beowulf*—a poem replete with troublesome 'episodes and digressions' and shot through with heterogeneous genres and registers.[20] Brodeur distinguishes three distinct types of narrative material in the poem ('folk-tale, heroic legend, and historical tradition'), along with passages that read like individual set-piece elegies.[21] Brodeur ultimately resolves these heterogeneous inclusions as producing the contrast, anticipation, and irony (that ultimate fetish of the New Criticism) which shape the unity of the narrative as well as the individuality of a poet who is 'a man of his age, yet greater than his age'.[22] But for Blaser and Spicer they also point to the possibility of a long poem that strangely coheres as a sequence of discrete fragments. Reciprocally, this mode of composition, which Blaser and Spicer call the 'serial poem', offers a strategic framing that allows us to finally forget the question of structural or thematic unity and to ask about the non-representational functions of the poem's narrative aesthetics.

In what follows here, I first consider the aesthetics of Blaser's and Spicer's accounts of the serial poem against the larger backdrop of mid-century structuralist narratology. The rest of the chapter then turns directly on how a serial poetics might comprehend the aesthetics of narrative in *Beowulf* along two vectors. First, I identify a latent narrative of fire and flame that interrupts the 'main' narrative (in which the 'heat' that Blaser ascribes to 'that story' will finally be legible in a conventional, nominal reference to the tactile experience of thermal sensation). This is not only a narrative of fire as such, but a fragmentary, meta-aesthetic narrative about the poem's sensological aesthetics of fire. Burning holes in the poem's narrative *ductus*, this aesthetics of fire will mark an attempt to align the poem's sensological aesthetics with an Outside to narrativity. With the aesthetics of fire serving as an emblem for one possible way to think about *Beowulf* as a serial poem, the second vector directly examines the phenomenal gaps, boundaries, divisions, or edges that fall around and within narrative units as points of entry for non-narrativity and the non-narrativized sensorium. I thus explore the porous boundaries of stylistically articulated 'verse-movements' and manuscript fitt-divisions in and around the so-called 'Finn episode'—one of the most notorious of the poem's 'episodes', and one we know Brodeur had Blaser and Spicer consider carefully—as the marks of a latent seriality. Enacting a mode of seriality not precisely equated to that of Blaser and Spicer, but nonetheless rendered legible by it, the narrative aesthetics of *Beowulf* yield a poem of variably determinable, partially overlapping discrete units that constitute an interruptible narrative vulnerable to and traversed by an un-narrativizable corporeality. As a function of its latent seriality, the heat of this story will locate the poem's sensology in its lyric, rather than narrative processes.

Serial composition and the aesthetics of structure

Although practices of and pronouncements about what came to be known as the 'serial poem' circulate ubiquitously under the large umbrella of the New American Poetry, the serial poem was particularly contested and generative for Blaser and Spicer, along with their Berkeley Renaissance companion, Robert Duncan. A serial poem is a long poem, composed in discrete, 'serialized' segments (although, in Duncan's work, segments appear across any number of discrete books). Joseph Conte's influential study generalizes the serial poem in the work of several poets as '"protean" and provisional', a form that 'incorporates random occurrences without succumbing to formlessness'.[23] Fitting the serial poem into the early critical investment in immanence in post-war American poetics (Robert Creeley's 'form is never more than an extension of content'), Conte emphasizes that '[e]ach element ... is not assigned by any external scheme'.[24] Distinguished from mere *sequence* by a militant parataxis, the serial 'can be described in semiotic terms as a poetic form in which the syntagmatic relation of the sign is predominant'.[25]

In the poetry of the Berkeley Renaissance, the serial poem was from the first yoked to medievalism in the community's performance and contestation of its inaugural myths, especially around Robert

Duncan's early book, *Medieval scenes* (1950), a text composed over several evenings of séance-like sessions of dictation.[26] Spicer's practice would draw explicitly on analogies to mid-century popular media like serial radio and television formats, which drew fire from Duncan as 'lowbrow' and led Conte to contrast Duncan's investment in 'an articulation of parts which is intentionally incomplete' to a view of Spicer's serial as a finite and episodic series.[27] More recently, however, Christopher Nealon reframed Spicer's sense of seriality in terms of an 'unrealizable' poetic whole,[28] while Katz argues that 'the "book" and the "serial poem" also militate more generally for a poetics of deferral, displacement, and spillage of poetry into its historically opposed others'.[29] These revisions help refocus questions about serial composition further away from the temptation to lapse into tacit reliance on a content-form dyad and towards exploring a non-representational porosity at the level of structure.

For Spicer, serial composition is partly a matter of the pragmatics of 'dictation' (wherein the poet attempts to allow what is radically 'Outside' the poet to write their poems for them).[30] Writing this way, as Spicer explains during his 'Vancouver lectures', is difficult to sustain over any length of time, and one has 'a better chance of being an empty vessel' by writing in shorter, discrete sittings.[31] But Spicer also advocates serial composition because, as he writes in an often-quoted letter to Robin Blaser included in his *Admonitions* (cited as Spicer's self-conscious attempt to divide his early and mature work), 'there is really no single poem' and 'poems should echo and re-echo against each other'.[32]

As an application of 'dictation' to larger scales of poetic composition, Spicer's Vancouver lectures develop two metaphors by which serial composition articulates a phenomenology of narrative and structure that positions either poet or reader in a kinesthetic and proprioceptive process. In the first,

> I'm going into the woods on a path that I have no idea about. I'm not going to look backwards on the path at all … Not looking backwards. Letting the poem look forward. Just following the bloody path to see where it goes.[33]

The second, which Spicer attributes to Blaser (and which Blaser will later use in a long, foundational essay on Spicer's work),[34] gives us the serial as a haunted house or a kind of inverted grail-procession:

it's as if you go into a room, a dark room. A light is turned on for a minute. Then it's turned off again and you go into a different room where a light is turned on and off.[35]

In both metaphors, a corporeal experience of a *ductus,* of *being led* through linearized factical space, is overlaid by the possibility of fugue-like recurrence, not as memory, return, or pattern, but as unexpected interruption—yielding something like narrative as an emergent phenomenon.

Blaser's account of the heat of *Beowulf,* phrased as 'the heat of that *story*' (italics mine), is embedded within an account of serial composition as a narratological poetics:

I'm interested in a particular kind of narrative—what Jack Spicer and I agreed to call in our own work the serial poem—this is a narrative which refuses to adopt an imposed story line, and completes itself only in the sequence of poems, if, in fact, a reader insists upon a definition of completion which is separate from the poems themselves. The poems tend to act as a sequence of energies which run out when so much of a tale is told. I like to describe this in Ovidian terms, as a *carmen perpetuum,* a continuous song in which the fragmented subject matter is only apparently disconnected.[36]

This description of emergent narrative from 'only apparently' disconnected matter may seem to imply more continuity or completion than Spicer's 'series of rooms'. But Blaser's meandering, deferring attempt to clarify the 'sequence of energies' that generates seriality also reorients the entire process of narrative around non-representational, worldly interruptions of a laminar phenomenology:

The sequence of energies may involve all kinds of things—anger may open a window, a sound from another world may completely reshape the present moment, the destruction of a friendship may destroy a whole realm of language or the ability to use it—each piece is in effect an extended metaphor (another word is probably needed), because in the serial poem the effort is to hold both the correspondence and the focus that an image is, and the process of those things coming together—so that the light from a white linen tablecloth reflects on the face of one's companion, becomes light, fire, and the white moth which happens to be in the room is also light in the dark around the table, and is thus both the light and the element of light that destroys it. I ask you to remember that every metaphor involves as least four elements—which are a story, and the bringing them together is an activity, a glowing energy if stopped over, if entered.[37]

On the level of narrative, 'energies' of the serial correspond loosely to the aleatory 'heat of the meeting' in the poem as a series of inclusions. The serial becomes discrete by this radical interruptability, and narrative then emerges as an effect of the poem's translative process.

Against the backdrop of mid-century structuralism, the phenomenological texture of such narrative evinces much less compatibility with any form/content dyad than with Roland Barthes' mid-1960s structuralist narratology. In his essay appearing in a landmark issue of *Communications* on structuralism and narrative in 1966, Barthes expounds a similarly interruptive structure that operates in even the smallest narrative units (for Barthes, these are 'sequences', made up in turn of individual 'functions'):[38]

> what calls for special attention is that some terms belonging to several sequences can easily dovetail into each other. Before a sequence is completed, the initial term of a fresh sequence can be introduced: sequences proceed according to a contrapuntal pattern. Functionally, the structure of narrative is that of the fugue: narrative 'pulls in' new material even as it 'holds on' to previous material.[39]

The polyfunctionality and dystaxy within and between these levels of structure mean that 'narrative integration does not offer the appearance of smooth regularity, like that of a fine architectural design, which would lead, from the infinite variety of simple elements through a symmetrical network of detours, up to a few complex masses'.[40] The stable, Tolkienian tower-poem, for example, could only be *an incidental effect* at the level of the narration or narrative discourse. On the micrological level, narrative depends on a 'structural "limping", a constant interplay of potentials, whose "falls" impart "tone" or *energy* to the narrative' (emphasis mine).[41] At the same time, Barthes' most reduced formulation of the genesis of narrative logic underscores an asymmetrical directionality: 'the necessity to vary and to outgrow the first *form* that man [*sic*] ever came by, namely repetition'.[42]

As for the ontology of narrative itself, right on the seam of Barthes' structuralist and poststructuralist modes, the emergent, productive activities of narrative (as in the above model of differential movement) keep overtaking those of reference and mimesis:

> in any narrative, imitation remains contingent. The function of narrative is not to 'represent'; it is to put together a scene which still retains a

certain enigmatic character for the reader, but does not belong to the mimetic order in any way. The 'reality' of the sequence does not lie in the 'natural' order of actions that make it up, but in the logic that is unfolded, exposed, and finally confirmed, in the midst of the sequence.[43]

Narrative as such is thus realized *without* referential relation to 'the real':

> What goes on in a narrative is, from the referential (real) point of view, strictly *nothing*. What does 'happen' is language per se, the adventure of language, whose advent never ceases to be celebrated.[44]

These still stunning claims are accounted for, in part, by Barthes' almost perversely strict observance of the structuralist isolation of 'the ultimate, self-designating, form of narrative' as the limit of properly narrative analysis: '[j]ust as linguistics stops at the sentence, the analysis of narrative stops at the analysis of discourse: from that point on, it is necessary to resort to another semiotics'.[45] So, conceived within the frame of 'the structurality of structure',[46] narrative is by definition *not* open to the a-semiotic world, and the only *relation* it accrues is to a meaning lent to it when referred to a higher semiotic level. But in exhausting the logic of this structure so precisely, Barthes exposes a semiotic infrastructure for the aesthetics of narrative. I would suggest that on limping seams and fugal lapses of this differential movement, precisely where a referential relationship to 'the real' is an absolute impossibility, the text may exhibit a more radical porosity to a kind of corporeal experience not fully integrated by its semiotics—akin to Barthes' concept, from his later semiotics of the photograph, of the *punctum*, the 'accident which pricks me' (disrupting the mild-mannered 'interest' of that he calls *studium*).[47]

When it comes to *Beowulf*, limping seams and fugal lapses of both texture and macrostructure have never desisted from asserting themselves in the critical literature—whether as anxiety about the 'episodes and digressions', attempts to solve textual problems, or glee at the ensuing complexity.[48] John A. Nist's account of the poem's eschewal of 'straight narration' is closer to accounts of interlace and ring composition, and defends the authorial unity of the poem, but also compares what he identifies as a cyclical narrative structure to a musical 'fugue'.[49] More forcefully, and resonant with what follows here, Mannish Sharma's study of (narratological) metalepsis in the poem concludes that 'the narrative of *Beowulf* is structured by the very resistance that the text poses to narrative structuration'.[50]

When Brodeur gave Blaser and Spicer the 'Finn episode' assignment discussed in the introduction and the first chapter, he probably aimed, with Bonjour's *The digressions of Beowulf*, at inoculating them against any remaining gasps of the nineteenth-century *Liedertheorie* (song-theory) of the poem's composition as a patchwork of short lays:[51]

> 4. Analyze the previous passage [*Beowulf*, line 1107–1124] as you would a modern poem both as a unit in itself and as part of the *Beowulf* poem.
>
> 5. How does the Finn episode fit into *Beowulf* as an aesthetic whole? Compare the use of this episode with the use of other episodes. If the Finnsburgh [*sic*] fragment had been inserted in place of the Finn episode, how would you show that it did not fit aesthetically into the poem as a whole?[52]

It would be interesting to know if this same assignment had been given to Stanley B. Greenfield, but as Hadbawnik notes, for Spicer such questions 'hint at the adulteration and fragmentation of the text, its mixture of the self-contained lyric and the sequential epic, as well the poet's ability to repackage and incorporate other poems into his work'.[53] It is likely to have done something similar for Blaser, too, whose approach to the lyric, as Nichols writes, 'modifies it to let in a wide range of historical and cultural content that is not traditional to the genre'.[54] However inadvertently, the prompt and questions as much as dare Blaser and Spicer to imagine a digression on a heroic Scandinavian feud-narrative as a discrete unit within the nascent serial poetics that they were in the midst of developing. In further prompting the poets to directly experiment with replacing the episode by inserting the fragmentary Old English poem on the same subject known as the 'Finnsburg fragment' or 'The fight at Finnsburg' in the place of the episode (something we know, as Hadbawnik notes, that Spicer did do, inserting his translation of the fragment into his *Beowulf* materials),[55] the assignment invites consideration of such serial adulteration at the level of narrative structure as a kind of seam by which *Beowulf* might already be capable of perceiving and including its poetic others (folktale, lyric, history, etc.). It is not, I would suggest, incidental that Mary Kate

Hurley points to *Beowulf*'s numerous episodes and digressions as a sign of the poem's 'pervasive obsession' with narrative transmission and loci of translative logic in a text that is not a translation.[56] But what could serial poetics practically look like in the Old English poem, and with what concrete aesthetic implications?

Fire and the aesthetics of what is outside narrative

                                        other step-stone
      holes in the world
                              the work folding
      a dragon   at the edge   of the sea   my enlargement
      of the pond
                        where   the story went
      wild   fiery   under the leaves
                  Blaser, 'Image-Nation 12 (Actus'[57]

To the extent that *Beowulf* contributes to a kind of mid-twentieth-century *Lieder*-poetics in the work of Blaser and Spicer, we might expect to find the phenomenological porosity of the serial poem at work in *Beowulf* in interruptions of the laminar flow of the main narrative. Although seldom noticed as such, among the most pervasive, confusing, and persistent interruptions in *Beowulf* are allusions to stories about fire as well as fragmentary references to fire that recall those allusions in turn. Along with the possibility that these flames (including those of the poem's unavoidable dragon) contribute to the spark behind Blaser's description of the 'heat' of this story, they become especially interesting as points that interrupt the *ductus* of the main narrative not only with a story about fire as a represented object but also with a kind of implicit metanarrative pointing to an aesthetic field traced by the poem's robust poetic lexicon for fire and flame. In tracing these pervasive, if irregular flare-ups, a story about narrativity and aesthetics emerges in discrete installments across the poem.

Almost as soon as the story that will eventually involve Beowulf in the affairs of Heorot begins, the narrator interrupts the encomium informing us that the newly completed hall 'hilfade/ heah ond horngeap' (ll. 81b–82a) (soared up high and horn-gabled) with the grim irony that it already 'heaðowylma bad,/ laðan liges' (ll. 82b–83a) (awaited war-surges,/ enemy fires). The fleeting allusion opens up one of the larger caverns of incomplete legendary material that Frank calls the poem's 'mysterious dark matter'.[58] Bonjour felt that its placement was crucial in constructing a complex, but (he assumed) entirely clear pattern of eventually tragic dynastic struggles, and Brodeur similarly classed it as one of the poem's many 'anticipations' that prepare us for 'the bloody division within a dynasty' and contribute to the poem's thematic unity.[59] But, within the poem itself, as Frank notes, in this 'first indication that things will not end well for the Scyldings … [t]he timing of the conflagration is left open, perhaps to accommodate different versions of the story in circulation'.[60] And without denying the possibility of its place within a mnemotechnical macrostructure, in the local experience of what James Earl calls the 'phenomenology of reading' *Beowulf*, 'as it opens slowly before us', [61] this fire is an alarming intrusion—an obsessive historian interrupting the entertainment with a grim correction but then trailing off before even explaining why it was so important.

Fire interrupts the story again once Grendel enters Heorot for the last time—another cause célèbre for mid-century critics. Brodeur canonized the tripartite narration of this approach to the hall as a 'design for terror'—identifying it as 'an extension of variation' within a narratology of horror that one might suspect is informed by his familiarity with pulp novel genres: [62]

> Suspense can be maintained without withholding all knowledge of an action's outcome until the final moment: it resides in the degree and quality of emotional tension imposed upon the listener … That conflict must engross the imagination, must tax its capacity to endure, but must never exceed its limits of toleration. Too much unrelieved horror blunts the response, and induces incredulity or indifference.[63]

This affective tension is underscored by a cinematographic-like narratology that cuts back and forth between the point of view of Grendel approaching and of the men inside,[64] and by a subtle manipulation of syntax and meter that stage the polarity and confrontation of Grendel and the men in the hall.[65] But when Grendel finally bursts into the hall, two references to fire puncture this thickly absorptive narrative style:

> Duru sona onarn
> fyrbendum fæst,   syþðan he hire folmum æthran;

onbræd þa bealohydig,   ða he gebolgen wæs,
recedes muþan.   Raþe æfter þon
on fagne flor   feond treddode,
eode yrremod;   him of eagum stod
ligge gelicost   leoht unfæger. (ll. 721b–727)

The door sprung open,
resilient in fire-bands [fire-forged bands], after he lay to it with his
    hands;
Then, violent-minded, he swung open—when he was swollen with rage—
the mouth of the hall. Instantly after this
the enemy put foot to the flashing floor,
went angry-minded; from his eyes arose,
most like flame, a light un-beautiful.

Grendel stands swollen in the mouth of the building as if something
it must either swallow or vomit out, toxic to the point that the
iron-reinforced door springs apart so violently that it may as well
liquefy (*oniernan* can mean 'to give' or 'uncoil', but also occurs as
a gloss on Latin *currere*, 'pour forth').[66] Yet the *fyr-* (fire-) of the
unique compound *fyrbendum* (fire-forged bands), without referencing
any actual fire in the narrative present, is like a tiny distracting
spark, a shard of another, more obscure narrative. The description
of the door as 'fyrbendum fæst' (resilient in fire-forged bands)
interrupts the skein of this present sequence with a very subtly ironic
reminder: the previous introduction to the hall now threatened by
Grendel was followed too soon with a forecast of its eventual
combustion. The fire which could not make Heorot strong enough
to withstand Grendel will eventually consume the great hall.[67] If
this mere component of a compound seems too slight to disturb the
narrative flow, recall that about sixty lines later, when Grendel and
Beowulf's fight seems like it might break the hall apart, the narrator
ironically reminds us that nothing could destroy the iron-reinforced
building, 'nymþe liges fæþme/ swulge on swaþule' (ll. 781b–782a)
(unless the embrace of flame/ swallowed [it] in heat).

And then, in the darkness, as if a synecdoche for all of Grendel's
breaches of the hall, a pair of eyes appears with the capacity to
provoke astonishing claims about literary history; for Renoir, 'the
last image evoked here—two dots of fire against a veil of blackness—is
probably the simplest in the English literature; it is also one of the
most effective'.[68] Up to this point, the specific tenor of the 'terror'

of the sequence depends upon a marked deprivation of the visual register, with Grendel gliding along 'under misthleoþum' (l. 710b) (under the cloak of dark; lit. slopes of fog). The point of view shifts between that of those Grendel approaches, then of Grendel on the approach,[69] but, as Michael Lapidge notes in further comparing the sequence to the techniques of horror fiction and art-horror cinema, 'the poet, far from wishing to adopt criteria for visualising Grendel, exercised great care in choosing language that would prevent such visualisation'.[70] The eyes thus become the fulcrum around which everything seems to grind to a halt—the spell of story pierced by an eruption of a specific sensory register. The narrator, as Renoir notes, 'says nothing of the claws and teeth, the gigantic stature and the murderous looks'; rather, '[t]hough we cannot see the monster, himself the sight of his eyes gives us the distressing sensation that *he* can see us; and then, under the circumstances the light that glows in these eyes is of a terrifying nature'.[71] Although the intriguing parallel between Grendel and the *draugr* or *haugbúi* that haunt later medieval Old Norse sagas is tempting here, these eyes are not creepy like the cold light in the moon-reflecting eyes of those living dead creatures.[72] Instead, the simile and lingering description that fully arrests the narrative pace compares the eyes—superlatively—to *flame* that is modified in turn with the litotes 'un-beautiful'. The two glowing orbs thus disrupt the story of unseen forward motion with an object of sudden and total visual fixation. But is *this* the apotheosis of the terror everyone is talking about—this frozen, epistemologically abyssal moment before the gore? Or might it again reflect the larger, hotter, final fire that awaits Heorot—as two hot embers of another story boring through this one and disrupting the immersive aesthetics of the sequence?

We might underscore the adjective *unfæger* (un-beautiful, ugly), as a judgment about the aesthetic qualities of *lig* (flame) when enfolded with affects of terror. The widely attested noun *lig* implies not only light and heat but unpredictable shape and movement, restlessness and instability, as in the 'wæfran' (restless) flames into which Hananiah, Azariah, and Mishael are consigned in the Junius manuscript poem *Daniel*.[73] The adjective *wæfre* modifies affective experience as well, as in the Finnsburg episode, in which, as Irving argues, a 'wæfre mod' (l. 1150b) (restless spirit) contributes to a 'latent image of fire' that threads through that story, suggesting in particular a 'fiery heart that blazes up out of its confinement'.[74] Moreover, *lig* can convey a sense of sharpness, too—even amidst billowing shape—as in the 'weallendne lig' (billowing/surging flame) that accompanies the gashing bites of serpents inflicted on the 'byrnendra scole' (burning pack) of the damned in the Exeter Book *Christ* poems.[75]

The attempted dynastic aesthetics of the 'medoærn micel' (l. 69a) (huge mead-house) stand in stark contrast to such fire. When it is built, Hrothgar commands the people to 'folcstede frætwan' (l. 76a) (adorn the people-place), rendering its static monumentality palatable for his followers. But more importantly, the aesthetics of Heorot should generate and sustain—and be sustained by—narrative. The narrator reports that they 'gefrægn' (l. 74a) (learned by asking) about the command to adorn the hall. As a *micel* (huge) hall, it is one that 'yldo bearn æfre gefrunon'(l. 70) (the children of men will forever learn about).[76] In these cases, the verb *gefrignan* echoes its occurrence in the poem's opening lines, where it marks the transmission of narratives about the Scylding Dynasty in its poetic sense of 'learning by asking'—a consummate signal of inaugural communal knowledge transmitted by narrative in Old English poetry.[77] The fiery eyes and their un-beauty mark the failure of Heorot's project of narrative and its narrative aesthetics—recalling, however fragmentarily, the fire that eventually consumes the structure and interrupting the story of Grendel's present threat.

The Old English poetic corpus routinely opposes fire to the waters of the Biblical flood in drawing out its eschatological connotations, but *Beowulf* associates Grendel (and the whole first part of the poem) with water and the flood,[78] further throwing the fires of his eyes into relief—not as a world-ending fire but as those flames that approach all too soon *within* the historical time of the hall yet *beyond* the time of the poem's main narrative. The 'unfæger' aesthetics of the eyes— in their materiality as a signifier—exhibit a flickering non-identity with self that burns something akin to two wormholes through the temporal order of narrative to whatever is properly outside it. If, as Lapidge argues, the approach of Grendel attempts to evoke 'the sensation of terror that is experienced in nightmares',[79] the simile comparing the eyes to flame attempts to alight for a moment precisely on the hallucinatory sensory-affective texture of the prenarrativized dream material. The fiery eyes enact the aesthetic fallout of a deterritorialization of narrative by the ecstatic operations of lyric. In terms of the units of Barthes' narratology, 'indices' (usually understood as providing information about the world of a story) are 'truly semantic units … [that] refer to a signified' rather than to an operation of the sequence at hand or to one further down the line.[80] As an index, the fiery eyes become a zero-point of semantic verticality, a vortex of lyricism whose aesthetics attempt to sense what something other than narrative—or that resists narrative—might feel like.

It is too tempting not to remark that, in the accidents of history, fire quite literally marks the outside of the narrative of *Beowulf* in its materiality as a manuscript truly beset with fire, singed from its brush with combustion in the 1731 Cotton Library fire, in which it found safety only in defenestration.[81] But this aside, narrative-piercing fire already spreads within the world of the poem. Stacy Klein argues that the victor in the Finnsburg episode is 'the fire itself, symbol of an ethos of insatiable violence'.[82] Moreover, as Christine Rauer notes, 'imagery of fire, heat and burning … occurs in almost every reference to the dragon', and, although the association of dragons with heat and fire is widely attested, it 'is not usually given the same prominence as in *Beowulf*'.[83] Indeed, in the unique compound *fyrdraca* (fire-dragon, l. 2689a), the dragon that quite literally ends Beowulf's narrative is joined to fire at the level of the lexeme. Almost never does the poem associate fire with anything pleasing. When the dragon 'wearp wælfyre' (launched out slaughter-fire), the result involves an unpleasant fluid-like spreading described with the verb *springan*—'wide sprungon/ hildeleoman' (battle-light spread/burst-forth/dispersed on all sides) (ll. 2582–2583a)—used elsewhere in the poem to describe how Grendel's 'hra wide sprong' (l. 1588b) (corpse burst all over) in death, and the way that 'swat ædrum sprong' (blood swiftly spread) (l. 2966b) from under Ongentheow's hair at Ravenswood. As Irving writes, fire is the dragon's 'most memorable attribute' and 'is never associated with heroic energy'.[84]

Up to and especially in the mouth of the dragon, the poem's lexicon of fire and flame accrues as the soft locus of a meta-aesthetic discourse, incompletely entangling the aesthetics of poetic diction and narrative. This lexicon for fire and heat adumbrates a phenomenal field at and beyond the limits of the human sensorium—references to which interrupt the main narrative with lyrical inclusions, indirectly registering an aesthetics of vulnerable corporeality that remains resistant to narrativity itself. All told, the poem employs at least nineteen different terms for fire, flame, or fire or flame with specific functions (a number of which are unique to the poem)—as well as two additional terms for human reactions to fire that may be read as referring to fire (i.e. compounds that take a 'fire-word' as the base-word) and two figurative epithets for fire (see Appendix). A lexical study on the granular level of the classic contributions of Brodeur's student Caroline Brady is not possible here,[85] but a brief survey of the most salient terms will be helpful.

Common words for fire and flame in *Beowulf* can suggest sensations of snagging, enveloping, and, as in the case of the serpent-bite flames above, sharpness. In two of the eight occurrences of garden variety *fyr* (fire)—a common word across the Old English corpus—the word is collocated with the past participle of the verb *befon* (ll. 2274a, 2595a) (enclose, ensnare, surround, seize), as is one instance of *lig* (l. 2321b) (flame), another relatively common term.[86] This sense of fire as enveloping can additionally register the flickering speed and the fractal curve and point of flame. In the latter collocation of *fyr* with *befon*, the 'nacod niðdraca' (smooth enemy-dragon) takes to the night sky 'fyre befangen' (l. 2273–2274a) (enveloped in fire). As Hideki Watanabe points out, this description of the dragon as both *nacod* (smooth? bare?—the term has given critics some difficulty)[87] and wreathed in fire resonates with the sword-epithet *hildeleoma* (battle-flame) so that, insofar as an unsheathed (*nacod*) sword is a battle-flame, the fire-sheathed dragon is 'assimilated to an unsheathed sword'.[88]

Elsewhere, the dragon's *fyr* suggests a further accelerated corporeal kinesthetics. The dragon is 'fyre gefysed' (l. 2309a) (impelled by fire).[89] From the perspective of oral-formulaic composition, Guillemette Bolens argues that the text invokes a logic of corporeal fire production that prioritizes abnormal or contorted bodily mobility over 'a form consisting of organs', and maintains that, rather than the mouth or head, 'the dragon's intellect is the source of flames because fire is produced not by organs but by a psychophysical event'.[90] For Bolens, when 'fyr unswiðor/ weoll of gewitte' (ll. 2881b–2882a) (fire less potently/ spilled from the head/mind/senses [of the dragon]) after the dragon is injured, we should imagine the fire as generated not from an organ in the head but from an intellect embodied in the dragon's wheeling movements.[91] However we conceive of the fire-producing mechanism, the shapes traced by the dragon's enclosing *fyr* are deeply associated with its coiling shape and its 'furious movements'—on which the poem focuses much more than the creature's motivation or symbolic import.[92] The *woh-bogen* (l. 2827a) (twist-bent) dragon is a *hring-boga* (coiled-creature) (l. 2561a),[93] whose movements include wheeling around or orbiting the outside of its barrow (*ymbe-hweorfan*, l. 2296b),[94] a serpentine sliding or slithering (*scriðan*, l. 2569b), and not only flying or flapping (*swingan*, l. 2264a) but also performing a kind of 'meteoric swerving, spinning flight' (as one critic finds in the description of the creature's flight as 'lacende hwearf' l. 2832b).[95]

The dragon also orbits the barrow 'hat ond hreohmod' (l. 2296a) (hot and fierce-minded). Especially in light of this description, other, more rare compounds with base-words that unmistakably refer to the dragon's fire, but take -*wylm* (surge, seething) as their limiting term, recall the surging and burning in descriptions of negative affective states from Old English vernacular psychology: *Bryne-wylm* (l. 2326b) (burning-surge), *fyr-wylm* (l. 2671a) (fire-surge), and *heaðo-wylm* (ll. 82b, 2819a) (battle-surge). In the case of the compounds *lig-egesa* and *gled-egesa* (both compounds unique to *Beowulf*), the reverse is true, as words that would in isolation seem to be primarily affect-words (both meaning something like *flame-terror* or *fire-terror*), seem to refer, in context, to the fire itself.[96] After the dragon is dead, the narrator explains that prior to its demise, it 'ligegesan wæg / hatne for horde, hioroweallende' (ll. 2780b–2781) (carried flame-terror, hot before the hoard,/ boiling over with violence; lit. sword-boiling, seething).[97] While Beowulf struggles alone with the dragon, Wiglaf exhorts the other warriors 'helpan hildfruman þenden hyt sy,/ gledegesa grim' (ll. 2649–2650a) (to help [our] battle-leader as long as the heat may be,/ the grim fire-terror'.[98] The latter example might be believably construed as a reference to the emotion that Beowulf endures at that moment. But since, in the first example, the flame-terror that the dragon carried before the hoard is *hat* (hot) and, in the second example, *gledegesa grim* can be taken as a variation of *hyt* (heat), it would seem that in both cases the dragon spreads fear of fire and fire itself,[99] or fire as terror materialized and sensorial—a lexical emulsion of the vocabulary of physical heat, elemental flame, and a discourse of sensory-affective experience.

Common words for flame and fire in the poem—*gled* (fire or flame in poetic diction, but prosaically live coals or embers),[100] along with *lig* and *fyr*—also adhere to a disturbingly gustatory register, especially as they attach to the verb *fretan* (devour, eat voraciously, consume).[101] Before Beowulf's funeral, Wiglaf laments, '[n]u sceal gled fretan/—weaxan wonna leg—wigena strengel' (ll. 3114b–3115) (now embers must devour—the dark flames flourish—the ruler of warriors). *Gled* also attaches to the gustatory register in the dragon's flame-production when we hear that it 'ongan gledum spiwan' (l. 2312) (began to vomit up flames). Despite the poetic context, *spiwan* is an inescapably gustatory/digestive verb, occurring widely with the sense of vomiting the contents of a diseased stomach, especially in medical contexts where it appears with (as here) a dative object.[102] The more rare, poetic terms *brond* (fire, a burning object) and *æled* (fire, as an element that can be kindled) also collocate with *fretan*, as when we learn that the dragon's hoard will burn with Beowulf's corpse, we are told that 'þa sceall brond fretan,/ æled þeccean'(ll. 3014b–3015a) (then the burning must devour, the fire conceal). And, on the pyre of Hildeburh's brother and son, fire as *lig* and, metaphorically, a *gæst* (spirit, breath, gust) seems hungry when 'lig ealle forswealg [the corpses]/ gæsta gifrost' (ll. 1122b–1123a) (flame entirely swallowed [the corpses]/ the greediest of spirits), consuming both bodies and treasure.

This paradoxically textured, cutting, fluid, gustatory, sonic, thermal, terrifying, angry, and sorrowful field reinforces the sense that the aesthetics of fire mark a lyric disruption and an aporia in the operations of narrative—specifically, in the narrativization of corporeal experience. When it is not interrupting the flow of the main narrative in Grendel's approach to Heorot, fire quite literally overwhelms and devours the human sensorium. Of course, the dragon's fire heralds total destruction, as when it pulverizes (*forgrindan*) Beowulf's fortress and Wiglaf's shield (ll. 2335a, 2677a), and nothing about the dragon shares a 'dependence on the limits of human perception'.[103] The poem's cremations, too, take their place alongside the allusions to the burning of Heorot and the references to the flames of the dragon as discrete nodes in a story about the aesthetics of fire. There, the sensory and affective terms that accrue to fire especially emphasize its over-saturation of corporeal sensory-affective experience. At Beowulf's 'bælfyra mæst' (l. 3143b) (largest of crematory fires), for example, the represented drama about the defeat of Beowulf's heroic male body and the likely impending sufferings of the Geats is shouted down by the lyrical, aural, and affective complexion of 'swogende leg/ wope bewunden' (ll. 3145b–3146a) (whooshing flame entwined with weeping).

But this narrative of fire and the human sensorium is perhaps nowhere more marked than in Hildeburh's brother's and son's noisy cremation at the heart of the Finn episode, where 'wælfyra mæst/ hlynode for hlawe' (ll. 1119b–1120a) (the biggest of slaughter-fires/ roared before the [grave] mound). Since the prosodical alliteration in line 1120 is carried by *h*- alone (*hlynode ... hlawe ... Hafelan*), the breath hissing from the extraprosodical repetition of the entire *hl*- consonant cluster serves to emphasize, if by pale imitation, that it is as if the sound of the fire is enough to consume the bodies. Kindling this lyrical eruption, in what critics often consider Hildeburh's one moment of agency:

> Het ða Hildeburh   æt Hnæfes ade
> hire selfre sunu   sweoloðe befæstan
> banfatu bærnan,   ond on bæl don
> eame on eaxle. (ll. 1114–1117a)

> Hildeburh then commanded that on Hnæf's funeral pile
> her own son be secured to the burning mass,
> to burn the bone-vessel, and to give [him] to the pyre
> at the shoulder of [his] uncle.[104]

It is hard for me to agree with Brodeur that this is 'stately', or 'one of the most majestic scenes in early literature'.[105] By this point, references to the bodies outnumber the three words for fire. And then, in the loud, huge conflagration, '[h]afelan multon,/ bengeato burston ðonne blod ætspranc,/ laðbite lices' (ll. 1120b–1122a) (heads melted, wound-openings burst, then blood spurted out from the hostile bites in the body). Hurley reads this moment within an account of Hildeburh 'as a limit case of the poem's ongoing negotiation of the limits of human agency per se',[106] and we might also read it as a limit case of the capacity to narrativize the human sensorium. By calling the fire a *gæst* (as discussed above), the text figuratively grants it animating spirits and the status of a narrative actor.[107] Unlike many of the animated 'things' of Old English poetry, whose 'voices', as Paz argues, enable a 'human-nonhuman dialogue' (however much it

is not 'easily contained by human discourse'), this fire is loud, but
mute.[108] It has no message, and is all aesthetics, yet its sensations
cannot be endured or translated for the human sensorium by narrative.
Here, Hurley argues, the story 'expends its force on the active role
played by the fire that swallows ('forswelgan') (1122) the bodies,
breaking them down to their component parts'[109]—reducing the
sensing corpus to the shoulders, bones, head, and hot fluids of the
senseless corpse. If vomited, fluid, sharp fire cannot taste very good,
here fire does the tasting—consuming, translating, and displacing
the locus of vulnerable corporeal experience.

Digressions, movements, and *fitts*: the heat of layered serialities

We can thus trace a kind of incipient, serialized narrative about the
poem's aesthetics of fire—and the limits of narrativizing the corporeal
sensorium—that emerges across the poem in a discrete sequence of
lyric fragments. Additionally, the interruptive aesthetics of fire, which
yield a kind of spacing in the flow of the main narrative, offer an
emblem of sorts for one of the components and aesthetic functions
of seriality. But does it make sense to look for a more marked
form of seriality in *Beowulf,* a spaced sequencing that conditions a
poetics of perceptual porosity on a larger scale? Put otherwise, how
seriously might we take *Beowulf* as a serial poem? Presumably with
something different in mind, Kenneth Sisam argued (in the same year
that Spicer gave his lectures on the serial poem in Vancouver) that
'[t]he extant form [of *Beowulf*] suggests a serial in three installments'.[110] But by what logic could a Blaser or a Spicer read the
Finnsburg episode as a unit in a serial poetics? It would be impractical
to expect any such units to resemble or to signify like Blaser's and
Spicer's serial units, which should be comprehended as shaped by
material historical conditions specific to post-war poetics—twentieth-
century popular media (television, radio) formats, twentieth-century
discourses of epic and totalitarianism, the shifting commodity status of
poetry at mid-century, etc.[111] However, both our general understanding
of the composition of Old English verse and the *Beowulf* manuscript
furnish us with some leads.

Pasternack's theory that Old English inscribed verse can be performed in 'movements' of (usually) fifteen to twenty-two lines could provide a heuristic for such boundaries—although without the certainty of typographically fixed sections that conventionally precede the performance of the modern printed poem. Since such movements are legible only as functions of an exceedingly 'writerly' text—in which the reader must combine minimal graphic cues in the manuscript with aural, prosodical, linguistic, conceptual, and narrative elements to discern and perform their boundaries as such[112]—the resulting 'marked breaks' are thus also 'the points at which readers enter the text to play with relationships among the movements, producing their own text or texts'.[113] There are probably not an infinity of viable boundaries, since the implied expression of 'tradition' will inevitably shape the coherence of a given verse-sequence,[114] and the obviousness of some boundaries to the trained reader may make some movements appear 'like building blocks that might be put together differently at another time'.[115] Yet, 'with no voice laying claim to the text, it belongs to its finders',[116] and so, when the signals do not clearly coincide, 'readers must decide the limits of the sequence according to desire as well as judgement of conventions'.[117] Pasternack's comparison of the structure of *Beowulf* to Paul C. Bauschatz's model for the atemporality of Germanic mythology as 'like a string or arrangement of beads'[118] suggests a model for the Old English serial poem—except that it would not always be immediately clear how to distinguish one bead from another.

In the case of *Beowulf*, another scheme of fixed, larger units potentially competes with, combines with, or overlays a serial reading of the poem by movement: the graphic division of the manuscript text into sections marked by roman numerals (accompanied by spacing, punctuation, and capitals that all vary between the manuscript's two scribes), which scholarly consensus presumes were referred to as *fitta* in Old English.[119] The word *fitt* may be taken generally to refer to a section or part but, on the basis of an Old Saxon cognate and the attestation of the Old English term as a gloss for the Latin *una lectio* (a reading, the reading-portion for a particular session of reading), the word may be taken more precisely as referring to a song-segment or poem-segment—in the sense of a 'canto'.[120] Ranging from 43 to 141 lines, although more often between 60 and 90, *Beowulf*'s fitts would have to be composed of a sequence of multiple 'movements'. Other Old English manuscripts also divide poems with punctuation, capitalization, and/or spacing—a small few with numerals (although only two with numbering pertaining to what modern editors take as individual poems).[121] Depending on how one tallies them, *Beowulf* has between forty-two and forty-three *fitts*.[122]

Debate continues about the extent to which these divisions are integral to the poem and relevant to its interpretation, especially focused on whether they are the sole work of the manuscript's two scribes, are copied from divisions in an exemplar, or can be identified in some way as 'authorial'.[123] Among those who accept that the divisions may be important to understanding the poem, a secondary debate concerns the extent to which they have a structural function and whether they can be aligned to chiastic structures, 'tectonic' schemes, and/or the distribution of major themes.[124] The heart of the primary debate lies in a persistent suspicion that the fitt-divisions 'may justly be called arbitrary and inappropriate' or are even evidence that whoever divided the poem failed to understand the poem's structure.[125] In noting that the poet 'felt at liberty to pause at places where we would not', Klaeber himself qualifies the remark with a reminder that the poet's 'conceptions of structure were different from our modern notions'.[126] The current editors more confidently assert without qualification that '[t]he person(s) responsible for the divisions felt at liberty to mark pauses at places where we would not, as well as to proceed without interruption where we would think a pause indispensable'.[127]

However, as a question of style comprehended in terms of corporeal experience rather than as a score along an abstracted continuum of appropriateness (whatever its historicity), and in the context of what Pasternack calls the 'unauthored' nature of Old English verse (as well as what we know about the role of scribes in shaping the production of manuscript texts),[128] whether or not the divisions are authorial as such ceases to be a necessary question. Both of the manuscript's scribes saw fit to preserve them from any presumed exemplar, and there is not, to my knowledge, any evidence that a reader contemporary to the manuscript would ignore them completely—so the burden of proof lies with those arguments that, finding the divisions ill fitting within a given theory of the poem's genesis or structure, deem them unworthy of any attention.[129] Even if the fitt-divisions are entirely the work of one or both of the scribes, and if even the scribes exhibit a poor comprehension of the poem (something Kiernan's account of their careful work would seem to counter),[130] the divisions shape how we encounter the only extant version of the poem. For example—and as a hint that we are on the right track—in examining the narrative patterns surrounding fitt-divisions which interrupt battle sequences, Sylvia Huntley Horowitz finds a suspense structure comparable to that of radio serials.[131] Without discounting previous studies of chiastic structures rendered legible by the fitt-divisions when viewed, as it were, from above, we might reconsider them as possible markers of a discrete seriality when they are met with in the phenomenology of sequential reading. More specifically, we might consider fitt-divisions in their coincidence with or aloofness to the potentially multiple boundaries of smaller verse-movements.

In lieu of a complete reevaluation of all the fitt-divisions of the poem, the remainder of this section considers the aesthetics that arise in the multivalent junctions of multiply overlaid—or incompletely overlapping—narrative units, fitt-divisions, and viable verse-movement boundaries in and around the Finnsburg episode. Taking the Finnsburg episode as a test case not only has the benefit of directly echoing Brodeur's critical preoccupations and the assignment recorded in Spicer's notebook. The episode also provides a coherent segment of the poem that traverses multiple fitts, includes an example, as discussed above, of the narrative-interrupting aesthetics of fire, and perennially raises questions about the relationship of the 'digressions' to the surrounding main narrative.[132] Moreover, despite ongoing disagreements about a number of textual problems and major elements of the narrative,[133] the episode has a tight chiastic structure.[134] Finally, as suggested by the fragmentary survival of 'The fight at Finnsburg' (a completely separate poem on the same subject), we can assume that the source material comprises an appropriate topic for a discrete *gid* (song, speech, recitation).[135]

Yet the whole of the episode does not coincide neatly with the two fitts that it traverses, nor, at either end, do these divisions necessarily line up with the only stylistic points of entry into the verse-sequences. Since critics continue to debate aspects of the allusively told narrative, I will try to sketch the main elements diplomatically. We pick up amidst the festivities in Heorot between the killing of

Grendel and his mother's retaliation. One of the songs recited by
the *scop* is that of Hildeburh, given in marriage by her people, the
Half-Danes, to Finn, the leader of a group of Frisians, in an effort
to secure peace between the two kin-groups. At Finn's court, the
peace breaks down, and after the ensuing conflict (which also involves
a group of 'Jutes' whose identity is the subject of debate) Hildeburh
oversees the gruesomely depicted cremation of her son and Hnæf,
her brother. When hostilities erupt again between the two parties,
who remain together over the winter under a tense truce, the
Frisians—including Finn—are slaughtered by the Half-Danes, now
under the command of Hengest, and Hildeburh is taken back to
the Danish court.

The fitt juncture between Fitt xvi and Fitt xvii bisects the narrative
in the middle of the stalemate between Hengest and Finn,[136] so the
narrative that the *scop* recites (or the report of the narrative they
recite) is not coincident with a self-contained fitt. On the front end,
Fitt xvi opens with a transition into the scene of the festivities (ll.
1050–1062), before the passage that explicitly frames the recitations
of the *scop* and the start of the episode proper (ll. 1063–1070). At
the end of the episode, a very brief transition marking the end of
the report of the *scop*'s performance (ll. 1159b–1162a) precedes a
remarkable description of Wealhtheow's circulation in the hall
(coincident with a rare instance of hypermetric lines) and the arrangement of the men at the high seat before Wealhtheow's speech and
the division at the end of Fitt xvii (ll. 1162b–1191).

Following the start of Fitt xvi, there are at least one, if not two
stylistic/narrative boundaries before the narrative of the episode
itself begins. In the manuscript, under the placement of 'xvi' according
to the usual practice of the first scribe (on its own line, surrounded
by points, just slightly left of center) (Figure 5.1),[137] a brief verse-
movement describes how festivities slowly ramp-up while Hrothgar
arranges for rewards and compensations for the events of the previous
night. The movement concludes with a maxim on fate and forethought
(the passage is given here with plausible Sievers verse-types marked
in superscript, for reference below):

[C]Ða gyt æghwylcum   [A]eorla drihten
[C]þara þe mid Beowulfe   [E]brimlade teah
[C]on þære medubence   [A]maþðum gesealde,
[A]yrfelafe,   [B]ond þone ænne heht

^Agolde forgyldan,   ^Bþone ðe Grendel ær
^Amane acwealde—   ^Cswa he hyra ma wolde,
^Bnefne him witig God   ^Awyrd forstode
^Bond ðæs mannes mod.   ^{D2}Metod eallum weold
^Agumena cynnes,   ^Cswa he nu git deð.
^AForþan bið andgit   ^Aæghwær selest,
^Aferhðes foreþanc: ^Afela sceal gebidan
^Aleofes ond laþes   ^Bse þe longe her
^Con ðyssum windagum   ^Aworolde bruceð. (ll. 1050–1062)

At this point, the lord of earls—to each
of those (that took the sea-voyage with Beowulf)
on the mead-benches—gave treasures,
heirlooms, and then commanded someone
to pay in gold for the man that Grendel before
put to death—as he (Grendel) would have done to more of them
except that the wise God stood against fate
(along with one man's spirit). The Maker controlled all
of human kind, as he still does now.
Therefore understanding is best in everything,
deliberation of the spirit: one must await a lot
of love and of hate, who long here
in these struggle-days, endures the world.

The temporality of the maxim underscores its function as a boundary, suspending the narrative time of the ða (then) that opens the unit by supplying the epochal temporal scale of fate (which easily spans the narrative ða and nu [then and now] of 'ðyssum windagum' [these struggle-days]).[138] Additionally, the gnomic mode itself supplants narrative sequence with the cognitive and meditative discourses of *andgit* (understanding) and *ferhðes foreþanc* (deliberation/forethought of the spirit).[139] Prosody too marks the maxim as a kind of punctuation, since the b-verse that opens the maxim can be scanned as a D2 type verse (/ l/x\) (breaking the pattern of preceding verse-types with a type seldom found in the b-verse in general),[140] and is followed by five lines bookended by an A-C and a C-A pattern (basic A-type: /xl/x, basic C-type: x/l/x), between which every half-line but one is an A-type.

This brief movement is followed by what might plausibly be read as an even briefer movement that describes the *scop*'s performances and has a relatively porous boundary with the beginning of the episode itself:

Þær wæs sang ond sweg   samod ætgædere
fore Healfdenes   hildewisan,
gomenwudu greted,   gid oft wrecen,
ðonne Healgamen,   Hroþgares scop
æfter medobence   mænan scolde
Finnes eaferan;   ða hie se fær begeat,
hæleð Healf-Dena,   Hnæf Scyldinga
in Freswæle   feallan scolde.
Ne huru Hildeburh   herian þorfte ... (ll. 1063–1071)

There was song and noise together at once
before the battle-wise one of the Halfdanes,
the harp-wood (was) touched, poems (were) often recited,
when Hrothgar's *scop* would ['was accustomed to'] recount
a hall-entertainment among the mead-benches
about the descendants of Finn. When the disaster befell them,
the warrior of the Halfdanes, Hnæf the Scylding,
had to fall in a Frisian-slaughter.
Not in the least did Hildeburh need to praise ...[141]

In the manuscript, a point follows 'worolde bruceð' (in the passage discussed above), preceding the opening of this movement with 'Þær wæs sang ond sweg' (there was song and noise) (Figure 5.1), which we can take as a principle clause in an a-verse with a clause-initial prosodical dip.[142] Since, as Daniel Donoghue has found, points in the *Beowulf* manuscript very often interact with verse syntax and occur before an a-verse that begins a clause, and, of these, most also precede a prosodical dip (seemingly providing a place for a reader's eye to pause while scanning ahead),[143] this point may simply serve to help clarify this break in the verse syntax. But while most points in Old English verse manuscripts seem to have very localized functions, this one is not strictly necessary to mark a new clause (the dip, *Þær wæs*, can do that), or for other likely uses (e.g. breaking up an alliterative run to help indicate the end of a line).[144] So, especially since this is the first point after the fitt boundary, it is worth noting, as Donoghue reports, that the majority of clauses following a point are principle clauses, and modern editors take many of these as the start of a new verse-paragraph.[145] It is possible then that some readers might encounter this point as emphasizing the coincidence of a narrative, syntactic, and stylistic boundary between the maxim and the return to the main narrative.[146]

Following this movement boundary and the scene of the *scop* performing, the poem begins to introduce the episode. Many scholars take the episode as a direct quotation of the *scop*'s performance, 'though there is little agreement where the performance begins'.[147] Presumably prompted by Brodeur, Spicer himself attempted to read the episode as a discrete unit but remained unsure of its boundaries; he inserted a footnote into his translation at the caesura of line 1068, reading 'Inserted. Does story begin here, 1069 or 1071?' (Figure 5.2).[148] Moreover, where the story begins is less certain to the extent that it is not immediately clear whether the poem reports the *scop*'s direct speech, a summary thereof, or, as Brodeur has it, 'as an illustration of the songs which furnished entertainment' (taking the episode as serving the poem's larger thematics, and not the Danish audience in Heorot).[149] Although direct speech in Old English poetry is marked quite differently than that of classical sources or the modern novel,[150] Brodeur's position might draw support from the relatively conspicuous absence of an introductory formula in the mode of the 'Beowulf maðelode' (e.g. l. 2510) (Beowulf speechified) type that would sharply demarcate the beginning of a quoted performance.

In any case, well-trodden textual difficulties further complicate the problem of where the episode begins. Most of these concern issues internal to syntactic units rather than the relationships between them, and their resolution would not totally eliminate the ambiguities of stylistic and structural boundaries.[151] Does the assertion that Hrothgar's *scop* 'mænan scolde/ Finnes eaferan' (ll. 1067b–1068a) (would ['was accustomed to'] recount, about the descendants of Finn) indicate that the following b-verse picks up with the matter of the episode proper, or does it merely elaborate the identification of the story as 'Finnes eaferan' ([about] the descendants of Finn)? The syntactic refrain between 'æfter medobence mænan scolde' (l. 1067) (would recount among the meadbenches) and 'in Freswæle feallan scolde' (l. 1070) (should fall in Frisian slaughter) may suggest a stronger stylistic boundary, contrasting the pleasantness of poetic recitation in Heorot with the unpleasantness recounted in the recitation that follows (which would then begin in the following line, in an a-verse with a clause-initial dip). Yet, the following line, 'ne huru Hildeburh herian þorfte', may either emphasize or soften this boundary, depending on whether we read *huru* as an emphatic adverb

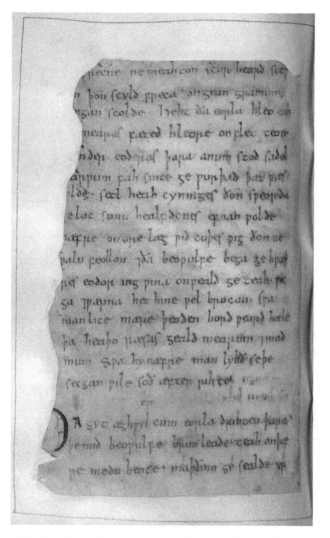

Figure 5.1 The *Beowulf* manuscript at Fitt xvi (British Library, Cotton MS Vitellius A XV), fols. 152v and 153r [BL fols. 155v-156r].

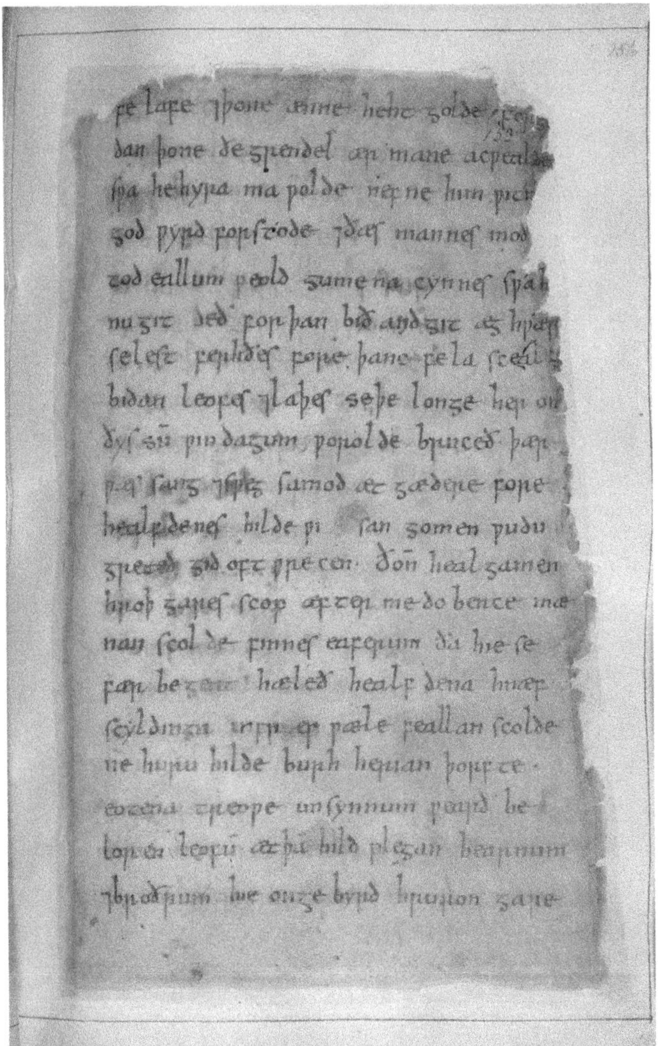

Figure 5.1 (Continued)

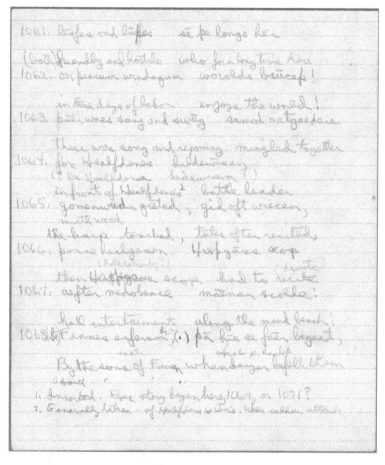

Figure 5.2 Page from Jack Spicer's translation of *Beowulf*,
ll. 1061–1068, with notes.

(*Indeed*, Hildeburh did not ...) or in collocation with *ne* as a
coordinating conjunction syntactically linked to the previous lines
(*Nor indeed* did Hildeburh ...).[152]

After the introduction of Hildeburh's name, it seems—for at least
a few lines—that we finally slip fully into the episode. And yet, one
last potential movement boundary remains:

Ne huru Hildeburh   herian þorfte
Eotena treowe;   unsynnum wearð
beloren leofum   æt þam lindplegan
bearnum ond broðrum;   hie on gebyrd hruron
gare wunde;   þæt was geomuru ides!
Nalles holinga   Hoces dohtor ... (ll. 1071–1076)

Not in the least did Hildeburh need to praise
the faith of Jutes. Guiltlessly she became
deprived of her dear ones in the shield-play
of children and brothers; they rushed to their ends
wounded by spears. That was a grief-stricken Lady!
Not at all did the daughter of Hoc, without care ...

These lines might be taken as beginning the episode proper, continuing the summary of the episode, or alternately as reorienting the summary of the episode around Hildeburh's grief and position in the feud.[153] Furthermore, the exclamatory *þæt was* ... (that was ...) construction is, as Bartlett notes, a conspicuous device for concluding entire poems.[154] In this case (occupying a single b-verse and followed by a new clause with an initial dip), the construction conspicuously echoes 'þæt was god cyning' (l. 11b) (that was a good king), which marks the end of the opening movement in the present poem. Whether one begins the episode proper before or after this line may depend on whether the reader takes Hildeburh as essential to a summary of the episode.

The conclusion of Fitt xvi—punctuated by the movement detailing the cremation of Hildeburh's son and Hnæf (ll. 1107–1124)—both interrupts or suspends the continuity of the episode and, as Horowitz argues, creates suspense around the outcome of the overall conflict.[155] At the same time, the cremation, with the interruptive aesthetics of fire discussed above, and as an occasion to pause over grief, coincides with this junction as a narrative boundary *within* the episode.

The end of the episode proper does not coincide with the end of Fitt xvii, which concludes after some thirty-two and a half additional lines. However, in comparison to the uncertainty about the point at which we enter the episode, once Hengest and his men avenge Hnæf, the end of the episode is explicitly marked in an abrupt shift back to the narrative time and space of the celebrations in Heorot:

                                   Hie on sælade
      drihtlice wif   to Denum feredon,
      læddon to leodum.
                                   Leoð wæs asungen,
      gleomannes gyd.   Gamen eft astah,
      beorhtode bencsweg;   byrelas sealdon
      win of wunderfatum. (ll. 1157b–1162a)

                                   They, on the sea-path
      transported the lordly woman to the Danes,
      carried [her] to [her] people.
                                   The song was sung through,
      the harp-man's recitation. Joy-sounds mounted-up after,
      bench-noise glittered; cup-bearers offered
      wine from wonder-cups.

If one were to read the episode as direct speech, there would be no
difficulty about where to put final quotation marks in a modern
translation—the discourse of the frame narrative clearly returns.

But even as the end of the episode is implicitly demarcated on
the level of pragmatics, it is not starkly differentiated from the
end-frame narrative by a stylistic boundary. The half-line that ends
the episode and the half-line that returns us to the main narrative
are both Sievers type-A verses and are hinged together as the a- and
b-verses of a prosodically continuous line. Only in the next line,
'gleomannes gyd. Gamen eft astah …'—whose a-verse ('gleomannes
gyd') is not precisely enjambed with, but in variation with *leoð* in
the preceding half-line—does the rhythm shift, with a type E a-verse
(/\x//) followed by a type D2 b-verse (///x/), both relatively less common
in those positions.[156] Although the shift of voice rings clear, this
overlaying of what we might think of as syntactic and prosodical
'hinges' stylistically softens the boundary between episode and main
narrative.[157]

This note is almost immediately drowned out by the stylistic
eruption that introduces Wealhtheow's speech and describes the
seating arrangement of the men she addresses:

      … win of wunderfatum.   Þa cwom Wealhþeo forð
      gan under gyldnum beage   þær þa godan twegen
      sæton suhtergefæderan;   þa gyt wæs hiera sib ætgædere,
      æghwylc oðrum trywe.   Swylce þær Unferþ þyle
      æt fotum sæt frean Scyldinga;   gehwylc hiora his ferhþe treowde,

þæt he hæfde mod micel,   þeah þe he his magum nære
arfæst æt ecga gelacum.   Spræc ða ides Scyldinga:
'Onfoh þissum fulle ... (ll. 1162–1169a)

... wine from wonder-cups. Then Wealhtheow came forth,
went out under a golden crown where those two good ones
sat, paternal-nephew and uncle; then their kinship was yet at one,
each faithful to the other. Likewise, there Unferth the spokesman
sat at the feet of the lord of the Scyldings; each of them trusted his
     spirit,
that he had a great mind, though he had not been, to his kin-people,
merciful in the commotion of swords. The Scylding lady then spoke:
Receive this full (cup) ...

If the previous lines did not, these loudly restart the time of the
main narrative. The adverb *þa* (then) recalibrates the temporal scale,
while the prosody of the whole half-line ('Þa cwom Wealhþeo forð',
which I scan as type-B, xx/lx/), with a clause-initial two-syllable
dip in a b-verse (clarified in the manuscript by a less common
mid-line point),[158] allows a brief hush before the sudden appearance of Wealhtheow. The announcement of the Queen's advent
then spills over into a variation that leads off one of the poem's
three groups of hypermetric lines (with six instead of four stressed
positions).

Yet this coordinated eruption of the main narrative and stylistic
pomp does not herald a new absorptive succession of events in the
narrative present, and critics often detect an ironic disjunction
between, on the one hand, the lavish hypermetric prosody and, on
the other, the lines of cryptic references to the future demise of
Heorot and the litotes concerning Unferth's history of kin-slaying.[159]
Moreover, by its nature as direct speech, Wealhtheow's ensuing
remarks (ll. 1169–1187) further slow the pace of the main narrative
we have only just re-entered, multiplying its multivalencies. As
Overing argues, this series of ambiguous directives (speech acts
which attempt to move others to do something) addressed to the
warriors on the bench have outcomes that are variously 'contradic-
tions', unknown, or that remain outside the action of the poem
itself.[160] Perhaps even as a direct function of the gendered semiotics
that Overing identifies in this exposing of 'linguistic promises',[161]
the directives thus erode the narratological distinction between context
and drama.

The final line of the speech is followed by a last view of the warriors (ironically united in peace) focalized through the queen, echoing the scene described in the hypermetric verses and offering a clear end-boundary for the verse-movement:

Hwearf þa bi bence,   þær hyre byre wæron,
Hreðric ond Hroðmund,   ond hæleþa bearn,
giogoð ætgædere;   þær se goda sæt,
Beowulf Geata   be þæm gebroðrum twæm. (ll. 1188–1191)

She turned then by the bench where her boys were,
Hrethric and Hrothmund, and the son of the warrior,
the youths together; where the good one sat,
Beowulf of the Geats, between the two brothers.

Finally, the boundary of the stylistic unit, the narrative unit, and the fitt-division coincide. So, although it was not at first quite clear where it began, this final movement of the fitt becomes retrospectively legible as a cohesive, semi-discrete unit.

Beowulf relies, at least in part, on inclusions of verse-movements that are composed of narrative's others (lyrics, maxims) and layered with localized stylistic effects in order to inscribe boundaries and breaches in the narrative. Partly for this reason, the search for seriality around the Finnsburg episode has met with a series of successive, variably marked aesthetic edges that herald fragments or shards breaching the texture of narrativity. 'From above', the well-known readings of envelope or similar mnemonic structures certainly help to make sense of this array of ambiguous boundaries bookending these fitts. But, as met with in the successive sequence of reading, around the fitt-divisions and the boundaries of the 'episode', one encounters a series of provisional, then dissolving, incompletely overlapping stylistic, formal, and narrative boundaries, as if several serial schemes were laid on top of each other. And where the sequencing of Blaser's and Spicer's serial arises from pure spacing—most akin to the fitt-divisions—at least in manuscript form, the narrative of *Beowulf* combines such boundaries with intrusions of non-narrative composition. The relative 'softness' of these boundaries as entry- or exit-points from a verse-sequence yields a certain kind of continuity, as, for example, when one becomes suddenly aware that the episode proper is underway, but, looking back, one cannot pinpoint precisely where they entered it. But this porousness also allows that what functions as a boundary might suddenly multiply or interrupt itself, so that one shudders through emergently discrete units on the way in and out of the episode.

Shorter units like verse-movements may seem more viable as a unit of composition for Old English poetry, rendering the fitts themselves perhaps less useful as discrete units from which to read *Beowulf* as a type of 'serial poem'. But the interplay of boundaries on the levels of pragmatics, narrative functions, and style—in such marked proximity to the fitt-divisions—suggests a kind of latent, emergent, uneven seriality. This emergent seriality may have a practical, if not uncomplicated, function in providing units of the poem for reading and performance—just as, for Spicer, serial composition made the possibility of composition by dictation more viable. Taken as a perceptual process of the poem, a function of the heat of *Beowulf*, this emergent seriality—a fundamental intteruptability or 'enterability' of the poem—marks a narrative aesthetics whose texture functions as the ground against which its inclusions get to play figure.

But as an operation of the heat of *Beowulf* scaled to narrative structure, the concretely sensorial dimension of this process is not immediately clear. If, for Spicer, seriality is the principle by which the 'book' is 'structured by dictation and not by the poet'[162]—which is to say, that elusive, indigestible Outside—then perhaps this structure registers some incompatibility of narrativity itself with a non-representational sensorial poetics. To phrase it in terms of the poem's incipient narrative of fire examined earlier in the chapter, these variably overlapping pseudo-serial units may be a result of a long narrative poem besieged by the role played by the aesthetics of fire in that story—that resistance of sensoriality to narrativity.

Representationally, of course, *Beowulf* is not 'about' these things, even though, as we saw early on, the synesthetic, multisensorial world that the poem is 'about' may lie beyond the scope of conventional representational poetics. Even so, this does not mean that, in the end, the heat of *Beowulf* is indistinguishable from human sensory experience. Unlike the aesthetics of compounds and variation that invoked specific regions of the non-human world and/or of corporeal experience, the aesthetics of these narrative inclusions most concretely circumscribe modulations of styles, genres, or occasions. Yet, Blaser writes, 'an actual directive of all serial poems is that the series is other than, not simply more than, its parts'.[163] Accordingly, in the poem's interruptive resistance to narrative, its aesthetics may become—although no less corporeal—both more lyric and *less human*.

My contention here is not that *Beowulf* is somehow indistinguishable from these mid-century poetics or would somehow, ahistorically, comprehend itself as the kind of serial poem that emerges in Blaser's and Spicer's poetry. But by thus thinking comparatively with the serial poem, we learn something about the always partial and so necessarily serial and aleatorily iterative entanglements of poetry and *not-poetry* in *Beowulf*. We learn that an early medieval poem *could* enact a narrative poetics in such a way to contest, or at least dialectically complicate, the aesthetic processes of narrative poetics. Blaser argues that 'the serial poem constantly circumscribes an absence that brings its presences to life'.[164] In its heat, Beowulf does this too, at once exposing and assisting the limits of vulnerable corporeality, attempting to reach—or rather, to translate—the heat that lies beside what it as a poem conceives of as poetry.

Notes

1 Bachelard, *The Psychoanalysis of fire*, p. 111.
2 *AOB*, p. 87.
3 Tolkien, 'Monsters', pp. 29–30.
4 Leyerle, 'The interlace structure of *Beowulf*', pp. 7, 13. Leyerle is not the only critic to dismiss the terminology of 'digressions'; see Stanley, 'The narrative art of *Beowulf*', p. 64; Stevick, 'Representing the form', p. 14.
5 Bartlett, *The larger rhetorical patterns*, pp. 9–29. And see, e.g., Hieatt, 'Envelope patterns'; Howlett, 'Form and genre'.
6 Niles, 'Ring composition', p. 933 n. 7. Cf. Tonsfeldt, 'Ring structure'.
7 E.g. Hart, '*Ellen*: some tectonic relationships'; Carrigan, 'Structure and thematic development'; Howlett, 'Form and genre'; Hieatt, 'Envelope patterns'; Huppé, *The hero in the earthly city*, p. 89.
8 Stevick, 'Representing the form', p. 5.
9 Hill, 'Episodes such as the Offa of Angeln passage', p. 29.
10 Stevick, 'Hunting the Anglo-Saxon aesthetic', pp. 145, 134, 160.
11 Hill, 'On aesthetics', p. 10. The remark is made with respect to the interests of Hill's work along with that of Hart and Stevick.

12 Niles, 'Ring composition', p. 931.
13 *Ibid.*, p. 932.
14 E.g. Bartlett, *The larger rhetorical patterns,* pp. 9–29; Du Bois, 'The unity of *Beowulf*', pp. 402, 405.
15 Niles' work is particularly emblematic in this regard, e.g. Niles, *Homo narrans.*
16 E.g. Barnes, 'Folktale morphology'; Shippey, 'The fairy tale structure of *Beowulf*'; Rosenburg, 'Folktale morphology and the structure of *Beowulf*'. More recently, see Aguirre, 'Phasing *Beowulf*'.
17 Todorov, 'The two principles of narrative', p. 39.
18 Shklovsky, *Theory of prose,* p. 170.
19 *AOB,* p. 221.
20 Hadbawnik, 'Introduction: "*Beowulf* is a hoax"', pp. 4–5.
21 *AOB,* pp. 132, 229.
22 *Ibid.,* see pp. 223–35, at p. 223.
23 Conte, *Unending design,* p. 11. For Creeley's quote, see Olson, 'Projective verse', p. 240.
24 Conte, *Unending design,* p. 21. And see Altieri, 'From symbolist throught to immanence'.
25 Conte, *Unending design,* pp. 20–2.
26 The debate, too labyrinthine to represent here, ranges from who was or was not present at the *Medieval scenes* sessions, to whether or not this work was an inaugural serial poem for the group, to which of their later works are truly serial poems. Duncan's accounts are various (and sometimes contradictory), including the printed preface in *Medieval scenes* (1979 reprint), typescript and manuscript notes for the Medieval scenes papers at Kent State University, and several interviews. See Duncan, *A poet's mind,* e.g. pp. 17, 75, 77–8, 109–10. Cf. *AT,* p. 69; *House,* pp. 52–3, 55–6; Jarnot, *Robert Duncan,* pp. 101–5; Nichols, *A literary biography,* pp. 42–4; *PBLG,* pp. 12, 20.
27 Conte, *Unending design,* pp. 49, 63. He does not consider Blaser in his own right.
28 Nealon, *The matter of capital,* p. 32.
29 Katz, *The poetry,* pp. 21, 48 n. 3.
30 E.g. *House,* pp. 4–48; see Gizzi, 'Afterword', pp. 185–9.
31 *House,* p. 55.
32 *MV,* p. 163.
33 *House,* p. 54.
34 See *TF,* p. 119.
35 *House,* p. 55.
36 *TF,* p. 5.
37 *Ibid.,* pp. 5–6.

38 Barthes, 'An introduction', pp. 244–6.
39 *Ibid.*, p. 255.
40 *Ibid.*, p. 270.
41 *Ibid.* p. 270.
42 *Ibid.*, p. 271.
43 *Ibid.*
44 *Ibid.*
45 *Ibid.*, pp. 264–5.
46 Derrida, 'Structure, sign, and play', pp. 278, 280.
47 Barthes, *Camera lucida*, pp. 25–7. It would be disingenuous not to imagine that Dinshaw's invocation of the punctum informs my thinking here, however different the context. See *Getting medieval*, pp. 40–54.
48 See Sisam, *The structure of Beowulf*. And see, e.g., Duncan, 'Epitaphs for æglæcan'. More recently, Joy and Ramsey, 'Liquid *Beowulf*', pp. xxx–lxvii, xxxvii; Cronan, 'Narrative disjunctions'. For post-*Liedertheorie* theories of compositional disunity, see Magoun, '*Beowulf* A', and '*Béowulf* B'; and Kiernan, *Beowulf and the Beowulf manuscript*, pp. 249–57. And see Kisor, 'The aesthetics of *Beowulf*', p. 245
49 Nist, 'The structure of *Beowulf*', p. 312.
50 Sharma, 'Metalepsis and monstrosity', pp. 246–8, 279.
51 The theory originates with Ludwig Ettmüller, but becomes more indelibly associated with Karl Müllenhoff. In 1979, Calder clocks the earliest attempts to disprove the theory to Karl Schemann in 1882 ('The study of style', p. 24).
52 JSB.
53 Hadbawnik, 'Introduction: "*Beowulf* is a hoax"', p. 7.
54 Nichols, *Radical affections*, p. 172.
55 '"*Beowulf* is a hoax"', p. 7 n. 8.
56 Hurley, *Translation effects*, p. 154.
57 Blaser, *The holy forest*, p. 182.
58 Frank, '*Beowulf* and the intimacy of large parties,' p. 57.
59 Bonjour, *The digressions*, pp. 45–6; *AOB*, p. 228.
60 Frank, '*Beowulf* and the intimacy of large parties', p. 60.
61 Earl, 'The Swedish wars in *Beowulf*', pp. 32–3.
62 *AOB*, pp. 88–106. The phrase spawns a whole 'design for terror' industry in *Beowulf* criticism. See Renoir, 'Point of view'; Greenfield, 'Grendel's approach'; Lapidge, '*Beowulf* and the psychology of terror'; Storms, 'Grendel the terrible'; O'Brien O'Keeffe, '*Beowulf*: lines 702b–836'.
63 *AOB*, p. 89.
64 Renoir, 'Point of view', pp. 162–3.
65 Greenfield, 'Grendel's approach', p. 283.

66 JH, s.v. *oniernan*.
67 On detecting irony in 'formulaic' descriptions, see Liuzza, 'Iron and irony', p. 60.
68 Renoir, 'Point of view', p. 165.
69 *Ibid.*, pp. 162–3.
70 Lapidge, '*Beowulf* and the psychology of terror', p. 399 n. 27.
71 Renoir, 'Point of view', p. 166.
72 Lapidge, '*Beowulf* and the psychology of terror', pp. 376–7. On the phenomenology of 'moon eyes', see Ármann Jakobsson, *The troll inside you*, pp. 37, 44, 45, 49, 134, 136; on 'moon eyes' as a narratological problem, Eriksen, 'Traversing', pp. 96–7.
73 *Daniel*, l. 240.
74 Irving, *A reading*, p. 173. Irving too references *Daniel*, l. 241.
75 *Christ*, ll. 1250–1251.
76 This reading draws on Liuzza, who follows Mitchell and Robinson's edition here. See Liuzza, *Beowulf*, l. 70, p. 55 n. 2; Mitchell and Robinson, *Beowulf*, l. 70.
77 DOE, s.v. *ge·frignan*, B., B.1. See Hurley, *Translation effects*, pp. 151–4; Saltzman, 'Community', pp. 46–7; Magennis, *Images of community*, pp. 1–2. These are *figured* examples, not reflections of historical modes of performance. See Frank, 'The search for the Anglo-Saxon oral poet'; Niles, 'The myth of the Anglo-Saxon oral poet'.
78 See Anlezark, *Water and fire*, pp. 292–366.
79 Lapidge, '*Beowulf* and the psychology of terror', pp. 391–2.
80 Barthes, 'An introduction', p. 247.
81 Kl. 4, p. xxvi; Prescott, '"Their present miserable state"'.
82 Klein, *Ruling women*, p. 94.
83 Rauer, *Beowulf and the dragon*, p. 33. Cf. Lawrence, 'The dragon and his lair', p. 549; and, on the necessarily *imaginary* nature of the dragon, Du Bois, 'The dragon', p. 821. And see Ogura, 'OE *wyrm, nædre,* and *draca*', p. 118, who argues that the dragon's fire differentiates it from a venomous *nædre* (serpent).
84 Irving, *A reading*, p. 216.
85 Brady, 'The synonyms for "sea" in *Beowulf*'; 'Weapons in *Beowulf*'. On other groups of synonyms see Kl. 4, pp. cxiv–cxv.
86 DOE, s.v. *fyr*.
87 Sisam objects to 'smooth' as an 'unlikely translation' for what he assumes is a modifier for reptilian, scaled skin. See Sisam, 'Beowulf's fight', p. 134.
88 Watanabe, 'Sword, fire, and dragon', p. 199.
89 See Lawrence, 'The dragon and his lair', p. 549.
90 Bolens, 'The limits of textuality', pp. 109, 122.

91 *Ibid.*
92 Irving, *A reading*, p. 216. But see Du Bois, 'The dragon in *Beowulf*', pp. 819–22; Bonjour, *Twelve Beowulf papers,* pp. 97–113.
93 Critics debate the particulars of the dragon's serpentine or lizard-like shape. See Sisam, '*Beowulf*'s fight', 143; Shilton, 'The nature of Beowulf's dragon', pp. 68, 71; Keller, 'The dragon in *Beowulf* revisited', p. 220; Brown, 'The firedrake in *Beowulf*', pp. 439–41.
94 But see Huppé, who finds this action 'grimly humorous'. See *The hero in the earthly city*, p. 54,
95 Brown, 'The firedrake in *Beowulf*', p. 453. But see Klaeber, 'The Christian elements of *Beowulf*', pp. 63–4. Klaeber contends that *lacende hwearf* means merely 'flying'.
96 Following the logic of most noun-noun nominal compounds of this type, the *DOE* analyzes the word *gled-egesa* as terror *caused by* fire.
97 The participial compound *hioroweallende* is particularly challenging to construe in Present Day English, since the limiting word, *heoru-* (as a simplex, a poetic term for *sword*), is particularly productive of compounds which make sense in terms of literal swords (e.g. *heorudolg*, lit. sword-wound). Both the *DOE* and JH solve the problem by taking *heoru-* as a metonymic abstraction, giving, respectively, 'seething with destruction' and 'gushing with destruction'. See *DOE,* s.v. *heoruweallende*; JH, s.v. heoruweallende.
98 Here I follow Kl. 4 in reading *hyt* as 'heat' and not a third person pronoun (p. 253, n 2649b; glossary, s.v. *hyt(t)*).
99 On merging of 'fact and figure' in OE poetry, see Stanley, 'Old English poetic diction', regarding *weallan/wylm*, at pp. 472–3.
100 *DOE,* s.v. *gled.*
101 *DOE,* s.v. *fretan.*
102 See BT, s.v. *spiwan*, 1, 1b. The occurrences in *Bald's leechbook* are too numerous to list here and are easily found with a *DOE Corpus* search. One can *spiwan* a wide range of things, from worms, to blood, to—as penitentials suggest—too much drink, e.g. Raith, *Die altenglische Version,* p. 241.
103 Calder, 'Setting and ethos', p. 35. And see Amodio, 'Affective criticism', pp. 65–7. Cf. Bonjour, *Twelve Beowulf papers,* pp. 98–9, 107; Whitelock, *The audience of Beowulf*, p. 95; Lawrence, 'The dragon and his lair', pp. 549–50; Shilton, 'The nature of Beowulf's dragon', p. 71. But, cautioning against such suppositions, see Brown, 'The firedrake in *Beowulf*', p. 450.
104 On Hildeburh's agency, see, e.g.: Hill, 'Þæt wæs geomuru ides!', p. 241; Porter, 'The social centrality of women in *Beowulf*'; Hurley, 'Elemental intimacies', pp. 150–3.

105 Brodeur, 'Design and motive', pp. 16, 18.

106 Hurley, 'Elemental intimacies', p. 151.

107 *Ibid.*, p. 148.

108 Paz, *Nonhuman voices,* p. 29.

109 Hurley, 'Elemental intimacies', p. 151.

110 Sisam, *The structure of Beowulf,* p. 4.

111 See Conte, *Unending design*, pp. 3, 103; Gizzi, 'Afterword', pp. 181, 187–9; Nealon, *The matter of capital,* pp. 126–9; *PBLG*, pp. x, 4.

112 Pasternack, *Textuality,* pp. 10–11, 21–7, 120–1.

113 *Ibid.*, pp. 120–1.

114 *Ibid.*, pp. 19, 24, 146.

115 *Ibid.*, p. 44.

116 *Ibid.*, pp. 148, 120.

117 *Ibid.*, p. 168.

118 *Ibid.*, pp. 121–3, citing Bauschatz, *The well and the tree*, p. 97.

119 See Kl. 3, pp. c–ci; Kl. 4, pp. xxxiii–xxxv.

120 Kl. 4, p. xxxiii n. 5; Timmer, 'Sectional divisions', pp. 320–1.

121 The editors of Kl. 4 assume that 'all the longer Old English poems' are fitted (p. xxxiii). See also Timmer, 'Sectional divisions'; Owen-Crocker, *Four funerals*, p. 138; Fulk, 'The origin of the numbered sections', pp. 105–7; Pasternack, *Textuality,* p. 149. In the Junius Manuscript, the numbering is continuous across the entire sequence of *Genesis, Exodus,* and *Daniel*. See *ASPR* 1, pp. xviii–xxi.

122 The first section is not preceded by a number, and three numerals seem to be omitted. Some of the numerals have been altered by erasure and overwriting. Kl. 3 counts forty-three, excepting the first section (p. c); Kl. 4 counts forty-two, excepting the first section (p. xxxiv). Horowitz counts 'forty-three (or forty-four with the numbered exordium)'. Owen-Crocker believes the numerals of the first scribe refer retrospectively through *Fitt* xii, and so includes the first section (labeled as fitt 0) in her total count of forty-four. See Horowitz, 'Interrupted battles', p. 296; Owen-Crocker, *Four funerals*, p. 142.

123 See Kl. 3, p. ci; cf. Kl. 4, p. xxxv. See also Bradley, 'The numbered sections', p. 165; Carrigan, 'Structure and thematic development'; Willard, 'Review', pp. 622–3; Timmer, 'Sectional divisions', pp. 321–2; Boyle, 'The Nowell Codex and the poem of *Beowulf*', p. 30; Kiernan, *Beowulf and the Beowulf manuscript*, pp. 243–78; Conner, 'The section numbers in the *Beowulf* manuscript'; Huppé, *The hero in the earthly city*, pp. 61–102; Eliason, 'Review'; Wells, 'The sections in Old English poetry'; Howlett, 'Form and genre in *Beowulf*'; Howlett, 'New criteria for editing *Beowulf*'; Horowitz, 'Interrupted battles', pp. 295–304; Mitchell and Robinson, *Beowulf*, pp. 6–7; Owen-Crocker, *Four funerals*,

pp. 133–57; Fulk, 'The origin of the numbered sections'. See Fulk's essay for extended bibliography.

124 Huppé, *The hero in the earthly city*, p. 63. For chiastic and 'tectonic' readings of the fitts, see Carrigan, 'Structure and thematic development'; Owen-Crocker, *Four funerals*, pp. 133–57; Hieatt, 'Envelope patterns', pp. 249–65; Hart, 'Ellen: some tectonic relationships'.

125 Kl. 4, p. xxxv. Fulk, 'The origin of the numbered sections', pp. 96, 104.

126 Kl. 3, p. ci.

127 Kl. 4, p. xxxv.

128 Pasternack, *Textuality*, pp. 12–21; and see O'Brien O'Keeffe, *Visible song*, pp. 46–7, 193.

129 My thanks to Daniel Donoghue for helping me to clarify this logic. Any problems in this argument remain my own.

130 Kiernan, *Beowulf and the Beowulf manuscript*, pp. 10–11, 171, 193–218.

131 Horowitz, 'Interrupted battles', p. 296.

132 Uncharacteristically, Brodeur thought that the immediate surrounding sequence was not important in this case ('Design and motive', p. 41), and that the episode 'is self-contained, and in itself quite independent of the main story. Yet it is highly appropriate in context' (*AOB*, p. 140). Elsewhere, Brodeur seems to equivocate, suggesting that the choice of poem may be significant in the presence of Wealhtheow (*AOB*, pp. 119–20). See also Sisam, *The structure of Beowulf*, pp. 33–9; Benskin, 'The narrative structure', p. 61. Cf. Bonjour, *The digressions*, pp. 59–62; Lawrence, *Beowulf and epic tradition*, pp. 109–10; Fry, 'Finnsburh: a new interpretation'; Gwara, 'The foreign Beowulf'; Irving, *A reading*, pp. 136–7; Overing, *Language*, pp. 88–101.

133 Relevant literature dates back quite a way, but many continuing debates can be traced to Brodeur's disagreements in 'Climax' and 'Design and motive', with Malone, 'The Finn episode in *Beowulf*' and Williams, *The Finn episode in Beowulf*. See also Malone, 'Hildeburg and Hengest'; Fry, 'Finnsburh'; Kaske, 'The *eotenas* in *Beowulf*'; Fulk, 'Six cruces'; Bammesburger, 'Hildeburh's son'.

134 See Benksin, 'The narrative structure'; and on its function as *gid* see Gwara, 'The foreign Beowulf', pp. 198–201.

135 Neither text seems to draw directly on the other. See the discussion and references in Kl. 4, pp. 277–9, and 273 n. 1–2. It is worth noting, in the context of this chapter, that the fragment opens with moonlight (reflecting off advancing warriors) negatively compared to fire: 'ne her draca ne fleogeð,/ ne her ðisse healle hornas byrnað' (Kl. 4, ll. 3b–4) (nor here does a dragon fly,/ nor here do the gables of this hall burn).

136 All fitt numbers refer to Kl. 4.

137 Owen-Crocker, *Four funerals*, p. 140.

138 On verse-boundaries and the breaking of linear time, see Pasternack, *Textuality*, pp. 132–4.

139 On similar uses of gnomic utterance see Paternack, *Textuality*, pp. 37, 88.

140 I scan the line with the first stressed element, *Metod*, with two short syllables, carrying a resolved stress.

141 Ll. 1066–1067 include the cruces around MS 'heal gamen' (taken variously as hall-joy, or the proper name of Hrothgar's *scop*), and the uncertain sense of 'mænan'. See Kl. 4, pp. 180–1 n. 1066–70. I defer here to Liuzza's translation, which follows a number of other editors; e.g. Kl. 3, ll. 1066–1067; Wrenn, ll. 1066–1067. But see Fulk, 'Six cruces', pp. 195–8.

142 Function words that occur at the beginning of a clause in Old English poetry are typically unstressed, and here the verse can be read as a C-type (xx/lx/). The basic principle here concerns 'Kuhn's laws', but for major proposed modifications, see Momma, *The composition of Old English poetry*; Mines, 'An examination'; Hutcheson, 'Kuhn's law'. For a more recent endorsement, Weiskott, 'Old English'. For a remarkably lucid summary, see Donoghue, *How the Anglo-Saxons*, pp. 89–107.

143 Donoghue, *How the Anglo-Saxons*, pp. 110–14.

144 *Ibid.*, p. 125.

145 *Ibid.*, p. 114.

146 It should be noted that only a few lines later, another point precedes 'ðonne Healgamen' (l. 1066a) (Fig. 4), an a-verse with a clause-initial dip, with the likely effect, I think, of helping to clarify a clause boundary.

147 Kl. 4, p. 180 n. 1063–1159.

148 JSB. Spicer regularly uses 'Br.' to attribute information to Brodeur's lectures. On this page his notation is confused.

149 Brodeur, 'Design and motive', p. 42. More recently, Benskin softly echoes Brodeur, claiming the 'Biblical style' of the episode renders it 'hardly a story Hroðgar's scop would have sung'. See 'The narrative structure', pp. 61, 39. But see Fry, 'Finnsburh', pp. 2, 12; Gwara, 'the foreign Beowulf', p. 129.

150 See Louviot, *Direct speech*, pp. 24–100.

151 These include whether to emend MS *eaferum* to *eaferan*, the meaning of *mænan* and its object, and the related question of whether to read MS *heal gamen* as a common noun ('hall entertainment') or the name of Hrothgar's *scop*. See Kl. 4, pp. 180–1 for an overview. Taking *mænan* as intransitive and not emending *eaferum* would alter a syntactic boundary, but only by a half-line. This could make the

reading of elaboration/variation that I suggest below less likely but would not necessarily resolve whether or not the following lines begin the episode proper or continue to identify the particular story recited.

152 The relevant *DOE* entry highlights this latter possibility, see s.v. *huru*, 1.b.ii. Liuzza's translation takes it as merely emphatic; see Liuzza, *Beowulf*, l. 1071. Hurley reads *ne huru* as 'nor', but takes it as an appropriate beginning to the episode ('Elemental intimacies', p. 151).

153 Earlier critics, even one as sensitive to the poem's attention to Hildeburh's grief as Brodeur (e.g. 'Design and motive', p. 15), found her importance to the episode negligible: 'Hildeburh is not essential to the plot' (p. 16). Cf. Chance, *Woman as hero*, pp. 3, 10, 100–6; Overing, *Language*, pp. 68–107; Hill, 'Þæt wæs geomuru ides!', pp. 240–1; Klein, *Ruling women*, pp. 95–9; Hurley, 'Elemental intimacies'.

154 As Pasternack argues, 'the same devices that end poems also end movements'. See Pasternack, *Textuality*, pp. 125, 125 n. 18, citing Bartlett, *The larger rhetorical patterns*, p. 96.

155 Horowitz, 'Interrupted battles', p. 300.

156 Statistics on frequency of Sievers verse types from Kiernan, *Electronic Beowulf*.

157 See Donoghue, *How the Anglo-Saxons*, p. 113, on the possibility of an 'interesting interplay between metrical phrasing and syntactic phrasing, especially where the syntax spills over from one line to the next, as it often does in enjambed clauses of *Beowulf*'.

158 On mid-line points in *Beowulf*, see O'Brien O'Keeffe, *Visible song*, p. 175; Kl. 4, p. xxxii. And see Kiernan, *Electronic Beowulf*, f. 155v.

159 See *AOB*, pp. 119–20; on the meter and irony, see Irving, *A reading*, p. 137; Kl. 4, pp. clx–clxi.

160 Overing, *Language*, pp. 96–9.

161 *Ibid.*, p. 99.

162 *House*, p. 54.

163 *TF*, p. 33.

164 *TF*, p. 34.

Afterword

And yet they too break hearts. These humans—uncoded, uncyphered, their sheer presences. Beyond the word 'Beauty'.

They are the makers of man's enterprise. Beyond the word 'blowtorch,' the two of them, holding a blowtorch at all beauty.

Spicer, *A textbook of poetry*[1]

So what is the heat of *Beowulf*? It is multisensory, complexional, synesthetic, and not necessarily determined by early medieval sensory hierarchies, equally capable of extending or impairing, assisting or deforming the human sensorium and the experience of corporeality. It is an unstable *ductus*, a permutational diction, a porous structure. It is congruent with *ruminatio* and with the early medieval cardiocentric psychological model, and probably implies a monkish reader of a post-Benedictine-reform manuscript. It is not indifferent to the heat represented in the many fires of *Beowulf*—burning homes, treasures, and bodies (and we wonder whether Blaser and Spicer, West Coast poets reading *Beowulf* at mid-century, might have thought of heat and fire differently now that the climate catastrophe has brought the worsening and seemingly endless season of fires to that edge of North America). Its operations on different scales of the poem's structure overlap incompletely. It shuttles between the historically conditioned human sensorium and a larger non-human outside—what lies beyond that sensorium not in the Kantian sense of the beautiful, but as phenomenological fact. The heat of *Beowulf* insists on poetry as that which, paradoxically, includes what is emphatically not poetry—even in a poetry determined by a distinct poetic lexicon and a traditional system of expression.

The heat of *Beowulf* also points to that Old English poem's capacity to shape poetics a millennium after it was copied in its ment—not because of its stability, potency, or 'excellence', but because it releases, in the present, what Blaser called 'the passage of a wildness'.[2] In recognizing this, the complex of Blaser's and Spicer's encounter with the poem has been ironically much more 'medieval' than the critical practices of their contemporaries in professional Old English studies. This recognition offers us a literary historiography of the *longue durée* without transhistorical phenomena. It also offers an unexpected kind of scholarly 'accuracy' in helping us to translate, on a more granular level—however speculatively—a plausible early medieval experience of *Beowulf* that we can comprehend corporeally now.

By cultivating a greater critical capacity to detect and explore the non-representational capacities and orientations of medieval poems without immediately reinscribing them within a representational teleology, we are able to perceive them at work in an energetic world. In understanding medieval poems as *active* in this way, we also have that much more of a chance of doing what I believe Brodeur wanted to do for *Beowulf* in constructing a fragile framework for the study and appreciation of its aesthetics at mid-century: that is, to translate the poem—in the sense of allowing it to recrystallize—in the present as a work that 'promises that a great deal more will be held'. On this count, there is a growing corpus of contemporary poetry whose medievalisms are worth taking seriously as possible theoretical horizons for the medieval literature on which they draw and to which they address themselves.[3]

At the same time, I doubt that the legibility of 'heat' as a term for the aesthetic processes discussed here can be usefully transported very far from Blaser's corpus, and my focus on the process of following the contours of *Beowulf*'s aesthetics has meant avoiding more exegetical reading or generalized critical intervention. Even so, these admittedly idiosyncratic readings do harbor larger, generalizable implications for the practice of poetics beyond reading *Beowulf*. In ending the book, I want to point to three related examples on which my commentarial reading practices have not allowed sufficient direct discussion.

1. Once reframed as a question of perception rooted in historical sensology, aesthetics becomes an inescapably ecopoetical inquiry. While the ecopoetic must always start with an Outside, and may so often set out as a corrective to anthropocentricsm, it is all too

easy to forget that the human sensorium remains ineluctably primary in meeting the non-human world. The capacity for poetics to translate that world into sensorial processes reinvests ecopoetics with the vulnerable corporeality of the human body. For medievalists, late or early, these possibilities may point us in directions not traditionally sought by ecocriticism within a horizon of purely representational poetics: on the one hand, physiology, sensology, and/or health, and, on the other, translation.[4] As we saw in passing in Chapter 2, in a text like the Alfredian *Boethius*, we encounter both sides of this question as a condition for thinking about how both people and poems process sensory experiences of the non-human world. It is likely that ecocritical analyses also lie in wait within the latent phenomenologies of other early texts that consider rhetorical tropes and discussions of physical phenomena, like Byrhtferth's *Enchiridion*. Also of interest in this respect are the monastic theatrical, pedagogical, and hermeneutic practices of attention and distraction that Erica Weaver has considered.[5] If taken as conditioning a poetics of encountering the physical non-human world as much as a religious orthopraxis, we might expect such practices to articulate a kind of perceptual temporality outside of and modifying the experience of worldly human corporeality.

This last possibility in particular is also ripe for comparative reading between twentieth-century poetics and the medieval—and here I am thinking about the temporalities of two very different New York School-associated poets, John Ashbery and Bernadette Mayer. On the first page of Ashbery's long poem, *Flow chart*, we read, '*It seems I was reading something;/* I have forgotten the sense of it or what the small/ role of the central poem made me want to feel. No matter'.[6] From here the poem goes on for more than 200 pages with lines broken as verse but often stretched so long as to look like prose—becoming, as Ben Lerner describes it, 'one of the most exciting books I've ever read … also often boring'.[7] And yet, '[t]his boredom, however, is integral to the effect. If the book is "about" any one thing, it's about time, and isn't boredom, when time is emptied, the condition in which we experience temporality as such?'[8] Add to this another twentieth-century text, Bernadette Mayer's *Midwinter Day*—a bewildering book in six parts written entirely on December 22, 1978 that delves micrologically into the temporalities of the quotidian, opening up pockets of inhuman time with a very human domestic space and deforming the very temporality of the human sensorium:

> Often memory
> Lends images to looking past the town close to the threes
> Into the forest I saw while rehearsing for this narration,
> It's a piece or a dream or a story or a book, exciting invention,
> We cross the street getting a line for a poem from right of way
> But the neat dry bank is always the same big loss, even today
> Though the pigeons from our roof feed in the yard next door
> We are still as poor ...[9]

Taken together, such texts might offer a fascinating comparative node with which to better understand the poetics of human and inhuman temporality and attention in Old English and early Anglo-Latin monastic texts (for example, *horaria*) and orthopraxis.[10]

2. This convergence of sensology, phenomenology, and ecopoetics also makes possible a thicker consideration of ideologies and historical experiences of different forms of (especially sensory) impairment as a crucial horizon of non-representational aesthetics. This is not a question of perceiving or even historicizing 'beauty', but of what a poem can or cannot perceive, and how it can assist or impair the historical human sensorium. The assumed dominance of the visual in Old English poetry and in medieval hierarchies of the senses—as well as its place in the reflexive sensory register of our critical lexicon—set against all the non-visually oriented and synesthetic perceptual processes of *Beowulf* and the historical reality of vision impairment in early medieval England, presents a case in point. The all-too-brief attention I was able to pay to the intersection of sensory hierarchies and vision impairment in early medieval contexts can thus bear quite a bit more consideration, especially as a context for reevaluating assumptions about the dominance of the visual register—and the inclusion or occlusion of impaired and unimpaired multisensorial experience—in Old English verse.

Here, early medieval legal and medical texts, including the *Leechbooks* and the formerly maligned *Lacnunga,* still have more to tell us about potential counternarratives to hierarchies of the senses in Old English verse and early medieval material culture—not in a capitulation to a 'medical model' of disability but as textual traces of embodied experiences and concrete contexts for Old English sensorial poetics. Despite the mountains of scholarship on orality and aurality in medieval verse, as Garner points out, 'not everyone would have been able to participate equally in this oral/aural culture'.[11] Garner's effort to begin remediating the audism of 'much oral tradition scholarship' examines (as noted briefly in Chapter 2) medical and legal texts as it explores 'the intersections of Deaf studies and oral theory within the context of early medieval England in particular'.[12] Detailing an early medieval understanding of a wide spectrum of hearing loss and deafness during the period, alongside a diversity of social responses to those experiences,[13] such work suggests the need to consider how hearing loss and congenital hearing impairments may have shaped the sensorial aesthetics of Old English verse. Especially given my attention to Brodeur's recitations of *Beowulf*, such work may also enable comparative considerations of the aesthetics of Old English verse, aurality and poetic performance in the *longue durée*, and recent attention to deafness, error, and mishearing in contemporary poetics.[14]

Finally, in discussing especially the potentially impairing functions of the aesthetics of *Beowulf*, my vocabulary often implies a phenomenon of tactility and/or vision that deserves more attention across medieval studies, and which here I only have space to name: *texture*—what, for Eve Kosofsky Sedgwick comprised 'an array of perceptual data that includes repetition, but whose degree of organization hovers just below the level of shape or structure'.[15]

3. Lastly, to the extent that the heat of *Beowulf* is a phenomenon of medieval literary history as generated by twentieth-century avant-gardes, Blaser's and Spicer's implicit revisions of Pound's turn to the medieval also point to a very particularized non-representational capacity of Old English poetry. Pound's loss of interest in *Beowulf* can be linked to his gradual adherence to an account of medieval aesthetics congruent with the explicitly anti-ornamental purity of his 'radiant world where one thought cuts through another with a clean edge'[16]—as in the Vorticism deemed necessary, in part, because '[o]ne is tired of ornamentations'.[17] Accordingly, and in a manner that concerns the queer aspects of their poetics that have been less salient for much of this book, in admitting *Beowulf* back into the canon of companion texts for the avant-garde, Blaser and Spicer also implicitly reopen that poetics of radiant energy to the queerly coded, ornamental, medieval aesthetics rejected by Pound as 'bulging

and bumping and indulging in bulbous excrescence'.[18] An attention to the ornamentality of Old English poetics would require readings that emphasize the phenomenologically robust functions of supposedly superficial qualities of the text (i.e. rhetoric, aesthetics)—not because they are 'actually not' superficial, but in their very superficiality. What if we understood decoration and ornamentation not as a 'feature' or topic of Old English poetry, but as one of its primary non-representational functions?

Nowhere is this possibility more apparent than in the Exeter Book riddles, where a capacity to elicit wonder-responses to the everyday world already suggests a thick sensorial and phenomenological lexicon.[19] In the most radically non-representational functions of the riddles, they engage Pound's radiant world by decorating it. Take, for example, Riddle 31—whose 'solution' is by no means settled but might be reasonably taken as a bagpipe (or, as Niles gives it in Old English, *blæst-pipe):[20]

Is þes middangeard   missenlicum
wisum gewlitegad,   wrættum gefrætwad.
Ic seah sellic þing   singan on ræcede;
wiht wæs nower   werum on gemonge,
sio hæfde wæstum   wundorlicran.
Niþerweard   wæs neb hyre,
fet ond folme   fugele gelice;
no hwæþre fleogan mæg   ne fela gongan,
hwæþre feþegeorn   fremman onginneð,
gecoren cræftum,   cyrreð geneahhe
oft ond gelome   eorlum on gemonge,
siteð æt symble,   sæles bideþ,
hwonne ær heo cræft hyre   cyþan mote
werum on wonge.   Ne heo þær wiht þigeð
þæs þe him æt blisse   beornas habbað.
Deor domes georn,   hio dumb wunað;
hwæþre hyre is on fote   fæger hleoþor,
wynlicu woðgiefu.   Wrætlic me þinceð,
hu seo wiht mæge   wordum lacan
þurh fot neoþan,   frætwed hyrstum.
Hafað hyre on halse,   þonne hio hord warað,
bær, beagum deall,   broþor sine,
mæg mid mægne.   Micel is to hycgenne
wisum woðboran,   hwæt sio wiht sie.[21]

This middle-earth is in a variety
of ways made-radiant, decorated with ornaments.
I saw a strange thing singing in the hall.
There was nowhere a creature in the company of men
who had a more-wondrous issue.
Downward was her beak,
feet and hands alike to [those of] a bird.
However, she cannot fly, nor walk very much;
yet, foot-eager [yearning for locomotion], she endeavors to perform,
chosen with skill, she turns again
and again in the company of famous men,
sits at the feast, awaits that appointed time
when she may soon make her skill known
to the men in the meadow. Nor does she partake
of that which the men have in happiness.
A noble thing, eager for fame, she remains silent;
yet on her foot is a fair sound,
a joyous song-gift. It is *wrætlic* [wondrous, lit. ornament-like] to me,
how that creature may leap with words
by means of a foot beneath, [the creature] adorned with decorations.
She has her brothers on her neck when she guards treasure,
[her] naked [neck], exultant with rings,
—[she] the kinswoman with strength. It is great to consider,
for the wise speech-carrier, what the creature may be.[22]

The riddle opens with the fundamentally ornamental cosmology alluded to in Chapter 4, and then proceeds not to represent that cosmos so much as to produce it, *ornamenting the world* with a series of incompletely overlapping and variously scaled metaphors.[23] To the extent that this world appears, it appears ornamentally, and to the extent one wants to render it sensible in language, to entangle a poem with it, one must elaborate language into an ornamental surface. It is also the case that once 'solved', the riddle may harbor a 'central' metaphor that is key to 'unriddling' it, but in a non-hermeneutic mode, read for its sensory-affective activity and not its not-insignificant secrets, we encounter a series of incompletely overlapping implicit metaphors and similes that describe different parts or aspects of the 'creature'—and which we do not necessarily encounter at first glance as belonging to a single integrated metaphorical register.[24] Read in light of the stylistic commitments announced in the opening formula of the poem, we might experience successive similes, metaphors, and their partial overlapping as the poem's effort to hang so many gems or baubles on the variously physical or conceptual aspects of the 'solution'. The interruption of a more gnomic style near the end of the poem suggests as much, reflecting the results of what the poem has done: *it is amazing that this thing coated with decoration now appears as such—in and through the poem's capacity to ornament it.* It isn't that we readers of Old English verse are insensitive to ornament, although we do tend to like to 'rescue' it from 'mere' ornamentality, eager to move on from the first stage of sense-making to its semiotic functions. But we rarely pause to consider the ecopoetical dimensions of a poem whose function is to decorate the world.

The heat of *Beowulf* is not necessarily complicit in such decoration—although the fabric of the poem also includes secrets and riddles,[25] and we might find space to read these too in terms of the sensorial functions of hermeneutic experiences rather than the other way around. Nor am I trying to argue for some kind of moratorium on mimetic or representational readings. But the specificity and idiosyncrasy that inheres in the range of implications and directions that I enumerate above are perhaps part of the point. The process of reading *Beowulf* with Blaser, Spicer, and Brodeur has perhaps suggested both that readers of twentieth-century literature can always expand their archive backwards and that practitioners of early medieval studies might more commonly entertain critical practices oriented less around a unitary thesis than particularized processes of reading. In turning to twentieth-century poetics as a theoretical discourse for reading medieval literature, and in turning towards a more premodern sense of aesthetics, what we gain more than anything else is perhaps the potential to expand and particularize our critical lexicon for the experience of medieval literature, in the past, in the twentieth century, and now. As high-minded as it sounds, this particularization of our critical vocabulary may help us better understand how poetry extends and impairs how we feel the world.

Notes

1   *MV,* p. 312.
2   *TF,* p. 29.

3 Patience Agbabi's work is well known to medievalists. Beyond the texts engaged in Old English cited in the introduction, see Moina Pam Dick, *Moira of edges / Moira the tart*; Pattie McCarthy's *margerykempething* and *qweyne wifthing;* kari edwards' *dôNrm'-lä-püsl*; and I want to point to Karen Coonrod and Paul Vasile's (in progress) *Judith*, a 'Music/Text/ Chamber/Hybrid/Opera'. I regret not having the space to speak to each of these in the main text and thank an anonymous reader for urging me to gesture to them more concretely.

4 It is worth reiterating that Hurley's recent book similarly lands on questions of the non-human in *Beowulf* through questions of translation; see Hurley, *Translation effects,* pp. 151–82.

5 Weaver, 'Performing (in)attention'.

6 Ashbery, *Flow chart,* p. 3.

7 Lerner, 'The reflection of a reading', p. 373.

8 *Ibid.*

9 Mayer, *Midwinter Day,* p. 43.

10 I am grateful to Erica Weaver for the conversation in which this constellation emerged, and in which she suggested Mayer's *Midwinter Day*. And see Weaver, 'Performing (in)attention)'.

11 Garner, 'Deaf studies', p. 22.

12 *Ibid.*, pp. 34, 22, and see 26.

13 *Ibid.*, p. 34.

14 E.g. Davidson, *Distressing.*

15 Sedgwick, *Touching feeling,* p. 16.

16 Pound, *Literary essays,* p. 154.

17 Pound, *Early writings,* p. 285.

18 Pound, *Literary essays,* pp. 150–1.

19 See Dailey, 'Riddles, wonder and responsiveness'; Ramey, 'Crafting strangeness', pp. 201–2; Ramey, 'The riddle of beauty', p. 480.

20 Riddle 31, and see ASPR 3, p. 338 n. 31; see also Niles, *Old English enigmatic poems,* p. 146 n. 10.

21 I have adjusted the punctuation of lines four and five from the ASPR text in accordance with my translation below.

22 I follow the ASPR 3 editors in taking *sio* in the final line as a relative pronoun.

23 See Remein, 'Decorate'.

24 On 'unriddling' central metaphors in Old English riddles, see Murphy, *Unriddling,* pp. 23, 77. On the hermeneutics of secrecy in the Old English riddles, see Saltzman, *Bonds of secrecy,* pp. 161–83.

25 Saltzman, 'Secrecy'.

Appendix: catalog of 'fire' and 'heat' words in *Beowulf*

FP = disproportionately frequent in poetry
P = occurs only in poetry
U = unique to *Beowulf*
'occurrences' = in the Old English corpus
(Information on frequency from Kl. 4, glossary, and *DOE*, when available; further estimates, for heuristic use only, based on *DOE Web Corpus* searches and Bessinger, *A Concordance*.)

In all quotations, all 'fire words' are in bold and all nouns and adjectives denoting 'heat' are underscored.

Nouns referencing *fire*

- *ad*, 55 occurrences, FP (specifically funerary fire)
  '**Ad** wæs geæfned' (l. 1107a)
  'Æt þæm **ade** wæs eþgesyne/ swatfah syrce ...' (ll. 1110–1111a)
  'Het ða Hildeburh æt Hnæfes **ade**/ hire selfre sunu sweoloðe befæstan' (ll. 114–115)
  'Him ða gegiredan Geata leode/ **ad** on eorðan unwæclicne' (ll. 3137–3138)
- *æled*, 12 occurrences, P (fire or flame, the element that can be kindled, usually destructive)
  'þa sceall **brond** fretan,/ **æled** þeccean' (ll. 3014b–3015a)
- *bæle*, 30 occurrences, FP (fire or flame of execution and sacrifice, also funerary fire)
  'ac mid **bæle** for,/ **fyre** gefysed' (ll. 2308b–2309a)
  'Hæfde landwara **lige** befangen,/ **bæle** ond **bronde**' (ll. 2321–2322a)

'beorhtne æfter **bæle**' (l. 2803a)

'Here-Scyldinga/ betst beadorinca wæs on **bæl** gearu' (ll. 1108b–1109)

'ond on **bæl** don/ eame on eaxle' (ll. 1116b–1117a)

'Denia leode/ **bronde** forbærnan, ne on **bel** hladan/ leofne mannan' (ll. 2125a–2127a)

'ær he **bæl** cure,/ <u>hate</u> **heaðowylmas**' (ll. 2818b–2819a)

●*bæle-fyr*, 3 occurrences, P (sacrificial-fire, funerary-fire, pyre)

'Ongunnon þa on beorge **bælfyra** mæst/ wigend weccan' (ll. 3143–3144a)

●*brond*, 50 occurrences, FP, also frequent in glosses (fire or flame, alternately a firebrand or burning object; figuratively, sword)

'þa sceall **brond** fretan,/ **æled** þeccean' (ll. 3014b–3015a)

'Denia leode/ **bronde** forbærnan, ne on **bel** hladan/ leofne mannan' (ll. 2125b–2127a)

'Hæfde landwara **lige** befangen,/ **bæle** ond **bronde**' (ll. 2321–2322a)

'**bronda** lafe' (l. 3160b)

as sword-epithet:

'þæt hine syðþan no/ **brond** ne beadomecas bitan ne meahton' (ll. 1453b–1454)

'Forgeaf þa Beowulfe **brand** Healfdenes' (l. 1020)

●*bryne-leoma*, 1 occurrence, U (beam of fire, burning flame, gleam of fire)

'**bryneleoma** stod/ eldum on andan' (ll. 2313b–2314a)

●*bryne-wylm*, 3 occurrences, P (surge of fire, surging flame, fire-wave, fire-swell, burning-swell)

'þæt his sylfes ham,/ bolda selest, **brynewylmum** mealt' (ll. 2325b–2326)

●*fyr*, 1625 occurrences (fire as physical phenomenon, combustion, one of four elements, etc.)

'þæt ðæt **fyr** ongon/ sweðrian syððan' (ll. 2701b–2702a)

'in **fyres** fæþm' (l. 185a)

'oððe **fyres** feng' (l. 1764a)

'**fyre** befangen' (l. 2274a)

'ac mid **bæle** for,/ **fyre** gefysed' (ll. 2308b–2309a)

'nearo ðrowode/ **fyre** befongen se ðe ær folce weold' (ll. 2594b–2595)

'**fyr** on flode' (l. 1366a)

•*fyr-wylm*, 1 occurrence, U (surge of fire, fire-swell, fire-wave)
'fyrwylmum fah' (l. 2671a)

•*gæst*, ca. 3100 occurrences, most not referring to fire (ghost, spirit, breath, *gust, movement in air, blast, demon*; figuratively, fire)
'lig ealle forswealg,/ **gæsta** gifrost' (ll. 1122b–1123a)

•*gled*, 110 occurrences (live coal, ember, bed of coals; in poetry, fire, flame; in glosses, spark, torch)
'þæt minne lichaman/ mid minne goldgyfan **gled** fæðmie' (ll. 2651b–2652)
'Nu sceal **gled** fretan/—weaxan wonna **leg**—wigena strengel' (ll. 3114b–3115)
'Ða se gæst ongan **gledum** spiwan' (l. 2312)
'**gledum** forgrunden' (l. 2335a)
'**gledum** forgrunden' (l. 2677a)
'wæs se legdraca/ grimlic gryrefah **gledum** beswæled' (ll. 3040b–3041)

•*gled-egesa*, 1 occurrence, U (flame-terror, fire-terror—but see OED, which suggests that it refers to a terror caused by fire and not to fire itself)
'þenden <u>hyt</u> sy,/ **gledegesa** grim' (ll. 2649b–2650a)

•*hilde-leoma*, 2 occurrences, U (battle-light; flames, fire; figuratively, sword)
'wide sprungon,/ **hildeleoman**' (ll. 2582b–2583a)

•*heaðo-fyr*, 2 occurrences, U (fierce fire, battle-fire)
'ac ic ðær **heaðufyres** <u>hates</u> wene' (l. 2522)
'wæs þær burnan **wælm**/ **heaðofyrum** hat' (ll. 2546b–2547a)

•*heaðo-wylm*, 7 occurrences, P (fierce flame, intense heat, battle-surge, battle-wave, battle-swell)
'[Sele] **heaðowylma** bad/ laðan **liges**' (ll. 82b–83a)
'ær he bæle cure,/ <u>hate</u> **heaðowylmas**' (ll. 2818b–2819a)

•*lig*, very frequent in poetry and prose (fire, flame, lightning)
'**lig** ealle forswealg,/ **gæsta** gifrost' (ll. 1122b–1123a)
'Nu sceal **gled** fretan/—weaxan wonna **leg**—wigena strengel' (ll. 3114b–3115)
'[Sele] **heaðowylma** bad/ laðan **liges**' (ll. 82b–83a)
'nymþe **liges** fæþm/ swulge on swaþule' (ll. 781b–782a)
'wolde se laða **lige** forgyldan/ drincfæt dyre' (ll. 2305–2306a)
'Hæfde landwara **lige** befangen,/ **bæle** ond **bronde**' (ll. 2321–2322a)

'lind wið **lige**' (l. 2341a)
'**ligge** gelicost' (l. 727a)
'for dracan **lege**' (l. 2549b)

•*lig-egesa*, 1 occurrence, U (fire-terror, but used with reference to the substance of the fire itself, see *gled-egesa*)
'**ligegesan** wæg/ <u>hatne</u> for horde' (ll. 2780b–2781a)

•*lig-yð*, 1 occurrence, U (fire-wave, flame-wave)
'**Lig-yðum** for' (l. 2672b)

•*swaþul*, 1 occurrence, U (flame, heat)
'nymþe **liges** fæþm/ swulge on **swaþule**' (ll. 781b–782a)

•*sweoloð*, U? [closely related words appear in poetry/prose] (heat, flames)
'hire selfre sunu **sweoloðe** befæstan,/ banfatu bærnan, ond on **bæl** don/ eame on eaxle' (ll. 1115–1117a)

•*swioðol*, U? [closely related words appear in both poetry and prose; see *swaþul*] (fire, flame)
'wudurec astah/ sweart ofer **swioðole**' (ll. 3144b–3145a)

•*wæl-fyr*, 2 occurrences, U (deadly fire, slaughter-fire)
'wearp **wælfyre**' (l. 2582a)
'Guðrec astah/ wand to wolcnum; **wælfyra** mæst/ hlynode for hlawe' (ll. 1118b–1120a)

•*wylm*, at least 29 occurrences in poetry, perhaps twice as many occurrences in prose (boiling, seething, welling, billow, steam; burning, flame)
'wæs þær burnan **wælm**/ heaðofyrum <u>hat</u>' (ll. 2546b–2547a)

Adjectives and nouns referencing *heat*

•*hat*, adj., ca. 350 occurrences (hot)
'wyrm <u>hat</u> gemealt' (l. 897b)
'<u>hat</u> ond hreohmod hlæw oft ymbehwearf' (l. 2296)
'wæs þære burnan **wælm**/ heaðofyrum <u>hat</u>' (ll. 2546b–2547a)
'<u>hat</u> hildeswat' (l. 2558a)
'<u>hat</u> ond heaðogrim' (l. 2691a)
'<u>hat</u> on hreðre' (l. 3148a)
'wæs þæt blod to þæs <u>hat</u>/ ættren ellorgæst se þær inne swealt' (ll. 1616b–1617)
'ac ic ðær **heaðufyres** <u>hates</u> wene' (l. 2522)

'atol yða geswing eal gemenged/ <u>haton</u> heolfre heorodreore weol'
   (ll. 848–849)

'<u>hatan</u> heolfre' (l. 1423a)

'**ligegesan wæg**/ <u>hatne</u> for horde' (ll. 2780b–2781a)

'ær he **bæle** cure,/ <u>hate</u> **headowylmas**' (ll. 2818b–2819a)

'<u>hatost</u> heaþoswata' (l. l668a)

•*hat*, noun, 11 occurrences, FP (heat)

   '[Wiglaf] geseah his mondryhten/ under heregriman <u>hat</u> þrowian'
   (ll. 2604b–2605)

•*hyt*, noun, unique form (?) (heat, see Kl. 4, glossary, s.v. *hyt(t)*)

   'þenden <u>hyt</u> sy,/ **gledegesa** grim' (ll. 2649b-2650a)

Bibliography

Editions and primary sources

Allen, Donald (ed.), *The new American poetry 1945–1960* (Berkeley, CA: University of California Press, 1999).

Ashbery, John, *Flow chart* (New York: Knopf, 1991).

Baraka, Amiri, 'State/meant', in *The LeRoi Jones/Amiri Baraka reader*, ed. William J. Harris (New York: Thunder's Mouth Press, 1991), pp. 169–70.

Bede, *Historiae ecclesiastica gentis Anglorum*, in J. E. King (ed.), *Bede: Opera historica* IV, Loeb Classical Library (Cambridge, MA: Harvard University Press, 1930).

Brodeur, Arthur G., Notes, *Selections from Beowulf read by Arthur G. Brodeur*, LP Audio Recording, 12 in., 33 1/3 rpm, published by Brodeur's Students and the University of California, 1955.

Brodeur, Arthur G., with Farnham Bishop, *The altar of the legion* (Boston, MA: Little Brown, 1926).

Blaser, Robin, *The astonishment tapes: talks on poetry and poetics with Robin Blaser and friends*, ed. Miriam Nichols (Tuscaloosa, AL: University of Alabama Press, 2015).

Blaser, Robin, *The fire: the collected essays of Robin Blaser*, ed. Miriam Nichols (Berkeley, CA: University of California Press, 2006).

Blaser, Robin, *The holy forest: the collected poems of Robin Blaser*, ed. Miriam Nichols (Berkeley, CA: University of California Press, 2006).

Blaser, Robin, 'Non-learned, non-ecclesiastical words in Old English from Latin and Romance sources: a quantitate approach', Robin Blaser fonds, Simon Fraser University Special Collections and Rare Books, MSA-103201, MSA-103205.

Chapman, George, *Bussy d'Ambois*, in Thomas Marc Parrott (ed.), *The plays and poems of George Chapman: the tragedies* (London: George Routledge and Sons, 1910), pp. 1–74.

Christ, in George Philip Krapp and Elliott Van Kirk Dobbie (eds), *ASPR*, Vol. 3 (New York: Columbia University Press, 1936), pp. 2–49.

Coonrod, Karen (librettist), and Paul Vasile (music), *Judith: Music/Text/ Chamber/Hybrid/Opera from the Anglo-Saxon Epic*, Workshop Performance, MIT Center for Art, Science and Technology, Cambridge, MA, March 5, 2019.

Daniel, in George Philip Krapp (ed.), *ASPR*, Vol. 1 (New York: Columbia University Press, 1931), pp. 11–132.

Dick, Moina Pam, *Moira of edges / Moira the tart* (Brooklyn, NY: Organism for poetic research, 2019).

The dream of the rood, in George Philip Krapp (ed.), *ASPR*, Vol. 1 (New York: Columbia University Press, 1931), pp. 61–5.

Duncan, Robert, 'The Chimeras of Gerard de Nerval' in *Poetry/Audit* 4.3 (1967), 38–64.

Duncan, Robert, *The collected early poems and plays*, ed. Peter Quartermain (Berkeley, CA: University of California Press, 2012).

Duncan, Robert, 'From a notebook', in James Maynard (ed.), *Robert Duncan: collected essays and other prose* (Berkeley, CA: University of California Press, 2014), pp. 44–6.

Duncan, Robert, 'The homosexual in society', in James Maynard (ed.), *Robert Duncan: collected essays and other prose* (Berkeley, CA: University of California Press, 2014), pp. 5–18.

Duncan, Robert, *Medieval scenes* (Kent, OH: Kent State University Press, 1979).

Duncan, Robert, *Medieval scenes* papers. Robert Edward Duncan Papers, Kent State University Libraries Special Collections and Archives.

Duncan, Robert, *A poet's mind: collected interviews with Robert Duncan, 1960–1985*, ed. Christopher Wagstaff (Berkeley, CA: North Atlantic Books, 2012).

Edwards, kari, *dôNrm'-lä-püsl dôNrm'-lä-püsl*, ed. Tina Žigon (Kuwait City: eth press, 2017).

Eliot, T. S., *Collected poems, 1909–1962* (New York: Harcourt, 1991).

Exodus, in George Philip Krapp (ed.), *ASPR*, Vol. 1 (New York: Columbia University Press, 1931), pp. 91–107.

'Fellowship awards, 1952–53', *Journal of the American Association of University Women* 45.4 (1952), 226.

Fenollosa, Ernest, and Ezra Pound, *The Chinese written character as a medium for poetry: a critical edition*, ed. Haun Saussy, Jonathan Stalling, and Lucas Klein (New York: Fordham University Press, 2011).

Genesis, in George Philip Krapp (ed.), *ASPR*, Vol. 1 (New York: Columbia University Press, 1931), pp. 3–87.

Ginsberg, Allen, *Allen Ginsberg reads Howl and other poems*, LP Audio Recording, 12", 33 1/3 rpm. Fantasy Records #7006, 1959.

Guthlac, in George Philip Krapp and Elliott Van Kirk Dobbie (eds), *ASPR*, Vol. 3 (New York: Columbia University Press, 1936), pp. 49–88.

Heaney, Seamus (trans.), *Beowulf: a new verse translation* (New York: Norton, 2001).

The homilies of Wulfstan, ed. Dorothy Bethurum (Oxford: Clarendon, 1957).

Isidore of Seville, *Etymologiarum sive originum libri xx*, ed. R. M. Lindsay, 2 vols (Oxford: Oxford University Press, 1911).

Kantorowicz, Ernst, Lecture notes for 'medieval England', 'English constitutional history', English constitutional history II', Ernst Kantorowicz Collection. Leo Baeck Institute Archives, New York Boxes 4–5.; via the Internet Archive, https://archive.org/details/ernstkantorowicz00reel01 (accessed June 21, 2019).

Kerouac, Jack, *The Dharma bums* (New York: Penguin, 1986).

Kiernan, Kevin (ed.), *Electronic Beowulf* 4.1, The British Library and the University of Kentucky College of Arts and Sciences, 2019, https://ebeowulf.uky.edu/ebeo4.0/CD/main.html (accessed April 9, 2021).

Liuzza, R. M. (trans.), *Beowulf: a new verse translation*, 2nd edn (Peterborough, ON: Broadview, 2012).

Liuzza, R. M. (trans.), *Old English poetry: an anthology* (Peterborough, ON: Broadview, 2014).

Mayer, Bernadette, *Midwinter Day* (New York: New Directions, 1982).

McCarthy, Pattie, *margerykempething* (Kuwait City: eth press, 2017).

McCarthy, Pattie, *queyne wifthing* (Kuwait City: eth press, 2017).

Meyer, Thomas (trans.), Beowulf: a translation (Brooklyn, NY: punctum books, 2011).

Mitchell, Bruce, and Fred C. Robinson (eds), *Beowulf: an edition* (Malden, MA: Blackwell, 1998).

Morgan, Edwin (trans.), *Beowulf: a verse translation into modern English* (Berkeley, CA: University of California Press, 1952).

Morris, William, and A. J. Wyatt (trans.), *The tale of Beowulf: sometime king of the Weder Geats* (Hammersmith: Kelmscott, 1895).

Morris, William, and EiríkrWilliamMagnusson (trans.), *Grettis saga: the story of Grettir the Strong* (London: F. S. Ellis, 1869).

The Old English Boethius: an edition of the Old English versions of Boethius' De consolation philosophiae, ed. Malcolm Godden and Susan Irvine, 2 vols (Oxford: Oxford University Press, 2009).

Olson, Charles, 'Against wisdom as such', in Donald Allen and Benjamin Friedlander (eds), *Charles Olson: collected prose* (Berkeley, CA: University of California Press, 1997), pp. 260–4.

Olson, Charles, 'Projective verse', in Donald Allen and Benjamin Friedlander (eds), *Charles Olson: collected prose* (Berkeley, CA: University of California Press, 1997), pp. 239–49.

The panther, in George Philip Krapp and Elliott Van Kirk Dobbie (eds), *ASPR*, Vol. 3 (New York: Columbia University Press, 1936), pp. 169–71.

Pound, Ezra, *Ezra Pound: poems and translations*, ed. Richard Sieburth (New York: Library of America, 2003).

Pound, Ezra, *ABC of reading* (New York: New Directions, 1960).

Pound, Ezra, *The cantos of Ezra Pound* (New York: New Directions, 1993).

Pound, Ezra, *Early writings* (New York: Penguin, 2005).

Pound, Ezra, *Literary essays of Ezra Pound*, ed. T. S. Eliot (New York: New Directions, 1935).

Pound, Ezra, 'The music of Beowulf': a digital critical edition and introduction*, ed. Maxwell Gray (Madison, WI: Center for the History of Print and Digital Culture, 2019), https://uw.digitalmappa.org/57 (accessed September 10, 2020).

Pound, Ezra, 'The music of *Beowulf*', Ezra Pound papers, American literature collection, Beinecke rare book and manuscript library, Yale University, YCAL MSS 43, Box 69, folder 3045, TS.

Raith, Josef (ed.), *Die altenglische Version des Halitgar'schen Bussbuches (sog. Poenitentiale Pseudo-Ecgberti)*, Bibliotek der angelsächsischen Prosa 13 (Hamburg: H Grand, 1933, [repr. Darmstadt 1964]).

Riddle 31, in George Philip Krapp and Elliott Van Kirk Dobbie (eds), *ASPR*, Vol. 3 (New York: Columbia University Press, 1936), p. 196.

Riddle 33, in George Philip Krapp and Elliott Van Kirk Dobbie (eds), *ASPR*, Vol. 3 (New York: Columbia University Press, 1936), p. 197.

Riddle 40, in George Philip Krapp (eds), *ASPR*, Vol. 1 (New York: Columbia University Press, 1931), pp. 200–3.

Robin Blaser fonds, Simon Fraser University Special Collections and Rare Books, MSA-1.

Skeat, W. W. (ed.), *The Holy Gospels in Anglo-Saxon, Northumbrian, and Old Mercian Versions*,Vol. 4 (Cambridge: Cambridge University Press, 1871–87, [repr. Darmstadt 1970]).

Spicer, Jack, *Be brave to things: the uncollected poetry and plays of Jack Spicer*, ed. Daniel Katz (Middletown, CT: Wesleyan University Press, 2021).

Spicer, Jack, *The collected books of Jack Spicer*, ed. Robin Blaser (Santa Barbara, CA: Black Sparrow Press, 1975).

Spicer, Jack, *The house that Jack built: the collected lectures of Jack Spicer*, ed. Peter Gizzi (Middletown, CT: Wesleyan University Press, 1998).

Spicer, Jack, *Jack Spicer's Beowulf*, ed. David Hadbawnik and Sean Reynolds, *Lost and found: CUNY Poetics documents initiative* 2.5, Part 1–2 (Spring 2011).

Spicer, Jack, Letter to Robin Blaser, Bancroft Library, BANC MSS 2004/209, Box 1, folder 7.

Spicer, Jack, *My vocabulary did this to me: the collected poetry of Jack Spicer*, ed. Peter Gizzi and Kevin Killian (Middletown, CT: Wesleyan University Press, 2008).

The whale, in George Philip Krapp and Elliott Van Kirk Dobbie (eds), *ASPR*, Vol. 3 (New York: Columbia University Press, 1936), pp. 171–4.

Widsith, in George Philip Krapp and Elliott Van Kirk Dobbie (eds), *ASPR*, Vol. 3 (New York: Columbia University Press, 1936), pp. 149–53.

The wife's lament, in George Philip Krapp and Elliott Van Kirk Dobbie (eds), *ASPR*, Vol. 3 (New York: Columbia University Press, 1936), pp. 210–11.

Williams, William Carlos, *Spring and all* (New York: New Directions, 2011).

Wordsworth, William, and Samuel Taylor Coleridge, *Lyrical Ballads: 1798 and 1802*, ed. Fionna Stafford (Oxford: Oxford University Press, 2013).

Wrenn, C. L. (ed.), *Beowulf with the Finnesburg fragment*, revised by W. F. Bolton (New York: St. Martin's Press, 1973).

Wyatt, A. J. (ed.), *Beowulf: edited with textual foot-notes, index of proper names, and alphabetical glossary* (Cambridge: Cambridge University Press, 1894).

Zupitza, J. (ed.), *Ælfric's Grammatik und Glossar*, Sammlung englischer Denkmäler 1, repr. with intro. by H. Gneuss (Berlin: Niehans, 1966).

Secondary sources

Abram, Christopher, 'At home in the fens with the Grendelkin', in Daniel C. Remein and Erica Weaver (eds), *Dating Beowulf: studies in intimacy* (Manchester: Manchester University Press, 2020), pp. 120–44.

Abram, Christopher, 'New light on the illumination of Grendel's mere', *JEGP* 109.2 (2010), 198–216.

Aguirre, Manuel, 'Phasing *Beowulf*: an aspect of narrative structure in fairytale and epic', *Studia Anglica Posnaniensia* 37 (2002), 359–86.

Allfrey, Francesca, Francesca Brooks, Joshua Davies, Rebecca Hardie, Carl Kears, Clare Lees, Kathryn Maude, James Paz, Hana Videen, and Victoria Walker, 'New ways to know the medieval: creativity, pedagogy, and public engagement with *Colm Cille's Spiral*', *Old English Newsletter* 46.3 (2015), www.oenewsletter.org/OEN/issue/46-3_allfrey.php (accessed February 19, 2019).

Altieri, Charles, 'From symbolist thought to immanence: the ground of postmodern American poetics', in Paul A. Bové (ed.), *Early postmodernism: foundational essays* (Durham, NC: Duke University Press, 1995), pp. 40–76.

The American heritage dictionary of the English language, 5th edn (Boston: Houghton Mifflin Harcourt, 2018).

Amodio, Mark C., 'Affective criticism, oral poetics, and Beowulf's fight with the dragon', *Oral Tradition* 10.1 (1995), 54–90.

Amodio, Mark C., *Writing the oral tradition: oral poetics and literature culture in medieval England* (Notre Dame, IN: University of Notre Dame Press, 2004).

Anlezark, Daniel, *Water and fire: the myth of the flood in Anglo-Saxon England* (Manchester: Manchester University Press, 2012).

Arac, Jonathan, *Huck Finn as idol and target: the functions of criticism in our time* (Madison, WI: University of Wisconsin Press, 1997).

Ármann Jakobsson, *The troll inside you: paranormal activity in the medieval north* (Santa Barbara, CA: Punctum Books, 2017).

Austin, J. L., *How to do things with words*, 2nd edn, ed. J. O. Urmson and Marina Sbisà (Cambridge, MA: Harvard University Press, 1975).

Ayoub, Lois, 'Old English *wæta* and the medical theory of the humors', *JEGP* 94 (1992), 332–46.

Bachelard, Gaston, *The psychoanalysis of fire*, trans. Alan C. M. Ross (Boston, MA: Beacon, 1968).

Backhouse, Janet, and Leslie Webster, *The making of English: Anglo-Saxon art and culture, AD 600–900* (London: British Museum, 1991).

Backhouse, Janet, D. H. Turner, and Leslie Webster, *The golden age of Anglo-Saxon art, 966 to 1066* (London: British Museum, 1964).

Bammesburger, Alfred, 'Hildeburh's son', *Notes and Queries* 53.1 (2006), 14–17.

Banchetti-Robino, Marina Paola, 'Ibn Sīnā and Husserl', *Philosophy East and West* 54.1 (2004), 71–82.

Barnes, Daniel R., 'Folktale morphology and the structure of *Beowulf*', *Speculum* 45 (1970), 416–34.

Barr, Rebecca, 'Resurrecting Saxon things: Peter Reading, 'species decline', and Old English poetry', in David Clark and Nicholas Perkins (eds), *Anglo-Saxon culture and the modern imagination* (Woodbridge, Suffolk: Boydell and Brewer, 2010), pp. 225–78.

Barthes, Roland, *Camera lucida: reflections on photograph*, trans. Richard Howard (New York: Hill and Wang, 1981).

Barthes, Roland, 'An introduction to the structural analysis of narrative', trans. Lionel Duisit, *New Literary History* 6.2 (1975), 237–72.

Bartlett, Adeline Courtney, *The larger rhetorical patterns of Anglo-Saxon poetry*, Columbia University Studies in English and Comparative Literature 122 (New York: Columbia University Press, 1935).

Bauschatz, Paul C., *The well and the tree: the world and time in early Germanic culture* (Amherst, MA: University of Massachusetts Press, 1982).

Bayless, Martha, 'The Fuller brooch and Anglo-Saxon depictions of dance', *ASE* 45 (2016), 183–212.

Bennett, Jane, *Influx and efflux: writing up with Whitman* (Durham, NC: Duke University Press, 2020).

Bennett, Jane, *Vibrant matter: a political ecology of things* (Durham, NC: Duke University Press, 2010).

Benskin, Michael, 'The narrative structure of the Finnsburh episode in *Beowulf*, *Amsterdam beiträge zur älteren Germanistik* 77 (2018), 37–64.

Benson, Larry D., 'The literary character of Anglo-Saxon poetry', *PMLA* 81.5 (1966), 334–41.

Bergvall, Caroline, *Meddle English* (New York: Nightboat, 2011).

Bernstein, Charles, 'Afterword', in Robin Blaser, *The holy forest: the collected poems of Robin Blaser*, ed. Miriam Nichols (Berkeley, CA: University of California Press, 2006), pp. 507–10.

Bernstein, Charles, 'Against National Poetry Month as such', in *Attack of the difficult poems: essays and inventions* (Chicago, IL: University of Chicago Press, 2011), pp. 27–32.

Bernstein, Charles, *A poetics* (Cambridge, MA: Harvard University Press, 1992).

Bernstein, Charles, 'The practice of poetics,' in *Attack of the difficult poems: essays and inventions* (Chicago, IL: University of Chicago Press), pp. 73–9.

Bessinger, Jess B., *A concordance to the Anglo-Saxon poetic records* (Ithaca, NY: Cornell University Press, 1978).

Blomfield, Joan, 'The style and structure of *Beowulf*, *Review of English Studies* 14.56 (1938), 396–403.

Bolens, Guillemette, 'The limits of textuality: mobility and fire production in Homer and *Beowulf*, *Oral tradition* 16.1 (2001), 107–28.

Bolton, W. F., '"Variation" in *The battle of Brunanburh*', *Review of English Studies* 19.76 (1968), 363–72.

Bonjour, Adrien, *The digressions of 'Beowulf'* (Oxford: Basil Blackwell, 1950).

Bonjour, Adrien, 'Jottings on *Beowulf* and the aesthetic approach', in Robert P. Creed (ed.), *Old English poetry: fifteen essays* (Providence, RI: Brown University Press, 1967), pp. 179–92.

Bonjour, Adrien, *Twelve Beowulf papers 1940–1960* (Neuchâtel: Faculté des Lettres, Neuchâtel, 1962).

Bonner, Joshua H., 'Toward a unified critical approach to Old English poetic composition', *Modern Philology* 73.3 (1975–76), 219–28.

Boyle, Leonard E., 'The Nowell Codex and the poem of *Beowulf*, in Colin Chase (ed.), *The dating of Beowulf* (Toronto: University of Toronto Press, 1981), pp. 23–32.

Bradley, Henry, 'The numbered sections in Old English poetical MSS', *Proceedings of the British Academy* 7 (1915), 165–87.

Brady, Caroline, 'The Old English nominal compounds in -*rád*', *PMLA* 67.4 (1952), 538–71.

Brady, Caroline, 'The synonyms for "sea" in Beowulf', in *Studies in honor of Albert Morey Sturtevant* (Lawrence, KS: University of Kansas Press, 1952), pp. 22–46.

Brady, Caroline, 'Weapons in *Beowulf*: an analysis of the nominal compounds and an evaluation of the poet's use of them', *ASE* 8 (1979), 79–141.

Braeger, Peter C., 'Connotations of (*earm*)sceapen: *Beowulf* ll. 2228–2229 and the shape-shifting dragon', *Essays in Literature* 13 (1986), 327–30.

Brodeur, Arthur G., *The art of Beowulf* (Berkeley, CA: University of California Press, 1959).

Brodeur, Arthur G., '*Beowulf*: one poem, or three?', in Jerome Mandel and Bruce E. Rosenburg (eds), *Medieval literature and folklore studies: essays in honor of Francis Lee Utley* (New Brunswick, NJ: Rutgers University Press, 1970), pp. 3–26.

Brodeur, Arthur G., 'The climax of the Finn episode', *University of California Publications in English* 8 (1943), 285–662.

Brodeur, Arthur G., 'Design and motive in the Finn episode', *University of California Publications in English* 14.1 (1943), 1–42.

Brodeur, Arthur G., 'The meaning of Snorri's categories', *University of California Publications in Modern Philology* 26 (1952), 129–48.

Brodeur, Arthur G. (trans.), *The Prose Edda by Snorri Sturluson* (New York: American-Scandinavian Foundation, 1916; reprint Dover Thrift, 2006).

Brodeur, Arthur G., 'The riddle of the runes', *University of California Publications in English* 3.1 (1932), 1–15.

Brodeur, Arthur G. 'Statement by Arthur G. Brodeur, ca. 1949', California Loyalty Oath Digital Collection, Online archive of California, www.oac.cdlib.org/view?docId=hb209nb4s7&query=&brand=oac4, accessed August 17, 2017.

Brodeur, Arthur G., 'The structure and unity of *Beowulf*', *PMLA* 68.5 (1953), 304–12.

Brooks, Francesca, 'Liturgy, performance, and poetry of the passion: David Jones and *The dream of the rood*', *Religion & Literature* 49 (2018), 83–92.

Brown, Alan K., 'The firedrake in *Beowulf*', *Neophilologus* 64 (1980), 439–60.

Buchanan, Peter, 'Cædemon and the gift of song', *postmedieval* 6.3 (2015), 165–73.

Buchanan, Peter, 'Phenomenal Anglo-Saxons: perception, adaptation, and the poetic imagination' (PhD dissertation, University of Toronto, 2013).

Buttigieg, Joseph, 'The exemplary worldliness of Antonio Gramsci's literary criticism', *boundary 2* 11.102 (1982–83), 21–39.

Calder, Daniel G., 'Setting and ethos: the pattern of measure and limit in *Beowulf*', *Studies in Philology* 69.1 (1972), 21–72.

Calder, Daniel G., 'The study of style in Old English poetry: a historical introduction', in Daniel G. Calder (ed.), *Old English poetry: essays on style* (Berkeley, CA: University of California Press, 1979), pp. 1–65.

Cameron, M. L., *Anglo-Saxon medicine* (Cambridge: Cambridge University Press, 1993).

Cameron, M. L., 'The sources of medical knowledge in Anglo-Saxon England', *ASE* 11 (1982), 135–55.

Carberry, Matthew, *Phenomenology and the late twentieth-century American long poem* (Cham, Switzerland: Palgrave, 2019).

Carrigan, Eamon, 'Structure and thematic development in *Beowulf*', *Proceedings of the Royal Irish Academy* 66 C (1967), 1–51.

Carruthers, Mary, *The book of memory: a study of memory in medieval culture*, 2nd edn (Cambridge: University of Cambridge Press, 2008).

Carruthers, Mary, 'The concept of *ductus*, or, journeying through a work of art', in Carruthers (ed.), *Rhetoric beyond words: delight and persuasion in the arts of the Middle Ages* (Cambridge: Cambridge University Press, 2010), pp. 190–213.

Carruthers, Mary, *The craft of thought: meditation, rhetoric, and the making of images, 400–1200* (Cambridge: University of Cambridge Press, 2000).

Carruthers, Mary, *The experience of beauty in the Middle Ages* (Oxford: Oxford University Press, 2013).

Carruthers, Mary, '*Varietas*: a word of many colours', *Poetica: Zeitschrift für Sprachund Literaturwissenshaft* 41.1–2 (2009), 11–32.

Cesalli, Laurent, and Hamid Taieb, 'Brentano and medieval ontology', *Phenomenological Studies (Revista da abordagem gestáltica)* 24 (2018), 417–28.

Chaganti, Seeta, 'Vestigial signs: inscription, performance, and the *Dream of the rood*', *PMLA* 125.1 (2010), 48–72.

Chamberlain, Lori, 'Ghostwriting the text: translation and the poetics of Jack Spicer', *Contemporary Literature* 26.4 (1985), 426–42.

Chance, Jane, *Woman as hero in Old English literature* (Syracuse, NY: Syracuse University Press, 1986).

Chapman, Don, 'Composing and joining: how the Anglo-Saxons talked about compounding', in Antonina Harbus and Russell Poole (eds), *Verbal encounters: Anglo-Saxon and Old Norse studies for Roberta Frank* (Toronto: University of Toronto Press, 2005), pp. 39–54.

Clarke, George, 'The traveler recognizes his goal: a theme in Anglo-Saxon poetry', *JEGP* 64.4 (1965), 645–59.

Clemoes, Peter, 'Action in *Beowulf* and our perception of it', in Daniel G. Calder (ed.), *Old English poetry: essays on style* (Berkeley, CA: University of California Press, 1979), pp. 148–68.

Cohen, Jeffrey Jerome, *Medieval identity machines* (Minneapolis, MN: University of Minnesota Press, 2003).

Cole, Norma, 'A minimum of matter: notes on Robin Blaser, "the fire", and "the moth poem"', in Miriam Nichols (ed.), *Even on Sunday:*

essays, readings, and archival materials on the poetry and poetics of Robin Blaser (Orono, ME: National Poetry Foundation, 2002), pp. 125–33.

Conner, P. W., 'The section numbers in the *Beowulf* manuscript', *ANQ* 24.4 (1985), 33–8.

Conte, Joseph M., *Unending design: the forms of postmodern poetry* (Ithaca, NY: Cornell University Press, 1991).

Creed, Robert P., 'On the possibility of criticizing Old English poetry', *Texas Studies in Literature and Language* 3.1 (1961), 97–106.

Cronan, Dennis, 'Narrative disjunctions in *Beowulf*', *English Studies* 99.5 (2018), 459–78.

Cronan, Dennis, 'Old English *gelad*: "a passage across water"', *Neophilologus* 71 (1987), 316–19.

Crowne, David K., 'The hero on the beach: an example of composition by theme in Anglo-Saxon poetry', *Neuphilologische Mitteilungen* 61.4 (1960), 362–72.

Dailey, Patricia, 'Riddles, wonder and responsiveness in Anglo-Saxon literature', in Clare A. Lees (ed.), *The Cambridge history of early medieval English literature 500–1150* (Cambridge: Cambridge University Press, 2012), pp. 451–72.

Davidson, Michael, *Distressing language: disability and the poetics of error* (New York: NYU Press, 2022).

Davidson, Michael, *Guys like us: citing masculinity in cold war poetics* (Chicago, IL: University of Chicago Press, 2004).

Davidson, Michael, *The San Francisco Renaissance: poetics and community at mid-century* (Cambridge: Cambridge University Press, 1989).

Davies, Joshua, 'Re-locating Anglo-Saxon England: places of the past in Basil Bunting's *Briggflatts* and Geoffrey Hill's *Mercian Hymns*', in Julian Weiss and Sarah Salih (eds), *Locating the Middle Ages: the spaces and places of medieval culture* (London: Centre for Late Antique and Medieval Studies, Kings College London, 2012), pp. 199–212.

Davies, Joshua, *Visions and ruins: cultural memory and the untimely Middle Ages* (Manchester: Manchester University Press, 2018).

Davis, Kathleen, *Periodization and sovereignty: how ideas of feudalism and secularism govern the politics of time* (Philadelphia, PA: University of Pennsylvania Press, 2008).

Davis-Secord, Jonathan, *Joinings: compound words in Old English literature* (Toronto: University of Toronto Press, 2016).

De Campos, Haroldo, 'Translation as creation and criticism', trans. Diana Gibson and Haroldo de Campos, in de Campos, *Novas: Selected Writings*, ed. Antonio Sergio Bessa and Odile Cisneros (Evanston, IL: Northwestern University Press, 2007), pp. 312–26.

Deleuze, Gilles, *The fold: Leibniz and the baroque*, trans. Tom Conley (Minneapolis, MN: University of Minnesota Press, 1992).

Deleuze, Gilles, and Félix Guattari, *A thousand plateaus: capitalism and schizophrenia*, trans. Brian Massumi (Minneapolis, MN: University of Minnesota Press, 1987).

Derrida, Jacques, *Specters of Marx*, trans. Peggy Kamuf (New York: Routledge, 1994).

Derrida, Jacques, 'Structure, sign, and play in the discourse of the human sciences', in *Writing and difference*, trans. Alan Bass (Chicago, IL: University of Chicago Press, 1978), pp. 278–94.

Derrida, Jacques, 'Des Tours de Babel', trans. Joesph F. Graham, in *Psyche: inventions of the other*, Vol. 1, ed. Peggy Kamuf and Elizabeth Rottenberg (Stanford, CA: Stanford University Press, 2007), pp. 191–225.

Diamond, Robert E., 'Theme as ornament in Anglo-Saxon poetry', *PMLA* 76.5 (1961), 461–8.

Dinshaw, Carolyn, *Getting medieval: sexualities and communities pre- and postmodern* (Durham, NC: Duke University Press, 1999).

Dinshaw, Carolyn, *How soon is now: medieval texts, amateur readers, and the queerness of time* (Durham, NC: Duke University Press, 2012).

Donoghue, Daniel, *How the Anglo-Saxons read their poems* (Philadelphia, PA: University of Pennsylvania Press, 2018).

Donoghue, Daniel, 'The languages of *Beowulf* between Klaeber and Heaney', in Jana K. Schulman and Paul E. Szarmach (eds), *Beowulf at Kalamazoo: Essays on Translation and Performance* (Kalamazoo, MI: Medieval Institute Publications, 2012), pp. 15–29.

Donoghue, Daniel, *Style in Old English poetry: the test of the auxiliary* (New Haven, CT: Yale University Press, 1987).

Doyle, Conan, 'Anglo-Saxon medicine and disease: a semantic approach' (PhD dissertation, Corpus Christi College, Cambridge, 2011).

Du Bois, Arthur E. 'The dragon in *Beowulf*', *PMLA* 72.5 (1957), 819–22.

Du Bois, Arthur E. 'The unity of *Beowulf*', *PMLA* 49.2 (1934), 374–405.

Duggan, Lisa, and Laura Farina, 'Intimate senses/sensing intimacy', *postmedieval* 3.4 (2012), 373–9.

Dumistrescu, Irina, '*Beowulf* and *Andreas*: intimate relations', in Daniel C. Remein and Erica Weaver (eds), *Dating Beowulf: studies in intimacy* (Manchester: Manchester University Press, 2020), pp. 257–78.

Duncan, Ian 'Epitaphs for æglæcan: narrative strife in *Beowulf*' in Harold Bloom (ed.), *Beowulf: modern critical interpretations* (New York: Chelsea House, 1987), pp. 111–30.

Earl, James W., 'The forbidden *Beowulf*: haunted by incest', *PMLA* 125.2 (2006), 298–305.

Earl, James W., 'The Swedish wars in *Beowulf*', *JEGP* 114.1 (2015), 32–60.

Earl, James W., *Thinking about 'Beowulf'* (Stanford, CA: Stanford University Press, 1994).

Eliason, Norman E., 'Review of R. D. Stevick, *Suprasegmentals, meter, and the manuscript of Beowulf*', *Speculum* 45 (1970), 165–8.

Eliason, Norman E., 'Wulfhliþ (*Beowulf*, l. 1358)', *JEGP* 41.1 (1935), 20–3.

Ellard, Donna Beth, *Anglo-Saxon(ist) pasts, postsaxon futures* ([Brooklyn, NY]: punctum Books, 2019).

Ellard, Donna Beth, 'Communicating between species and between disciplines—lessons from the Old English *Seafarer*', *Exemplaria* 30.4 (2018), 293–315.

Ellingham, Lewis, and Kevin Killian, *Poet be like god: Jack Spicer and the San Francisco Renaissance* (Hanover, NH: Wesleyan University Press, 1998).

Eriksen, Sarah Bienko, 'Traversing the uncanny valley: Glámr in narratological space', in Ármann Jakobsson and Miriam Mayburd (eds), *Paranormal encounters in Iceland 1150–1400* (Boston, MA: Medieval Institute Publications, De Gruyter, 2020), pp. 89–108.

Eshleman, Clayton, 'The Lorca working', *boundary 2* 27.1 (1977), 31–49.

Estes, Heide, *Anglo-Saxon literary landscapes* (Amsterdam: Amsterdam University Press, 2017).

Faas, Eknert, *Young Robert Duncan: portrait of the poet as a homosexual in society* (Santa Barbara, CA: Black Sparrow, 1983).

Farnham, W. E. and A. E. Huston, 'Arthur Gilchrest Brodeur, English; German: Berkeley' (obituary), in *In Memoriam: University of California, July 1975*, University of California Academic Senate, pp. 17–18, University Archives, University of California Berkeley, Bancroft Library, online at California Digital Library, http://texts.cdlib.org/view?docId=hb9t1nb5rm; NAAN=13030&doc.view=frames&chunk.id=div00008&toc.depth=1&toc.id=&brand=calisphere (accessed July 5, 2017).

Ferhatović, Dennis, 'A portrait of the translator as Grendel's mother: the postcolonial feminist polyphony of Meghan Purvis' *Beowulf*', in Irinia Dumistrescu and Eric Weiskott (eds), *The shapes of early English poetry: style, form, history* (Kalamazoo, MI: Medieval Insititute Publications, 2019), pp. 59–81.

Foys, Martin, 'Ephemeral rings: Anglo-Saxon bells and immaterial media', conference paper, Biennial Meeting of the BABEL Working Group, University of Texas, Austin, November 6, 2010.

Foys, Martin, 'Hearing the bell in Anglo-Saxon England', Conference paper, International Society of Anglo-Saxonists, University of Wisconsin, Madison, WI, August 4, 2011.

Foys, Martin, 'A sensual philology for Anglo-Saxon England', *postmedieval* 5.4 (2014), 456–72.

Frank, Roberta, '*Beowulf* and the intimacy of large parties', in Daniel C. Remein and Erica Weaver (eds), *Dating Beowulf: studies in intimacy* (Manchester: Manchester University Press, 2020), pp. 54–72.

Frank, Roberta, 'King Cnut in the verse of his skalds', in Alexander Rumble (ed.), *The reign of Cnut: King of England, Denmark, and Norway* (London: Leicester University Press, 1994), pp. 106–24.

Frank, Roberta, '"Mere" and "sund": two sea changes in Old English literature', in Phyllis Rugg Brown, Georgia Ronan Crampton, and Fred C. Robinson (eds), *Modes of interpretation in Old English literature: essays in honor of Stanley B. Greenfield* (Toronto: University of Toronto Press, 1986), pp. 153–72.

Frank, Roberta, 'The search for the Anglo-Saxon oral poet', *Bulletin of the John Rylands Library* 75.1 (1993), 11–36.

Frank, Roberta, 'Terminally hip and incredibly cool: Carol, Vikings, and Anglo-Scandinavian England', *Representations* 100.1 (2002), 23–33.

Fredman, Stephen, *Poet's prose: the crises in American verse* (Cambridge: Cambridge University Press, 1983).

Frey, Charles, 'Lyric in epic: Hrothgar's depiction of the haunted mere', *English Studies* 58.4 (1977), 296–303.

Fry, Donald K., 'Finnsburh: a new interpretation', *Chaucer Review* 9.1 (1974), 1–14.

Fry, Donald K., 'Variation and economy in *Beowulf*', *Modern Philology* 65.4 (1968), 53–6.

Fulk, R. D., 'The origin of the numbered sections in *Beowulf* and in other Old English poems', *ASE* 35 (2006), 91–109.

Fulk, R. D., 'Six cruces in the Finnsburg fragment and episode', *Medium Ævum* 74.2 (2005), 191–204.

Gardner, Thomas, 'The Old English kenning: characteristic feature of Germanic poetical diction?', *Modern Philology* 67.2 (1969), 109–17.

Garner, Lori Ann, 'Deaf studies, oral tradition, and Old English texts', *Exemplaria* 29.1 (2017), 21–40.

Gelling, Margaret, 'The landscape of *Beowulf*', *ASE* 31 (2002), 7–11.

Gizzi, Peter, 'Afterword: Jack Spicer and the practice of reading', in *House*, pp. 173–225.

Glofelty, Cheryll, 'What is ecocriticism?', in 'Defining ecocritical theory and practice: sixteen position papers from the 1994 Western Literature Association meeting, Salt Lake City, Utah, 6 October, 1994', www.asle.org/wp-content/uploads/ASLE_Primer_DefiningEcocrit.pdf (accessed April 9, 2021).

Godden, Richard, 'Prosthetic ecologies: vulnerable bodies and the dismodern subject in *Sir Gawain and the green knight*', *Textual Practice* 30.7 (2016), 1273–90.

292   *Bibliography*

Godden, Richard, and Jonathan Hsy, 'Analytic survey: encountering disability in the Middle Ages', *New Medieval Literatures* 15 (2013), 313–39.

Gómez, Isabel C., 'Anti-surrealism? Augusto de Campos "untranslates" Spanish-American poetry', *Mutatis Mutandis* 11.2 (2018), 376–99.

Gómez, Isabel C., 'Brazilian transcreation and world literature: Macunaíma journeys from Sáo Paolo to Caracas', *Journal of World Literature* 1 (2016), 316–41.

Gómez, Isabel C., 'Transcreation / transcriasção. Cannibal translation of 'a mulher vai' by Angélica Freitas', *Jacket 2: commentaries*, ed. Kristin Dykstra, October 28, 2015.

Graff, Gerald, *Professing literature: an institutional history* (Chicago, IL: University of Chicago Press, 1987).

Greenfield, Stanley B., '"Beowulf" 207b–228: narrative and descriptive art', *Notes and Queries* n.s. 13 (1966), 86–90.

Greenfield, Stanley B., 'The formulaic expression of the theme of "exile" in Anglo-Saxon poetry', *Speculum* 30.2 (1955), 200–6.

Greenfield, Stanley B., 'Grendel's approach to Heorot: syntax and poetry', in Robert P. Creed (ed.), *Old English poetry: fifteen essays* (Providence, RI: Brown Univeristy Press, 1967), pp. 275–84.

Greenfield, Stanley B., *The interpretation of Old English poems* (London: Routledge, 1976).

Greenfield, Stanley B. (ed.), *Studies in Old English literature in honor of Arthur G. Brodeur* (Eugene, OR: University of Oregon Books, 1963).

Gwara, Scott, 'The foreign Beowulf and the "fight at Finnsburh"', *Traditio* 63 (2008), 185–233.

Hadbawnik, David, 'Differing intimacies: *Beowulf* translations by Seamus Heaney and Thomas Meyer', in Daniel C. Remein and Erica Weaver (eds), *Dating Beowulf: studies in intimacy* (Manchester: Manchester University Press, 2020), pp. 227–53.

Hadbawnik, David, 'Introduction: "*Beowulf* is a hoax": Jack Spicer's medievalism', in Hadbawnik and Sean Reynolds (eds), *Jack Spicer's Beowulf, Lost and found: CUNY Poetics documents initiative* 2.5, Part 1 (Spring 2011), 1–13.

Hadbawnik, David, 'Introduction: the opening of the field', in Hadbawnik (ed.), *Postmodern poetry and queer medievalisms: time mechanics* (Berlin: De Gruyter/Medieval Institute Publications, 2022), pp. 1–16.

Hadbawnik, David, 'Jack Spicer and the English department', *Paideuma* 46 (2019), 7–30.

Hadbawnik, David, 'Preface', in Thomas Meyer (trans.), *Beowulf: a translation* (Brooklyn, NY: punctum, 2012), pp. 1–3.

Hadbawnik, David, 'Speak like a child: Caroline Bergvall's medievalist trilogy', in Hadbawnik (ed.), *Postmodern poetry and queer medievalisms: time mechanics* (Berlin: De Gruyter/Medieval Institute Publications, 2022), pp. 179–203.

Hadbawnik, David, 'Time mechanics: the modern Geoffrey Chaucer and the medieval Jack Spicer', *postmedieval* 4.3 (2013), 270–83.

Hadbawnik, David, and Sean Reynolds, 'All times contemporaneous', *postmedieval* 6.2 (2015), 115–19.

Hadbawnik, David, and Sean Reynolds (eds), 'Contemporary poetics and the medieval muse', special issue, *postmedieval* 6.2 (2015).

Harris, Leslie A., 'Techniques of pacing in *Beowulf*', *English Studies* 62 (1982), 97–108.

Hart, Thomas, '*Ellen*: some tectonic relationships in *Beowulf* and their formal resemblance to Anglo-Saxon art', *Papers on Language and Literature* 6 (1970), 263–90.

Heaney, Seamus, *Death of a naturalist* (London: Faber, 1966).

Heinzel, Richard, *Über den Stil der altergermanischen Poesie*, Quelen und Forschungen 10 (Strasbourg: Karl J. Trübner, 1875).

Hejinian, Lyn, 'Reason', in *The language of inquiry* (Berkeley, CA: University of California Press, 2008), pp. 337–54.

Hieatt, Constance B., 'Envelope patterns and the structure of *Beowulf*', *English Studies in Canada* 1.3 (1975), 249–65.

Hill, John M., 'Episodes such as the Offa of Angeln passage and the aesthetics of *Beowulf*', *Philological Review* 34 (2008), 29–49.

Hill, John M. 'On aesthetics and quality: an introduction', in John M. Hill (ed.), *On the aesthetics of* Beowulf *and other Old English poems* (Toronto: University of Toronto Press, 2010), pp. 3–23.

Hill, John M. (ed.), *On the aesthetics of* Beowulf *and other Old English poems* (Toronto: University of Toronto Press, 2010).

Hill, Joyce, 'Þæt wæs geomuru ides! A female stereotype examined', in Helen Damico and Alexandra Hennesy Olsen (eds), *New readings on women in Old English* (Bloomington, IN: Indiana University Press, 1990), pp. 235–47.

Hoek, Michelle C. 'Anglo-Saxon innovation and the use of the senses in the Old English *Physiologus* poem', *Studia Neophilologica* 69.1 (1997), 1–10.

Hollis, Stephanie, 'Scientific and medical writings', in Phillip Pulsiana and Elaine Treharne (eds), *A companion to Anglo-Saxon literature* (Malden, MA: Blackwell, 2001), pp. 188–208.

Holsinger, Bruce, *The premodern condition: medievalism and the making of theory* (Chicago: Chicago University Press, 2005).

Holt, Kelly, '"In the sense of a lasting doctrine": Ernst Kantorowicz and the serial poetics of the Berkeley Renaissance' (PhD dissertation, University of California Santa Cruz, 2009).

Holt, Kelly, 'Spicer's poetic correspondence: a pun the letter reflects', in John Emil Vincent (ed.), *After Spicer: critical essays* (Middletown, CT: Wesleyan University Press, 2011), pp. 36–68.

Horowitz, Sylvia Huntley, 'The interrupted battles in *Beowulf*', NM 85.3 (1984), 295–304.

Howe, Nicholas, 'Praise and lament: the afterlife of Old English poetry in Auden, Hill, and Gunn', in Peter S. Baker and Nicholas Howe (eds), *Words and works: studies in medieval English language and literature in honor of Fred C. Robinson* (Toronto: University of Toronto Press, 1998), pp. 293–310.

Howe, Nicholas, 'Scullionspeak', *The New Republic*, February 28, 2000, pp. 32–4.

Howe, Nicholas, 'Who's afraid of translating *Beowulf*', in Jana K. Schulman and Paul E. Szarmach (eds), *Beowulf at Kalamazoo: Essays on Translation and Performance* (Kalamazoo, MI: Medieval Institute Publications, 2012), pp. 31–49.

Howe, Nicholas, *Writing the map of Anglo-Saxon England* (New Haven, CT: Yale University Press, 2007).

Howlett, David R., 'Form and genre in *Beowulf*', *Studia Neophilologica* 46 (1974), 309–25.

Howlett, David R., 'New criteria for editing *Beowulf*', in D. G. Scragg and P. E. Szarmach (eds), *The editing of Old English* (Cambridge: Brewer, 1994), pp. 69–84.

Hsy, Jonathan, Tory V. Pearman, and Joshua R. Eyler, 'Introduction: disabilities in motion', in Hsy, Pearman, and Eyler (eds), *A cultural history of disability in the Middle Ages*, A cultural history of disability, vol. 2 (London: Bloomsbury, 2020), pp. 1–18.

Hullbert, J. H., 'A note on the psychology of the *Beowulf* poet', in K. Malone and M. B. Rudd (eds), *Studies in English philology: a miscellany in honor of Frederick Klaeber* (Minneapolis, MN: University of Minnesota Press, 1929), pp. 189–95.

Huppé, Bernard F., *The hero in the earthly city: a reading of Beowulf* (Binghamton, NY: SUNY Binghamton Medieval and Renaissance Texts and Studies, 1984).

Hurley, Mary Kate, 'Elemental intimacies: agency in the Finnsburg episode', in Daniel C. Remein and Erica Weaver (eds), *Dating Beowulf: studies in intimacy* (Manchester: Manchester University Press, 2020), pp. 147–63.

Hurley, Mary Kate, *Translation effects: language, time, and community in medieval England* (Columbus, OH: Ohio State University Press, 2021).

Hutcheson, B. R., 'Kuhn's law, finite verb stress, and the critics', *Studia Neophilologica* 64 (1992), 129–39.

Irvine, Martin, 'Anglo-Saxon literary theory exemplified in Old English poems: interpretating the cross in "The dream of the rood" and "Elene"', *Style* 20.2 (1986), 157–81.

Irving, Edward B., Jr, *A reading of Beowulf* (New Haven, CT: Yale University Press, 1969).

Jakobson, Roman, 'On linguistic aspects of translation', in Lawrence Venuti (ed.), *The translation studies reader*, 2nd edn (New York: Routledge, 2004), pp. 138–43.

Jarnot, Lisa, *Robert Duncan, the ambassador from Venus: a biography* (Berkeley, CA: University of California Press, 2012).

Jones, Chris, 'Anglo-Saxonism in nineteenth-century poetry', *Literature Compass* 7 (2010), 358–69.

Jones, Chris, *Fossil poetry: Anglo-Saxon and linguistic nativism in nineteenth-century poetry* (Oxford: Oxford University Press, 2018).

Jones, Chris, 'Old English after 1066', in Malcolm Godden and Michael Lapidge (eds), *The Cambridge companion to Old English literature*, 2nd edn (Cambridge: Cambridge University Press, 2013), pp. 313–30.

Jones, Chris, *Strange likeness: the use of Old English in twentieth-century poetry* (Oxford: Oxford University Press, 2006).

Jones, Chris, 'While crowding memories came: Edwin Morgan, Old English and nostalgia', *Scottish Literary Review* 4.2 (2012), 123–44.

Jorgensen, Alice, 'Introduction', in Alice Jorgensen, Frances McCormack, and Jonathan Wilcox (eds), *Anglo-Saxon emotions: reading the heart in Old English language, literature, and culture* (Farnham, Surrey: Ashgate, 2015), pp. 1–17.

Jorgensen, Alice, 'The trumpet and the wolf: noises of battle in Old English poetry', *Oral Tradition* 24 (2009), 319–36.

Joy, Eileen A. [Fradenburg], 'Goodbye to all that: my own personal field of schizoid Anglo-Saxon Studies', *Heroic Age* 11 (May 2008), www.heroicage.org/issues/11/foruma.php.

Joy, Eileen A. [Fradenburg], and Mary K. Ramsey, 'Liquid *Beowulf*', in Eileen A. [Fradenburg] Joy and Mary K. Ramsey (eds), *The postmodern Beowulf: a critical casebook* (Morgantown, WV: West Virginia University Press, 2006), pp. xxxix–lxvii.

Joy, Eileen A. [Fradenburg] and Mary K. Ramsey (eds), *The postmodern Beowulf: a critical casebook* (Morgantown, WV: West Virginia University Press, 2006).

Kaske, R. E., 'The *eotenas* in *Beowulf*', in Robert P. Creed (ed.), *Old English poetry: fifteen essays* (Providence, RI: Brown University Press, 1967), pp. 285–310.

Katz, Daniel, *The poetry of Jack Spicer* (Edinburgh: Edinburgh University Press, 2013).

Kears, Carl, 'Eric Mottram and Old English: revival and re-use in the 1970s', *Review of English Studies* n.s. 69.290 (2018), 230–454.

Keller, Thomas L., 'The dragon in *Beowulf* revisited', *Aevum* 55.2 (1981), 218–28.

Kiernan, Kevin, *Beowulf and the Beowulf manuscript* (New Brunswick, NJ: Rutgers University Press, 1981).

Killian, Kevin, 'Spicer at the Mattachine', in John Emil Vincent (ed.), *After Spicer* (Middletown, CT: Wesleyan University Press, 2011), pp. 16–35.

Kim, Dorothy, 'The question of race in *Beowulf*', *Jstor daily*, September 25, 2019, https://daily.jstor.org/the-question-of-race-in-beowulf/ (accessed April 9, 2021).

Kim, Yookang, 'Demarcation of compounding and prefixation in Old English', *Linguistic Research* 32.2 (2015), 419–50.

Kisor, Yvette, 'The aesthetics of *Beowulf*: structure, perception, and desire', in John D. Hill (ed.), *On the aesthetics of Beowulf and other Old English poems* (Toronto: University of Toronto Press, 2010), pp. 227–46.

Klaeber, Frederick, *The Christian elements in Beowulf* ['Die christliche Elemente im *Beowulf*', *Anglia* 35 (1911), 111–36, 249–70, 453–82; 36 (1912), 169–99], trans. Paul Battles, *Old English newsletter subsidia* 24 (Kalamazoo, MI: Medieval Institute, 1996).

Kleege, Georgina, 'As if our friends felt the sun for us', *postmedieval* 3.4 (2012), 472–5.

Klein, Stacy, *Ruling women: queenship and gender in Anglo-Saxon literature* (South Bend, IN: University of Notre Dame Press, 2006).

Klein, Thomas, 'The coarser senses in Old English: the Old English verbs of tasting, smelling, touching and perceiving' (PhD dissertation, University of Toronto, 1998).

Klein, Thomas, '*Stonc æfter stane* ("Beowulf", l. 2888a): philology, narrative context, and the waking dragon', *JEGP* 106.1 (2007), 22–44.

Knapp, Ethan, 'Medieval studies, historicity, and Heidegger's early phenomenology', in Andrew Cole and D. Vance Smith (eds), *The legitimacy of the Middle Ages: on the unwritten history of theory* (Durham, NC: Duke University Press, 2010), pp. 159–93.

Kodish, Deborah G., 'Introduction', in Neil V. Rosenberg and Deborah G. Kodish (eds), liner notes, '*Folk-songs of America': The Robert Winslow Gordon Collection 1922–1932*, LP recording (Washington DC: Archive of Folksong, Library of Congress, 1978).

Ladrick, Alice, '*Tender* and changing', *postmedieval* 6.2 (2015), 200–9.

Lapidge, Michael, '*Beowulf* and the psychology of terror', in Helen Damico and John Leyerle (eds), *Heroic poetry in the Anglo-Saxon period* (Kalamazoo, MI: Medieval Institute Publications, 1993), pp. 373–402.

Lavezzo, Kathy, 'Whiteness, medievalism, immigration: rethinking Tolkien through Stuart Hall', *postmedieval* 12.1–4 (2021), 29–51.

Lawrence, W. W., *Beowulf and epic tradition* (Cambridge, MA: Harvard University Press, 1928).

Lawrence, W. W., 'The dragon and his lair in *Beowulf*', *PMLA* 33.4 (1918), 547–83.

Lees, Clare A., 'Basil Bunting, *Briggflatts*, Lindisfarne and Anglo-Saxon interlace', in David Clark and Nicholas Perkins (eds), *Anglo-Saxon culture and the modern imagination* (Woodbridge, Suffolk: Boydell and Brewer, 2010), pp. 111–28.

Lees, Clare A. 'In three poems: medieval and modern in Seamus Heaney, Maureen Duffy, and Collette Bryce', in Gillian R. Overing and Ulrike Wiethaus (eds), *American/medieval* (Göttingen: V&R unipress, 2016), pp. 177–202.

Lees, Clare A., and Gillian R. Overing, *The contemporary medieval in practice* (London: University College London Press, 2019).

Lerer, Seth, '*Beowulf* and contemporary critical theory', in Robert E. Bjork and John D. Niles (eds), *A Beowulf handbook* (Lincoln, NE: University of Nebraska Press, 1997), pp. 324–39.

Lerner, Ben, 'The reflection of a reading: *Flow chart* (1991)', *Conjunctions* 49 (2007), 372–6.

Leslie, R. F., 'Analysis of stylistic devices and effects in Anglo-Saxon literature', in Jess B. Bessinger Jr and Stanley J. Kahrl (eds), *Essential articles for the study of Old English poetry* (Hamden, CT: Archon Books, 1968), pp. 255–66.

Lewis, C. S., *The allegory of love* (Oxford: Oxford University Press, 1972).

Leyerle, John, 'The interlace structure of *Beowulf*', *University of Toronto Quarterly* 37.1 (1967), 1–17.

Liddell, Henry George and Robert Scott, *An intermediate Greek-English lexicon* (Oxford: Clarendon, 1889).

Lingus, Alphonso, 'Translator's preface', in Maurice Merleau-Ponty, *The visible and the invisible*, ed. Claude Lefort, trans. Alphonso Lingus (Evanston, IL: Northwestern University Press, 1968), pp. xl–lvi.

Liuzza, R. M., 'Iron and irony in *Beowulf*', in Jana K. Sculman and Paul E. Szarmach (eds), *Beowulf at Kalamazoo: essays on translation and performance* (Kalamazoo, MI: Medieval Institute, 2012), pp. 50–68.

Liuzza, R. M., 'Lost in translation: some versions of *Beowulf* in the nineteenth century', *English Studies* 83 (2002), 281–95.

Lockett, Leslie, *Anglo-Saxon psychologies in the vernacular and Latin traditions* (Toronto: University of Toronto Press, 2011).

Lomax, John, and Alan Lomax, *American ballads and folksongs* (New York: Macmillan, 1934).

Lord, Albert Bates, *The singer of tales* (Cambridge, MA: Harvard University Press, 1960).

Louviot, Elsie, *Direct speech in Beowulf and other Old English poems* (Cambridge: Boydell and Brewer, 2016).

Magennis, Hugh, *Images of community in Old English poetry* (Cambridge: Cambridge University Press, 1996).

Magennis, Hugh, *Translating 'Beowulf'* (Cambridge: D. S. Brewer, 2011).

Magoun, Francis P., Jr, '*Béowulf A'*: A Folk-Variant', *Arv* 14 (1958), 95–101.

Magoun, Francis P., Jr, '*Béowulf B*: a Folk-Poem on Béowulf's Death', in Arthur Brown and Peter Foote (eds), *Early English and Norse studies presented to Hugh Smith in honour of his sixtieth birthday* (London: Methuen, 1963), pp. 127–40.

Magoun, Francis P., Jr, 'The oral-formulaic character of Anglo-Saxon narrative poetry', *Speculum* 28.3 (1953), 446–67.

'Magoun perplexed at publication of cable', *Harvard Crimson*, November 26, 1934, www.thecrimson.com/article/1934/11/26/magoun-perplexed-at-publication-of-cable/ (accessed April 19, 2021).

Malone, Kemp, 'The Finn episode in *Beowulf*', *JEGP* 25.2 (1926), 157–72.

Malone, Kemp, 'Grendel and his abode', in A. G. Hatcher and K. L. Selig (eds), *Studia Philologica et Litteraria in honorem L. Spitzer* (Berne: Francke Verlag, 1958), pp. 297–308.

Malone, Kemp, 'Hildeburg and Hengest', *ELH* 10.4 (1943), 257–84.

Malone, Kemp, 'Review of Arthur Brodeur, *The art of Beowulf*', *Modern Language Notes* 75.4 (1960), 347–53.

Malone, Kemp, 'Review of Godfrid Storms, *Compounded names of peoples in Beowulf: a study in the diction of a great poet*', *English Studies* 41 (1960), 200–5.

Malone, Kemp, 'Variation in *Widsith*', *JEGP* 45.2 (1946), 147–52.

Marriott, David, 'A dialectics of the real', in Charles Watts and Edward Byrne (eds), *The recovery of the public world: essays on poetics in honour of Robin Blaser* (Burnaby, BC: Talonbooks, 1999), pp. 351–5.

McCaffery, Steve, 'Blaser's Deleuzian folds', *Discourse* 20.3 (1998), 99–122.

McCaffery, Steve, *The darkness of the present: poetics, anachronism, and the anomaly* (Tuscaloosa, AL: University of Alabama Press, 2012).

Merleau-Ponty, Maurice, *La phénoménologie de la perception* (Paris: Gallimard, 1945).

Merleau-Ponty, Maurice, *The phenomenology of perception*, trans. Colin Smith (London: Routledge, 2003).

Merleau-Ponty, Maurice, *The phenomenology of perception*, trans. Donald A. Landes (New York: Routledge, 2012).

Merleau-Ponty, Maurice, *The visible and the invisible*, ed. Claude Lefort, trans. Alphonso Lingus (Evanston, IL: Northwestern University Press, 1968).

Middleton, Peter, 'An elegy for theory: Robin Blaser's essay "The practice of outside"', in Miriam Nichols (ed.), *Even on Sunday: essays, readings, and archival materials on the poetry and poetics of Robin Blaser* (Orono, ME: National Poetry Foundation, 2002), pp. 179–206.

Mines, Rachel, 'An examination of Kuhn's second law and its validity as a metrical-syntactical rule', *Studies in philology* 99.4 (2002), 337–55.

Mitchell, David T., and Sharon L. Snyder, *Narrative prosthetics: disability and the dependencies of discourse* (Ann Arbor: University of Michigan Press, 2000).

Momma, Haruko, *From philology to English studies: language and culture in the nineteenth century* (Cambridge: Cambridge University Press, 2013).

Momma, Haruko, *The composition of Old English poetry* (Cambridge: Cambridge University Press, 1997).

Mossin, Andrew, 'In the shadow of Nerval: Robert Duncan, Robin Blaser, and the poetics of (mis)translation', *Comparative literature* 28.4 (1997), 673–704.

Mossin, Andrew, 'Recovering the public world: Robin Blaser, and the discourses of subjectivity and otherness in *Image nations 1-12*', Miriam Nichols (ed.), *Even on Sunday: essays, readings, and archival materials on the poetry and poetics of Robin Blaser* (Orono, ME: National Poetry Foundation, 2002), pp. 135–64.

Murphy, Patrick J., *Unriddling the Exeter riddles* (University Park, PA: Pennsylvania State University Press, 2011).

Nagel, Alexander, *Medieval modern: art out of time* (New York: Thames and Hudson, 2012).

Nealon, Christopher, *The matter of capital* (Cambridge, MA: Harvard University Press, 2011).

Newhauser, Richard, 'Introduction: the sensual Middle Ages', in Richard Newhauser (ed.), *A cultural history of the senses in the Middle Ages* (London: Bloomsbury, 2016), pp. 1–22.

Newhauser, Richard, '"Putten to ploughe": touching the peasant sensory community', in Fiona Griffiths and Kathryn Starkey (eds), *Sensory reflections: traces of experience in medieval artitfacts* (Berlin: De Gruyter, 2019), pp. 225–48.

Newhauser, Richard, 'The senses: the medieval sensorium, and sensing (in) the Middle Ages', in Albrecht Classen (ed.), *Handbook of medieval culture, Vol. 3* (Göttingen: De Gruyter, 2015), pp. 1560–75.

Nicholls, Peter, *Ezra Pound: politics, economics, and writing, a study of The Cantos* (Atlantic Highlands, NJ: Humanities Press, 1984).

Nicholls, Peter, 'Modernising modernism: from Pound to Oppen', *Critical Quarterly* 44.2 (2002), 41–58.

Nicholls, Peter, *Modernisms: a literary guide*, 2nd edition (New York: Palgrave, 2009).

Nicholls, Peter, 'The poetics of modernism', in Alex Davis and Lee M. Jenkins (eds), *The Cambridge companion to modernist poetics* (Cambridge: Cambridge University Press, 2007), pp 51–67.

Nichols, Miriam 'Introduction: reading Robin Blaser', in Miriam Nichols (ed.), *Even on Sunday: essays, readings, and archival materials on the poetry and poetics of Robin Blaser* (Orono, ME: National Poetry Foundation, 2002), pp. 25–76.

Nichols, Miriam, *A literary biography of Robin Blaser: mechanic of splendor* (Cham, Switzerland: Palgrave, 2019).

Nichols, Miriam, 'Love will eat the empire: a commentary', in Nichols (ed.), *The fire: the collected essays of Robin Blaser* (Berkeley, CA: University of California Press, 2006), pp. 369–400.

Nichols, Miriam, *Radical affections: essays on the poetics of outside* (Tuscaloosa, AL: Alabama University Press, 2012).

Niles, John D., *Beowulf: the poem and its tradition* (Cambridge, MA: Harvard University Press, 1983).

Niles, John D., 'Formula and formulaic system in *Beowulf*', in John Miles Foley (ed.), *Oral traditional literature: a Festschrift for Albert Bates Lord* (Columbus, OH: Slavica, 1981), pp. 394–415.

Niles, John D., *Homo narrans: the poetics and anthropology of oral literature* (Philadelphia, PA: University of Pennsylvania Press, 1999).

Niles, John D., 'Introduction', in Robert E. Bjork and John D. Niles (eds), *A Beowulf handbook* (Lincoln, NE: University of Nebraska Press, 1997), pp. 1–12.

Niles, John D., 'Introduction: negotiating the Anglo-Saxons' visual world', in John D. Niles, Stacy S. Klein, and Jonathan Wilcox (eds), *Anglo-Saxon England and the visual imagination*, Essays in Anglo-Saxon Studies 6 (Tempe, AZ: ACMRS, 2016), pp. 1–22.

Niles, John D., 'The myth of the Anglo-Saxon oral poet', *Western Folklore* 62.1/2 (2003), 7–61.

Niles, John D., *Old English enigmatic poems and the play of texts* (Turnhout: Brepols, 2006).

Niles, John D., 'Ring composition and the structure of *Beowulf*', *PMLA* 94.5 (1979), 924–35.

Niles, John D. (et al.), *Beowulf and Lejre* (Tempe, AZ: ACMRS, 2007).

Niles, John D., Stacy S. Klein, and Jonathan Wilcox (eds), *Anglo-Saxon England and the visual imagination*, Essays in Anglo-Saxon Studies 6 (Tempe, AZ: ACMRS, 2016).

Nist, John A., 'The structure of *Beowulf*', *Papers of the Michigan Academy of Sciences, Arts, and Letters* 43 (1958), 307–14.

Norwood, Stephen H., *The Third Reich in the ivory tower* (Cambridge: Cambridge University Press, 2009).

Oberman, Miller, *The unstill ones* (Princeton, NJ: Princeton University Press, 2017).

O'Brien O'Keeffe, Katherine, '*Beowulf*: lines 702b–836: transformations and the limits of the human', *Texas Studies in Language and Literature* 23.4 (1981), 484–94.

O'Brien O'Keeffe, Katherine, 'Diction, variation, the formula', in Robert E. Bjork and John D. Niles (eds), *A Beowulf handbook* (Lincoln, NE: University of Nebraska Press, 1997), pp. 84–104.

O'Brien O'Keeffe, Katherine, 'Hands and eyes, sight and touch: appraising the senses in Anglo-Saxon England', *ASE* 45 (2016), 105–40.

O'Brien O'Keeffe, Katherine, *Visible song: transitional literacy in Old English verse* (Cambridge: Cambridge University Press, 1990).

Ogura, Michiko, 'OE *wyrm*, *nædre*, and *draca*', *Journal of English Linguistics* 21.2 (1988), 99–124.

Orlemanski, Julie, 'Literary genre, medieval studies, and the prosthesis of disability', *Textual Practice* 30.7 (2016), 1253–72.

Osborn, Marijane, '"Verbal sea charts" and *Beowulf*'s approach to Denmark', in John Miles Foley (ed.), *De gustibus: essays for Alain Renoir* (New York: Garland, 1992), pp. 441–55.

Oshitari, Kinshiro, 'The sea in *Beowulf*', *Eibungaku kenkyū* (Studies in English Literature) 50 (1973), 3–18.

Otaño Gracia, Nahir I., 'Towards a de-centered global North Atlantic: blackness in *Saga af Tristram ok Ísodd*', *Literature Compass* 16.9–10 (2019), 1–16.

Overing, Gillian R., '*Beowulf*: a poem in our time', in Clare A. Lees (ed.), *The Cambridge history of early medieval English literature* (Cambridge: Cambridge University Press, 2013), pp. 309–21.

Overing, Gillian R., '*Beowulf* on gender', *New Medieval Literatures* 12 (2010), 1–22.

Overing, Gillian R., *Language sign and gender in Beowulf* (Carbondale and Edwardsville, IL: Southern Illinois University Press, 1990).

Overing, Gillian R., 'Reinventing Beowulf's voyage to Denmark', *Old English Newsletter* 21.2 (1988), 30–9.

Overing, Gillian R., and Marijane Osborn, *Landscape of desire: partial stories of the medieval Scandinavian world* (Minneapolis, MN: University of Minnesota Press, 1994).

Overing, Gillian R., and Ulrike Wiethaus (eds), *American/medieval: nature and mind in culture transfer* (Göttingen: V&R unipress, 2016).

Overing, Gillian R., and Ulrike Wiethaus (eds), *American/medieval goes north: earth and water in transit* (Göttingen: V&R unipress, 2019).

Owen-Crocker, Gale, *The four funerals in Beowulf* (Manchester: Manchester University Press, 2000).

Paetzel, Walther, *Die Variationen in der altgermanischen Alliteration Poesie*, Paltestra 48 (Berlin: Mayer and Müller, 1913).

Palazzo, Éric, 'Art, liturgy, and the five senses in the early middle ages', *Viator* 41.1 (2010), 25–56.

Parkes, Malcolm, *Pause and effect: punctuation in the west* (Berkeley, CA: University of California Press, 1993).

Pasternack, Carol Braun, 'Disjunction: a structural convention in Old English poetry' (PhD dissertation, University of California Los Angeles, 1983).

Pasternack, Carol Braun, 'Stylistic disjunctions in *The dream of the rood*', *ASE* 13 (1984), 167–86.

Pasternack, Carol Braun, *The textuality of Old English poetry* (Cambridge: Cambridge University Press, 1995).

Paz, James, *Nonhuman voices in Anglo-Saxon literature and material culture* (Manchester: Manchester University Press, 2017).

Pepper, Stephen C., *Aesthetic quality: a contextualistic theory of beauty* (New York: Scribners, 1938).

Pepper, Stephen C., 'Whitehead's "actual occasion"', in Robert C. Whitten (ed.), *Studies in Whitehead's philosophy* (The Hague: Martinus Nijhoff, 1961), pp. 71–88.

Persky, Stan, 'Reading Robin Blaser', in Persky and Brian Fawcett, *Robin Blaser* (Vancouver: New Start Books, 2010), pp. 3–45.

Pope, John C., *The rhythm of Beowulf: an interpretation of the normal and hypermetric verse-forms in Old English poetry* (New Haven, CT: Yale University Press, 1942).

Porter, Dorothy, 'The social centrality of women in *Beowulf*: a new context', *The Heroic Age* 5 (2001), www.heroicage.org/issues/5/porter1.html (accessed April 19, 2021).

Pratt, David, 'Persuasion and invention at the court of King Alfred the Great', in Catherine Cubitt (ed.), *Courtly culture in the early Middle Ages: proceedings of the first Alcuin conference* (Turnhout: Brepols, 2003), pp. 189–21.

Prescott, Andrew, '"Their present miserable state of cremation": the restoration of the Cotton Library', in C. J. Wright (ed.), *Sir Robert Cotton as collector: essays on an early Stuart courtier and his legacy* (London: British Library, 1997), pp. 391–454.

'Professors regret Hanfstaengl snub', *New York Times*, 1, 1934.

Quirk, Randolph, 'Poetic language and Old English meter', in Arthur Brown (ed.), *Early English and Norse studies: presented to Hugh Smith in honour of his sixtieth birthday* (London: Methuen, 1963), pp. 150–71.

Quirk, Randolph, and C. L. Wrenn, *An Old English grammar* (New York: Holt, Rinehalt, and Wintson, 1960).

Ramey, Peter, 'Crafting strangeness: wonder terminology in the Exeter Book Riddles and the Anglo-Latin Enigmata', *Review of English Studies* 69.289 (2018), 201–15.

Ramey, Peter, 'The riddle of beauty: the aesthetics of *wrætlic* in Old English verse', *Modern Philology* 114.3 (2017), 457–81.

Ramey, Peter, 'Variation and the poetics of oral performance in *Cædmon's hymn*', *Neophilologus* 96.3 (2012), 441–56.

Ramsey, Lee C., 'The sea voyages in *Beowulf*', *Neuphilologische Mitteilungen* 72.1 (1971), 51–9.

Rasula, Jed, *This compost: ecological imperatives in American poetry* (Athens, GA: University of Georgia Press, 2012).

Rauer, Christine, *Beowulf and the dragon: parallels and analogues* (Cambridge: D. S. Brewer, 2000).

Raulff, Ulrich, *Kreis ohne Meister: Stefan Georges Nachleben* (Munich: C. H. Beck, 2009).

Reed, David, sleeve notes, *Selections from Beowulf read by Arthur G. Brodeur*, LP Audio Recording, 12 in., 33 1/3 rpm, Issued by Brodeur's Students and the University of California, No publisher, California, 1955.

Remein, Daniel C., 'Auden, translation, betrayal: radical poetics and translation from Old English', *Literature Compass* 8 (2011), 811–29.

Remein, Daniel C., 'Decorate', in Jeffrey Jerome Cohen and Lowell Duckert (eds), *Veer ecology: a companion for environmental thinking* (Minneapolis, MN: University of Minnesota Press, 2017), pp. 90–104.

Remein, Daniel C., 'Human-tongued basilisks', in L. O. Aranye Fradenburg (ed.), *Staying alive: a survival manual for the liberal arts* (Brooklyn, NY: punctum, 2013), pp. 135–62.

Remein, Daniel C., 'Robin Blaser, Jack Spicer, and Arthur Brodeur: avant-garde poetics, the pedagogy of Old English at mid-century, and a counterfactual critical history, or, the importance of a broadly conceived English studies department', *postmedieval* 6.2 (2015), 174–90.

Remein, Daniel C., and Erica Weaver, 'Dons and dragons: *Beowulf* and "popular reading"', in Heather Blurton and Dwight F. Reynolds (eds), *Bestsellers and masterpieces: the changing medieval canon* (Manchester: Manchester University Press, 2022), pp. 49–78.

Remein, Daniel C., and Erica Weaver, 'Getting intimate', in Remein and Weaver (eds), *Dating Beowulf: studies in intimacy* (Manchester: Manchester University Press, 2019), pp. 1–28.

Renoir, Alain, *A key to old poems: the oral-formulaic approach to the interpretation of West-Germanic verse* (Philadelphia: University of Pennsylvania Press, 1988).

Renoir, Alain, 'Old English formulas as themes and tools for textual interpretation', in Phyllis Rugg, Georgia Ronan Crampton, and Fred

C. Robinson (eds), *Modes of interpretation in Old English literature: essays in honor of Stanley B. Greenfield* (Toronto: University of Toronto Press, 1986), pp. 65–79.

Renoir, Alain, 'The Old English *Ruin*: contrastive structure and affective impact', in Martin B. Green (ed.), *The Old English elegies: new essays in criticism and research* (Rutherford, NJ: Fairleigh Dickinson University Press, 1983), pp. 1148–73.

Renoir, Alain, 'Oral formulaic rhetoric and the interpretation of literary texts', in John Miles Foley (ed.), *Oral tradition in literature: interpretation and in context* (Columbia, MI: University of Missouri Press, 1986), pp. 103–35.

Renoir, Alain, 'Point of view and design for terror in *Beowulf*', NM 63.3 (1962), 154–67.

Renoir, Alain, 'Wulf and Eadwacer: a noninterpretation', in Jess Bessinger and Robert Creed (eds), *Fanciplegius: medieval and linguistic studies in honor of Francis P. Magoun Jr.* (New York: New York University Press, 1965), pp. 147–63.

Reynolds, Sean, 'Afterword: Jack Spicer's translation of *Beowulf* and the Lowghosts of a dead language', in David Hadbawnik and Sean Reynolds (eds), *Jack Spicer's Beowulf, Lost and found: CUNY Poetics documents initiative* 2.5, Part 2 (Spring 2011), 17–37.

Riebel, David A., 'A grammatical index to the compound nouns of Old English verse (based on the entries in Grein-Köhler, *Sprach-schatz der Angelsächsischen Dichter*)' (PhD dissertation, Indiana University, 1963).

Riedinger, Anita R., 'The formulaic relationship between *Beowulf* and *Andrea*', in Helen Damico and John Leyerle (eds), *Heroic poetry in the Anglo-Saxon period* (Kalamazoo, MI: Medieval Institute Publications, 1993), pp. 283–312.

Robertson, Lisa, *Debbie: an epic* (Vancouver: New Star Books, 1997).

Robinson, Fred C., *Beowulf and the appositive style* (Knoxville, TN: University of Tennessee Press, 1985).

Robinson, Fred C., 'Lexicography and literary criticism: a caveat', in James L. Rosier (ed.), *Philological essays: studies in Old and Middle English language and literature in honor of Herbert Dean Meritt* (The Hague: Mouton, 1970), pp. 99–110.

Robinson, Fred C., '"The might of the north": Pound's Anglo-Saxon studies and "The seafarer"', *Yale Review* 71 (1981), 199–224.

Robinson, Fred C. 'Two aspects of variation in Old English poetry', in Daniel G. Calder (ed.), *Old English poetry: essays on style* (Berkeley, CA: University of California Press, 1979), pp. 127–45.

Robinson, Fred C., 'Variation: a study in the diction of Beowulf' (PhD dissertation, University of North Carolina, Chapel Hill, 1961).

Rosenburg, Bruce A. 'Folktale morphology and the structure of *Beowulf*: a counterproposal', *Journal of the Folklore Institute* 11 (1974), 199–209.

Russom, Geoffrey, 'Artful avoidance of the useful phrase in "Beowulf", "The battle of Maldon", and "The fates of the apostles"', *Studies in Philology* 75.4 (1978): 371–90.

Russom, Geoffrey, 'At the center of *Beowulf*', in Stephen O. Glosecki (ed.), *Myth and early northwest Europe*, Medieval and Renaissance Texts and Studies 320 (Tempe, AZ: ACMRS, 2008), pp. 225–40.

Said, Edward, 'Opponents, audiences, constituencies, community', in *Reflections on exile and other essays* (Cambridge, MA: Harvard University Press, 2000), pp. 118–47.

Said, Edward, 'Reflections on exile', in *Reflections on exile and other essays* (Cambridge, MA: Harvard University Press, 2000), pp. 173–86.

Said, Edward, 'Representing the colonized', in *Reflections on exile and other essays* (Cambridge, MA: Harvard University Press, 2000), pp. 293–316.

Sakkis, John, 'John Sakkis interviews Robin Blaser', *The Poker* 5 (2005), 61–72.

Saltzman, Benjamin A., *Bonds of secrecy: law, spirituality, and the literature of concealment in early medieval England* (Philadelphia, PA: University of Pennsylvania Press, 2019).

Saltzman, Benjamin A., 'Community, joy, and the intimacy of narrative in *Beowulf*' in Daniel C. Remein and Erica Weaver (eds), *Dating Beowulf: studies in intimacy* (Manchester: Manchester University Press, 2020), pp. 31–53.

Saltzman, Benjamin, A., 'Secrecy and hermeneutic potential in *Beowulf*', *PMLA* 133.1 (2018), 36–55.

Sarrazin, Gregor, *Beowulf-Studien* (Berlin: Mauer and Müller, 1888).

Saussy, Haun, *The ethnography of rhythm: orality and its technologies* (New York: Fordham University Press, 2008).

Scully, Jackie Leach, 'Disability and vulnerability: on bodies, dependence and power', in Catriona Mackenzie (ed.), *Vulnerability: new essays in ethics and feminist philosophy* (New York: Oxford University Press, 2014), pp. 204–21.

Sedgwick, Eve Kosofsky, *Touching feeling* (Durham, NC: Duke University Press, 2003).

Serres, Michel, *The five senses: a philosophy of mingled bodies*, trans. Margaret Sankey and Peter Cowley (London: Bloomsbury, 2016).

Shaar, Claes, 'On a new theory of Old English poetic diction', *Neophilologus* 40.4 (1956), 301–5.

Sharma, Mannish, 'Metalepsis and monstrosity: the boundaries of narrative structure in *Beowulf*', *Studies in Philology* 102.3 (2005), 247–79.

Shaw, Lytle, *Fieldworks: from place to site in postwar poetics* (Tuscaloosa, AL: University of Alabama Press, 2013).

Shaw, Lytle, *Frank O'Hara: the poetics of coterie* (Iowa City: University of Iowa Press, 2006).

Shaw, Lytle, *Narrowcast: poetry and audio research* (Stanford, CA: Stanford University Press, 2018).

Sheehan, Jason, 'Bro. This is not the "Beowulf" you think you know'. *NPR Book Reviews*, August 27, 2020, www.npr.org/2020/08/27/906423831/bro-this-is-not-the-beowulf-you-think-you-know (accessed April 19, 2021).

Shilton, Howard, 'The nature of Beowulf's dragon', *Bulletin of the John Rylands Library* 79.3 (1997), 67–77.

Shippey, Thomas A., 'The fairy tale structure of *Beowulf*', *Notes and Queries* 214 (1969), 2–11.

Shklovsky, Viktor, *Theory of prose*, trans. Benjamin Sher (Normal, IL: Dalkey Archive, 1991).

Singer, Julie, *Blindness and therapy in late medieval French and Italian poetry* (Cambridge: Brewer, 2011).

Sisam, Kenneth, 'Beowulf's fight with the dragon', *Review of English Studies* 9.34 (1958), 129–40.

Sisam Kenneth, *The structure of Beowulf* (Oxford: Oxford University Press, 1965).

Skinner, Jonathan, 'Why ecopoetics', *Ecopoetics* 1 (2001), 105–6.

Smailbegović, Ada, 'Of the dense and rare', *Triple Canopy* (2013), www.canopycanopycanopy.com/contents/of_the_dense_and_rare/#title-page (accessed April 19, 2021).

Smith, Roger, 'Seafaring imagery in Old English poetry' (PhD dissertation, Stanford University, 1987).

Snediker, Michael, 'Prodigal son: (midway along the pathway)', *Criticism* 51.3 (2009), 489–594.

Snediker, Michael, *Queer optimism: lyric personhood and other felicitous persuasions* (Minneapolis, MN: University of Minnesota Press, 2008).

Sobchack, Vivian, 'A leg to stand on: prosthetics, metaphor, and materiality', in Marquard Smith and Joanne Morra (eds), *The prosthetic impulse: from a posthuman present to biocultural future* (Cambridge, MA: MIT Press, 2006), pp. 17–42.

Sobecki, Sebastian I., *The sea and medieval English literature* (Cambridge: D. S. Brewer, 2008).

Spanos, William V., 'Jack Spicer's poetry of absence: an introduction', *boundary 2* 6.6 (1977), 1–2.

Spanos, William V. (ed.), *Jack Spicer*, special issue, *boundary 2* 6.1 (1977).

Spiegelberg, Herbert, '"Intention" and "intentionality" in the scholastics, Brentano, and Husserl', trans. Linda L. McAlister and Margarete Schgttle, in Herbert Spiegelberg, *The context of the phenomenology movement*, Phaenomenologica 80 (The Hague: Martinus Nijhoff, 1981), pp. 3–26.

Stanley, Eric G., '*Beowulf*', in E. G. Stanley (ed.), *Continuations and beginnings: studies in Old English literature* (London: Thomas Nelson and Sons, 1966), pp. 104–41.

Stanley, Eric G., '"A very land-fish, a languagelesse, a monster": Grendel and the like in Old English', in K. E. Olsen and L. A. J. R. Houwen (eds), *Monsters and the monstrous in medieval northwest Europe* (Leuven: Peeters, 2001), pp. 79–92.

Stanley, Eric G., 'The narrative art of *Beowulf*', in Hans Bekker-Nielson et al. (eds), *Medieval narrative: a symposium* (Odense: Odense University Press, 1980), pp. 58–81.

Stanley, Eric G., 'Old English poetic diction and the interpretation of *The wanderer, The seafarer*, and the *Penitent's prayer*', in Jess B. Bessinger, Jr and Stanley J. Kahrl (eds), *Essential articles for the study of Old English poetry* (Hamden, CT: Archon Books, 1968), pp. 458–514.

Stanton, Robert, *The culture of translation in Anglo-Saxon England* (Cambridge: Brewer, 2002).

Steinhoff, Eirik, 'The making of the *Chicago Review*: the meteoric years (1948–1958)', *Chicago Review*, web feature on *Big table*, www.chicagoreview.org/big-table-web-feature/#steinhoff_making (accessed September 19, 2021).

Stevick, Robert D., 'Hunting the Anglo-Saxon aesthetic in large forms: a möbian quest', in John M. Hill (ed.), *On the aesthetics of* Beowulf *and other Old English poems* (Toronto: University of Toronto Press, 2010), pp. 135–60.

Stevick, Robert D., 'Representing the form of *Beowulf*', in Joah H. Hall, Nick Doane, and Dick Ringler (eds), *Old English and new, studies in language and linguistics in honor of Frederic G. Cassidy* (New York: Garland, 1982), pp. 3–14.

Storms, Godfrid, 'Grendel the terrible', *NM* 73.1/3 (1972), 427–36.

Strite, Victor L., 'Old English sea-terms: a word-list and a study of definitions' (PhD dissertation, University of Missouri–Columbia, 1970).

Taylor, Paul Beekman, 'Themes of death in *Beowulf*' in Creed (ed.), *Old English poetry: fifteen essays* (Providence, RI: Brown University Press, 1967), pp. 249–74.

Timmer, B. J., 'Sectional divisions in poems in Old English manuscripts', *Modern Language Review* 47.3 (1952), 319–22.

Todorov, Tzvetan, 'The two principles of narrative', trans. Philip E. Lewis, *Diacritics* 1.1 (1971), 37–44.

Tolkien, J. R. R., '*Beowulf*: the monsters and the critics', Sir Israel Gollancz Memorial Lecture, Proceedings of the British Academy 22 (Oxford: Oxford University Press, 1936).

Tonsfeldt, H. Ward, 'Ring structure in *Beowulf*', *Neophilologus* 62 (1977), 443–52.

'Translation of "Deutsche Allgemeine Zeitung" story gives cables sent by Mellon and Magoun', *Harvard Crimson*, November 23, 1934, www.thecrimson.com/article/1934/11/23/translation-of-deutsche-allgemeine-zeitung-story/ (accessed April 19, 2021).

Trilling, Renée R., *The aesthetics of nostalgia: historical representation and Old English verse* (Toronto: University of Toronto Press, 2009).

Tripp, Raymond P., Jr, *More about the fight with the dragon: Beowulf 2208b–3182* (Lanham, MD: University Press of America, 1983).

Tuan, Yi-Fu, *Topophilia: a study of environmental perception, attitudes, and values* (New York: Columbia University Press, 1990).

Tupper, Frederick (ed.), *The riddles of the Exeter Book* (Boston, MA: Ginn and Co., 1910; reprint, Darmstadt: Wissenshcaftliche Buchgesellschaft, 1968).

Turner, Sharon, *History of the Anglo-Saxons from the earliest period to the Norman conquest*, 5th edn, Vol. 3 (London: 1928).

Tyler, Elizabeth M., *Old English poetics: the aesthetics of the familiar in Anglo-Saxon England* (York: York Medieval Press, 2006).

Van Meurs, J. C., '*Beowulf* and literary criticism', *Neophilolologus* 39 (1955), 114–30.

Venuti, Lawrence, 'Translation as cultural politics: regimes of domestication in English', *Textual Practice* 7.2 (1993), 208–23.

Vilmar, A. F. C., *Deutsche Alterümer im Hêliand Als Einkleindung Der Evandelischen Geschichte* (Marburg: N. G. Elwert, 1845; reprint, 1862).

Vincent, John Emil (ed.), *After Spicer: critical essays* (Middletown, CT: Wesleyan University Press, 2011).

Wallace, Karen Bruce, 'Grendel and Goliath: monstrous superability and disability in the Old English corpus', in R. H. Godden and Asa Mittman (eds), *Monstrosity, disability, and the posthuman in the medieval and early modern world* (Cham: Palgrave, 2019), pp. 107–26.

Watanabe, Hideki, 'Sword, fire, and dragon: polysemous compounds in *Beowulf* reconsidered with special reference to *nacod nið draca* (2273) and *þæt wæs modig secg*', in Michiko Ogura (ed.), *Textual and contextual studies in medieval English: towards the reunion of linguistics and philology* (Bern: Peter Land, 2006), pp. 193–204.

Watts, Charles, and Edward Byrne (eds), *The recovery of the public world: essays on poetics in honor of Robin Blaser* (Burnaby, BC: Talonbooks, 1999).

Weaver, Erica, 'Performing (in)attention: Ælfric, Ælfric Bata, and the *Visitatio sepulchri*', *Representations* 152 (2020), 1–24.

Weiskott, Eric, 'Old English poetry, verse by verse', *ASE* 44 (2015), 95–130.

Wells, D. M., 'The sections in Old English poetry', *Yearbook of English Studies* 6 (1976), 1–4.

Whallon, William, 'The diction of *Beowulf*', *PMLA* 76.4 (1961), 309–19.

Whallon, William, 'Formulas for heroes in the *Iliad* and *Beowulf*', *Modern Philology* 63.2 (1965), 95–104.

Wheatley, Edward, 'Blindness: evolving religious and secular constructions and repsonses', in Jonathan Hsy, Tory V. Pearman, and Joshua E. Eyler (eds), *A cultural history of disability in the Middle Ages* (London: Bloomsbury, 2022), pp. 67–81.

Wheatley, Edward, *Stumbling blocks before the blind: medieval constructions of a disability* (Ann Arbor, MI: University of Michigan Press, 2010).

Whitelock, Dorothy, *The audience of Beowulf* (Oxford: Clarendon, 1951).

Whitman, F. H., 'The meaning of "formulaic" in Old English verse composition', *NM* 76.4 (1975), 529–37.

Wickham-Crowley, Kelley M., 'Living on the *ecg*: the mutable boundaries of land and water in Anglo-Saxon contexts', in Clare A. Lees and Gillian R. Overing (eds), *A place to believe in: locating medieval landscapes* (University Park, PA: University of Pennsylvania Press, 2006), pp. 85–110.

Willard, Rudolph, 'Review of *Beowulf with the Finnesburg fragment* by C. L. Wrenn', *JEGP* 53 (1954), 617–23.

Williams, R. A. *The Finn episode in Beowulf: an essay in interpretation* (Cambridge: Cambridge University Press, 1924).

Wrenn, C. L., 'Recent work on *Beowulf* to 1958: Ch I, Sutton Hoo and *Beowulf*', in R. W. Chambers (ed.), *Beowulf: an introduction to the study of the poem*, 3rd edn (Cambridge: Cambridge University Press, 1959), pp. 514–23.

Wright, Charles C., *The Irish tradition in Old English literature* (Cambridge: Cambridge University Press, 2010).

Yao, Steven G., *Translation and the languages of modernism: gender, politics, language* (New York: Palgrave, 2002).

Yates, Frances A., *The art of memory* (London: Routledge, 1966).

Young, Alex Trimble, '"The queen of the mad frontier": settler colonialism and Jack Spicer's queer politics', in Goia Woods (ed.), *Left in the west: literature, culture, and progressive politics in the American west* (Reno, NV: University of Nevada Press), pp. 254–74.

Young, Helen, 'Whiteness and time: the once, present, and future race', in *Studies in Medievalism* 24 (2015), 39–49.

Index